D1743633

Lecture Notes
in Business Information Processing   **498**

Series Editors

Wil van der Aalst⬛, *RWTH Aachen University, Aachen, Germany*
Sudha Ram⬛, *University of Arizona, Tucson, AZ, USA*
Michael Rosemann⬛, *Queensland University of Technology, Brisbane, QLD, Australia*
Clemens Szyperski, *Microsoft Research, Redmond, WA, USA*
Giancarlo Guizzardi⬛, *University of Twente, Enschede, The Netherlands*

LNBIP reports state-of-the-art results in areas related to business information systems and industrial application software development – timely, at a high level, and in both printed and electronic form.

The type of material published includes

- Proceedings (published in time for the respective event)
- Postproceedings (consisting of thoroughly revised and/or extended final papers)
- Other edited monographs (such as, for example, project reports or invited volumes)
- Tutorials (coherently integrated collections of lectures given at advanced courses, seminars, schools, etc.)
- Award-winning or exceptional theses

LNBIP is abstracted/indexed in DBLP, EI and Scopus. LNBIP volumes are also submitted for the inclusion in ISI Proceedings.

Tiago Prince Sales · Sybren de Kinderen ·
Hend*erik* A. Proper · Luise Pufahl ·
Dimka Karastoyanova · Marten van Sinderen
Editors

Enterprise Design, Operations, and Computing

EDOC 2023 Workshops

IDAMS, iRESEARCH, MIDas4CS, SoEA4EE, EDOC Forum,
Demonstrations Track and Doctoral Consortium
Groningen, The Netherlands, October 30 – November 3, 2023
Revised Selected Papers

Springer

Editors
Tiago Prince Sales 🆔
University of Twente
Enschede, The Netherlands

Sybren de Kinderen 🆔
Eindhoven University of Technology
Eindhoven, The Netherlands

Henderik A. Proper 🆔
Vienna University of Technology
Vienna, Austria

Luise Pufahl 🆔
Technical University of Munich
Heilbronn, Germany

Dimka Karastoyanova 🆔
University of Groningen
Groningen, The Netherlands

Marten van Sinderen 🆔
University of Twente
Enschede, The Netherlands

ISSN 1865-1348   ISSN 1865-1356 (electronic)
Lecture Notes in Business Information Processing
ISBN 978-3-031-54711-9   ISBN 978-3-031-54712-6 (eBook)
https://doi.org/10.1007/978-3-031-54712-6

This Springer imprint is published by the registered company Springer Nature Switzerland AG
The registered company address is: Gewerbestrasse 11, 6330 Cham, Switzerland

Paper in this product is recyclable.

Preface

For over twenty-five years, the EDOC conference has been the primary annual event for disseminating and discussing the latest developments in enterprise computing. In addition to the main track, EDOC 2023 offered a forum, a demonstration track, and a doctoral consortium. It also hosted five workshops of interest to the community. All of these events were held in person, together with the main conference in Groningen, The Netherlands.

The forum is a track within the main conference where authors are given a platform to present and discuss early-stage work. This year, we accepted four forum papers for presentation and publication in this proceedings volume.

The demonstration track offered a highly interactive outlet for researchers and practitioners to present prototypes and applications in the context of enterprise computing. This year, we accepted three tools for presentation, each of which was accompanied with a short paper published here.

The doctoral consortium is a track designed to encourage early-stage doctoral candidates to present their research projects and exchange with other researchers in their fields. Submitted projects are reviewed by senior researchers, who then provide valuable feedback to the candidates. This year, we accepted four projects for presentation and publication in this proceedings volume.

Workshops within EDOC cover more focused topics and allow for the presentation and discussion of work that is in the early development stages. As such, the workshops provide an excellent venue for discussing enterprise computing topics that may become important research streams in the future, as well as topics that are already important in a smaller and more focused setting. This year, we are proud to have hosted five workshops, namely:

- Insights in Data FAIRification Planning (BYOFO Workshop)
- Workshop on Intelligent Digital Architecture, Methods, and Services for Industry 4.0 and Society 5.0 (IDAMS)
- Workshop on Empirical Methodologies for Research in Enterprise Architecture and Service-Oriented Computing (iRESEARCH)
- Workshop on the Modelling and Implementation of Digital Twins for Complex Systems (MIDas4CS)
- Workshop on Service-oriented Enterprise Architecture for Enterprise Engineering (SoEA4EE)

These workshops were selected based on their fit with EDOC's topics of interest, their format and target audience, and their potential to attract high-quality papers. IDAMS, iRESEARCH, MIDas4CS, and SoEA4EE established their programs in collaboration with the workshop chairs and their accepted papers have undergone a rigorous reviewing and selection process. All in all, 14 workshop papers are published in this proceedings volume. They were accepted out of a total of 37 submissions.

The Insights in Data FAIRification Planning (BYOFO) Workshop adopted a different format than the other four. It consisted of a hands-on workshop inspired by the format of the "Bring Your Own Data" (BYOD) workshops, previously organized by the same authors within the rare diseases research community. This workshop was designed to guide participants through the critical "identifying your FAIRification objectives" step of the process of making data Findable, Acessible, Interoperable and Reusable (FAIR, and the FAIRification process). It introduced GO-Plan, a method that offers a systematic approach to identifying and developing a FAIRification plan. It also emphasized the advantages of producing resources that align with the FAIR principles.

We followed a "post-proceedings" format for this volume. That is, the authors published here could submit the final version of their papers after EDOC, allowing them to improve their papers based on the feedback they received from the reviewers and at the conference. We believe this led to better and more mature publications.

Lastly, we would like to thank everyone involved in the organization of EDOC 2023. Their contribution was key to the success of the conference and its satellite events. We give a special thanks to our workshop organizers, the chairs of the forum, doctoral consortium, and demonstrations track, as well as to the authors of the papers published here.

November 2023

Tiago Prince Sales
Sybren de Kinderen
Henderik A. Proper
Luise Pufahl
Dimka Karastoyanova
Marten van Sinderen

Organization

General Chairs

Dimka Karastoyanova   University of Groningen, The Netherlands
Marten van Sinderen   University of Twente, The Netherlands

Program Committee Chairs

Henderik A. Proper   TU Vienna, Austria
Luise Pufahl   TU Munich, Germany

Workshop Chairs

Tiago Prince Sales   University of Twente, The Netherlands
Sybren de Kinderen   Eindhoven University of Technology,
     The Netherlands

Demonstrations Track Chairs

Fadi Mohsen   University of Groningen, The Netherlands
Stefan Schoenig   University of Regensburg, Germany

Doctoral Consortium Chairs

Irene Vanderfeesten   KU Leuven, Belgium
Maria Iacob   University of Twente, The Netherlands

Industrial Chairs

Zoran Milosevic   Deontik/Best Practice Software, Australia
Pascal Ravesteijn   HU University of Applied Sciences,
     The Netherlands

Publicity Chair

Mirela Riveni   University of Groningen, The Netherlands

Proceedings Chair

João Luiz R. Moreira   University of Twente, The Netherlands

Website Chairs

Magda Piekorz   University of Groningen, The Netherlands
Mirela Riveni   University of Groningen, The Netherlands

Local Organization Committee

Ineke Schelhaas   University of Groningen, The Netherlands
Dimka Karastoyanova   University of Groningen, The Netherlands
Mirela Riveni   University of Groningen, The Netherlands
Fadi Mohsen   University of Groningen, The Netherlands

Steering Committee

João Paulo A. Almeida   Federal University of Espírito Santo, Brazil
Colin Atkinson   University of Mannheim, Germany
Remco Dijkman   Eindhoven University of Technology,
                                   The Netherlands
Georg Grossmann   University of South Australia, Australia
Giancarlo Guizzardi   University of Twente, The Netherlands
Sylvain Hallé   Université du Québec à Chicoutimi, Canada
Zoran Milosevic   Deontik, Australia
Selmin Nurcan   University Paris 1 Panthéon-Sorbonne, France
Stefanie Rinderle-Ma   University of Vienna, Austria
Marten van Sinderen   University of Twente, The Netherlands

BYOFO 2023 – Insights in Data FAIRification Planning

César Bernabé[1], Isadora Valle Sousa[2,3], Annika Jacobsen[1],
Luiz Olavo Bonino da Silva Santos[1,2], and Marco Roos[1]

[1]Leiden University Medical Centre, Leiden, The Netherlands
c.h.bernabe@lumc.nl
[2]Semantics, Cybersecurity & Services, University of Twente, The Netherlands
i.vallesousa@utwente.nl
[3]Free University of Bozen-Bolzano, Bolzano, Italy
l.o.boninodasilvasantos@utwente.nl, m.roos@lumc.nl

The Insights in Data FAIRification Planning (BYOFO 2023) Workshop adopted a different format than the other four. It consisted of a hands-on workshop inspired by the format of the "Bring Your Own Data" (BYOD) workshops, which were previously organized by the some of the BYOFO 2023 authors within the rare diseases research community [1]. This workshop was designed to guide participants through the critical "identifying your FAIRification objectives" step of the process of making data Findable, Acessible, Interoperable and Reusable (FAIR [3], and the FAIRification process [4]). It introduced the **G**oal-**O**riented FAIRification **Plan**ning method (GO-Plan) [2], which offers a systematic approach to identifying and developing a FAIRification plan. It also emphasized the advantages of producing resources that align with the FAIR principles.

The FAIR principles provide guidance for making data accessible, interoperable, and reusable for both humans and machines. Data that is made FAIR can be efficiently analysed and reused with other FAIR datasets. Consequently, adherence to the FAIR principles has become a valuable characteristic for research projects in several areas. However, FAIRification is multifaceted and multidisciplinary, and it can be accomplished through a variety of means. As a result, defining explicit FAIRification objectives at the onset of the process is critical to ensuring a successful and efficient process.

Currently, limited research has been conducted on effective methods for eliciting FAIRification objectives and their impact on FAIRification activities. Furthermore, there is a lack of studies examining the impact of poorly defined objectives on FAIRification realization. Considering these gaps in knowledge, GO-Plan was proposed. It builds on experience gained from recent FAIRification projects, including training on FAIR (e.g., [1]), and conducting FAIRification within single (e.g., [5]) and among multiple institutions (e.g., [6]), and feedback from experts on FAIR. It provides a systematic approach to identifying, refining and prioritizing FAIRification objectives.

By establishing clear objectives through GO-Plan, individuals conducting FAIRification can effectively guide and justify implementation decisions, as well as identify the necessary metadata and data components that need to be gathered and made available for facilitating the reusability of FAIR data. At the end of the workshop, participants created their own FAIRification plan and learned how to apply the method to their own needs.

Acknowledgments. We would like to thank all participants of BYOFO 2023, as well as the organizers of EDOC 2023 for their help with the organization of the workshop. We also thank the LUMC Biosemantics and the EJP RD FAIRification Stewards groups for constant feedback on this research. This initiative has received funding from the European Union's Horizon 2020 research and innovation program under grant agreement N°825575 and the Trusted World of Corona (TWOC; LSH Health Holland).

References

1. Bernabé, C., et al.: Building expertise on FAIR through evolving Bring Your Own Data (BYOD) workshops: describing the data, software, and management-focused approaches and their evolution. Data Intell. (2023). https://doi.org/10.1162/dint_a_00236
2. Bernabé, C., et al.: A goal-oriented method for FAIRification planning (2023). https://doi.org/10.21203/rs.3.rs-3092538
3. Wilkinson, M.D., et al.: The FAIR Guiding Principles for scientific data management and stewardship. Sci. Data (2016). https://doi.org/10.1038/sdata.2016.18
4. Jacobsen, A., et al.: A generic workflow for the data FAIRification process. Data Intell. (2000) https://doi.org/10.1162/dint_a_00028
5. Queralt-Rosinach, N., et al.: Applying the FAIR principles to data in a hospital: challenges and opportunities in a pandemic. J. Biomed. Semant. (2022). https://doi.org/10.1186/s13326-022-00263-7
6. dos Santos Vieira, B., et al.: Towards FAIRification of sensitive and fragmented rare disease patient data: challenges and solutions in European reference network registries. Orphanet J. Rare Diseases (2022). https://doi.org/10.1186/s13023-022-02558-5

Contents

Demonstrations Track

Doctoral Consortium

IDAMS

IDAMS – Intelligent Digital Architecture, Methods, and Services for Industry 4.0 and Society 5.0

Yoshimasa Masuda[1,2], Alfred Zimmermann[3], Rainer Schmidt[4], and Asif Gill[5]

[1]Carnegie Mellon University, USA
yoshi_masuda@keio.jp
[2]Keio University, Japan
[3]Reutlingen University, Germany
alfred.zimmermann@reutlingen-university.de
[4]Munich University of Applied Sciences, Germany
rainer.schmidt@hm.edu
[5]University of Technology Sydney, Australia
asif.gill@uts.edu.au

The digital transformation of global industries and value chains and the associated need for structured research and standardization has given rise to major global and national initiatives. These initiatives address the potential and challenges of digitalization. Enterprises and societies currently face crucial challenges, while Industry 4.0 becomes increasingly important in the global manufacturing industry. Industry 4.0 offers a range of opportunities for companies to increase the flexibility and efficiency of production processes.

The development of new business models can be promoted with digital platforms and architectures for Industry 4.0. Industry 4.0 is dedicated to research and practice for industry and supports the implementation of this vision, especially in manufacturing companies. According to the Japanese government, Society 5.0 is more general and can be defined as a fusion between cyberspace and physical space, addressing economic progress aligned with solving social problems by providing goods and services to meet repeated latent needs regardless of location, age, gender, or language.

Contemporary advances in the field of artificial intelligence have led to a rapidly growing number of intelligent systems that can operate entirely independently of human intervention or enable interactions of unprecedented complexity with humans. Data plays a central role in intelligent digital architecture and allows automation of decisions impacting all stakeholders.

The use of artificial intelligence techniques enables decisions that were previously reserved for humans to be made autonomously. Intelligent systems augment processes by creating automated interfaces to human beings and replacing human decision making with machine-based decision-making. Intelligent digital architectures support requests for, configuration of, and fulfillment of services.

Digitalization promotes the creation of intelligent systems and services with an intelligent digital architecture. Products based on intelligent digital architectures become aware of their environment, act upon it, are able to interact with human beings, and can change their functionality during their lifetime. Products and services based on intelligent digital architectures have local autonomous capabilities and extend them dynamically by accessing external services.

Platforms become feasible by matching the supply and demand of services, resources, and products. Intelligent digital architectures also enable and enhance business models by integrating resources and leveraging decision making in unprecedented ways, for instance, by applying a Digital Enterprise Architecture Framework such as the Adaptive Integrated Digital Architecture Framework (AIDAF). Public discourse on "autonomous" algorithms which work on "passively" collected data contributes to this view.

The EDOC Workshop – Intelligent Digital Architecture, Methods, and Services for Industry 4.0 and Society 5.0 – covers fundamental and practical aspects to support digital transformation. This disruptive change interacts with all information processes and systems, which for years have been important business enablers for the digital transformation. Intelligent digital architectures enable intense interaction with customers and products. The customer is closely integrated with business processes and interacts like a co-worker by using implicit touchpoints, which are provided by mobility and wearable systems and the Internet of Things. In this way, customer experience is fostered with disruptive transformation and continuous improvement.

The IDAMS 2023 workshop was a half-day workshop, held in conjunction with EDOC 2023. All submissions were peer-reviewed by at least three members of the EDOC 2023 and IDAMS international Program Committee.

Acknowledgments. We wish to thank all authors for having shared their work with us, as well as the members of the IDAMS 2023 Program Committee and the organizers of EDOC 2023 for their help with the organization of the workshop.

IDAMS Organization

Workshop Chairs

Yoshimasa Masuda   Carnegie Mellon University, USA
Keio University, Japan
Alfred Zimmermann   Reutlingen University, Germany
Rainer Schmidt   Munich University of Applied Sciences, Germany
Asif Gill   University of Technology Sydney, Australia

Program Committee

Abdellah Chehri   University of Quebec at Chicoutimi, Canada
Andreas Speck   Christian-Albrechts-University Kiel, Germany
Birger Lantow   University of Rostock, Germany
Christian Schweda   Reutlingen University, Germany
Dierk Jugel   Reutlingen University, Germany
Dimka Karastoyanova   University of Groningen, The Netherlands
Hironori Takeuchi   Musashi University, Japan
Janis Stirna   Stockholm University, Sweden
John Gøtze   IT University of Copenhagen, Denmark
Karlheinz Blank   T-Systems International, Germany
Kurt Sandkuhl   University of Rostock, Germany
Marco Aiello   University of Stuttgart, Germany
Matthias Wissotzki   Wismar University of Applied Sciences, Germany
Michael Möhring   Munich University of Applied Sciences, Germany
Milan Simic   RMIT University, Australia
Oliver Bossert   McKinsey & Company, Germany
Shuichiro Yamamoto   Nagoya University, Japan
Ulrike Steffens   Hamburg University of Applied Sciences, Germany

Multiple Use Case Analysis of an AI Hospital Using the AIDAF and Intelligence Amplification Design Canvas

Jean Paul Sebastian Piest[1]([✉]) [ID], Masahiro Jinzaki[2] [ID], Yoshimasa Masuda[3] [ID], Masako Toriya[3] [ID], Osamu Nakamura[3], and Tetsuya Toma[3] [ID]

[1] University of Twente, Drienerlolaan 5, 7522 NB Enschede, The Netherlands
j.p.s.piest@utwente.nl
[2] Keio Medical School, 35 Shinanomachi, Shinjuku-ku 160-8582, Tokyo, Japan
jinzaki@rad.med.keio.ac.jp
[3] Keio School of System Design and Management, 4-1-1 Hiyoshi, Kohoku-ku, Yokohama 223-8526, Kanagawa, Japan
{yoshi_masuda,masako.toriya,osamu}@keio.jp,
t.toma@sdm.keio.ac.jp

Abstract. In March 2023, the five-year AI Hospital Program in Japan was completed. Various AI-applications have been implemented in four model AI Hospitals. This paper contains the results of a multiple use case analysis of an AI Hospital using the AIDAF and the intelligence amplification design canvas. The aim of this research paper is two-fold to: 1) evaluate the utility of the AIDAF and intelligence amplification design canvas to analyse implemented AI-applications, and 2) conduct a multiple use case analysis in an AI Hospital. A focus group was created and developed a three-step process to analyse nine use cases and related AI-applications that have been implemented at Keio University Hospital using the AIDAF and intelligence amplification design canvas. First, each use case was analysed using the four guiding principles of the intelligence amplification design canvas. Second, conceptual representations were created for each use case. Third, an aggregated view of the AI Hospital was created. The results and findings were discussed in five focus group meetings. This study provides empirical support that the AIDAF and the intelligence amplification design canvas can effectively support the individual analysis of implemented AI-applications as well as conducting a multiple use case analysis. As such, this study provided insight in the current state of the AI Hospital and identified opportunities for extensions and future development in the second term of the AI Hospital Program and Open Healthcare Platform 2030 consortium. The current study was mainly based on qualitative analysis and comparison implemented AI-applications within a single organization and did not include in-depth user research. Future research may contribute to the analysis of similar use cases in other (AI-)hospitals to conduct a cross use case analysis.

Keywords: AI · Hospital · Intelligence Amplification · Design Canvas · Enterprise Architecture · Focus Group · Multiple Use Case Analysis · Digital Healthcare

© The Author(s), under exclusive license to Springer Nature Switzerland AG 2024
T. P. Sales et al. (Eds.): EDOC 2023 Workshops, LNBIP 498, pp. 5–22, 2024.
https://doi.org/10.1007/978-3-031-54712-6_1

1 Introduction

The vision of Society 5.0 as 'a human-centered society that balances economic advancement with the resolution of social problems by a system that highly integrates cyberspace and physical space' [1] is unfolding, providing opportunities for new value creation, amongst other sectors, for healthcare and caregiving [2]. Artificial Intelligence (AI), aimed at mimicking cognitive functions of humans with (assistance of) computers and machines, plays an essential role within the Society 5.0 vision and has been extensively reviewed in the healthcare domain [3–8]. Earlier work [9] identified 18 applications and six case studies in healthcare under Society 5.0 and proposed future research to conduct a multiple use case analysis.

In 2018, after a successful pilot, Keio University Hospital was selected as one of the four AI model hospitals in Japan, as part of the Strategic Innovation Promotion Program, promoted by Japan's Cabinet Office [10]. As part of this five-year AI Hospital Program, several use cases were explored and various concrete AI-applications have been implemented within the four AI model hospitals. The AI Hospital Program was completed in March 2023.

Earlier work provided the intelligence amplification design canvas [11], supporting design workshop [12], tutorial [13], and method using the Adaptive Integrated Digital Architecture Framework (AIDAF) and ISO 9241-210:2019 for human-centred design of interactive systems [14]. At present, the intelligence amplification design canvas is mainly applied for the conceptualization of ideas for new applications utilizing human-centred AI. However, the design workshop and method have not yet been thoroughly tested for the analysis of existing AI-applications and, more specifically, for the purpose of a multiple use case analysis. The completed AI Hospital Program provided the opportunity to conduct such a study and connect to work in the Open Healthcare Platform 2030 (OHP2030) consortium. This paper contains the results and findings related to the multiple use case analysis at Keio University Hospital.

Extending earlier work, the aim of this research paper is twofold: 1) evaluate the utility of the intelligence amplification design canvas to analyse use cases of implemented AI-applications, and 2) recursively use the intelligence amplification design canvas as part of the AIDAF to perform a multiple use case analysis in an AI Hospital. In line with this twofold aim, the following research questions will by addressed in this paper:

RQ1: Can the intelligence amplification design canvas and its four guiding principles be used to analyse and conceptualize use cases related to implemented AI-applications and (iteratively) conduct a multiple use case analysis?

RQ2: How can the AIDAF support the alignment of the digital transformation strategy and directions of the management and CIO of an AI Hospital?

The remainder of this paper is structured as follows. Section 2 contains relevant related and earlier work. Section 3 describes the research methodology. Section 4 contains the results of the AI hospital use case analysis with the intelligence amplification design canvas. Section 5 discusses the results and findings in relation to related work. Section 6 concludes and discusses areas for future research.

2 Related and Earlier Work

This section discusses related work in Sect. 2.1 and earlier work in Sect. 2.2.

2.1 AI in Healthcare and Medicine

AI has been extensively reviewed in healthcare and is developing rapidly. This subsection highlights the insights from a selection of well-cited and recent reviews.

A survey from 2017 [3] of AI in healthcare, based on PubMed data from 2013–2016, focused on the motivation for applying AI in healthcare, data types for analysis with AI-techniques, mechanisms to provide meaningful results, and disease types that are addressed. Motivations that were briefly mentioned, amongst others, include learning features from large datasets, obtaining insights for clinical decision making, providing abilities to learn and correct based on feedback, and assist specialists by providing up-to-date medical information. The survey identified data from diagnostic imaging, genetic testing/diagnosis, and electrodiagnosis as the main data types. Based on their sample from PubMed, Machine Learning (ML), in specific Support Vector Machines (SVM) and Neural Networks (NN), and Natural Language Processing (NLP), utilizing text processing and classification, are the main techniques to subsequently process structured and unstructured data. Additionally, the rise of Deep Learning (DL) was noted. Literature mainly concentrated on cancer, nervous system diseases, and cardiovascular diseases. A conceptual model is proposed to develop a roadmap from clinical data generation to clinical decision-making using ML and NLP. Additionally, the survey mentions obstacles for real-life implementation, including regulations and data exchange.

A survey from 2018 [4] highlights historical developments, including rule-based AI-systems, medical expert systems, ML approaches, and the rise of DL. Similar to [3], image-based diagnosis is presented as the main application area for medical AI, and examples are discussed within the practice of radiology, ophthalmology, dermatology, and pathology. Additional examples include genome interpretation, ML for biomarker discovery, clinical outcome prediction, patient monitoring, inferring health status through wearable devices, and autonomous robotic surgery. More specifically, the survey presents four models for information flow in conventional decision support systems, integrative decision support systems, and fully automated clinical systems. Additionally, the survey provides examples of the different development stages of medical AI applications and clinical integration. Technical challenges that were discussed are the (large) data requirements, difficulties to include contextual data, black box models, integration of multiple (external) data sources, transfer learning, preserving privacy of patients, and creating a highly scalable and secure computing environment. Social benefits can result in reducing fatigue and administrative burden. However, the implementation of AI is non-trivial and comes with several risks/hazards. In addition to careful design and implementation, certification of clinical AI-systems is often required before large-scale deployment. Moreover, consent and privacy frameworks are needed to securely process and/or share patient data. The survey calls for a multidisciplinary and multi-sector collaboration to foster development of medical AI.

More recent reviews from 2020 [5], 2021 [6], 2022 [7], and 2023 [8], provide similar overviews and note, amongst other developments, the use of Reinforcement Learning

(RL) [5] and Federated Learning (FL) [7]. Furthermore, the transition towards care a home require the selection and integration of supporting hardware and network technologies [5]. Internet of Things (IoT) devices are being deploying within hospitals and wearables are provided for individual use by patients [6]. As AI is being implemented in practice, real-world AI applications are reviewed, illustrating a wide spectrum of AI use cases and their implementations in case studies [6].

2.2 Intelligence Amplification Design Canvas and AIDAF

Earlier work introduced the intelligence amplification design canvas [11]. The main aim of the intelligence amplification design canvas is to support the conceptualization of human-centred AI-applications during the initial design thinking stages emphasize, define, and ideate [11]. The intelligence amplification design canvas is developed using action design research and evaluated in different workshop settings with a variety of use cases and domains. Guiding principles and questions related to the thirteen elements were deducted, as described in earlier work [11–14], to effectively support practitioners and IT experts to conceptualize ideas for human-centred AI-applications in four iterations.

To increase the utility of the above-mentioned design approach, the intelligence amplification design canvas and workshop approach has been incorporated in the AIDAF [14]. Additionally, the design approach has been mapped to the four design activities and six principles of the ISO 9241-210:2019 for human-centred design of interactive systems. More specifically, its potential use for design thinking and enterprise software development were explored, resulting in a set of seventeen testable propositions for future evaluation in case study research [14]. Furthermore, the AIDAF is utilized for digital transformation towards healthcare ecosystems [16].

Next, the research methodology will be described.

3   Methodology

This section describes the use of the AIDAF in Sect. 3.1, the focus group meetings in Sect. 3.2, and the three-step process for multiple use case analysis in Sect. 3.3.

3.1   Use of the AIDAF

Building upon earlier work [14], the AIDAF was utilized to establish a focus group (see Sect. 3.2) and guide a three-step process (see Sect. 3.3) to conduct the multiple use case analysis with the intelligence amplification design canvas, conceptualize individual use cases and the overview of the current state of the AI Hospital.

More specifically, an adaptive enterprise architecture cycle and design thinking approach was processed to facilitate iterative use case analysis, discussion, verification, and refinement. From a managerial and CIO perspective, the integration between the current state and the target architecture will be very important to align the digital IT strategy of the CIO during the architecture review phase of the adaptive enterprise architecture cycle. The use of AIDAF will be further discussed in Sect. 4.2 and 4.6.

3.2 Focus Group Meetings

A focus group was established to conduct confirmatory qualitative research. The main aim of the focus group was to determine the utility of the intelligence amplification design canvas for the analysis of multiple implemented AI-applications. More specifically, the use of the four guiding principles and guiding questions related to the thirteen elements of the intelligence design canvas were evaluated.

The scope was set to use cases that were implemented as part of the AI Hospital Program and actually in use. The iterative approach and already existing guiding open-ended questions of the intelligence design canvas were applied to analyse each use case. This way, a structured multiple case analysis could be conducted. Table 1 presents an overview of the five focus group meetings that were held.

The first author analysed the use cases with the intelligence amplification design canvas. The second author provided background materials, answered questions, and verified the results for each use case from the CIO perspective. The focus group meetings were led by the third author. The fourth, fifth, and sixth author were involved as subject matter experts to discuss the results.

3.3 Multiple Use Case Analysis

Each use case was analysed using the four guiding principles and questions related to the thirteen elements of the intelligence design canvas. The focus group members selected nine use cases that were implemented as part of the AI Hospital Program and currently in use within different departments of the Keio University Hospital, utilizing a variety of AI-technologies, digital tools, and supporting IT.

Then, a three-step process was agreed upon, as shown in Fig. 1. The first step was to complete the thirteen elements of the intelligence amplification design canvas for each individual use case, as described in earlier work [12, 13]. The second step was to conceptualize each use case in a conceptual representation, including the main users, systems, interfaces, and interactions. The third step was to aggregate the conceptual representations of the use cases in a high-level overview of the AI Hospital project.

Table 1. Overview of focus group meetings.

Date	Focus group meeting topics	Location	Duration
24-02-2023	Introduction AI Hospital Program	Keio University Hospital	90 min
17-03-2023	Discuss scope and methodology	Keio University Hospital	60 min
27-04-2023	Determine use cases for analysis	Hybrid	60 min
21-06-2023	Discuss and verify use case 1 and 2	Hybrid	60 min
20-07-2023	Discuss and verify use case 3–10	Hybrid	90 min

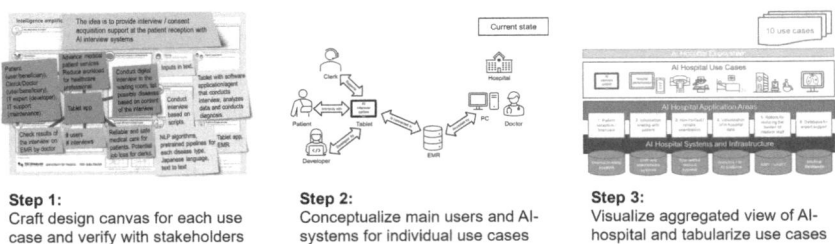

Step 1:
Craft design canvas for each use case and verify with stakeholders

Step 2:
Conceptualize main users and AI-systems for individual use cases

Step 3:
Visualize aggregated view of AI-hospital and tabularize use cases

Fig. 1. Three-step process for multiple use case analysis.

4 Multiple Use Case Analysis

This section presents the results and findings of the multiple use case analysis at Keio University Hospital in Tokyo. Section 4.1 introduces the AI Hospital Program. Section 4.2 explains the use of the AIDAF for the purpose of this study. Section 4.3 presents the nine analysed use cases. Section 4.4 contains a detailed use case analysis of three selected use cases. Section 4.5 presents an aggregated view of the current AI Hospital project. Section 4.6 describes the approach for future developments.

4.1 AI Hospital Program

The AI Hospital Program was initiated by the Government of Japan and implemented within four selected AI model hospitals [10]. In the special episode of NHK's science view, the program manager Dr. Yusuke Nakamura explains that "ai" means "love" in Japanese, which relates to the main aim of the AI Hospital Program to "bring back humanity in the medical system using AI and digitalization" [10]. A broad variety of use cases and concrete AI-applications were demonstrated in this special episode.

This study has been conducted within Keio University Hospital in Tokyo. The main objective was to construct an AI Hospital model by implementing and/or combining various AI and supporting IT that have emerged in recent years to provide: (1) reliable and safe medical care for patients, (2) advanced medical services for patients, (3) reduced workload for healthcare professionals, and (4) advanced support for community and/or home healthcare. Figure 2 presents the governance structure that was established to support the realization of the AI Hospital model. The AI Hospital Committee consisted of a small headquarter and broad decentralized organization by involving more than 25 departments. All these members were stimulated to develop AI-initiatives and attend an information exchange meeting every two months.

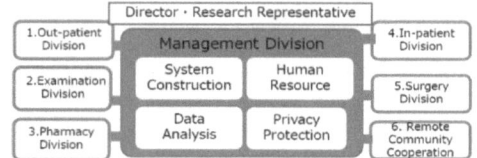

Fig. 2. AI Hospital Committee at Keio University Hospital.

4.2 Multiple Use Case Analysis with the AIDAF

As introduced in Sect. 3.1, the AIDAF was used to guide the multiple use case analysis as part of the AI Hospital Program [10]. Figure 3 visualizes the use of the AIDAF for this study. The other three AI model hospitals (light) were not analysed.

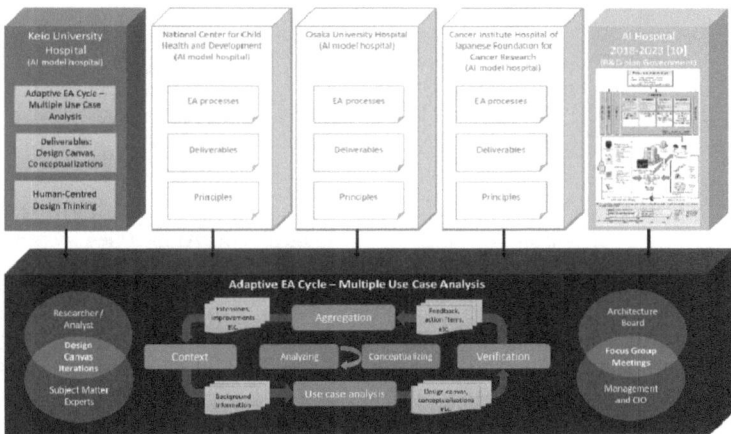

Fig. 3. Application of the AIDAF for multiple use case analysis.

A reversed variant of the adaptive enterprise architecture cycle was agreed upon by the focus group as described in Sect. 3.2 and shown in Fig. 3. Here, the intelligence amplification design canvas was used by the researcher together with subject matter experts to analyse use cases based on background materials that were provided by the CIO. The four guiding principles were applied to complete a design canvas and conceptualization for each use case. The results were discussed and verified during the focus group meetings. An initial version of the aggregated overview of the AI Hospital was created based on the first focus group meeting and iteratively refined.

Using the AIDAF and the adaptive enterprise architecture cycle, described in Sect. 4.2, and the four guiding principles of the intelligence amplification design can be mapped to the six principles of the ISO 9241-210:2019 for human-centred design of interactive systems: (1) design based on explicit understanding of users, tasks, and environments, (2) user involvement throughout design and development, (3) design driven by user-centred evaluation, (4) iterative processes, (5) design that addresses the whole experience, and (6) design team with multidisciplinary skills and perspectives.

4.3 Use Case Analysis

This section provides a brief overview of the nine use cases that were analysed using the intelligence amplification design canvas and its four guiding principles. Subsequently, the context of use, main users and goals have been summarized for each use case together with the conceptualization.

Use Case #1: AI Interview System. The idea behind this use case (Fig. 4), is to provide interview and consent acquisition support at the patient reception with AI interview systems. The main users are the patient, clerk, and doctor. The goals are to (1) advance medical patient services and (2) reduce workload for healthcare professional.

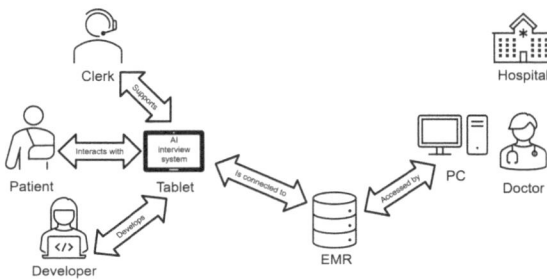

Fig. 4. Conceptualization of the use case related to the AI interview system.

Use Case #2: Digital Patient Information Service. The idea behind this use case (Fig. 5) is to establish efficient information sharing with the patient by providing digital information services via smartphones. The main users are the patient, clinics, and doctor. The goals are advance medical patient services, (2) reduce workload for healthcare professional, and (3) advance support for home care.

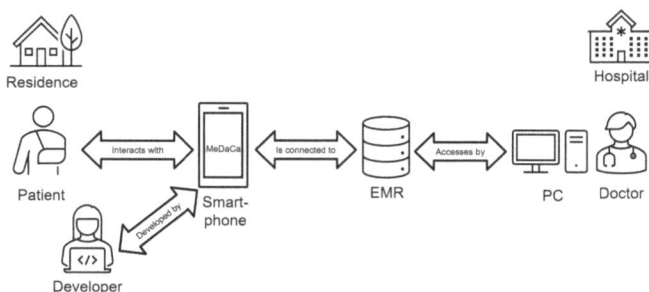

Fig. 5. Conceptualization of use case for digital patient information service.

Use Case #3: Robot Assisted Coronary Angiography. The idea behind this use case (Fig. 6) is to reduce the radiation exposure of the cardiologist by separating the X-ray area and the control area for robot-assisted angiography. The main user is the cardiologist. The main goal is to reduce radiation exposure.

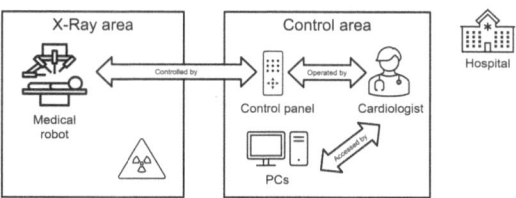

Fig. 6. Conceptualization of use case for robot assisted coronary angiography.

Use Case #4: Upright Remote CT Scan. The idea behind this use case (Fig. 7) is to realize a remotely operated, non-contact upright CT scan of patients in a standing position. The main users are the patient and the radiographer. The main goals are to (1) reduce the time to take CT scans and (2) reduce the exposure to radiation.

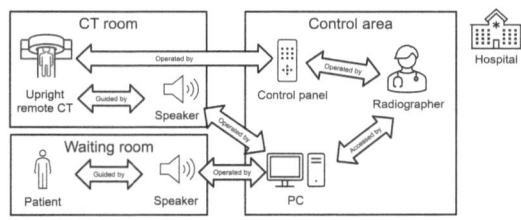

Fig. 7. Conceptualization of use case with upright remote CT scan.

Use Case #5: Optimizing Bed Management. The idea behind this use case (Fig. 8) is to centrally analyse and visualize in-hospital sensor data from bed wheels. The main users are the hospital management and operators in the command center. The main goals are to (1) optimize bed management and (2) predict bed occupation.

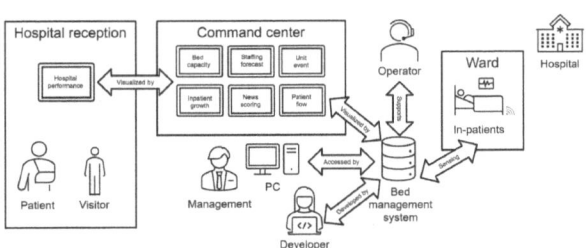

Fig. 8. Conceptualization of use case for optimizing bed management.

Use Case #6: Improving US, CT, and MRI Equipment Efficiency. The idea behind this use case (Fig. 9) is to improve the efficiency of US, CT, and MRI equipment by analysing sensor data. The main users are hospital management and data analysts. The main goals are to (1) improve equipment utilization and (2) reduce costs.

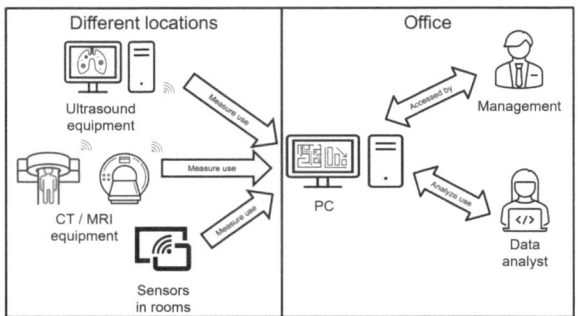

Fig. 9. Conceptualization of use case for improving US, CT, and MRI equipment efficiency.

Use Case #7: Drug Delivery Robot. The idea behind this use case (Fig. 10) is to introduce delivery robots to bring medicines to the ward. The main users are pharmacists and nurses. The main goal is to reduce the workload for medical staff.

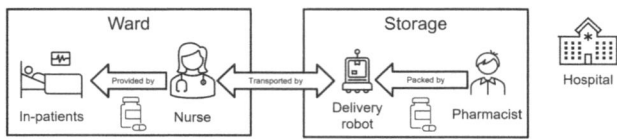

Fig. 10. Conceptualization of use case for drug delivery robot.

Use Case #8: Automatic Picking Robot. The idea behind this use case (Fig. 11) is to ensure accurate drug dispensing by introducing an automatic picking robot. The main users are pharmacists and logistics employees. The main goals are to (1) improve medical safety, (2) reduce mistakes, and (3) reduce workload.

Fig. 11. Conceptualization of the use case with the automatic picking robot.

Use Case #9: AI Self-driving Wheelchair. The idea behind this use case (Fig. 12) is to transport patients with physical impairments to appointments by introducing an AI self-driving wheelchair. The main user is the patient. The main goals are to (1) improve patient mobility and (2) reduce the burden for medical staff.

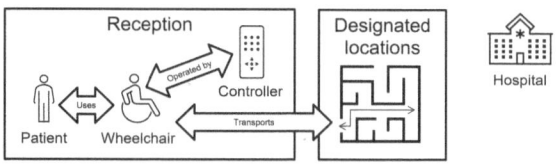

Fig. 12. Conceptualization of the use case for the AI self-driving wheelchair.

4.4 Detailed Use Case Analysis

This section presents the results of a detailed use case analysis that was done using the four guiding principles of the intelligence amplification design canvas: (1) human-centric design, (2) agent embodiment, (3) data driven enhancement, and (4) human in the loop. Due to page restrictions, the following three use cases, that utilize different AI-technologies, will be discussed in more detail: (1) AI Interview System, (2) Optimizing Bed Management, and (3) AI Self-driving Wheelchair.

In the next subsections, the use of the intelligence amplification design canvas is demonstrated to iteratively define the selected use cases using its thirteen elements. The colours correspond to the four design activities of the ISO 9241-210:2019 for human-centred design of interactive systems: (1) understand and specify the context of use (green), (2) specify the user requirements (red), (3) produce design solutions (yellow), and (4) evaluate the design (blue).

Use Case #1: AI Interview System. Following the context of use and conceptualization in Subsect. 4.3, Fig. 13 presents the results of the four iterations using the guiding principles of the intelligence amplification design canvas for use case #1.

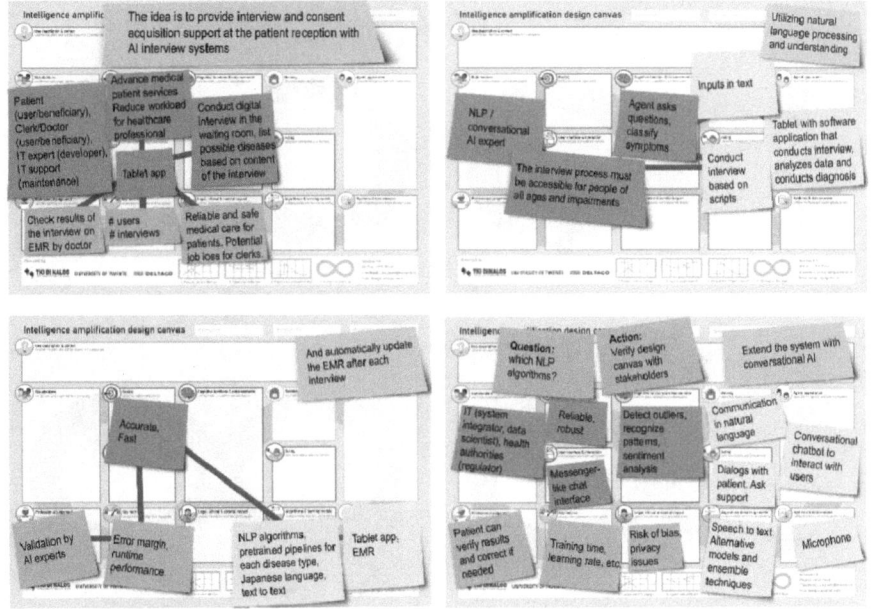

Fig. 13. Results of the four iterations for the analysis of use case #1.

First, the human-centred use of the tablet app was defined. Patients, supported by clerks, use the AI Interview System to complete digital interviews in the waiting room to prepare the consultation or examination by the doctor. The doctor can check the results in the Electronic Medical Record (EMR) of the patient along with possible diseases. This way, the doctor can prepare and focus on communication with the patient during the consultation or examination, which contributes to bring back humanity as explained in Sect. 4.1 and the NHK special episode [15]. The use of AI to identify possible diseases has several ethical implications. Each disease classification using AI should be carefully designed, developed, and evaluated.

Second, the current design solution was defined. The current AI Interview System uses NLP algorithms to process input of patients and conducts interviews based on interview scripts. Revisiting the first iteration defined which tasks are handled by the AI system and refined the user interface requirements and required expertise.

Third, the core systems and algorithms were defined. Here, the iteration helped to refine goals and metrics from the perspective of data driven enhancement.

Fourth, the consistency of the use case analysis was checked and possible extensions were ideated. This resulted in the idea to extend the current AI Interview System with conversational AI.

Use Case #5: Optimizing Bed Management. Following the context of use and conceptualization in Subsect. 4.3, Fig. 14 presents the results of the iterative analysis of use case #5.

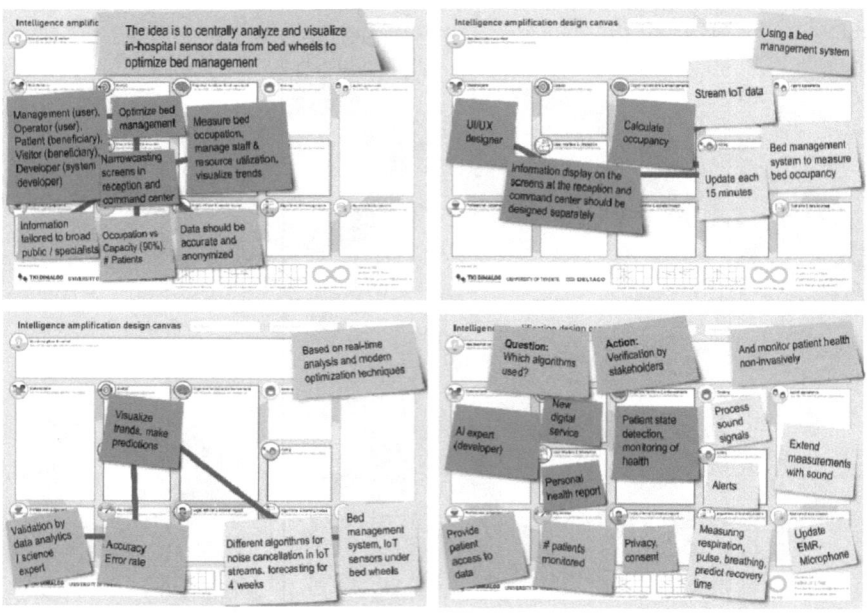

Fig. 14. Results of the four iterations for the analysis of use case #5.

First, the human-centred use of narrowcasting screens in the command center by operators and management was analysed. The bed management system provides up-to-date insight in the current occupation and predictions for the next four weeks. This information is used to optimize the utilization of the available bed capacity. Additionally, meaningful information is shared with medical staff, patients, and visitors.

Second, the data collection with IoT sensors underneath bed wheels was analysed. Revisiting the first iteration identified the need of UI/UX knowledge.

Third, the main functionality of the bed management system was discussed. In the current set-up, the bed occupation is updated each 15 min and predictions are made for four weeks ahead. Data analytics techniques can be useful here to visualize trends. Potentially other optimization techniques can be applied.

Fourth, the verification revealed that the bed management uses sophisticated noise cancellation algorithms, developed by university researchers, to extract data to detect the patient state. Algorithms were developed to measure respiration and heart pulse non-invasively. This contributes to reducing patient stress and well-being, as demonstrated in the NHK special episode [15]. In the future, additional sensors could be added to improve remote patient monitoring. Additionally, the data could also be used to develop patient-centred reports and update the EMR. Here, privacy and consent acquisition are important design aspects to evaluate next to algorithm performance.

Use Case #9: AI Self-driving Wheelchair. Following the context of use and conceptualization in Subsect. 4.3, Fig. 15 presents the results for use case #9.

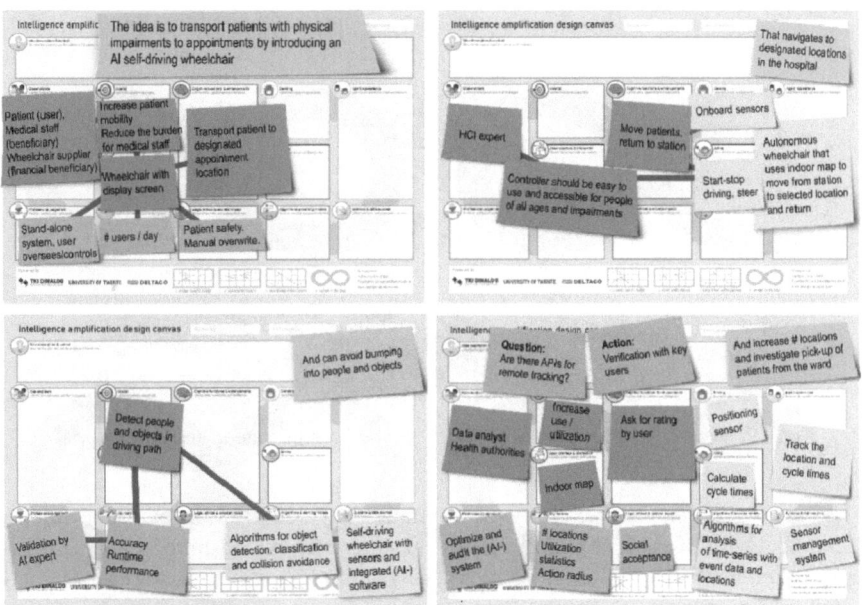

Fig. 15. Results of the four iterations for the analysis of use case #9.

First, the use of the AI Self-driving Wheelchair by impaired visitors and/or patients was defined. This fully autonomous wheelchair transports people to designated locations, increasing patient mobility whilst reducing the burden for medical staff. The wheelchair is a stand-alone system with built-in safety measures. The person driving the wheelchair is in control and can control the wheelchair using a display.

Second, the solution design was analysed. The AI Self-driving Wheelchair uses an indoor map and onboard sensors. Revisiting the first iteration added the requirement of universal access to ensure that the wheelchair can be used by people of all ages and impairments. This requires expertise regarding human computer interaction.

Third, the use of AI-techniques was defined. Here, algorithms are in use for detecting people, obstacles, or objects in the driving path and collision avoidance. Although the wheelchair does not drive fast, timely and accurate functioning of these algorithms is important to ensure safety.

Fourth, scaling up the use of the AI Self-driving Wheelchair was explored. This resulted in ideas for on-demand use by patients to leave the ward and for example go to appointments or facilities. Additionally, sensors could be attached to the AI Self-driving Wheelchair for asset tracking and optimalization of its utilization. Further-more, a simple user feedback system could be introduced to measure patient satisfaction and collect user input for improvement of patient mobility services.

4.5   Aggregated Overview AI Hospital

After analysing the nine use cases, the current state of the AI Hospital was conceptualized in an aggregated view, as shown in see Fig. 16.

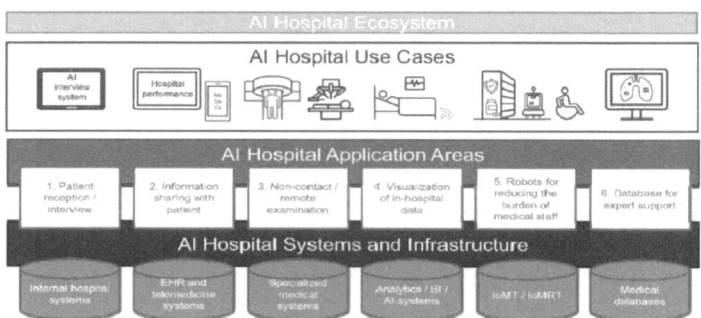

Fig. 16. Aggregated high-level overview of the current state of the AI Hospital.

The aggregated high-level overview contains a layered view, integrating functional and technical building blocks within the current state of the AI Hospital at Keio University Hospital. The analysed use cases were categorized in six application areas: (1) patient reception interviewing, (2) information sharing with patients, (3) non-contact and/or remote examination, (4) visualization of in-hospital data, (5) robots for reducing the burden of medical staff, and (6) databases for expert support. The main supporting systems are presented in the infrastructure layer, including internal hospital systems, EMR and telemedicine systems, specificized medical systems, systems for analytical purposes (e.g., Business Intelligence, AI), Internet of (Medical Robotic) Things (IoT/IoMRT), and medical databases.

The current high-level overview highlights the AI Hospital ecosystem layer. Although this layer was not within the primary scope of the AI Hospital implementation at Keio University Hospital, the role of external stakeholders is clearly visible based on the analysed use cases. Current work in progress aims to explore the ecosystem layer as part of research and development work in the OHP2030 consortium.

Next, the proposed approach of the AIDAF for the development of future AI-applications for the 2nd generation AI Hospital Program will be discussed.

4.6 Developing Future AI-Applications with the AIDAF

The AI Hospital Program will be continued. Figure 17 presents the proposed use of the AIDAF to support the development of the 2nd generation AI Hospital Program and collaborate with the OHP2030 consortium to create an AI-Hospital Ecosystem.

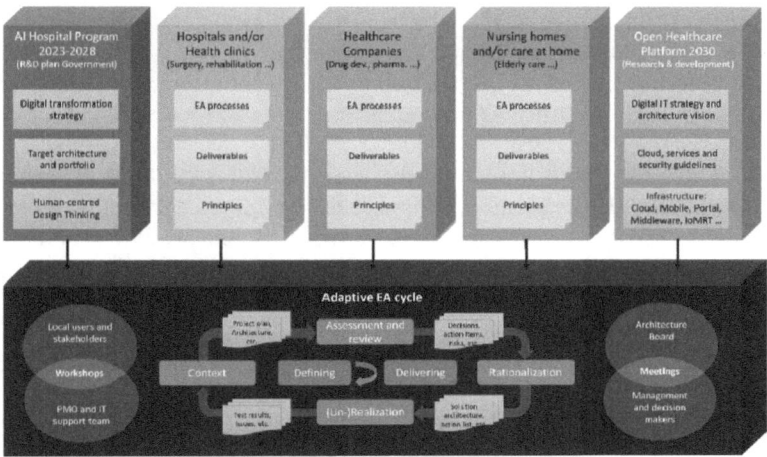

Fig. 17. Proposed use of the AIDAF for the development of the 2nd generation AI Hospital.

Similar to the proposed use of the AIDAF within the OHP2030 consortium [9], the AI Hospital Program can leverage the AIDAF and human-centred design thinking approach, as described in [14, 16], to support the development of new AI-applications for the 2nd generation AI Hospital. Current work in progress focuses on the development of a digital transformation strategy, target architecture, and portfolio of projects. Here, the intelligence amplification design canvas can be used to organize workshops with local users and ecosystem partners. The adaptive enterprise architecture cycle can be used to guide the design and development processes, (solution) architecture reviewing, and related managerial decision making. The established focus group can be extended and transformed to function as an architecture board for the AI Hospital Committee and fulfil a governance function for projects.

The next section will discuss the results in relation to related work.

5   Discussion

This study evaluated the use of the intelligence amplification design canvas and AIDAF for the analysis of multiple use cases and implemented AI-applications within Keio University Hospital as part of the completed five-year AI Hospital Program.

The use of AI within healthcare and medicine has been extensively reviewed and is continuing to develop rapidly. The broad variety of application areas, use cases, and AI-techniques are well-reflected in the current AI Hospital Program and concrete implementations within Keio University Hospital. Here, digitalization, supporting IT, and IoT sensors enable sophisticated use of data-driven AI-techniques. Additionally, modern robotics have proven to be effective and safe to address current needs within the context of hospitals. The current study resulted in a conceptualization of the current state of an AI Hospital and identified areas for future research and development.

Regarding RQ1, the intelligence amplification design canvas and the AIDAF have together proven to be effective to analyse existing AI-applications and conduct a multiple use case analysis. Regarding RQ2, the adaptive enterprise architecture cycle provided a three-step process to analyse, discuss and review individual use cases and recursively conceptualize an aggregated overview based on a managerial and CIO perspective. This approach could easily be repeated and might provide a common ground for cross use case analysis in other (AI model) hospitals.

However, there are some limitations that must be addressed. First, it must be noted that in the current study design the intelligence design canvas does not include in-depth user evaluation and/or case study research. Furthermore, the level of granularity of the conceptualizations is limited and based on informal representations. Additionally, the three-step process should be tested in other organizations.

Next, the study will be concluded.

6   Conclusion

This study provides empirical support that the intelligence amplification design canvas, and more specifically its four guiding principles, and the AIDAF can effectively support the processes to conduct a use case analysis of implemented AI-applications as well as conducting a multiple use case analysis. Regarding RQ1, the study analysed nine use cases and resulted in an aggregated view of the AI Hospital project within Keio University Hospital as part of the five-year AI Hospital Program. The use of the intelligence amplification design canvas has proven effective to create conceptual representations. Three selected use cases were discussed in more detail to demonstrate the utility of the intelligence amplification design canvas for the analysis of existing use cases. Regarding RQ2, the use of the AIDAF was positioned and demonstrated for the purpose of a multiple use case analysis and future development of AI-applications. Here, the adaptive enterprise architecture cycle has proven effective in combination with the focus group meetings. The recursive use of the intelligence design canvas, based on the three-step process that was applied as an adaptive enterprise architecture cycle within the AIDAF, effectively supported the creation of an aggregated view and also provided useful new insights.

This study contributes to the fast-growing AI knowledge base in healthcare and medicine with a timely multiple use case analysis. As such, scholars and healthcare professionals can leverage the research methodology and results of the multiple use case analysis both as a reference and a potential starting point to explore potential AI use cases within the context of a hospital. The approach can be applied and tested in other organizations and potentially be extended to a new method for analysing and modelling digital architectures and services. This way, the results of this study are also considered relevant for the information systems research discipline. More specifically, this study can contribute to the development of new or improved intelligent digital architectures, methods, and services for Society 5.0.

The present study has some limitations that need to be addressed. The main limitations of the multiple use case analysis is the application within a single organization. Additionally, the use case analysis is not based on an in-depth user evaluation. Furthermore, although quantification is addressed within the intelligence amplification design canvas, the current study is mainly based on a qualitative use case analysis.

From a practical point of view, this study provided insight in the current state of development of the AI Hospital project at Keio University Hospital and identified opportunities for extensions and future development. Building upon earlier work and the current study, the intelligence amplification design canvas and AIDAF can be used for the development of the 2nd generation of the AI Hospital Program and co-develop an AI-ecosystem together with the OHP2030 consortium.

Future research may contribute to analyse similar use cases in other (AI-)hospitals for a cross use case analysis. Therefore, the authors aspire to establish a working group for collaborative research, development, and evaluation of generalizable use cases as part of the AI Hospital Program and the OHP2030 consortium. Furthermore, future research can investigate alignment with established standards and methods for in-depth user evaluation and case study research. More specifically, future research can contribute to extract (generic) software patterns and (reusable) AI mechanisms based on the multiple case analysis and/or other use cases.

References

1. Cabinet Office (2023). Society 5.0. https://www8.cao.go.jp/cstp/english/society5_0/index. html
2. Cabinet Office (2023). Examples of Creating New Value in the Fields of Healthcare and Caregiving (Society 5.0). https://www8.cao.go.jp/cstp/english/society5_0/medical_e.html
3. Jiang, F., Jiang, Y., Zhi, H., et al.: Artificial intelligence in healthcare: past, present and future. Stroke Vasc. Neurol. (2017). https://doi.org/10.1136/svn-2017-000101
4. Yu, K.H., Beam, A.L., Kohane, I.S.: Artificial intelligence in healthcare. Nat. Biomed. Eng. **2**, 719–731 (2018). https://doi.org/10.1038/s41551-018-0305-z
5. Rong, G., Mendez, A., Bou Assi, E., Zhao, B., Sawan, M.: Artificial intelligence in healthcare: review and prediction case studies. Engineering **6**(3), 291–301 (2020). https://doi.org/10. 1016/j.eng.2019.08.015. ISSN 2095-8099

6. Lee, D., Yoon, S.N.: Application of artificial intelligence-based technologies in the healthcare industry: opportunities and challenges. Int. J. Environ. Res. Public Health **18**(1), 271 (2021). https://doi.org/10.3390/ijerph18010271
7. Rajpurkar, P., Chen, E., Banerjee, O., et al.: AI in health and medicine. Nat. Med. **28**, 31–38 (2022). https://doi.org/10.1038/s41591-021-01614-0
8. Thayyib, P.V., et al.: State-of-the-art of artificial intelligence and big data analytics reviews in five different domains: a bibliometric summary. Sustainability **15**(5), 4026 (2023). https://doi.org/10.3390/su15054026
9. Piest, J.P.S., Masuda, Y., Nakamura, O.: Healthcare under society 5.0: a systematic literature review of applications and case studies. In: Chen, Y.W., Tanaka, S., Howlett, R.J., Jain, L.C. (eds.) Innovation in Medicine and Healthcare. KES InMed 2023. Smart Innovation, Systems and Technologies, vol. 357. Springer, Singapore (2023). https://doi.org/10.1007/978-981-99-3311-2_8
10. Cabinet Office: Cross-ministerial Strategic Innovation Promotion Program. SIP Innovative Artificial Intelligence (AI) Hospital System (2019). https://www8.cao.go.jp/cstp/english/10_aihospital_rdplan.pdf
11. Piest, J.P.S., Iacob, M.E., Wouterse, M.J.T.: Designing intelligence amplification: a design canvas for practitioners. In: Ahram, T., Taiar, R. (eds.) Human Interaction & Emerging Technologies (IHIET 2022): Artificial Intelligence & Future Applications. International Conference. AHFE Open Access, vol. 68. AHFE International, USA (2022). https://doi.org/10.54941/ahfe1002714
12. Piest, J.P.S., Iacob, M.E., Wouterse, M.J.T.: Designing intelligence amplification: organizing a design canvas workshop. In: Ahram, T., Taiar, R. (eds.) Human Interaction & Emerging Technologies (IHIET 2022): Artificial Intelligence & Future Applications. International Conference. AHFE Open Access, vol. 68. AHFE International, USA (2022). https://doi.org/10.54941/ahfe1002739
13. Piest, J.P.S., Iacob, M.E., Wouterse, M.J.T.: Tutorial: conceptualizing intelligence amplification in human-centred AI applications using the design canvas. In: Ahram, T., Taiar, R. (eds.) Human Interaction and Emerging Technologies (IHIET-AI 2023): Artificial Intelligence and Future Applications. International Conference. AHFE Open Access, vol. 70. AHFE International, USA (2023). https://doi.org/10.54941/ahfe1002937
14. Piest, J.P.S., Masuda, Y., Nakamura, O., Karaca, K.: Human-centred design thinking using the intelligence amplification design canvas and the adaptive integrated digital architecture framework. In: Zimmermann, A., Howlett, R., Jain, L.C. (eds.) Human Centred Intelligent Systems. KES-HCIS 2023. Smart Innovation, Systems and Technologies, vol. 359. Springer, Singapore (2023). https://doi.org/10.1007/978-981-99-3424-9_15
15. NHK Science view (2023). Special Episode: AI Hospitals - A Step Towards the Future. https://www3.nhk.or.jp/nhkworld/en/ondemand/video/2015303/
16. Masuda, Y., Jain, R., Zimmermann, A., Schmidt, R., Nakamura, O., Toma, T.: Applying AIDAF for digital transformation toward ecosystem in global enterprise. In: Zimmermann, A., Howlett, R., Jain, L.C. (eds.) Human Centred Intelligent Systems. KES-HCIS 2023. Smart Innovation, Systems and Technologies, vol. 359. Springer, Singapore (2023). https://doi.org/10.1007/978-981-99-3424-9_16

Driving Innovation in Industry 4.0 Through Business Model Simulation

Paula Velandia$^{(\boxtimes)}$ (iD), Andrea Herrera (iD), L. María José Bonilla, Mario Sánchez (iD), and Jorge Villalobos (iD)

Universidad de los Andes, Bogotá, Colombia
`pa.velandiar@uniandes.edu.co`

Abstract. In the dynamic Industry 4.0 landscape, organizations aim to enhance economic performance and sustainability. Business Model Innovation (BMI) plays a vital role, enabling firms to integrate disruptive technologies and maintain competitiveness. However, current BMI research mostly focuses on static Business Models (BMs), neglecting the dynamic interactions between BMs components. However, dynamic BM analysis is critical in the era of Industry 4.0 as it is a valuable decision-making tool supporting strategic planning in complex BMs. In this work, we propose a novel approach to conceptualize dynamic BM scenarios through a metamodel. Then, we present a model to demonstrate the use of our approach in the context of Industry 4.0. Finally, we discuss the practical implications that our proposal has on equipping firms with mechanisms to foster innovation and adaptability and respond to market volatility and competition.

Keywords: Industry 4.0 · Business Model Innovation · Business Model Simulation

1 Introduction

In the industry 4.0 model, the main objective of organizations is to improve their economic and operational performance while being more sustainable. In particular, manufacturing firms have become increasingly interested in incorporating this concept to their business model (BM) [1]. Moreover, researchers have also recognized this concept as the main driver for innovation in the manufacturing industries in the coming decades [2]. With this goal in mind, firms have focused on using various disruptive technologies to influence their production and value delivery [3]. For instance, firms have attempted to incorporate artificial intelligence, robotic process automation (RPA) or augmented reality [4] into their processes.

Along those lines, the concept of Business Model Innovation (BMI) has become relevant in this context. Particularly, as new BMs are regularly generated [5], firms have become interested in understanding how these innovations can be incorporated into their own particular BMs. In other words, BMI is now seen as an essential capability for organizations seeking to drive growth, revitalize a lagging core or defend against industry disruption [5]. Therefore, in Industry 4.0 is an essential tool for acquiring and

T. P. Sales et al. (Eds.): EDOC 2023 Workshops, LNBIP 498, pp. 23–38, 2024.
https://doi.org/10.1007/978-3-031-54712-6_2

maintaining competitive advantage [6]. Research on BMI advocates the need to rethink traditional BMs [7] in order for firms to develop the necessary capabilities to become part of Industry 4.0 [8]. Furthermore, the concept of BMI has gained relevance among researchers and practitioners as it can be implemented in any firm, regardless of their size or the product they sell [9]. In this sense, multiple small and medium-sized manufacturing firms can also benefit from the innovation of their BMs.

In general, research on BMI has been divided into two points of view. The first corresponds to the static dimension of the BMs, which focuses on describing a business as a set of components and their relationships [11], leaving aside the interactions between them. The second, corresponds to the dynamic dimension of the BMs, which seeks to represent the evolution of the business over time by analyzing the interactions between its components [4, 10]. This type of work has gained momentum since it allows to understand both how value is created among the components of a business over time, and how changes in these components impact the rest of the BM [1]. Particularly, some authors recognize its importance, since humans are unable to mentally infer dynamic behaviors, as well as to recognize causal feedback relationships distant in time and space [3].

In the context of Industry 4.0, dynamic analysis is considered as a support tool for decision making, strategic planning, and for the modeling and execution of complicated systems by evaluating multiple scenarios [11, 12]. In other words, since business are complex systems, it is necessary to analyze them taking into account their dynamic behavior [3] since several components of BMs are time sensitive or depend on other relationships [7]. Therefore, the static representation is not sufficient to correctly analyze complex businesses [7]. And, in Industry 4.0, being able to understand and innovate BMs is crucial to effectively respond to market volatility, and intense competition [3, 13]. Consequently, research on the dynamic dimension of BMs is highly valued in Industry 4.0 as it saves time and resources by providing reliable estimates of business performance, which is one of the most useful indicators for decision making [3, 14].

However, as mentioned, BMI research has limitations, as it has been mostly focused on the static dimension of BMs [14]. Some researchers have proposed different approaches to perform dynamic analysis using for example system dynamics [5], which have allowed to evaluate specific Industry 4.0 business scenarios [15]. Nevertheless, these approaches are not particularly focused on BMI. Therefore, they lack common guidance on how firms can analyze their own BMs from a dynamic point of view.

In this paper, we present an approach that enables the translation of static BMs to dynamic BMs. Then, we model multiple scenarios to analyze how dynamic analysis techniques enhance BMI in the context of Industry 4.0 and we present one of them. The remaining sections of this document are organized as follows: Sect. 2 provides an overview of the existing literature on static and dynamic BMs and their role on BMI in the Industry 4.0 context. Section 3 describes the metamodel, which is the basis of the proposed approach and the scenario that was built to exemplify its application. Section 4 presents the simulation results and Sect. 5 discusses their implications in practice. Finally, Sect. 6 presents conclusions, limitations, and directions for future research.

2   Business Models and Simulation in Industry 4.0

BMI research calls for a review of current BMs and the approaches used to innovate them [1]. Moreover, authors such as [16] recognize the need to use existing BMs as inspiration to achieve innovation. Thus, an increasing number of researchers are becoming interested in understanding BMI for this purpose. However, most research on BMI is not particularly focus on Industry 4.0 but on a more general point of view, covering both the static and dynamic dimensions of BMs in multiple industries.

In the static dimension of BMs, [5] has focused on analyzing BMs from a structural point of view determining their key components and the relationships between them. Along the same path, [15] described how the components of BMs are organized and how they can communicate with each other to generate value and revenue. Even if most research is not focused on Industry 4.0, their contributions can be used to understand manufacturing BMs and leveraging on these for Industry 4.0 innovations. For instance, a well-recognized research on static BMs is the Business Model Canvas [17] by Osterwalder. It has been widely used as a tool to define and evaluate BMs [1, 13, 15]. Moreover, the Business Model Canvas allows specifying BMs both in the Industry 4.0 or other contexts.

Only a few authors have focused on studying BMs on Industry 4.0. For instance, [18] provides a taxonomy to describe, analyze and classify BMs in Industry 4.0. Other authors have focused on specific types of BMs in the context of Industry 4.0. For instance, circular BMs [19], open BMs [20], sustainable BMs [21] or the BM's of technology providers [22]. In addition, some authors explore the impact of particular technologies in BMs such as digital platforms [23] or additive manufacturing [24].

However, static BMs have a significant drawback in that they lack the ability to analyze inter-component behavior and their responses to events. To overcome this limitation, some authors suggest enhancing static representations by incorporating dynamic characteristics and conducting simulations for specific business scenarios [6]. Consequently, BMI research has shifted its focus towards understanding the dynamic aspects of BMs. Especially, researchers have explored the dynamics of Digital Enterprises [25] and sustainable BMs [26] while others have concentrated on small and medium-sized enterprises [27]. Despite conducting an initial search using keywords such as "BMI" and "dynamic elements", we found a lack of relevant results in academic papers. Hence, it appears that existing research on BMI insufficiently addresses the incorporation of dynamic elements, failing to provide adequate support for BMI in this context.

Researchers state that it is necessary to create models for exploration, discovery and analysis of BMs on Industry 4.0 [10]. In general, research on dynamic aspects in Industry 4.0 focuses on providing a theoretical basis [28], simulating BMs in specific industries [29] or with specific technologies [30]. However, it is not clear how firms can use or replicate these results in their own BMs to make more informed decisions.

In conclusion, the significance of BMI within the context of Industry 4.0 cannot be overstated. Nonetheless, the existing body of research in this domain seems to lack sufficient emphasis on Industry 4.0's specific context. The prevailing focus on static (BM) modeling is limiting the potential for innovation, as it hinders a comprehensive analysis of business component behavior within specific and practical business scenarios. To fully harness the transformative potential of Industry 4.0 and BMI, there is an evident need for academic endeavors that address the dynamic aspects of BMs and their relevance in the context of contemporary industrial landscapes. By incorporating dynamic elements into the related research, we can foster a more profound understanding of the intricate interplay between various business components and enhance the efficacy of decision-making processes in an increasingly complex and evolving business environment.

3 Proposal

In this section, we present how simulation can be used to validate innovations on BMs in Industry 4.0 improving decision-making processes. Figure 1 presents our approach. To start with, from [12], we define the metamodel of the elements of a static BM. Then, we identify the fundamental concepts of Discrete Event Simulation (DES) which is the selected approach as it can provide exclusive insights for predicting outcomes of multiple scenarios [31]. These are the concepts that are then incorporated to the metamodel. Finally, we use an example to demonstrate the use of our proposal to facilitate decision making processes for a firm in the context of Industry 4.0.

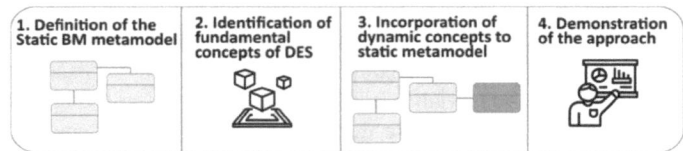

Fig. 1. Methodological approach.

As mentioned, we define the static metamodel by relying on [12]. This metamodel proposes the elements to model the structural part of a BM. First, *Components* represent stocks of information, value and/or money that exchange items with other components. This exchange is achieved through *Channels*, which represent how a component sends and receives the exchanged item. Each channel must have a type: (1) Provisioning channels that allow one component to supply goods to another, (2) Transformation channels that allow raw materials to be transformed to produce the exchanged items, (3) Distribution channels that allow one component to deliver exchanged items to another, (4) Relationship channels that allow information to be exchanged between two components and (5) Monetization channels that allow money to be received for the item sold. Each channel performs a group of activities related to its objective. For instance, the activities of the monetization channel could be "receive payment" or "deliver a receipt".

To include the dynamic part, we first stablish the elements of DES [32]. *Entities* are the elements under study (e.g., customers). They move through the system, can hold different states, and interact with other entities. Additionally, there are *Activities*, which are the actions performed in the system. Finally, there are *Parameters*. These can be defined over entities (e.g., customer demand), over activities (e.g., processing time) or over the whole system (e.g., time of operation). And they can be updated when an event or trigger occurs.

Next, is imperative to stablish the relation between the static concepts and the dynamic ones. For this purpose, we define Business Scenarios (BSc). These are specific processes that occur in a BM (e.g., provisioning process or product sale). We define that a BM can have multiple BSc and that a BSc is the implementation of a group of activities in a particular order. Depending on the BSc of interest, the components in the static part can become *Entities* of the dynamic part (e.g., customer). In that case, the correspondent parameters will have to be defined. As parameters can also be defined over activities this relationship must exist in the metamodel as well. Finally, a BSc has a set of triggers that initiates activities in the scenario (e.g., the creation of an order initiates the manufacturing activities). Of course, these triggers also have a set of parameters defined over them (e.g., an order is created every hour). The extended metamodel is presented in Fig. 2. The concepts of the dynamic part are in blue. As the fundamental elements of DES are included, we argue this metamodel is sufficient to incorporate dynamic elements into static representations of BMs. Consequently, this metamodel allows to easily define the parameters, triggers, and activities in a BSc. Thus, easing the translation process into simulation scenarios which are then used in decision-making processes.

To illustrate this approach, we use a BM constructed from the theory proposed by [1] regarding BMI in Industry 4.0. In our case, we present a manufacturing BM with a user-driven approach and an interest in innovating by improving its customer interface. First, we create the BM that conforms to the static part of the metamodel. Second, we add the dynamic elements. And third, we use a simulation software to analyze the impact that the proposed innovation may have on the firm.

The example firm, Casey, sells customized mobile phone cases to its customers. At their current operation, they have a point of sale where customers first describe to an employee the design, they want their case to have. The employee then sends the specifications to the warehouse where the case is customized. Once these activities are completed, the case is delivered to the customer. If the case design is satisfactory, the customer pays and leaves the point of sale. If it is not, the customer re-specifies their requirements, and the employee generates a new order for a new case. If the case does not meet the customer's expectations for a second time, the customer leaves. This is the current scenario. However, Casey is interested in innovating its selling process by improving its customer interface. By implementing an AI-enhanced website for customers to provide a detailed design of case they want aiming to be able to serve more customers, minimize errors in the design-to-manufacturing process and provide a better customer experience. In the future scenario, customers will enter the new website, design their case, and pay for it. Then, they will wait until Casey receives the order, designs the case, and delivers it at their home. To evaluate the impact that this initiative has on the current BM, we use our approach.

First, we provide a visual representation for the static part of this BM, using the language defined by [12]. In their work, *Components* are represented as boxes and *Channels* as lines between them. Dotted lines are digital channels. Activities are not represented for simplicity. Then, we add the dynamic elements to the model (see Fig. 3). In this example, we model two BSc: BSc1, highlighted in purple, groups, and orders the activities for provisioning process, and BSc2, highlighted in pink, focuses on the sale process, including design, payment, and distribution activities. Each scenario has

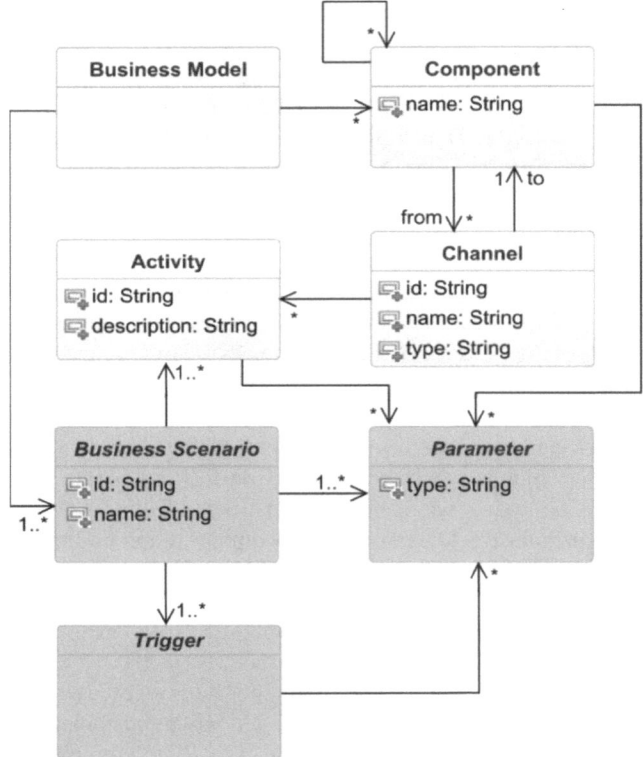

Fig. 2. Dynamic BMs Metamodel

the order of the activities in each channel. For instance, in BSc1 the order is sent to the customer (see Fig. 3 BSc1 – 1) and then the provider sends the products (see Fig. 3 BSc1 – 2). For BSc2, we analyze the behavior of the customer. Thus, this component is the *Entity* of interest. Figure 3 also presents the parameters defined for activities A.1 and A.2. For instance, A.2 is the activity in which the customer provides the information and requirements to design the case. For this activity, we define the time it will take to complete using a time parameter, which we also set for all the other activities in the model. Finally, we define the parameters for the triggers. For example, Trigger 1 initiates the relationship activities when the customer enters the interface. For this trigger, we define the capacity parameter which is understood as how many customers can specify their requirements at the same time, the same is done for each Trigger.

Once we define the dynamic elements of the scenarios, we select Simio as the simulation software to study their behavior. This selection is due to Simio's use of a discrete event simulation model and ease of access for the research team. However, as the dynamic elements do not depend on the simulation software, any other software with the same simulation model can be used. This is a fundamental step to effectively analyze BScs. By correctly and completely defining the dynamic elements in the static representation,

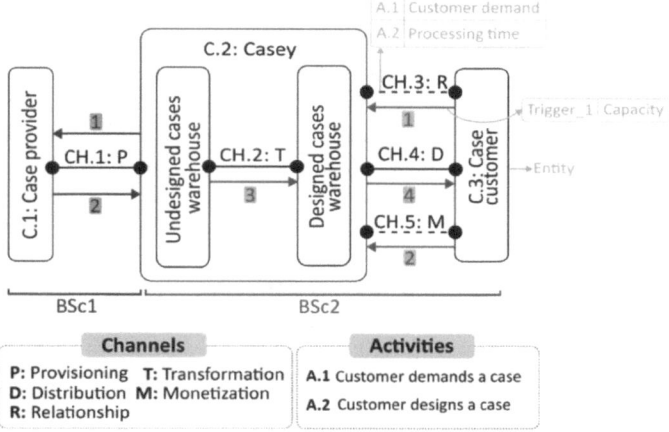

Fig. 3. Casey's BM.

the translation to any simulation software should be done almost automatically. As mentioned, our approach is not focused on Simio. In the future, tools for translating the static representation into any software should be developed.

In this example, we translate the elements in Fig. 3 to Simio's elements. In this software, channels become *Servers* where activities are performed by customers. All defined parameters are assigned to the customer entity, to the servers or to the entire system. Additionally, we model the processes that enable the activities to be synchronized internally, corresponding to the BSc1. For example, the provisioning process when inventory is decreasing. The resulting model for Casey in Simio is also shown in Fig. 4.

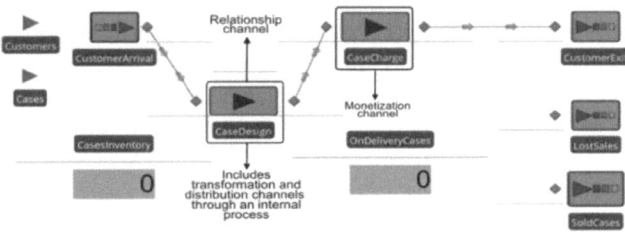

Fig. 4. Casey's BM in Simio

In this model, we have a *Source (CustomerArrival)* that generates the customers that flow through the channels. Then, we model the relationship channel as a server *(CaseDesign)*, which represents the new customer interface where the design activities take place. Internally, when a customer finishes its design, the server starts the manufacturing and distribution process. Meanwhile, the customer flows to the *CaseCharge* server, where monetization activities take place. In the end, the *Sinks (CustomerExit,*

LostSales and SoldCases) are updated once a transaction is completed. As it will be presented in Section IV, this allows us to obtain meaningful information about the scenario. In addition, the model allows to see the number of cases in Inventory (*CasesInventory*) and the number of cases that are in distribution *(OnDeliveryCases)* at each moment.

To effectively analyze the impact that a customer interface improvement could have on Casey's current BM, we simulate both the current and future scenarios. In both cases, we simulated 48 h of Casey's operation, and we maintained the parameters to ease comparison. This allows us to compare the average number of cases in inventory, the number of customers, the time it takes a customer to obtain a case, the utilization of the relationship channel, the average time of a design process instance and the number of lost sales. With our approach, we can provide Casey with valuable information about the impact that a customer interface innovation may have on its current BM. Thus, the approach allows the firm to make more informed decisions on the implementation of an innovation, as we will see on the simulation results, presented in the following section.

4   Results

As mentioned in Section III, we model both the current and future situation for Casey. Consequently, we can analyze the impact that a customer interface innovation has on Casey's BM. The specific indicators that were analyzed are: (1) Average cases in inventory, (2) Average Cases that entered the inventory, (3) Average time in station of the cases in inventory, (4) Average time in system of customers, (5) Case Design Scheduled Utilization, (6) Case Charge server average time of processing, (7) Case Design server average time of processing, (8) Average customers that exited Casey, (9) Average sold cases and (10) Average frustrated customers. The results are presented next.

Firstly, we analyzed the behavior of the inventory. To do this, we started by understanding the *number of average cases in inventory*. This indicator allows us to see how many cases are available for sale at a certain point in time. As can be seen in Table 1, the average number of cases in inventory decreased in the future situation. This can be interpreted to mean that innovation in the new customer interface innovation allows Casey to have a higher frequency of customer arrivals. Consequently, it allows the firm to have a higher number of sales. Thus, obtaining a higher inventory rotation.

Table 1. Average cases in inventory.

Situation	
Current	*Future*
14.46 ± 0.66 u	10.72 ± 0.36 u

Secondly, we complement the former results with the number of average cases that entered the inventory shown in Table 2 and the average time in inventory of a case shown in Table 3. Table 2 shows that for the future situation, Casey´s inventory is replenished more frequently since a higher demand arrives. However, the results on Table 3 allows us to see that even though more cases are entering the inventory, they are remaining less time in it. Thus, confirming that with this kind of innovation the firm obtains a higher rotation rate in its inventory.

Table 2. Average cases that entered the inventory.

Situation	
Current	*Future*
22.07 ± 1.13 u	34.1 ± 2.21 u

Table 3. Average time of cases in inventory.

Situation	
Current	*Future*
23.65 ± 1.77 hr	17.5 ± 1.73 hr

Thirdly, we analyzed the impact that the new customer interface has on the customer behavior. Specifically, we analyzed their *average time in the system*. This represents how long it took a customer, on average, to go through each *Server* in the system and arrive to the *Sink*. In other words, this indicator allows us to know what was the average time that a customer took to enter the page, design its case, pay for it and, finally, exit Casey's page. The results can be seen on Table 4.

Table 4. Average time in system.

Situation	
Current	*Future*
125.56 ± 4.21 min	43.46 ± 0.35 min

As can be observed, after improving the customer interface, the average time it takes a customer to go through Casey´s system has a significant improvement. In the current situation a customer would take almost 3 times the time of the future situation. This is explained by the fact that, after the implementation of this new interface, some steps are eliminated. To start with, this interface can ensure that the customer's design is clearly understood by both customer and firm. Therefore, the customer does not have to go through a review process or rework their design. In other words, this innovation allows Casey to eliminate human error in Casey's side. As a result, the customer can substantially reduce its time in Casey's system, which has various implications: (i) with this result the customer who receives an enhanced shopping experience by not having to spend as much time on the design and purchase process. And (ii), the new interface allows Casey to receive a higher number of customers and, consequently, increases its sales and revenue.

Fourth, we analyzed the *use of the case design server.* As explained, this server is responsible for receiving customers and allowing them to design their case. In the current situation, as this process takes place in a physical point of sale, customers depend on the availability of the employees. If a customer arrives and the employee is busy, they will have to wait until the employee is free to design their case. Specifically, the simulation shows that the server will be busy the 1.56% of the time. However, since the hypothetical innovation is focused on providing a new customer interface, the future situation will not have a limited customer capacity. This allows customers to design their case without waiting for an employee, this indicator drops to cero in the future situation, as is shown in Table 5.

Table 5. Case design server use.

Situation	
Current	*Future*
1.56 ± 0.22%	0%

Fifth, we complemented the previous analysis by studying how long it took for customers to design their case. The results of this analysis are shown in Table 6, which can be interpreted to mean that by improving the customer interface, it will take longer for customers to design their cases because they will have to become familiar with this new design tool. In other words, customers will have to go through the process of learning how the interface works and how to review the final design and, place and confirm their orders. However, as observed in Table 5, customers will never have to wait in line in order to design their case. Furthermore, we also analyzed the behavior of the activities in the monetization channel, as shown in Table 7, it will take less time for the customer to make the payment in the future situation.

Table 6. Average time of case design processing.

Situation	
Current	*Future*
29.96 ± 0.33 min	39.97 ± 0.34 min

In addition, we analyzed the number of customers who completed the process, or the number of customers that obtained a case. Table 8 shows these results, where this indicator increases in the future situation, which can be explained for two main reasons: (i) by making a customer interface innovation, the number of customers arriving at Casey's platform increases since the firm has more capacity to receive them. (ii) since customers do not need to wait in line to design their case or to pay for it, it is possible

Table 7. Average time of case charge processing.

Situation	
Current	*Future*
7.6 ± 0.21 min	3.49 ± 0.05 min

for two customers to perform these activities at the same time. Thus, in the same period, the future situation allows more customers to be served.

Table 8. Average customers that completed the process.

Situation	
Current	*Future*
11.7 ± 1.55 customers	25.23 ± 2.09 customers

Moreover, Table 9 shows the average number of cases sold. This indicator represents only the cases that have already been delivered to the customers. Thus, at the end of the simulation in the future situation there are some cases that have not yet being delivered to the customer. This occurs because the customers may have already finished their design and abandoned the new interface. However, the case is still in the process of manufacturing or packaging for distribution. Nonetheless, the customer has already paid for it. Consequently, in the future situation the number of cases sold increases (by about 4 units). But it does not match to the number of customers that left Casey's new interface (see Table 8), i.e. in Table 9. Not all the cases sold are quantified. However, it could be stated that the average number of cases sold increases because the case is already designed and paid for. Consequently, this innovation allows Casey to sell more cases which in turn translates into higher revenues for the firm.

Table 9. Average sold cases.

Situation	
Current	*Future*
11.73 ± 1.57 u	15.63 ± 1.39 u

Finally, we analyze the *number of frustrated customers*, which represent those customers who wanted to make a purchase but due to failures in the design or transformation process have decided not to complete the transaction with Casey. This occurs in the current situation, when a customer´s design has gone through two failed review processes and Casey´s employees have not been able to properly meet the customer's expectations. In the future situation, with the new customer interface, human error is completely eliminated. In the new situation, customers place their orders through a platform and not with an employee who can misinterpret their design and cause errors in the process. The results of this indicator are shown in Table 10.

In the current situation, there are approximately 4 customers who have not completed the transaction with Casey. This situation does not only represent 4 lost sales from unsatisfied customers. But each time the review process is performed, a new design needs to be made in a new case, which means that more than 4 cases were lost, and the inventory had to be replenished. However, this was not due to more cases being sold, but due to errors in the design process. By upgrading the customer interface, Casey benefits because sales are no longer lost, human error is eliminated, and no additional costs are incurred.

Table 10. Average number of frustrated customers.

Situation	
Current	*Future*
4.47 ± 0.71 customers	0 customers

Based on the aforementioned results, it becomes evident that the hypothetical innovation in the customer interface holds substantial potential to confer numerous advantages upon Casey across multiple dimensions. First, it enables the firm to provide better service to its customers. This is because it reduces the time for customers to design and pay for their cases. It also saves the firm from having to put the customer through a cumbersome and time-consuming process. With this innovation, customers will no longer have to wait in line or go through tedious review processes that may end up in a frustrating experience. Second, Casey's can gain operational and financial improvement, as this innovation allows them to eliminate human error and improve their capacity. In the future situation, they will be able to serve a greater number of customers, which in turn, will be reflected in an increased revenue and a reduced waste. With these results, Casey can understand the impact that this innovation has on their inventory, revenue and customers. If wanted, Casey could simulate other BScs to compare different innovations. With this information, it is possible for Casey to make more informed decisions saving time, people and financial resources. Consequently, this approach allows Casey to analyze a potential innovation and understand the impact it may have on their relationship with their customers.

5   Analysis and Discussion

In this work, we propose an extended metamodel that allows us to define dynamic BSc over static BMs representations. To illustrate this approach, we use Casey. A manufacturing firm with an interest in customer interface innovation. In this case, we only modelled one firm with one type of innovation. However, one could model different BMs with multiple types of innovations. For instance, as [1] state, firms in the context of Industry

4.0 can have a service-oriented approach, a network-oriented approach, a user-driven approach or a combination of these. In addition, we modelled a firm with a user-drive approach but firms with other contexts can also be explored, broadening the type of innovation that a firm is interested in applying. Particularly, this can be done in four ways: (1) optimizing its internal and external process, (2) improving its customer interface, (3) participating in new ecosystems and value networks and (4) creating completely new BMs.

Therefore, our approach is not limited to a company with a particular focus or a particular innovation in mind. For instance, imagine that Casey wants to incorporate an intelligent sensor into each case. This to obtain information about the product wear and tear. Using simulation, one could model the typical activities that a case goes through after delivery and obtain the case conditions by the end of the warranty. This would make it possible to analyze, for example, the quality of the materials used in the transformation process.

This approach can be extended to more complex BMs with other types of innovation. For instance, one might focus on modelling the flow of information through the different channels to validate an Analytics initiative or modelling an entire supply chain to address collaboration and synchronization issues. Moreover, the approach allows modeling both the current and future situations for comparison. In this sense, it can also be used to understand the behavior of a BM with or without an innovation initiative.

The proposed metamodel can also be further extended. For instance, the component entity can be detailed so that specific dynamic characteristics can be associated with inventory (e.g., revision timer) or providers (e.g., how many times is inventory reviewed). Moreover, if a specific software is used, it is possible to include the characteristics that a component, channel, or activity should have in that environment. This would allow the creation of more complex and detailed situations for modeling explicit innovation initiatives.

One fundamental element of this approach is the comprehensive definition of the static BM. In addition, to include the dynamic elements of a given situation, data on the behavior of real components need to be collected in order to correctly parameterize the elements of the situation. In general, this approach can be easily adopted by those familiar with a particular simulation software. However, the translation process can be complex if only static representations have been worked with. Even when similar results can be obtained with an empirical definition and translation process, the lack of formality and standardization forces researchers to perform a new assessment for each BSc. With this approach, BSc, entities, parameters and triggers are defined from the static representation and can be easily translated into simulation software.

As a result, our proposal focuses on providing firms with reliable information so that they can make more informed decisions. Just to reiterate, this approach allows firms to analyze and compare different situations for a BM without incurring in the costs associated with traditional what-if analysis, such as hiring personnel, investing in new infrastructure, procuring additional supplies, allocating time, and spending significant financial resources. Consequently, this allows firms to effectively innovate and adapt to ever-changing market conditions, while minimizing the risks typically associated with new implementations.

6 Limitations, Conclusions and Future Research

Since BMI is currently considered an essential capability for organizations [15], multiple researchers and practitioners have been interested in understanding BMs in the context of Industry 4.0 in order to innovate them [1, 5]. To this end, most authors have focused on understanding the static dimension of BMs in multiple industries. However, few researchers have focused especially on BMs in Industry 4.0. Although, it has been recognized that research on Industry 4.0 would benefit from incorporating dynamic elements as this would allow firms to understand the elements that make the business save time and resources [6]. Moreover, this incorporation allows improving and facilitating the decision-making process by providing reliable estimates of business performance [24].

In this paper, we propose an approach to translate static BMs into dynamic BMs by using the Simio simulation software. We then discuss how the approach can be used for a specific firm with an innovation idea in the context of Industry 4.0. We present the results of the simulation for the firm' current and future scenarios and discuss how these results can be extended to more complex scenarios or other innovation initiatives.

In terms of limitations, we have extended the metamodel proposed by [12] to create the dynamic scenario presented in this paper. However, when translating more complex business scenarios it may be necessary to incorporate new entities or attributes. On the other hand, straightforward scenarios, such as the one presented in this paper, may require an adaptation of the proposed metamodel if they are to be translated into another simulation software. Thus, future research may be focused on extending the proposed metamodel to provide practitioners with a solid conceptual basis for creating their own simulation scenarios.

Furthermore, the presented simulation is based on average empirical data. We argue that more accurate results can be obtained by looking more closely at the typical behavior of this type of BM. Further research along this path could focus on collecting data relevant for multiple BMs and using our approach to create simulation scenarios. For instance, data can be collected for several "Case design" firms. By using our proposal, researchers can benchmark among competitors. Furthermore, this can be done over other manufacturing BMs to perform more detailed analysis.

Yet, another limitation of this work is that it has focused on analyzing a customer interface improvement. However, the impact of the incorporation of other Industry 4.0 technologies can also be analyzed. Finally, this approach focused on understanding the impact to the customer. However, future research can concentrate on modeling other parts of the BM. For instance, improving internal and external processes (e.g., procurement) or creating a completely new product or service.

This demonstrates the need to further work on the dynamic elements of BMs in the context of Industry 4.0. In this work, we aim to provide a straightforward approach to create dynamic models from static BMs. Furthermore, we propose a base case to illustrate how this process can be carried out. We then present the results of the case. Our main objective is to provide a basis on which researchers can build knowledge and more complex scenarios can be modeled and thus contribute with tools to improve the innovation process of BMs especially in the context of Industry 4.0.

Acknowledgment. We express our sincere gratitude for the support and collaboration extended by Andrea Montoya throughout the duration of the first phase of this project.

References

1. Ibarra, D., Ganzarain, J., Igartua-Lopez, J.: Business model innovation through Industry 4.0: a review. Procedia Manuf. **22**, 4–10 (2018)
2. Kagermann, H.: Change through digitization—value creation in the age of industry 4.0 23–45 (2015)
3. Alrajhi, M., Liu, K., Tehrani, J., Alsoud, A.R., Chidzambwa, L.: Modeling dynamic behavior of business organisations - extension of BPM with norms (2012)
4. Industry 4.0: IntechOpen, Rijeka (2020)
5. Romero, M.C., Sánchez, M.E., Villalobos, J.: Executable business model blueprints. In: Americas Conference on Information Systems (2018)
6. Romero, M., Villalobos, J., Sánchez, M.: Simulating the business model canvas using system dynamics 527–534 (2015)
7. Rodič, B.: Industry 4.0 and the new simulation modelling paradigm. Organizacija **50** (2017)
8. Wortmann, A., Barais, O., Combebale, B., Wimmer, M.: Modeling languages in industry 4.0: an extended systematic mapping study. Softw. Syst. Model. **19** (2020)
9. Mittal, S., Khan, M.A., Romero, D., Wuest, T.: A critical review of smart manufacturing & industry 4.0 maturity models: implications for small and medium-sized enterprises (SMEs). J. Manuf. Syst. **49**, 194–214 (2018)
10. de Paula Ferreira, W., Armellini, F., De Santa-Eulalia, L.A.: Simulation in industry 4.0: a state-of-the-art review. Comput. Ind. Eng. **149**, 106868 (2020)
11. Sunkle, S., Roychoudhury, S., Rathod, H., KulKarni, V.: Toward structured simulation of what-if analyses for enterprise (2014)
12. Romero, M.C., Lara, P., Villalobos, J.: Evolution of the business model: arriving at open business model dynamics. J. Open Innov. Technol. Mark. Complex. **7**(1), 86 (2021)
13. Ammirato, S., Linzalone, R., Felicetti, A.: The value of system dynamics' diagrams for business model innovation. Manag. Decis. (2021). **ahead-of-print**
14. Xu, J., et al.: Simulation optimization in the era of Industrial 4.0 and the industrial internet. J. Simul. **10**(4), 310–320 (2016)
15. Demil, B., Lecocq, X.: Business model evolution: in search of dynamic consistency. Long Range Plann. **43**(2), 227–246 (2010)
16. Remane, G., Hanelt, A., Tesch, J.F., Kolbe, L.M.: The business model pattern database—a tool for systematic business model innovation. Int. J. Innov. Manag. **21**(01), 1750004 (2017)
17. Osterwalder, A., Pigneur, Y.: Business model generation: a handbook for visionaries, game changers, and challengers, vol. 1. Wiley (2010)
18. Weking, J., Stöcker, M., Kowalkiewicz, M., Böhm, M., Krcmar, H.: Leveraging industry 4.0 – a business model pattern framework. Int. J. Prod. Econ. **225**, 107588 (2020)
19. Toth-Peter, A., Torres de Oliveira, R., Mathews, S., Barner, L., Figueira, S.: Industry 4.0 as an enabler in transitioning to circular business models: a systematic literature review. J. Clean. Prod. **393**, 136284 (2023)
20. Grabowska, S., Saniuk, S.: Assessment of the competitiveness and effectiveness of an open business model in the industry 4.0 environment. J. Open Innov. Technol. Mark. Complex. **8** (2022). https://doi.org/10.3390/joitmc8010057
21. Karmaker, C.L., Aziz, R.A., Ahmed, T., Misbauddin, S.M., Moktadir, Md.A.: Impact of industry 4.0 technologies on sustainable supply chain performance: the mediating role of green supply chain management practices and circular economy. J. Clean. Prod. **419**, 138249 (2023)

22. Marcon, É., Le Dain, M.-A., Frank, A.G.: Designing business models for Industry 4.0 technologies provision: changes in business dimensions through digital transformation. Technol. Forecast. Soc. Change **185**, 122078 (2022)
23. Veile, J.W., Schmidt, M.-C., Voigt, K.-I.: Toward a new era of cooperation: how industrial digital platforms transform business models in Industry 4.0. J. Bus. Res. **143**, 387–405 (2022)
24. Elhazmiri, B., Naveed, N., Anwar, M.N., Ul Haq, M.I.: The role of additive manufacturing in industry 4.0: an exploration of different business models. Sustain. Oper. Comput. **3**, 317–329 (2022)
25. Yuana, R., Prasetio, E.A., Syarief, R., Arkeman, Y., Suroso, A.I.: System dynamic and simulation of business model innovation in digital companies: an open innovation approach. J. Open Innov. Technol. Mark. Complex. **7**(4), 219 (2021)
26. Bocken, N.M.P., Geradts, T.H.J.: Barriers and drivers to sustainable business model innovation: organization design and dynamic capabilities. Long Range Plan. **53**(4), 101950 (2020)
27. Cosenz, F., Bivona, E.: Fostering growth patterns of SMEs through business model innovation. A tailored dynamic business modelling approach. J. Bus. Res. **130**, 658–669 (2021)
28. de Paula Ferreira, W., Armellini, F., de Santa-Eulalia, L.A., Thomasset-Laperrière, V.: A framework for identifying and analysing industry 4.0 scenarios. J. Manuf. Syst. **65**, 192–207 (2022)
29. Mourtzis, D., Vasialkopoulos, A., Zervas, E., Boli, N.: Manufacturing system design using simulation in metal industry towards education 4.0. Procedia Manuf. **31**, 155–161 (2019)
30. Stavrinides, G.L., Karatza, H.D.: Cyber-physical systems, digital twins and Industry 4.0: the role of modeling and simulation. Simul. Model. Practic. Theory **124**, 102727 (2023)
31. Mostafa, S., Chileshe, N., Abdelhamid, T.: Lean and agile integration within offsite construction using discrete event simulation. Constr. Innov. **16**(4), 483–525 (2016)
32. Furian, N.M., O'Sullivan, C., Walker, S.V., Neubacher, D.: A conceptual modeling framework for discrete event simulation using hierarchical control structures. Simul. Model. Pract. Theory **56**, 82–96 (2015). https://doi.org/10.1016/j.simpat.2015.04.004

Developing and Deploying Federated Learning Models in Data Spaces: Smart Truck Parking Reference Use Case

Jean Paul Sebastian Piest[1]([⊠]) [iD], Willem Datema[2] [iD], Danniar Reza Firdausy[1] [iD], and Harrie Bastiaansen[2] [iD]

[1] University of Twente, Drienerlolaan 5, 7522 NB Enschede, The Netherlands
{j.p.s.piest,d.r.firdausy}@utwente.nl
[2] TNO, Anna Van Buerenplein 1, 2595 DA Den Haag, The Netherlands
{willem.datema,harrie.bastiaansen}@tno.nl

Abstract. Earlier work proposed a reference use case and data space architecture for smart truck parking and positioned future use of federated learning for competition-, privacy sensitive data sharing. However, there is limited research regarding the deployment of federated learning in data spaces. Extending earlier work, this paper documents the results of experimental development of a federated learning model for smart truck parking and its instantiation in a data space infrastructure. Two iterations were carried out to assess the development of a federated learning model and deployment in a data space environment for the smart truck parking use case. First, a data space infrastructure was instantiated, containing a federated learning orchestrator, connectors with data apps, and a metadata broker. Second, a prototype was developed on top of the metadata broker to support the provisioning of the required data space components to the involved participants. Taken together, the experimental development related to the smart truck parking case provides initial support for the suitability of federated learning in a data space environment and contributes to better understanding of the potential use, technical feasibility, required efforts, and practical implications. From a practical perspective, the study provides interested scholars and software developers access to a reference implementation. The current study is limited to one federated learning model and deployment in a small data space environment. Future work may contribute to comparing multiple federated learning models and evaluation in an operational data space.

Keywords: Federated Learning · Data Spaces · Smart Truck Parking

1 Introduction

Privacy Enhancing Technologies (PETs) are currently emerging for accessing and processing data in use cases in which the various data sources cannot always simply be shared between stakeholders. This may be the case when the amount of data to be transferred is too large or due to sensitivity, confidentiality, ethical, privacy, legal, or other

T. P. Sales et al. (Eds.): EDOC 2023 Workshops, LNBIP 498, pp. 39–59, 2024.
https://doi.org/10.1007/978-3-031-54712-6_3

issues. In such cases, the data that are feeding the processing algorithms must remain within the security domain of its provider or administrator and are not to be transferred to other organizations for processing. Thus, only controlled access to the data may be allowed instead of exchanging the sensitive data. PETs may be implemented by means of solutions such as Federated Learning (FL) and secure Multi-Party Computation (MPC). An overview and categorization of FL an MPC has recently been provided by the OECD [1]. This paper focuses on FL in data spaces.

The development of data spaces is at the core of the European Data Strategy [2]. The European Commission (EC) has expressed its ambition related to federative data sharing in the EU Data Strategy as a 'Common European Data Space', which can alternatively be summarized as the movement towards a federation of interoperable data spaces. The EC initiated supporting regulations (e.g., the Data Act [3], the Data Governance Act [4], the Digital Services Act [5], the Digital Markets Act [6] and the Artificial Intelligence Act [7]) and plays an active role in the actual development and deployment of data spaces [8]. In the logistics industry, there are several relevant data space initiatives, including the development of a common European mobility data space, and country specific initiatives such as the Basic Data Infrastructure (BDI) that is being developed for the logistics industry in the Netherlands [9].

The above-mentioned data space initiatives and the PETs pursue a common goal with regard to controlled data sharing, data sovereignty, and privacy. Moreover, from both perspectives synergetic effects can be realized through collaboration and alignment of development of data space and PET architectures [10]. As such, previous work has introduced smart truck parking as a reference use case for the combination of a data sharing utilizing PETs in a data space infrastructure [11]. More specifically, this earlier work positioned future use of FL for competition sensitive data sharing. However, FL is a relatively young field and there is limited related work in the logistics domain. More specifically, much work focuses on technical aspects and modeling, but does not report on the efforts and challenges to deploy solutions. Moreover, there is limited research regarding the deployment of FL in data spaces.

This paper builds upon the above mentioned earlier work and focuses on assessment of the efforts and the associated challenges of developing and deploying a FL use case within a data space infrastructure. The following research question is addressed in this paper: "What are the practical implications for development and deployment of FL solution architectures in a data space infrastructure, using the illustrative and representative use case of smart truck parking in the logistics domain?".

This study intends to contribute to better understanding of the potential use, technical feasibility, required efforts, and practical implications related to the deployment of FL models in data space environments. Therefore, this paper documents the results and findings of experimental development of a FL model for smart truck parking and its deployment in a data space infrastructure. As such, the study explores the ideas put forward in earlier work and provides an initial validation of the technological layer of the data space architecture for the smart truck parking reference use case [11]. The current study is considered of interest for scholars and practitioners that are developing PETs, in particular FL applications, within the context of the emerging common European data spaces. From a practical perspective, the study provides interested scholars and software developers access to a reference implementation.

The remainder of this paper is structured as follows. Section 2 summarizes related and earlier work. Section 3 describes the methodology. Section 4 presents the result of the experimental development of a FL model for smart truck parking, the deployment in a data space infrastructure, and the prototype to extend the metadata broker with functionality for provisioning data space components. Section 5 discusses the results in relation to related work. Section 6 concludes and positions future work.

2 Related Work

This section subsequently addresses earlier work regarding the smart truck parking case and related work regarding data space initiatives and FL.

2.1 The Smart Truck Parking Use Case

This paper builds upon earlier work in which a reference use case, data space architecture, and a prototype application for smart truck parking were introduced [11]. The reference use case was developed using the Fraunhofer use case methodology. The data space architecture was established based on the International Data Spaces (IDS) Reference Architecture Model (RAM) and ArchiMate framework. Based on a case study at A1 Truck Parking in the Netherlands, a prototype application was developed for smart truck parking using 1.5 years of historical data. This prototype demonstrated the main components in the application layer of the data space architecture for smart truck parking. The previous study was limited to deployment of the prototype on a local machine. Additionally, the potential use of FL was positioned as future work.

The current study builds upon the reference use case and data space architecture for smart truck parking. More specifically, the current focus lies on validation of the technology layer of the proposed data space architecture by instantiating a data space infrastructure, including connectors with data apps for data providers, consumers, and service providers for FL, a metadata broker, and supporting data space components.

2.2 Data Spaces

At present, a multitude of European data spaces are emerging, e.g. for individual sectors, application areas, or geographical regions. Being able to seamlessly share data over these data spaces yields clear advantages: It extends the reach and scope of accessible data and allows new business models and solutions to be developed across sectors and regions. Hence, the data spaces should pursue the common goal of being able to share data in a trusted manner between participants in different data space instances, whilst each individual data space instance has a high degree of autonomy in developing and deploying its own internal agreements and ICT landscape. For data spaces to seamlessly interconnect in a federation, an interoperability framework is needed to manage and coordinate trusted and controlled data sharing between participants in multiple data space instances. This goal is at the very core of the European Data Strategy of a 'Common

European Data Space' [2]. To pursue this goal, various EU initiatives are exploring and developing reference architectures for federative data sharing and data spaces, including the Open DEI initiative [12, 13], and supporting initiatives for federative data sharing, such as the International Data Spaces Association (IDSA) [14, 15], Gaia-X [16, 17], FIWARE [18], iSHARE [19, 20], and the Data Space Business Alliance (DSBA) [21, 22].

Currently, the EU Data Spaces Support Centre (DSSC) [23] is the main initiative working towards a blueprint for the emerging (federation of) data spaces in Europe. The DSSC defines a data space as 'an infrastructure that enables data transactions between different data ecosystem parties based on the governance framework of that data space' [24]. Data spaces should be generic enough to support the implementation of multiple use cases. Moreover, the EU Open DEI initiative has identified three types of building blocks to be part of a data space [12, 13]: (1) building blocks for data platforms, providing support for effective data sharing and exchange as well as for engineering and deployment of data exchange and processing capabilities, (2) building blocks for data marketplaces, where data providers can offer and data consumers can request data, as well as data processing applications, and (3) building blocks ensuring data sovereignty, i.e. the ability for each stakeholder to control their data by making decisions related to how digital processes, infrastructures, and flows of data are structured, built and managed, based on an appropriate governance scheme, enabling specification of terms and conditions.

The upcoming EU Simpl procurement project [25] will be the initiative to adopt the DSSC blueprint, develop the associated building blocks, and make these available as open source for large scale deployment in the various EU sectoral data space deployment initiatives [8]. For logistics, this may be part of the development of the European Mobility Data Space [26] and BDI.

2.3 Federated Learning

The field of FL is relatively young and growing. The term FL was initially coined by McMahan [27, 28] in 2016 and first developed by Google [29, 30]. FL can be defined as 'a machine learning setting where multiple entities (clients) collaborate in solving a machine learning problem, under the coordination of a central server or service provider. Each client's raw data is stored locally and not exchanged or transferred; instead, focused updates intended for immediate aggregation are used to achieve the learning objective.' [31]. Alternatively, FL can be defined more concise as 'privacy-preserving decentralized collaborative machine-learning techniques' [29]. FL approaches are commonly categorized as horizontally FL, vertically FL, and federated transfer learning [27, 29]. In the case of horizontally FL, the participants share the feature space, but provide different samples. In vertically FL, the feature space (partly) differs per participant and participants share sample ID spaces. In the case of FL transfer, both the feature and sample space differ (or overlap little) and participants develop models in larger spaces under a federation.

FL is often used in environments where data are distributed, not independent and identically distributed, and unbalanced [27]. Although generic architectures exist for FL, there are significant differences between the three types of FL [29]. A recent review categorized FL systems in a taxonomy covering six aspects: (1) data distribution, (2) machine learning model, (3) privacy mechanism, (4) communication architecture, (5) scale of federation, and (6) motivation for federation [32].

FL is initially applied in healthcare, telecom, and banking [33]. More specifically, FL is regularly associated with blockchain [29, 32]. Up to date, there is limited research regarding the deployment of FL in data spaces. One specific related work proposed a data space architecture utilizing FL for privacy-preserving distributed collaborative condition monitoring and predictive maintenance [30].

3 Methodology

This section describes the methodological approach.

3.1 Fraunhofer Use Case Methodology

The current study builds upon the reference use case for smart truck parking that was developed based on the Fraunhofer use case methodology, as described in earlier work [11]. Reference use cases are abstract, simplified representations of real-world scenarios and mainly used for research, feasibility studies, and experimental development. Extending earlier work, the current study established a data space infrastructure for the development, deployment, and evaluation of an experimental FL model. The main goal of the experimental development was to assess the feasibility of FL for the smart truck parking use case and required efforts to implement a solution.

3.2 CRISP-DM

Extending earlier work [11, 34], the CRoss Industry Standard Process for Data Mining (CRISP-DM) was utilized to guide the experimental development of the FL model and deployment of the required data space components in a data space infrastructure.

Leveraging the business understanding and stakeholder analysis from earlier work, two subsequent development iterations were carried out to develop and deploy a federated learning model in a data space environment for the smart truck parking use case. First, a data space infrastructure was instantiated, containing a federated learning orchestrator, connectors with data apps, and a metadata broker. Second, a prototype was developed on top of the metadata broker to provide functionality for provisioning of the required data space components to the involved participants. Based on the results of these two iterations, the efforts to develop, evaluate, and deploy the FL-model in a data space infrastructure are reported.

Given the experimental nature of this study, the scope of deployment is limited to a controlled environment. However, this data space infrastructure and environment can serve as an industrial testbed for future evaluation and potentially be transferred to an enterprise use case implementation.

4   Results

This section presents the data space infrastructure setup, the main results and findings from the experimental development of the FL model, and the developed prototype following the steps of the CRISP-DM. The data apps for FL can be found on the Gitlab repository of the TNO Security Gateway [35, 36].

4.1   Data Space Infrastructure

Based on the proposed data space architecture from earlier work [11, 34] and the IDS RAM, a data space infrastructure was instantiated in two steps. The setup for the first step consists of a metadata broker, and three connectors, as shown in Fig. 1.

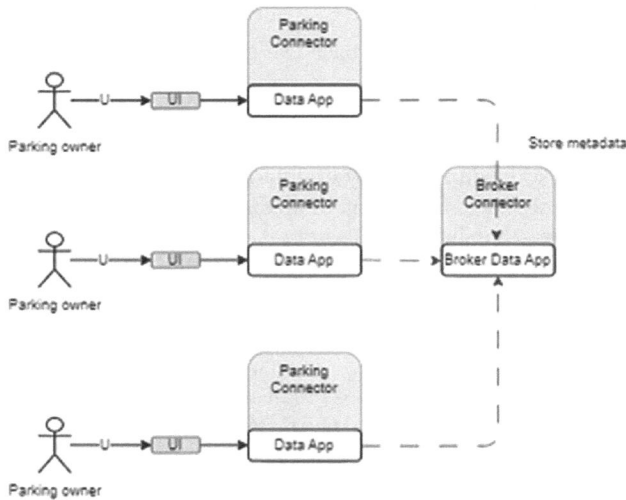

Fig. 1. First step of the process to share data for FL.

Each connector belongs to a different actor in the data space. Three connectors belong to the parking owners. The parking owners upload their data in the form of a Comma-Separated Values (CSV) file utilizing the User Interface (UI), shown in Fig. 3, of the data app.

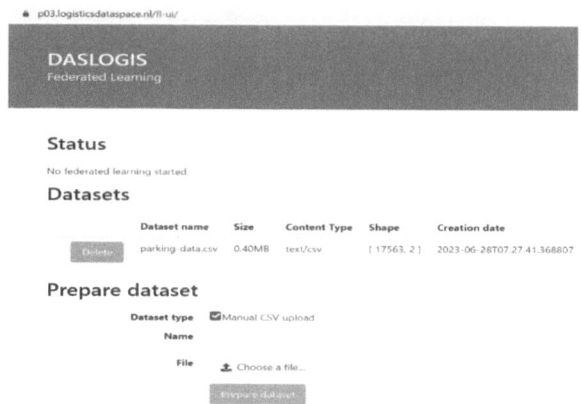

Fig. 2. Screenshot of the UI for parking owners (example P3).

Next, the solution architecture for developing the FL model was realized, as visualized in Fig. 2. In the second step, a connector is assigned to a researcher.

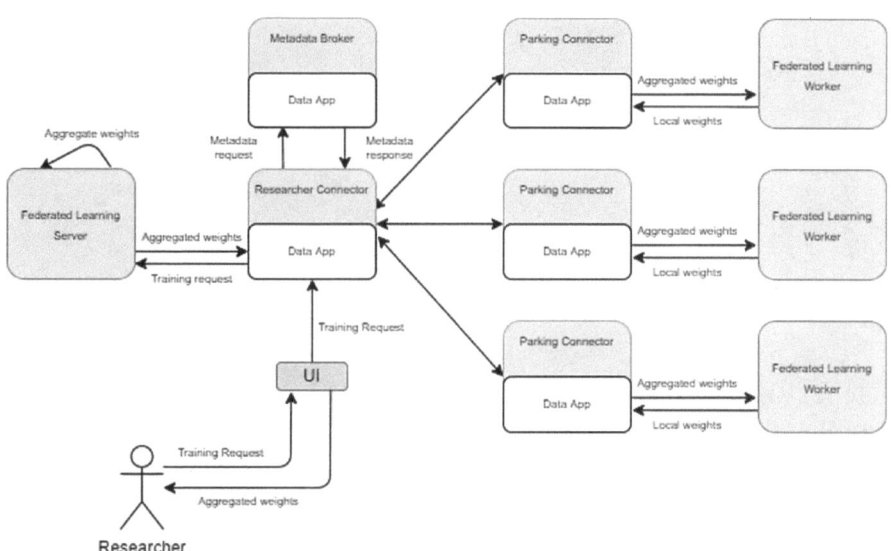

Fig. 3. Second step of the flow for Federated Learning.

In the context of this study, a researcher is defined as someone who has knowledge of machine learning, and whose task is to develop a model suitable for truck parking occupancy prediction. From the UI, shown in Fig. 4, the researcher can search for data providers, obtain meta data, request access to datasets, and subsequently develop, train, and evaluate FL models by modifying model configurations and parameters.

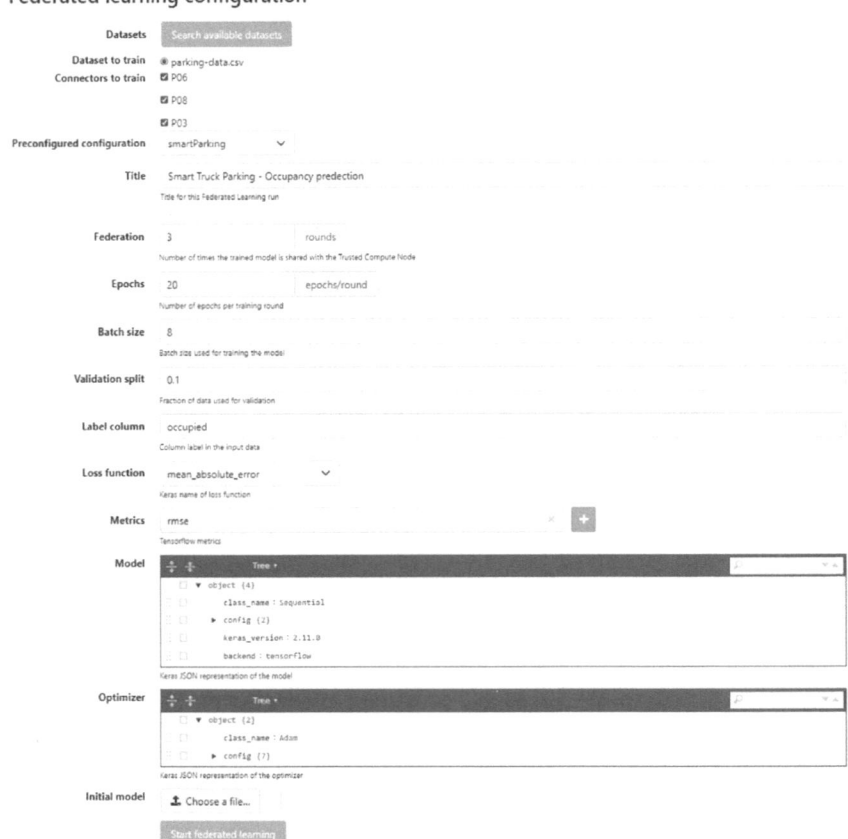

Fig. 4. Screenshot of the UI for the Researcher.

To see which parking owners have uploaded data, the researcher requests and uses information from the metadata broker. Afterwards, the researcher decides on which data sets to train one or multiple models. The selected model, which can be any model from the Keras library in Python, is then uploaded to the UI [37]. For example, how many epochs should be used per local run or how many rounds of FL should be run to train the model. After initial configuration of the parameters for training, the model is trained over the number of rounds set by the researcher. The progress of the training can be monitored in the UI for the Researcher. After the training, the final evaluation metrics for the training can be assessed. If the scores are satisfying for the researcher, they can download the model for further development, deployment, and use (i.e. inference). The above-mentioned process is visualized in a sequence diagram, shown in Fig. 5. An overview of available endpoints is provided in Table 1.

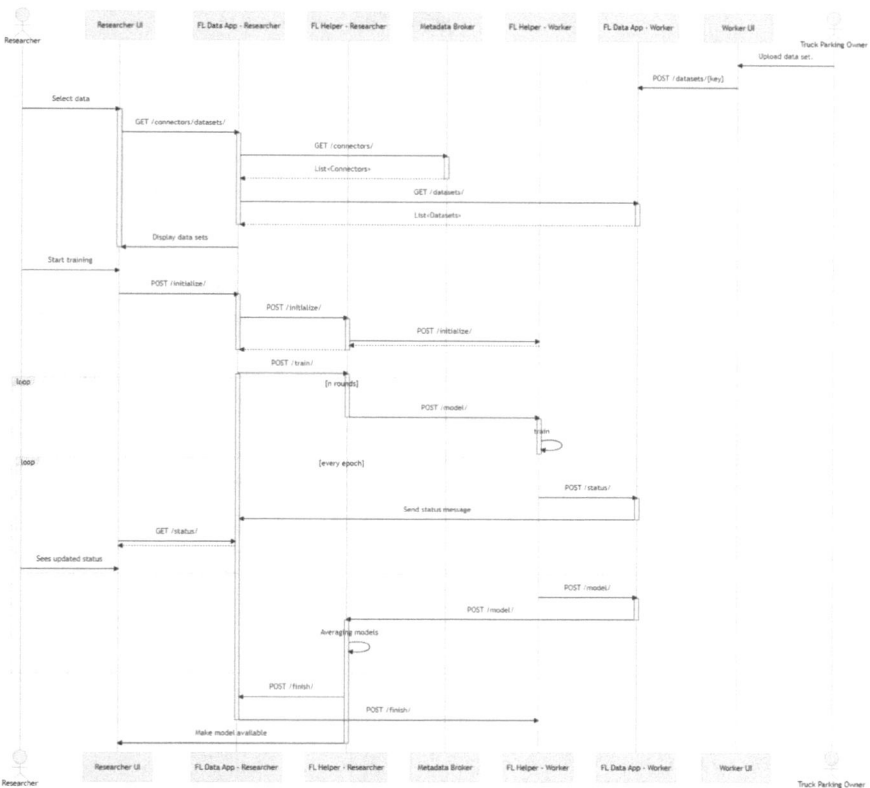

Fig. 5. Sequence diagram of FL in the data space infrastructure.

The actors have been assigned to the roles as defined in the IDS-RAM focusing on the Data Provider, which is assigned to the parking owner, and the Data Consumer, which is assigned to a researcher. The Dynamic Attribute Provisioning Service (DAPS) is left out for readability purposes. However, the identity of each connector is checked according to the IDS-RAM specifications.

Table 1. Overview of endpoints.

Component	Mode	Endpoint	Method	Description
FL data app	Researcher	/connectors	GET	Retrieve connectors in data space
		/connectors/datasets	GET	Retrieve datasets and connectors
		initialize	POST	Start FL process with parameters
		train	POST	Start training of the FL model
		status	GET	Check status of FL process
		model	GET	Download the model in h5 format
	Worker	/status	POST	Share metrics of FL epoch
		/model	POST	Send trained model to researcher
FL helper	Researcher	initialize	POST	Start FL process with parameters
		train	POST	Start training of the FL model
		model	GET	Download the model in h5 format
			POST	Share the FL model
		status	GET	Check status of FL process
	Worker	initialize	POST	Start FL process with parameters
		model	POST	Start training of the FL model
		finish	POST	Finish FL process
		status	GET	Check status of FL process
		/datasets/{key}	POST	Store dataset on file system
			DELETE	Deletes dataset from file system
		/datasets	GET	List all datasets of the worker

4.2 Dataset and Preparation

To demonstrate the use of FL over multiple truck parkings in a data space, a relatively simple experiment was conducted with publicly available data of three parkings in Bolzano, Italy [38]. The parkings that were selected for this experiment are located near to each other, specifically, P03, P06, and P08. The measurements were taken from the 26th of August 2022 until the 25th of October 2022, with the data available in CSV format. The first column contains the timestamp of the measurement. The second column contains the amount of used parking spaces. The occupancy of the parkings was measured roughly every 5 min for P03 and P08, resulting in 17,561 and 17,562 values respectively. For P06, some data points have a 10-min interval. Therefore, only 10,922 values are available between the selected dates. This data set is suited for FL where the data should be hidden from the researcher, because the input data only has two columns. Thus, providing such data should be relatively easy for data providers.

4.3 Feature Engineering

Similar to earlier work [34], feature engineering was used to create the features 'dayOfWeek', and 'hour' from the timestamps. The occupancy was calculated as a fraction of the total available parking spaces. Table 2 shows a sample of the data for P08.

Table 2. Sample of the CSV data as fed to the model.

Index	Occupied	Day of Week	Hour
0	0.176303	4	0
1	0.175355	4	0

4.4 Modeling

In the case of smart truck parking, the data are distributed, not independent and identically distributed, and unbalanced among truck parkings. However, based on earlier work, truck parkings are likely to have a similar feature space [34]. Therefore, it was decided to develop a horizontal FL model.

To demonstrate and evaluate the combination of FL in a data space, an experiment was conducted that trains a relatively simple horizontal FL Multi-Layer Perceptron model based on open parking data. As the goal was to predict a continuous variable, a simple regression model was created using the Sequential model from the Keras library in Python [37].

The developed Sequential model consists of three layers: (1) a Dense layer with 64 units, (2) a Dropout layer with a ratio of 0.2, and (3) another Dense layer with 6 units. These settings are based on experimental findings. The Dropout layer was used as a simple way to prevent overfitting [39]. The Adam optimizer was selected and used with a learning rate of 0.00001. The summary of the model was obtained by running model.summary() function of the Keras library [40], as shown in Table 3. In total, there are 582 parameters, which are all trainable.

Table 3. Model summary for sequential model.

Layer (type)	Output Shape	Param #
Reshape	(None, 2)	0
Dense	(None, 64)	192
Dropout	(None, 64)	0
Dense	(None, 6)	390

4.5 Evaluation

Three rounds of federation were runned, with each 20 epochs per round, to evaluate the developed Sequential model. The validation split was set to 10%, meaning 10% of the data was used to validate the model. To calculate the loss, the mean absolute error was used. The Root Mean Squared Error (RMSE) metric was used to assess the model after each epoch. The total training time is around 4 min. The final results were a RMSE of 0.187 for P03, 0.196 for P08, and 0.28 for P06. The results of the experiment are shown in Fig. 6.

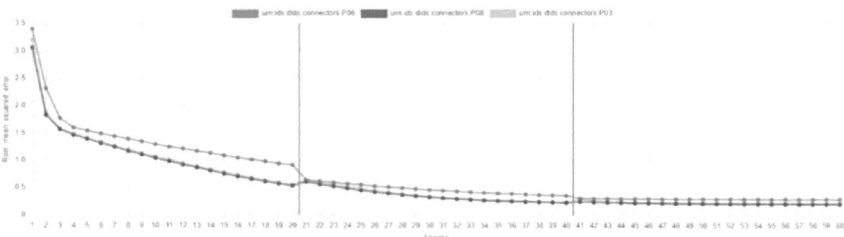

Fig. 6. Root mean squared error per connector after every epoch.

The data set with the least amount of data points has a higher error rate compared to the data sets with more data points. However, a clear effect of the averaging of the three models is visible after each round since the error rate of P06 is significantly lower after epoch 21 than after epoch 20. On the contrary, the error rates of P03 and P08 slightly increase. The same effect can be observed after epoch 41.

The experiment indicates that having more data points positively contributes to the overall results of the model. However, this experiment is conducted in a relatively simple setup. Therefore, it is necessary to add more data providers to extend the experiment with additional data sets and further proliferate the mutual benefits of this FL for smart truck parking.

4.6 Deployment

Given the large number of truck parking locations in Europe, fast onboarding of new data space participants is essential. To support this objective, similar to the UI for data space connectors, the implementation of the metadata broker and the provisioning of the essential data space components for the involved participants can be supported by a UI. Additionally to the development of the FL model, a prototype of such a UI was realized in a second development iteration, aiming to lower the barriers for parking owners to share data and increase the number of participants and data sets offered in the data space to improve the FL model.

The following components have been deployed as a result of the first iteration: the DAPS, a metadata broker, four connectors, along with the data apps comprising the connectors. The IDSA described that a standard metadata broker is responsible for registering, publishing, and supporting the discovery of metadata of data sources and services available in an IDS ecosystem [13]. The IDSA also prescribed that IDS Connectors are required for participants to offer, share, and consume data. Therefore, the provisioning of these components to support participants' onboarding and data resources selection should not be overlooked. With this in mind, a prototypical UI extension of the metadata broker has been developed, as shown in Fig. 7, to provide data space participants a so-called Connector Store.

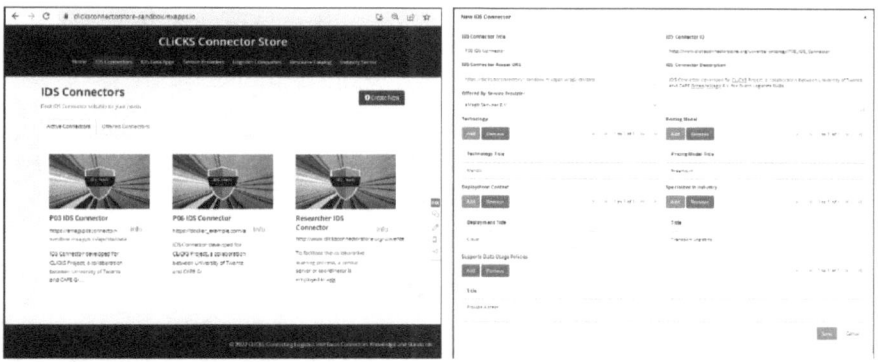

Fig. 7. Screenshots of the Connector Store UI listing active IDS Connectors in a data space (left) and functionality to create new IDS Connectors (right).

Extending earlier research [41], the Connector Store is responsible for supporting the selection and the provisioning of the suitable IDS Connectors for the participants based on contextual information. Respecting the technical specification of a standard metadata broker, the Connector Store leverages semantic web and linked data technologies to describe IDS Connectors, IDS Data Apps, and their software or service providers. Such technologies have been implemented in an increasing variety of contexts in recent years for enhancing the discoverability and accessibility of resources on the web [42]. As such, the Connector Store annotates the connectors and data apps with semantic layers that form subject-predicate-object triples in conformance to the Resource Description Framework (RDF) format.

In the smart truck parking case, the implementation of the Connector Store is aimed at supporting the onboarding process of prominent actors (e.g. truck-parking owners, truck drivers, etc.) in the data space by providing the necessary components suitable to their context. Following the onboarding, the involved actors can observe, in the UI, and query, through their respective IDS Connectors, the Connector Store for actively participating IDS Connectors in the data space, as shown in Fig. 8. This helps participants to explore opportunities of optimizing their operation by means of data sharing with partners. Next to that, the Connector Store also provides its data resource brokering service to the data space participants. This service is provided by (1) receiving the metadata of the truck parking datasets from the truck parking owners, acting as the data owners, and then (2) publishing meta data and resources to the data space to be used by researchers for the development of FL models and data apps, and (3) distribute data apps for transport planners for trip planning and truck drivers for dynamic rerouting as part of the reference use case in earlier work [11].

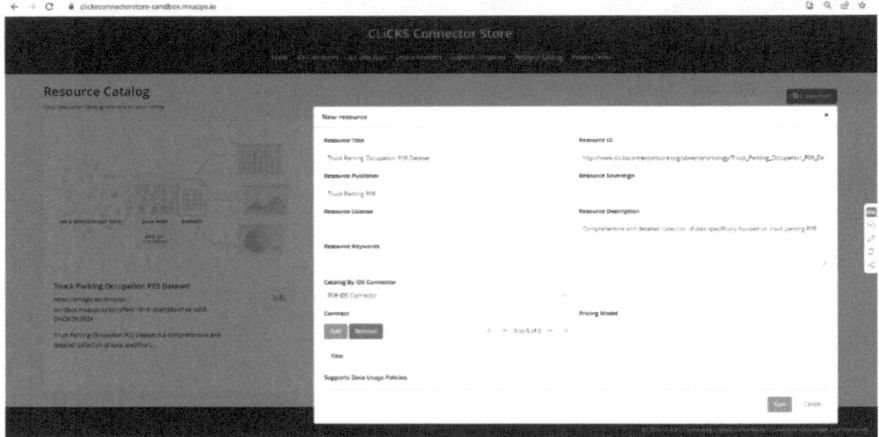

Fig. 8. The Connector Store publishing the metadata of data sets provided by the connectors of the truck parking providers.

Figure 8 illustrates how the Connector Store publishes the metadata of the truck parking datasets for other data space participants looking for more resources to train their model and optimize their occupancy. Additionally, via the Connector Store, the resulting model, trained using the shared data sets in the data space, can also be seen as a value adding resource and offered as such to stakeholders in the smart truck parking ecosystem (e.g., truck parking platforms). This generates a potential business ecosystem where actors in the smart truck parking data space will be stimulated to further cultivate the value of their data, e.g., (1) truck-parking owners or trucking companies (acting as data owners) offering their data to the data space and (2) researchers (acting as data users or service providers) provide their FL model to data space participants.

In the current work, the business model and economic agreements in the data space are not yet investigated. However, these aspects are important to consider for implementation and adoption. Here, collaboration with/between platform providers (e.g., Bosch Secure Truck Parking and TRAVIS Road Services) can potentially contribute to scaling up the use of smart truck parking solutions in the current real-world practice as indicated in earlier work [11].

4.7 Efforts, Challenges, and Open Issues

Additionally to the CRISP-DM cycle, the efforts, challenges, and open issues have been elaborated, as shown in Table 4. The experimental development in this study has been carried out by the five authors (see Declaration of authorship). The study was initiated in the third quarter of 2022 and completed in the second quarter of 2023. The initial research was conducted in the fourth quarter of 2022. Following, the FL model was developed and experiments were conducted in the first quarter of 2023. The prototype of the Connector Store was developed in the second quarter of 2023.

Table 4. The efforts, challenges, and open issues for each step of CRISP-DM.

Description	Efforts in hours	Challenges	Open issues
Deploy the federated learning data apps	±4	Combining knowledge of Kubernetes, IDS components and FL	Advanced workflow management. Evaluation by IDS
Business Understanding	- (Done in previous work)	Willingness to share data and invest in data sharing. Achieving large scale coverage	Development of a suitable business model and incentives to share data
Data Understanding	±4	Find data with overlapping time periods, without gaps. Verify the data quality	Automation of data collection and analysis of parking occupancy
Data Preparation	±6	Derive features from timestamps (e.g., day of week)	Semantic interoperability
Modeling	±16	Assess which features are beneficial for the FL model	Comparison with other FL models and alternative approaches
Evaluation	±2	Determine when the model scores sufficient	Increase number of data providers

(*continued*)

Table 4. (*continued*)

Description	Efforts in hours	Challenges	Open issues
Deployment	±0.25 (for each IDS Connector registration) ±0.50 (for each data resources metadata publication)	Proficiency and readiness level of semantic web and linked data technologies used by the metadata broker to annotate and manage the metadata of offered datasets submitted by participating IDS Connectors. Deployment at scale (e.g., tens of thousands of available parkings, real-time updates of parkings' availability, etc.)	Integration with participants' existing systems and business processes. Development of an application that uses the outcome of the model for operational use and decision support. Recommender feature of suitable resources (e.g., datasets, parking spots, etc.) based on their properties and data users' needs

The actual efforts, summarized in Table 4, are expressed in the number of hours that were needed to configure and deploy the data apps, develop the FL model, and conduct the experiments as described in this section. Compared to the lead time of the study, the actual development efforts were limited for a number of reasons, which will be briefly discussed.

First, and most important, the current study leveraged an existing representative data space testing environment at TNO. Thus, the efforts as mentioned in Table 4 do not include the efforts for realizing the data space infrastructure itself. Hence, the figures indicate the effort for the deployment of data apps in an existing and operational data space and the creation of the FL model. Such a scenario is considered representative for real-life situations, for instance when deploying data apps to the European Mobility Data Space [8, 26].

Second, the business understanding part for the current study was already researched in previous work.

Third, the Data Understanding part was also relatively short (4 h), because the input data only contained two columns and researchers benefitted from the results and insights from earlier work.

Fourth, the Modeling part also leveraged earlier work to determine which features were beneficial and was limited to the selected FL model and three data providers.

In case of a real-world application, the number of hours is expected to be higher, because internal systems and processes need to be aligned, and more effort is required to find the best possible model.

5 Discussion

In this section, the results are reiterated and possible explanations for the findings are discussed. Furthermore, the implications of the findings are highlighted.

The results of this study show that orchestrating FL through IDS communication is technically feasible. This was demonstrated by a simple FL model that predicts the occupancy of a parking lot, based on the architecture that was presented in earlier work [11, 34]. In case a data space is operational, it takes around 40 h to set up an environment where a FL model can be trained over datasets from multiple parties, while preserving data sovereignty for the data providers. The setup that was used in this study provides initial support for the technical feasibility. However, the operational feasibility to solve the truck parking problem requires further development and evaluation. The economic feasibility remains an open issue.

The adoption of the solution in a real-world setting requires the FL model to be incorporated in an application, as proposed in earlier work [11, 34], which can be queried in real-time to provide predictions regarding truck parking occupancy. The number of hours to realize such an application is expected to be higher for real-world applications, as the modeling will be more complex due to the increased number of variables, datasets, and more advanced FL models. Furthermore, the implementation requires integration with the participants' existing systems and alignment of interorganizational processes. Moreover, the development of a data ecosystem is expected to take most of the time and effort as there are tens of thousands of parkings in Europe.

To reach a critical mass, the onboarding of participants should require minimal time, effort, and technical knowledge. Providing a supporting UI, such as the Connector Store, is expected to contribute to lowering the barriers for participants.

The results show that the IDS architecture is suitable for training a FL algorithm, while preserving the data sovereignty for the parties involved. The use of data apps provides benefits for developers of FL models, because the governance, rules, and infrastructure for the orchestration are handled by the data spaces architecture and its components, leaving more time for the actual model development. This is also relevant for data space developers because the results show that it requires relatively little effort to offer a new service to a data space.

6 Conclusion

The main objective of this paper was to report the first results and findings regarding the assessment of the technical feasibility and deployment of FL models in a data space infrastructure. The combination of FL (or more in general PETs) and data spaces allows the privacy sensitive data to be accessed without the need to be shared between the stakeholders.

The assessment of the representative smart truck parking reference use case has demonstrated the technical feasibility and improved the understanding of the potential use and benefits of developing and deploying FL models (and more general PETs) in data spaces. Leveraging earlier work, a data space infrastructure was instantiated to deploy the DAPS, metadata broker, and three connectors. Datasets of three parkings were obtained and prepared. Next, the Sequential model from the Keras Python library was used to develop and evaluate a simple regression model. Three rounds of FL were run, illustrating a clear improvement regarding the training scores after each round among three parkings. Extending the metadata broker, a supporting Connector Store was developed to support the distribution and provisioning of IDS connectors and data resources among participants.

This study presents one of the first use cases of FL in a logistics data space. As such, it can serve as a reference for interested scholars and developers of FL models. More generally, it may contribute to enhancing more widespread application of privacy-preserving analytics, FL, and PETs in data spaces. However, the current study has been conducted in a controlled environment using one FL model. This setup can easily be extended to an industrial testbed with possibilities to assess its organizational feasibility, improving both efficiency and scalability to enable large scale adoption. Such a testbed can also be used to compare different FL models and potential solution alternatives.

The current study indicated specific challenges and open issues that can be addressed in future work. Future work may contribute to the evaluation of the FL model in an operational environment and make the final step of adopting the proposed architecture to realize a real-world business case. This requires the setup to be integrated with the systems of participants and extended with an application to provide real-time predictions based on the trained model. The development of APIs to provide access to the sensitive data as part of the data space environment could significantly improve the effectiveness thereof. Additionally, the organizational and economic feasibility are considered interesting areas for future work. Here, onboarding strategies can be developed and an appropriate business model can be developed together with the stakeholders, including incentives for participants. More specifically, the Connector Store implementation can be extended with pre-configured workflows and standardized system connectors (e.g., Transport Management Systems).

To optimally support the PETs in a data space environment, more advanced workflow management capabilities are required as multiple interaction patterns need to be supported, providing capabilities to define, control and manage the ordering of data processing steps and their inputs and outputs. It requires not only governance on data, but smart workflow management and orchestration of the services, running on the premises of different organizations. This implies further research on the data processing patterns and models of PETs to be optimally supported in the data space environment, with the goal to develop 'generic solutions' enabling (semi-)automatic deployment and improved monitoring.

Furthermore, in [1] it is argued that the adoption of PETs may also need legislation such as the Data Governance Act (DGA), and the need to make clearer in the DGA how PETs could increase the level of trust and control of data holders over their personal data.

Finally, a formal IDS evaluation and/or certification procedure can be conducted.

Declaration of Authorship
All authors discussed the results and contributed to the manuscript. The authors agreed on the final manuscript and declared no conflict of interest. **J.P.S. Piest** Ideator of the main idea. Scientific lead and supervision of the project. Structure and coverage of the

manuscript. Related work section regarding FL. Methodology section. Verification of the developed FL model and prototype. **W.P. Datema** Instantiated the data space infrastructure. Developed the FL model. Carried out experiments. Results section. Discussion section. **D.R. Firdausy** Developed the Connector Store prototype. Results section. **H. Bastiaansen** Co-supervision of the project. Introduction section. Related work section regarding data spaces. Conclusion section.

Acknowledgements. This paper is the result of the joint efforts of several research and innovation projects, the DASLOGIS project (2020-1-237TKI) and the CLICKS project (439.19.633), and supported by the Dutch Centre-of-Excellence on Data Sharing and Cloud of the Dutch Ministry of Economic Affairs and Climate Policy.

Supplementary Materials
The reference implementation can be found on the Gitlab repository of the TNO Security Gateway [35, 36]. Interested scholars and software developers can replicate the setup either using the Docker image (docker.nexus.dataspac.es/data-apps/federated-learning:1.0.0) or by building an OpenAPI data app using Gradle. The repositories of TNO provide stepwise guidance how to build, deploy, and configure the FL data app and FL helper.

References

1. Organization for Economic Cooperation and Development (OECD): Emerging Privacy Enhancing Technologies - Current Regulatory & Policy Approaches. https://www.oecd.org/publications/emerging-privacy-enhancing-technologies-bf121be4-en.htm
2. European Commission: A European strategy for data (2020). https://digital-strategy.ec.europa.eu/en/policies/strategy-data
3. European Commission: European Data Act (2022). https://ec.europa.eu/commission/presscorner/detail/en/ip_22_1113
4. European Commission: European Data Governance Act (2022). https://digital-strategy.ec.europa.eu/en/policies/data-governance-act
5. European Commission: European Digital Services Act (2022). https://commission.europa.eu/strategy-and-policy/priorities-2019-2024/europe-fit-digital-age/digital-services-act-ensuring-safe-and-accountable-online-environment_en
6. European Commission: European Digital Markets Act (2022). https://commission.europa.eu/strategy-and-policy/priorities-2019-2024/europe-fit-digital-age/digital-markets-act-ensuring-fair-and-open-digital-markets_en
7. European Union: European Artificial Intelligence Act (2021). https://eur-lex.europa.eu/legal-content/EN/TXT/?uri=celex%3A52021PC0206
8. EU PrepDSpace4Mobility Coordination and Support Action (Mobility Data Space CSA). "First Public Stakeholder Forum". https://mobilitydataspace-csa.eu/wp-content/uploads/2023/03/psf-28february.pdf
9. Piest, J.P.S., De Alencar Silva, P., Bukhsh, F.A.: Aligning Dutch logistics data spaces initiatives to the international data spaces: discussing the state of development. In: Proceedings of the Workshop of I-ESA 2022 (CEUR Workshop Proceedings, vol. 3214). CEUR (2022). http://ceur-ws.org/Vol-3214/WS6Paper1.pdf
10. Dutkiewicz, L., et al.: Privacy-preserving techniques for trustworthy data sharing: opportunities and challenges for future research. In: Curry, E., Scerri, S., Tuikka, T. (eds.) Data Spaces. Springer, Cham (2022). https://doi.org/10.1007/978-3-030-98636-0_15

11. Piest, J.P.S., Slavova, S., van Heeswijk, W.J.A.: A reference use case, data space architecture, and prototype for smart truck parking. In: Proceedings of the 22nd CIAO! Doctoral Consortium, and Enterprise Engineering Working Conference Forum 2022 Co-located with 12th EEWC 2022, pp. 1–15. [1] (CEUR Workshop Proceedings, vol. 3388). CEUR (2023). https://ceur-ws.org/Vol-3388/paper1.pdf
12. EU Open DEI Project: Aligning Reference Architectures, Open Platforms and Large-Scale Pilots in Digitising European Industry. https://www.opendei.eu
13. EU Open DEI Project: Design Principles for Data Spaces – Position Paper (2021). https://design-principles-for-data-spaces.org
14. International Data Spaces Association (IDSA): International Data Spaces: Reference Architecture Model Version 3 (2019). https://www.internationaldataspaces.org/wp-content/uploads/2019/03/IDS-Reference-Architecture-Model-3.0.pdf
15. International Data Spaces Association (IDSA): International Data Spaces: Reference Architecture Model Version 4 (2022). GitHub: https://github.com/International-Data-Spaces-Association/IDS-RAM_4_0
16. EU Gaia-X Initiative: Gaia-X Federation Services – GXFS. https://www.gxfs.eu/specifications
17. EU Gaia-X Initiative. Gaia-X - Architecture Document - 22.04 Release. https://gaia-x.eu/wp-content/uploads/2022/06/Gaia-X-Architecture-Document-22.04-Release.pdf
18. FIWARE. Components. https://www.fiware.org/catalogue
19. Dutch Neutral Logistics Information Platform (NLIP): iSHARE Data Sharing Initiative. https://www.iSHAREworks.org/en
20. iSHARE. Benefits For Data Spaces. https://ishare.eu/ishare/benefits/for-data-spaces
21. Data Space Business Alliance (DSBA): Unleashing the European Data Economy. https://data-spaces-business-alliance.eu
22. Data Space Business Alliance (DSBA): Technical Convergence Discussion Document. https://data-spaces-business-alliance.eu/dsba-releases-technical-convergence-discussion-document
23. EU Digital Europe Programme: Data Spaces Support Centre (DSSC). https://dssc.eu
24. EU Data Spaces Support Centre (DSSC) Initiative: DSSC Glossary, March 2023. https://dssc.eu/wp-content/uploads/2023/03/DSSC-Data-Spaces-Glossary-v1.0.pdf
25. EU Digital Europe Programme: SIMPL: cloud-to-edge federations and data spaces made simple. https://digital-strategy.ec.europa.eu/en/news/simpl-cloud-edge-federations-and-data-spaces-made-simple
26. EU PrepDSpace4Mobility (European Mobility Data Space) Coordination and Support Action (EMDS CSA, PrepDSpace4Mobility). The European Mobility Data Space. PrepDSpace4Mobility. https://mobilitydataspace-csa.eu
27. Pfitzner, B., Steckhan, N., Arnrich, B.: Federated learning in a medical context: a systematic literature review. ACM Trans. Internet Technol. 21(2), 1–31 (2021). Article 50. https://doi.org/10.1145/3412357
28. Fan, C., Hu, J., & Huang, J. (2009). Private semi-supervised federated learning. In International Joint Conference on Artificial Intelligence (IJCAI) (Vol. 2015, p. 2022)
29. Yang, Q., Liu, Y., Chen, T., Tong, Y.: Federated machine learning: concept and applications. ACM Trans. Intell. Syst. Technol. 10(2), 1–19 (2019). Article 12. https://doi.org/10.1145/3298981
30. Farahani, B., Monsefi, A.K.: Smart and collaborative industrial IoT: a federated learning and data space approach. Digit. Commun. Netw. (2023). https://doi.org/10.1016/j.dcan.2023.01.022
31. Kairouz, P., et al.: Advances and open problems in federated learning. Found. Trends® Mach. Learn. 14(1–2), 1–210 (2021). https://doi.org/10.1561/2200000083

32. Li, Q., et al.: A survey on federated learning systems: vision, hype and reality for data privacy and protection. IEEE Trans. Knowl. Data Eng. **35**(4), 3347–3366 (2023). https://doi.org/10.1109/TKDE.2021.3124599

33. Liu, H., Zhang, X., Shen, X., Sun, H.: A federated learning framework for smart grids: Securing power traces in collaborative learning (2021). https://doi.org/10.48550/arXiv.2103.11870

34. Slavova, S., Piest, J.P.S., van Heeswijk, W.J.A.: Predicting truck parking occupancy using machine learning. Procedia Comput. Sci. **201**, 40–47 (2022). https://doi.org/10.1016/j.procs.2022.03.008

35. FL data app URL: https://gitlab.com/tno-tsg/data-apps/federated-learning

36. FL helper. https://gitlab.com/tno-tsg/helpers/federated-learning-helper

37. Keras. https://keras.io/

38. Analytics (Open Data Hub, 2023). https://analytics.opendatahub.com/

39. Srivastava, N., et al.: Dropout: a simple way to prevent neural networks from overfitting. J. Mach. Learn. Res. **15**(1), 1929–1958 (2014)

40. TensorFlow. https://www.tensorflow.org/js/guide/models_and_layers

41. Firdausy, D.R., de Alencar Silva, P., van Sinderen, M., Iacob, M.E.: A data connector store for international data spaces. In: Sellami, M., Ceravolo, P., Reijers, H.A., Gaaloul, W., Panetto, H. (eds.) Cooperative Information Systems. CoopIS 2022. LNCS, vol. 13591. Springer, Cham (2022). https://doi.org/10.1007/978-3-031-17834-4_14

42. Janowicz, K., Van Harmelen, F., Hendler, J.A., Hitzler, P.: Why the data train needs semantic rails. AI Mag. **36**(1), 5–14 (2015). https://doi.org/10.1609/aimag.v36i1.2560

An Open and Standards-Based Approach for the Digital Building Permit in Montevideo

Laura González[1]([✉]), Bruno Rienzi[1], Raquel Sosa[1], Valentina Cornelius[1],
Martín O'Neil[1], Lilián Navickis[1], Elizabeth González[1], Gustavo Guimerans[1],
Janet Cortés[1], Francisco Ponzoni[1], Fabricio Álvarez[1], Andrés Nebel[1],
Sandra Cotto[1], Yamila Aguiar[1], Mauricio Calcagno[2], Maximiliano Riva[2],
Federico Reale[2], Brian Puerta[2], Enrique Rodríguez[2], Carolina Viñas[3],
Ignacio Turcatti[3], Gabriel Díaz[3], Gerardo Agresta[4], Juan Jose Prada[4],
María Eugenia Corti[4], Álvaro Rettich[4], Álvaro Marques[4], Lucía Juambeltz[4],
and Joaquín González[4]

[1] Facultad de Ingeniería, Universidad de la República, Montevideo, Uruguay
`{lauragon,brienzi,raquels,vcornelius,moneil,navickis,elizabet,gusguime,`
`jcortes,fponzoni,falvarez,anebel,scotto,yaguiar}@fing.edu.uy`
[2] Pyxis, Montevideo, Uruguay
`{mauricio.calcagno,maximiliano.riva,federico.reale,brian.puerta,`
`enrique.rodriguez}@pyxis.tech`
[3] DICA & Asociados, Montevideo, Uruguay
`{cvinas,iturcatti,gdiaz}@dica.com.uy`
[4] Intendencia de Montevideo, Montevideo, Uruguay
`{gerardo.agresta,juan.prada,maria.corti,alvaro.rettich,alvaro.marques,`
`lucia.juambeltz,joaquin.gonzalez.milburn}@imm.gub.uy`

Abstract. Building permits (BP) are authorizations required to start the construction of building projects and granted by public authorities. BPs are still mostly processed manually, which presents drawbacks (e.g. subjective interpretation of regulations, long processing times). The digitalization of the BP process is promising towards the digital transformation of public administration and the sector of Architecture, Engineering and Construction (AEC). However, current Digital Building Permit (DBP) solutions aiming to automate this process are usually partial, tailored-made or tool-specific, which hinders their applicability, extensibility, interoperability and portability. This paper presents an open and standards-based approach for the DBP in Montevideo, which comprises a compliance life cycle and a DBP platform. The approach leverages Building Information Modeling (BIM), is based on open standards and technologies, and aims to be extensible regarding regulations, types of buildings, and geographic locations. The approach also encompasses interdisciplinary work between teams with DBP-related skills (e.g. AEC, BIM, software engineering) and coming from different sectors (i.e. public administration, academia, software and AEC industries). The proposal was assessed by a prototype, functional/non-functional assessments, and validation activities with end-users. Results confirmed the feasibility and suitability of our approach, and let foresee its benefits and challenges.

T. P. Sales et al. (Eds.): EDOC 2023 Workshops, LNBIP 498, pp. 60–76, 2024.
https://doi.org/10.1007/978-3-031-54712-6_4

Keywords: digital building permit · openBIM · compliance · standards

1 Introduction

Building permits (BP) are authorizations required for the construction of a building project, which are granted by public authorities after verifying that the project complies with regulations at building and urban levels [24]. These permits are still mostly processed manually worldwide, which makes them a subjective, error-prone and time-consuming activity [25], with the risk of ambiguity, inconsistency in assessments, and delays over the construction process [22].

The Municipality of Montevideo (i.e. Intendencia de Montevideo) is not foreign to these drawbacks, as it receives between 700 and 1500 BP requests per year, whose processing involves extensive periods of manual analysis [15].

In turn, the Architecture, Engineering and Construction (AEC) sector is advancing towards the digitalization of its activities, mostly leveraging Building Information Modeling (BIM). openBIM [3] extends the benefits of BIM by enabling collaborative design, realization and operation of buildings based on open workflows and standards, via vendor-neutral formats [3] (e.g. IFC [17], BCF [2]).

The digitalization of the BP process is promising towards the digital transformation of public administration and AEC sector [24]. Indeed, studies have reported economic and time savings as well as efficiency and transparency increase [25]. Saved resources may be then used to address complex cases, enhancing in this way the quality of the built environment and the job task [25].

However, current Digital Building Permit (DBP) solutions to automate this process are usually partial, tailored-made or tool-specific, hindering their applicability, extensibility, interoperability and portability [24–26]. In turn, current initiatives identified key aspects for DBP (e.g. interdisciplinary teams, interoperable technologies, open standards, and machine readable requirements) [25].

This paper presents an open and standards-based approach for the DBP in Montevideo, comprising a compliance management life cycle and a DBP platform. The proposal encompasses interdisciplinary work between teams with diverse DBP-related skills (e.g. AEC, BIM, software engineering) and from different sectors. Particularly, this work was developed from November 2022 to August 2023 by Intendendia de Montevideo: https://montevideo.gub.uy/ (public administration), Facultad de Ingeniería: https://www.fing.edu.uy/ (academia), Pyxis: https://pyxis.tech/ (SW industry), Dica: https://dica.com.uy/ (AEC industry).

The proposal aims to return an agile response to BP applicants, leverages BIM and is based on open standards/technologies. It focuses on new residential buildings within an urban and central area of Montevideo, but the proposal aims to be extensible regarding regulations, types of buildings, and locations.

The proposal was assessed by implementing a prototype (which provides a reference implementation of the platform), performing functional/non-functional assessments, and carrying out validation activities with potential end-users.

The results and assessments so far have confirmed the feasibility of our approach and let foresee benefits and challenges of DBP solutions.

The rest of the paper is organized as follows. Section 2 provides background. Section 3 describes the proposed approach. Section 4 presents assessment results. Section 5 analyzes related work. Section 6 presents conclusions and future work.

2   Background

2.1   Compliance Management

Compliance management aims to ensure that organizations act in accordance with regulations [35]. It comprises activities such as the modeling, implementation, maintenance, verification, reporting, explanation, and resolution of compliance requirements extracted from different sources (e.g. laws, standards) [6].

In particular, in our previous work we defined a compliance management life cycle comprising four main phases [11]: Setup, Engineering, Control and Analysis. Setup involves managing elements that enable the development of compliance solutions. Engineering focuses on the development of such solutions and comprises four sub-phases: Modeling, Specification, Development and Deployment. Control involves controlling compliance, based on the developed solutions. Finally, Analysis involves analyzing compliance control results.

2.2   Digital Building Permit

The Digital Building Permit (DBP) focuses on automating the BP via digital processes and data about buildings and the built environment [24]. Different DBP developments and initiatives are currently being developed worldwide [26].

A reference DBP workflow is described in [24], including eight steps: rule interpretation/digitalization, preparation of 3D city models and geographic information, BIM modeling and IFC export, IFC structure validation, conversion/integration with 3D City models, regulation checks/reporting, and notification.

The European Network for Digital Building Permits (EUnet4DBP) identified DBP pillars such as: interoperable technology, simple and machine-readable rules and requirements, efficiency of process, and empowerment of public officers [24].

2.3   Relevant Standards

Industry Foundation Classes (IFC) is an open international standard, developed by buildingSMART [17], whose main purpose is to facilitate the exchange of data between BIM-based software applications [1]. IFC provides a library of objects (e.g. IfcWall), properties (e.g. NominalHeight) and relationships to represent building projects through their life cycle [30]. IFC also enables the definition of properties and property sets (PSets) for addressing specific information needs.

buildingSMART also developed the Model View Definitions (MVD) standard, which enables the definition of IFC data schema subsets to fit data exchange requirements for specific scenarios [4]. There is a set of official MVDs provided by buildingSMART (e.g. Design Transfer View - DTV) [1].

BIM Collaboration Format (BCF) is a buldingSMART standard that enables BIM-based applications to report topics of concern among project collaborators [2]. Collaborators create BCF topics by selecting IFC objects (e.g. an IfcWall), which are identified by their Globally Unique Identifier (GUI), and filling in data such as topic type (e.g. "Issue"), status (e.g. "Active"), title, priority, etc.

The standard ISO 12006-2:2015 [16] defines a framework for built environment classification systems. Particularly, Uniclass 2015 [10] has codes that enable classifying spaces (e.g. Bedrooms) and elements (e.g. Walls), among others.

CityGML is an Open Geospatial Consortium (OGC) standard that defines a conceptual model and data exchange format for rendering, storing, and sharing 3D geospatial data (e.g. virtual city models) [27].

Decision Model and Notation (DMN) [28] is an OMG standard, which defines a modeling and notation language for precisely specifying business decisions and rules. DMN models can be shared between platforms/organizations and enable the collaboration between business analysts and rule developers on constructing decision services. DMN models are also executable on DMN engines.

3   Open and Standards-Based DBP Approach

The DBP approach was developed by an interdisciplinary team, integrating skills of AEC, BP, BIM, systems integration, interoperability, geographic information systems (GIS), compliance management, and software architecture. The work is framed within a program of challenges for public services innovation [15].

The approach was debeloped based on Design Science Research (DSR) [12] and its main artifacts are a compliance management life cycle and a DBP platform. Four iterations of the DSR process [29] were carried out, in order to successively address new BP requirements and to enhance the IT artifacts.

Section 3.1 provides a general description of the proposal, which is refined by going through the phases of the life cycle from Sect. 3.2 to Sect. 3.5. The application of the approach in Montevideo is also presented in these sections.

3.1   General Description

The DBP approach follows current guidelines for DBP solutions: interdisciplinary work, open standards, and simple/machine readable requirements. It also aims to support interoperability with different systems (e.g. BIM tools) and vendor neutrality (by enabling AEC applicants and municipalities to select standards-compliant products that best fit their needs and constraints). Finally, the approach aims to support extensibility regarding regulations, types of buildings, geographic locations and compliance mechanisms. Figure 1 presents an overview of the approach, including its main actors and elements.

The main actors are: i) AEC applicants (e.g. architects) aiming to carry out a building project; ii) BP experts who master BP regulations; iii) BIM experts who master BIM; and iv) IT experts (e.g. software engineers, developers).

The general idea is: i) AEC Applicants model a building project using BIM tools and following modeling guidelines (e.g. Uniclass 2015); ii) applicants export

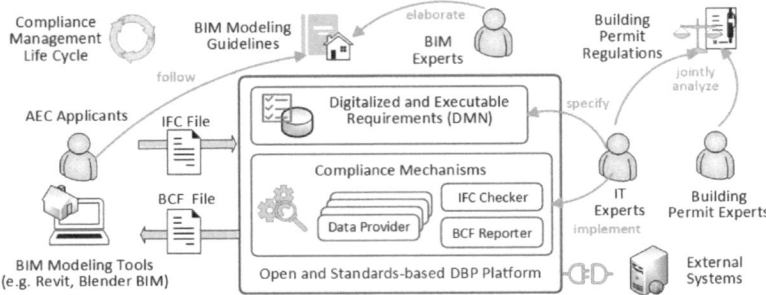

Fig. 1. General Overview of the Approach

the project to an IFC File using DTV; iii) applicants upload the file to the platform; iv) the platform validates its structure and verifies BP requirements; v) the platform generates a BCF File including compliance violations; vi) applicants download this file and load it into the BIM tool to visualize its content.

The DBP platform comprises two main elements: i) a repository of Digitalized and Executable BP Requirements (based on DMN); and ii) a set of Compliance Mechanisms, including an IFC Checker (to verify structure of IFC Files), a BCF Reporter (to generate BCF Files), and an extensible set of Data Providers (to obtain the required data to verify BP requirements).

The Compliance Management Life Cycle is an specialization of the life cycle defined in our previous work [11]. In particular, it has the same four main phases (i.e. Setup, Engineering, Control, Analysis), but it addresses DBP specific needs.

Several activities of the proposed life cycle have to be carried out so that the platform can verify BP requirements. BP and IT Experts have to jointly analyze BP regulations in order to identify BP requirements (e.g. buildings height cannot exceed the permissible maximum for the parcel) and the required data to verify them (e.g. building height, permissible maximum height of the parcel). BIM and IT experts have to determine how these data are specified on building models (e.g. building geometry) or obtained from calculations/external systems (e.g. an API that given a parcel number returns the permissible maximum height). BIM Experts have to elaborate BIM Modeling Guidelines so that applicants know how to specify the required data (e.g. use of LandID property to specify the parcel number). IT Experts have to specify and deploy BP requirements by leveraging the DMN standard, so that requirements become executable. IT Experts have to implement the required compliance mechanisms (e.g. a mechanism to invoke the aforementioned API to obtain the permissible maximum height of a parcel).

3.2   Compliance Setup

Compliance Setup involves configuring the DBP platform so that its elements can be used when verifying BP requirements. This configuration includes: i) which validations the IFC Checker performs (e.g. IFC files have to comply with IFC version 4); ii) the available data providers as well as the data that can be obtained from them; and iii) communication details (e.g. network address, message channel) to interact with the elements (i.e. IFC Checker, BCF Reporter, Data Providers, DMN Engine). This phase is mainly performed by IT Experts. Figure 2 presents the conceptual model associated to Data Providers.

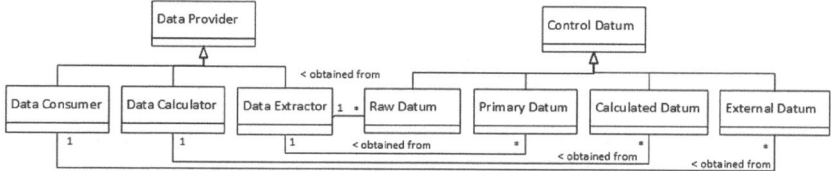

Fig. 2. Data Providers Conceptual Model

Data providers are in charge of obtaining the required data (i.e. control data) to verify BP requirements. They may be Data Extractors, Data Calculators or Data Consumers. Data Extractors process a digitalized building project (e.g. an IFC file) to extract raw data (i.e. directly obtained from IFC files) and primary data (i.e. obtained by simple calculations based on raw data). Data Calculators obtain calculated data, by leveraging specialized libraries (e.g. 3D libraries) in order to perform more advanced calculations. Data Consumers obtain external data by interacting with externals systems (e.g. a GIS).

The configuration of Data Providers requires specifying: a name, a description, a communication channel, a type, and the data it provides. Figure 3 presents the setup of the three data providers considered for the DBP in Montevideo.

Name	Description	commChannel	Type	Control Data
IFC-APY	IFC extractor based on IfcOpenShell	ifcapyChannel	extractor	parcelNumber, isMainBedroom, numberBedrooms buildingFloorArea, buildingTotalArea, buildingHeight buildingOpenings, spaceGeometry, openingGeometry
IDM-GIS	IDM Geographic Information System	idmgisChannel	consumer	parcelFar, parcelArea, parcelMaxHeight
GEOM-CAL	Geometry calculator based on SymPy	geomChannel	calculator	spaceDepth, spaceOpenings

Fig. 3. Data Providers for the DBP in Montevideo

IFC-APY is a data extractor which obtains raw data (e.g. parcel numbers) and primary data as simple calculations (e.g. counting the number of Bedrooms). It is based on IfcOpenShell: https://ifcopenshell.org/.

IDM-GIS is a data consumer which obtains external data (e.g. a parcel area given a parcel number) from the GIS of the Intendencia de Montevideo (IDM).

GEOM-CALC is a data calculator which obtains calculated data (e.g. space depth from its geometry) by leveraging SymPy: https://www.sympy.org/.

3.3 Compliance Engineering

This phase focuses on developing solutions to control BP requirements within the platform. It comprises Modeling, Specification, Development and Deployment.

Compliance Modeling. As shown in Fig. 4, compliance modeling involves three activities to be performed by different actors.

Activity	Reults	IT Expert	BIM Expert	BP Expert	AEC Applicant
Analysis of BP Regulations	BP requirements and associated control data	☑	☐	☑	☐
Analysis of control data	Additional control data, data dependencies, and modeling requirements	☑	☑	☐	☐
Elaboration of Modeling Guidelines	Modeling Guidelines	☐	☑	☐	☐

Fig. 4. Compliance Modeling Activities

The first modeling activity involves the analysis of BP regulations in order to identify BP requirements as well as the required data of buildings and their environment (i.e. control data) to verify such requirements. These activities are jointly performed by BP Experts and IT Experts. Figure 5 presents the conceptual model that was defined in order to perform this analysis.

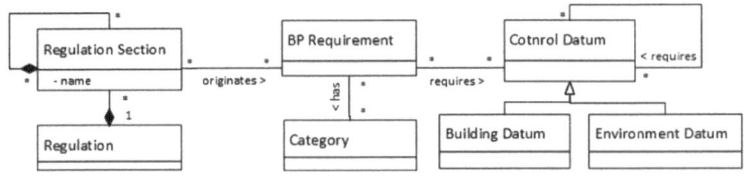

Fig. 5. Compliance Modeling Conceptual Model

BP Requirements may originate from various sections of different regulations. BP Requirements require data from the building/environment (i.e. control data) to be verified. BP Requirements are organized into categories (e.g. urban).

The result of this activity is a set of BP requirements modeled according to the conceptual model. Figure 6 presents a simplified version of how two BP requirements of Montevideo (analyzed within this work) were modeled.

ID	REQ-FAR
Name	Floor area ratio (FAR)
Regulations	Book II, ..., Section III (Municipal Normative)
Building Data	buildingFloorArea
Environment Data	parcelArea, parceFar
Category	urban

ID	REQ-BED
Name	Minimum area according to bedrooms
Regulations	Article 3 (National Normative)
Building Data	totalBuildingArea, numberBedrooms
Environment Data	
Category	building

Fig. 6. BP Requirements Modeling Examples

The requirement REQ-FAR establishes that "The relation between the floor area of a building and the area of the parcel where it is to be located, cannot be greater than the maximum floor area ratio (FAR) established for the parcel". REQ-FAR arises from a section of the Municipal Normative [14] and it belongs to the "urban" category. In order to be verified, REQ-FAR requires data from the building (buildingFloorArea) and from the environment (parcelArea, parcelFar).

The requirement REQ-BED establishes that "The total area of a building must exceed a minimum according to the number of bedrooms it has (1: 32 m², 2: 44 m², 3: 56 m², 4: 68 m²)". REQ-BED arises from "Article 3" of the National Normative [14] and it belongs to the "building" category. REQ-BED requires data from the building (totalBuildingArea, numberBedrooms) to be verified.

The second modeling activity involves the analysis of the identified control data in order to determine if other control data are required to obtain the already identified one (e.g. to obtain the parcel area, the parcel number is required). It also involves establishing which and how control data have to be specified by AEC applicants when modeling a building project. The results of this activity are additional control data, data dependencies, and modeling requirements. This activity is jointly performed by BIM Experts and IT Experts.

The third modeling activity involves the elaboration of modeling guidelines, in order to describe general structural requirements for building models (e.g. use of IFC version 4), and specific data needs to verify BP requirements. This activity is performed by BIM Experts and it has as result the modeling guidelines.

The modeling guidelines established for REQ-FAR and REQ-BED are: i) spaces whose function is Bedrooms have to be classified with the Uniclass 2015 code "SL_45_10_09 (Bedrooms)", as this enables obtaining "numberBedrooms"; ii) the parcel number where the building is to be located has to be specified using the LandID property (in PSetLandRegistration), as this enables obtaining "parcelFar" and "parcelArea" from the IDM-GIS data consumer; iii) there must be at least one floor at the ground level so that the building footprint can be calculated in order to obtain "buildingFloorArea"; and iv) all the inhabitable spaces must be correctly delimited so that "totalBuildingArea" can be calculated.

Note that during the setup phase, IFC Checker may be configured to verify IFC files comply with such modeling requirements (e.g. use of Uniclass 2015).

Compliance Specification As shown in Fig. 7, compliance specification involves two activities to be performed by different actors.

Activity	Reults	IT Expert	BIM Expert	BP Expert	AEC Applicant
Machine readable requirements specification	DMN-based requirements specification, validated by BP Experts	☑	☐	☑	☐
Modeling building models according to guidelines	Building model containing the required control data	☐	☐	☐	☑

Fig. 7. Compliance Specification Activities

The first activity involves the specification of BP requirements using a machine-readable format. The approach leverages DMN given that: it provides a graphical representation to bridge the gap between IT and business experts, it is an standard supported by different products, and DMN specifications are executable when deployed on DMN engines. This activity is jointly performed by IT Experts, who develop the specifications, and BP Experts, who validate them.

Figure 8 presents part of the DMN decision for REQ-BED within the KIE Sandbox (https://sandbox.kie.org/), including a DMN diagram (A), a decision table (B), and a dynamically generated web form to execute the decision (C).

In particular, the decision table indicates an evaluation result (i.e. true or false) according to the area and number of bedrooms of the building.

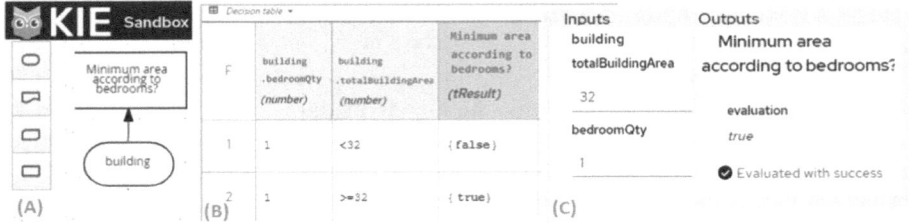

Fig. 8. DMN Decision for REQ-BED

The validation of DMN-based requirements by BP Experts is performed using: DMN graphical representations (e.g. diagrams, decision tables) and a web application that (inspired by KIE Sandbox) dynamically generates web forms for DMN-based requirements, enabling their online evaluation by BP Experts.

The second activity of this phase is performed by AEC applicants when modeling building projects with BIM tools. They have to include the required data in building models following the guidelines of the approach (e.g. spaces classification using Uniclass 2015, specification of parcel number using LandID).

DMN decisions developed for Montevideo, web forms to evaluate them, and videos showing how to specify control data in BIM tools are available in [8].

Compliance Development. This phase involves the implementation/extension of compliance mechanisms. Its activities are performed by IT Experts and may comprise: extending IFC Checker and BCF Reporter, extending data providers to obtain other data, and implementing/configuring new data providers. A new data provider has to receive data requests in a dedicated channel and send data responses to a predefined channel, adhering to a message structure. In turn, Fig. 9 shows how IFC-APY obtains the number of bedrooms (getBedroomsQty) and parcel number (getLandId) from an IFC file, by using IfcOpenShell.

```
def getBedroomsQty(model):
  referenceCode = "SL_45_10_09"  # Bedrooms
  result = 0
  spaces = model.by_type('IfcSpace')
  for space in spaces:
    refs = ifcopenshell.util.classification.get_references(space)
    for reference in refs :
      if reference[1] == referenceCode:
        result = result + 1
  return result
```

```
def getLandID(model):
  value=None
  sites = model.by_type('IfcSite')
  site = sites[0]
  psets = ifcopenshell.util.element.get_psets(site)
  if 'Pset_LandRegistration' in psets:
    psets2 = psets.get('Pset_LandRegistration')
    if 'LandID' in psets2:
      value = psets2.get('LandID')
  return value
```

Fig. 9. Obtaining Control Data from IFC File with IfcOpenShell

Compliance Deployment. This phase involves installing and leaving the compliance mechanisms (e.g. data providers) and executable requirements operational in the platform. These activities are performed by IT Experts.

3.4 Compliance Control

This phase involves the verification of BP requirements based on the solutions developed in the engineering phase. This verification is requested by AEC applicants and automatically performed by the DBP platform. Figure 10 presents the interactions within the platform when verifying the requirement REQ-FAR.

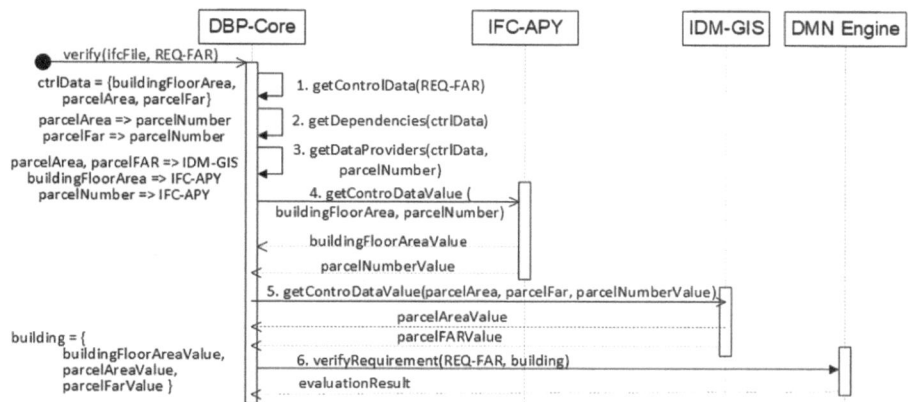

Fig. 10. Verifying REQ-FAR Requirement

After a verification request, the platform core component (DBP-Core) obtains the required data (buildingFloorArea, parcelArea, parcelFar) for REQ-FAR (1). DBP-Core obtains data dependencies for these data (2) (i.e. parcelNumber is required by parcelArea and parcelFar). DBP-Core obtains the Data Provider for the required data (3). DBP-Core interacts with IFC-APY to obtain the values of buildingFloorArea and parcelNumber (4). Using the parcelArea value, DBP-Core interacts with IDM-GIS to obtain values for parcelFar and parcelArea (5). Finally, DBP-core interacts with the DMN Engine to evaluate REQ-FAR based on the data values obtained for the building (6).

3.5 Compliance Analysis

This phase involves analyzing compliance control results and generating artifacts (e.g. reports) to ease the analysis. These activities are performed by the platform (generating BCF files) and by AEC applicants (analyzing BCF files content).

BCF Files generated by the platform include a topic of type "Issue" for each reason causing that a requirement verification fails. The GUID of the element generating the non-compliance is also included in the topic. Figure 11 shows how BCF topics can be analyzed using the BIM Collab plugin of Revit.

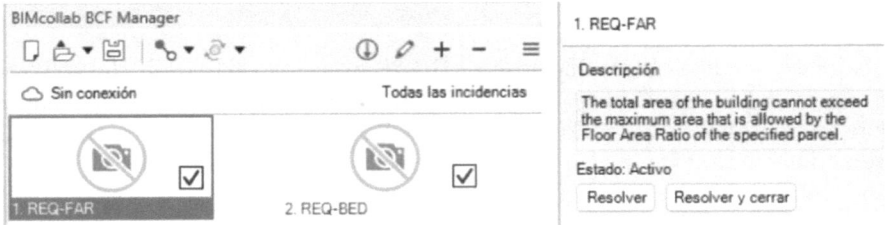

Fig. 11. Visualizing BCF Topics in Revit

4   Preliminary Assessment

4.1   Prototype Implementation

A prototype of the platform was developed to validate its technical feasibility.
Figure 12 presents its components and implementation products.

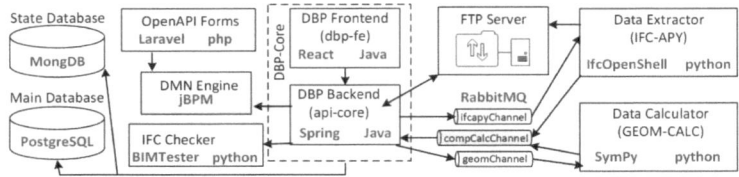

Fig. 12. Prototype Implementation

The core of the platform (DBP-Core) uses Java, React and Spring. A
PostgreSQL database is used to store requirements and setup data (e.g. data
providers). A MongoDB database is used to store state data of ongoing verification processes (e.g. obtained building data). jBPM is used as DMN Engine and
Laravel framework is used to automatically generate web forms to evaluate DMN
decisions. IFC Checker is based on BIMTester. Two Python-based data providers
are included: IFC-APY (based on IFCOpenShell) and Geom-CALC (based on
SymPy). RabbitMQ is used for asynchronous communication. An FTP server is
used to store uploaded IFC files. The prototype was deployed on Elastic Cloud
(https://minubeantel.uy/): a PaaS based on https://virtuozzo.com/.

The prototype supports the end-to-end verification of fifteen BP requirements
applying to Montevideo: four urban-related (e.g. FAR) and eleven building-
related (e.g. dimensions of rooms). Details of requirements are available in [8].

The prototype enabled the validation of the technical feasibility of the platform. It also enabled the identification of challenges regarding the maturity of
related products, which are still evolving (e.g. libraries to process IFC files), and
standards conformance in BIM tools (cf. Sect. 4.2).

4.2   Platform Assessment

The assessment of the platform comprised functional, interoprerability and performance aspects. The assessments leveraged the prototype and three main building models. These models are described in Fig. 13 and are available in [8].

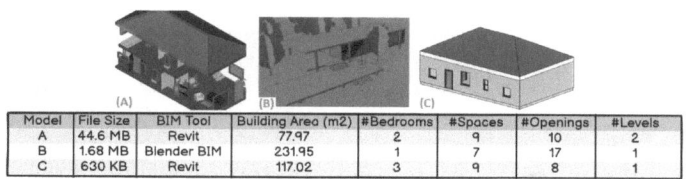

Model	File Size	BIM Tool	Building Area (m2)	#Bedrooms	#Spaces	#Openings	#Levels
A	44.6 MB	Revit	77.97	2	9	10	2
B	1.68 MB	Blender BIM	231.95	1	7	17	1
C	630 KB	Revit	117.02	3	9	8	1

Fig. 13. Test Data Building Models

Functional assessment focused on testing that the platform returns the expected evaluation of BP requirements according to the building model. Challenges arose given that the generation of test data involved the creation of complete building models. This issue was addressed by creating models as variations of models A, B and C, compliant with different requirements. This strategy resulted suitable and low-cost, in comparison with creating models from scratch.

Interoperability assessment focused on: i) verifying that the platform is able to obtain data from IFC files independently of the BIM tool used for generating such files, and ii) verifying that BCF files generated by the platform can be loaded in different BIM tools. IFC-related assessment was performed continuously given that test data included IFC files exported by two different tools: Revit and Blender BIM. Indeed, some issues impacted on modeling guidelines given that, by default, these tools exported some elements in different ways (e.g. IFC custom properties). In addition, the generation of BCF files by the platform presented some issues given that, although generated files were compliant with the BCF standard, they could not be loaded in Revit or Blender BIM. This had an impact on the amount of information returned on these files, as the platform is currently generating a minimal BCF file so that it can be loaded in these tools.

Finally, performance assessment focused on establishing a baseline for the processing time required to verify BP requirements, on a single user scenario and considering this transaction individually and without any competition. To this end, three groups of BP requirements were defined: i) basic: four BP requirements which do not require geometric operations; ii) geo: two BP requirements which require simple geometric operations (e.g. calculating space depth); iii) geo-int: two BP requirements which require geometries intersections. Figure 14 presents details of the Elastic Cloud environment over which these tests were performed and the results (i.e. processing times) of such tests (i.e. requesting the verification of each group of requirements for models A, B and C).

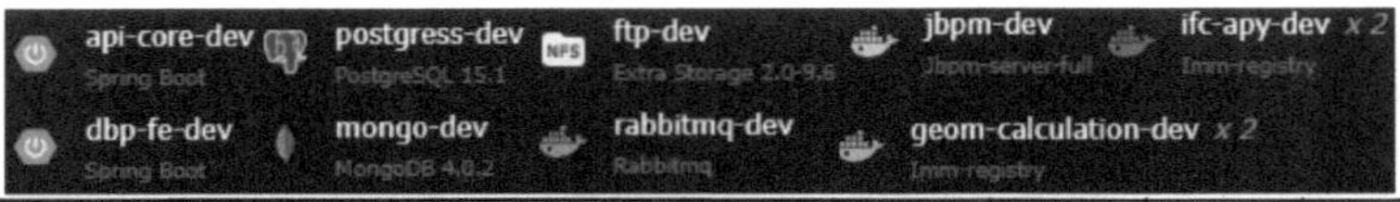

	api-core	dbp-fe	postgress	mongo	ftp	rabbitmq	jbpm	ifc-apy	geom-calc
RAM	2.25 GB	1.87 GB	768 MB	1 GB	768 MB	1.37 GB	3 GB	8 GB	4 GB
CPU	7.2 GHz	6 GHz	2.46 GHz	3.2 GHz	2.4 GHz	4.4 GHz	9.66 GHz	25.6 GHz	12.8 GHz
DISK	200 GB	200 GB	200 GB	200 GB	200 GB	200 GB	200 GB	400 GB	400 GB

basic (A)	basic (B)	basic (C)	geo (A)	geo (B)	geo (C)	geo-int (A)	geo-int (B)	geo-int (C)
14 s	5s	4s	2 min	20min	20min	32 min	59min	1h 6min

Fig. 14. Performance Tests Environment (Elastic Cloud) and Results

Performance tests were executed and monitored manually. During their execution, resource usage remained stable. However, processing times increased when performing geometric operations. These operations were also executed isolated from the platform in a PC (RAM: 8 GB, CPU: 2 GHz) and the processing time of getting data for geo-int was less than 3 min for all the models. Further analysis is required, but this increase may be caused by the available resources of the execution environment due to the type of subscription.

4.3 End-Users Assessment

The approach was assessed by conducting a focus group [18] with AEC professionals with experience in BPs. The goal of the activity was to gather opinions from them about the usability, viability and pertinence of the proposal, as well as about its potential impact in comparison with the traditional BP process.

Seven AEC professionals participated in the focus group (four of them without previous knowledge about the proposal). All participants had experience on BPs and some knowledge about BIM (three of them with concrete experience). All participants had used Autocad and three of them had also used Archicad or Revit. Three participants were working in companies and three as independent professionals. Three participants had teaching activity in universities. Participants had from 6 to 30 years of professional activity (most around 15 years).

The focus group had a duration of two hours and was performed virtually and recorded with Zoom. First, moderators provided a general description of the focus group. Then, participants had some minutes to comment information about themselves. Afterwards, moderators provided a general description of the proposal, by leveraging slides and by performing demos with BIM Tools/the prototype. Finally, a discussion period took place guided by a set of open questions performed by moderators and aligned with the goals of the activity.

All participants had positive opinions about the ease of use of the proposal, as well as regarding the benefits of the approach and its improvements in comparison with the traditional BP process. In addition, participants agreed that a more formal specification of BP requirements would reduce subjectivity. Participants also commented that it would be beneficial that the proposal could provide evaluation feedback about the simplest or most direct BP requirements, so that they can have more time for addressing complex requirements or cases.

Finally, all participants commented that the adoption of 3D modeling tools in order to use the proposal (e.g. to export IFC files) would not be an issue, since the new generation of professionals are already using these tools and the previous generations are starting to use them or willing to do so.

5 Related Work

There are few commercial tools that verify building code compliance [25]. Some are vendor-specific, such as SMARTreview APR [32] that checks compliance against the International Building Code (mainly in USA), and SoftTech BIMDCR [33], both of which are Revit plug-ins. Others are vendor-neutral and perform compliance checking on IFC files, such as Solibri Office [34] and Fornax Cloud [9]. Compared to our proposal, these tools manage rules in proprietary formats and rely on tool-dependent classifications for building objects [24].

In turn, the majority of large nationwide or citywide initiatives focus on developing bespoke open-source, standards-based solutions [24]. Many pilot projects are being developed worldwide, for instance in Finland (ECPIP) [13], Sweden (Smart Built Environment) [31], Germany (XPlanung and XBau) [19], France (Kroqi) [20] and Singapore (Intelligent Code Checking System based on Fornax Cloud). Our proposal is similar to them as it is based on standards. However, although it focuses on the Uruguayan normative, our platform aims to be extensible with respect to regulations, types of buildings and geographic locations.

Some works focus on checking regulations that require information about the surroundings of the planned building (e.g. urban plans, energy consumption policies) [5,7,23]. They rely on the use of commercial ETL software to perform manual transformations between IFC and CityGML models (among others). Since these transformations cannot be performed without human intervention, our approach favours the implementation of independent Data Extractors (or, eventually, Data Consumers) to retrieve the required data from each model type and Data Calculators to perform calculations on the combined data. In this way, data can be automatically combined from different model types on the fly without performing model transformations.

The rule interpretation and compliance checking is achieve through different approaches, many of which depend on Natural Language Processing techniques [21,36]. For instance, in [21], the original sentences from the building act are translated in several stages until an proprietary code is obtained. Our approach has the advantage that DMN decisions can be executed on any DMN-compliant engine, making the introduction of proprietary code unnecessary.

In addition, since October-2022 there are ongoing European research projects focusing on DBP (e.g. https://chekdbp.eu, https://accordproject.eu). As these projects advance, their results may complement ours. Finally, a distinguished characteristic of our work is that it provides an end-to-end approach to compliance management for DBP, as it covers: i) most typical compliance management phases (e.g. modeling, specification, verification, reporting) [6], and ii) most of the steps of the abstract DBP workflow defined in [24].

Finally, in the reviewed works, there is scarce information on other aspects that are addressed in our work, such as performance metrics (e.g. response or processing times), in-depth software architecture specification (e.g. detailed component interactions) and tool interoperability through the use of standards (e.g. models generated in different authoring tools).

6   Conclusions and Future Work

This paper presented a DBP approach, which comprises a life cycle and a DBP platform supporting compliance activities. Particularly, this work presented how this approach was applied to address specific BP requirements in Montevideo.

The proposal was assessed by a prototype, performing functional/non-functional assessments, and carrying out validation activities. These assessments enabled us to confirm the technical feasibility of implementing and operating the platform, the suitability of the selected standards, and the pertinence of the proposal for AEC professionals. Additionally, they enabled the identification of improvements (e.g. performance) and challenges (e.g. standards in tools).

The main contributions of this work are: the DBP specialization of the compliance life cycle, the proposal and development of the DBP platform to support the life cycle, and the application of both artifacts to address BP requirements in Montevideo. We believe that these results are a step forward on providing automated compliance verification solutions, which contribute to the areas of compliance management, DBP, and digital transformation of public services.

Such results enable us to argue that DBP solutions are promising towards the automation of the BP process, and the digital transformation of the AEC and public sectors. We confirmed how these solutions may reduce subjectivity regarding regulations, the advances of the area during last years, and the positive impact of DBP solutions for such sectors. We understand that these developments are challenging as they involve disparate and emerging technologies, as well as the interaction of teams from different disciplines and sectors. We consider that it is crucial to promote the seamless integration of capabilities of all actors, including municipalities, software and AEC industries, and academia.

Future work comprises addressing other BP requirements in Montevideo, and applying the proposal to other municipalities. We also plan additional assessment activities (e.g. workshops with end users) and prototype improvements, such as additional functionality, addressing performance issues, and implementing other data providers (e.g. based on CityGML to address urban-related requirements).

Acknowledgements. Supported by project DPU_S_2021_2_172901 funded by Agencia Nacional de Investigación e Innovación (ANII), Uruguay. We acknowledge Juan Castellar, Virgina de los Santos, and Marcio San Martín from Pyxis for their contribution to the prototype. We acknowledge Diana Pacheco for her contribution to the building models. We acknowledge ANTEL for providing promotional codes for Elastic Cloud within a FING-ANTEL agreement.

References

1. Borrmann, A., König, M., Koch, C., Beetz, J. (eds.): Building Information Modeling: Technology Foundations and Industry Practice. Springer, Cham (2018). https://doi.org/10.1007/978-3-319-92862-3
2. buildingSMART: BCF. https://technical.buildingsmart.org/standards/bcf/
3. buildingSMART: What is openbim? https://www.buildingsmart.org/about/openbim/
4. buildingSMART: mvdXML (2016). https://standards.buildingsmart.org/MVD/
5. Chognard, S., Dubois, A., Benmansour, Y., Torri, E., Domer, B.: Digital construction permit: a round trip between GIS and IFC. In: Smith, I., Domer, B. (eds.) EG-ICE 2018. LNCS, vol. 10864, pp. 287–306. Springer, Cham (2018). https://doi.org/10.1007/978-3-319-91638-5_16
6. El Kharbili, M.: Business process regulatory compliance management solution frameworks: a comparative evaluation. In: Asia-Pacific Conference on Conceptual Modelling, APCCM 2012 (2012)
7. Eriksson, H., et al.: Requirements, development, and evaluation of a national building standard-a Swedish case study. ISPRS Int. J. Geo-Inf. **9**(2), 78 (2020)
8. FING - PYXIS - DICA - IDM: Complementary material: code and videos (2023). https://www.fing.edu.uy/owncloud/index.php/s/8o9RRYSkWNRsJ7C
9. Fornax: Fornax Cloud. https://fornaxcloud.com
10. Gelder, J.: The design and development of a classification system for BIM. Build. Inf. Modell. (BIM) Design Constr. Oper. **149**, 477-491 (2015)
11. González, L., Ruggia, R.: A comprehensive approach to compliance management in inter-organizational service integration platforms. In: Proceedings of the 13th International Conference on Software Technologies. SCITEPRESS (2018)
12. Hevner, A.R., March, S.T., Park, J., Ram, S.: Design science in information systems research. MIS Q. **28**(1), 75-105 (2004)
13. Hirvensalo, A., Kaste, K., Maunula, A.: ECPIP Finland final report. WorkingPaper 24, Helsinki University of Technology (2008)
14. IDM: Digesto departamental. https://normativa.montevideo.gub.uy/indice/51202
15. IDM: Verificación automática del permiso de construcción en Montevideo (2021). https://innovacionpublica.anii.org.uy/desafios/construccion-inteligente/
16. ISO: ISO 12006-2:2015 (2015). https://www.iso.org/standard/61753.html
17. ISO: ISO 16739-1:2018 (2018). https://www.iso.org/standard/70303.html
18. Kontio, J., Bragge, J., Lehtola, L.: The focus group method as an empirical tool in software engineering. In: Shull, F., Singer, J., Sjøberg, D.I.K. (eds.) Guide to Advanced Empirical Software Engineering, pp. 93–116. Springer, London (2008). https://doi.org/10.1007/978-1-84800-044-5_4
19. Krause, K.U., Munske, M.: Geostandards xplanung und xbau. ZfV-Zeitschrift für Geodäsie, Geoinformation und Landmanagement (2016)
20. Kroqi: Kroqi. https://kroqi.fr/en
21. Lee, H., Lee, J.K., Park, S., Kim, I.: Translating building legislation into a computer-executable format for evaluating building permit requirements. Autom. Constr. **71** (2016). https://doi.org/10.1016/j.autcon.2016.04.008
22. Malsane, S., Matthews, J., Lockley, S., Love, P.E., Greenwood, D.: Development of an object model for automated compliance checking. Autom. Constr. **49**, 51–58 (2015). https://doi.org/10.1016/j.autcon.2014.10.004
23. Mandrile, M.: BIM as multiscale dacilitator for built environment analysis. Master's thesis, Univerza v Ljubljani (2020)

24. Noardo, F., et al.: Unveiling the actual progress of digital building permit: getting awareness through a critical state of the art review. Build. Environ. **213**, 108854 (2022)
25. Noardo, F., et al.: Integrating expertises and ambitions for data-driven digital building permits-the EUNET4DB. Int. Arch. Photogram. Remote Sens. Spat. Inf. Sci. **44**, 103–110 (2020)
26. Noardo, F., Malacarne, G.: Digital building permit: a state of play - I EUN-NET4DBP international workshop on digital building permit. Technical report, EUNnet4DBP (2021)
27. OGC: CityGML. https://www.ogc.org/standards/citygml
28. OMG: Decision model and notation (2021). https://www.omg.org/spec/DMN/
29. Peffers, K., Tuunanen, T., Rothenberger, M.A., Chatterjee, S.: A design science research methodology for information systems research. J. Manage. Inf. Syst. **24**(3), 45–77 (2007)
30. Sacks, R., Eastman, C., Lee, G., Teicholz, P.: BIM Handbook: A Guide to BIM for Owners, Managers, Designers, Engineers, and Contractors. Wiley, Hoboken (2018)
31. Smart Built Environment: Smart Built Environment. https://www.smartbuilt.se
32. SMARTreview APR: SMARTreview APR. https://www.smartreview.biz
33. SoftTech: BIMDCR. https://softtech-engr.com/bimdcr
34. Solibri: Solibri Office. https://www.solibri.com/solibri-office
35. Tran, H., Zdun, U., Holmes, T., Oberortner, E., Mulo, E., Dustdar, S.: Compliance in service-oriented architectures: a model-driven and view-based approach. Inf. Softw. Technol. **54**(6), 531–552 (2012)
36. Zhang, J., El-Gohary, N.M.: Integrating semantic NLP and logic reasoning into a unified system for fully-automated code checking. Autom. Constr. **73**, 45–57 (2017)

iRESEARCH

iRESEARCH – First Workshop on Empirical Methodologies for Research in Enterprise Architecture and Service-Oriented Computing

Maya Daneva[1] and Faiza A. Bukhsh[2]

[1] Semantics, Cybersecurity & Services, University of Twente, The Netherlands
m.daneva@utwente.nl
[2] Data Management & Biometrics, University of Twente, The Netherlands
f.a.bukhsh@utwente.nl

In the past decades, the EDOC conference and its co-located workshops have presented many research initiatives in which Enterprise Architecture (EA) and Service-Oriented Computing (SOC) scholars carried out empirical studies with practitioners and for practitioners in industry. The various industry-university collaborations that have been represented at EDOC have opened up a conversation about the evaluation of frameworks, approaches, and tools and the comparison of their resilience, sustainability, usefulness, and effectiveness in specific practical contexts. In particular, service-oriented approaches and EA approaches are increasingly more often applied in the context of new areas, such as Artificial-Intelligence-enabled enterprise computing, Internet of Things, digital ecosystems, digital twins, green and cloud computing, among others. The EDOC community's heightened interest in empirical evaluation has led to the accumulation and publication of empirical evidence through design science research, exploratory and confirmatory case studies, interview-based studies, focus groups and surveys.

The purpose of the first International Workshop on Empirical Methodologies for Research in Enterprise Architecture and Service-Oriented Computing (iRESEARCH) at EDOC 2023 was to initiate the conversation on the interfaces of the disciplines of EA/SOC and Empirical Research Methodologies (ERM). The workshop goals were:

(a) to open up the interdisciplinary debate on the steadily moving frontiers in empirical methodologies in support of EA and SOC research projects, and
(b) to expand the network of researchers designing and conducting empirical studies in EA and in the sub-fields of SOC, which in turn will lead to the cross-fertilization between these two fields and ERM.

The targeted outcomes of this workshop included the identification of open research problems and the possible solutions to these problems, regarding:

i. evaluation and comparison of EA and service-oriented methods, processes and tools in context;
ii. emerging research methods;

iii. new and unexpected forms of collaboration with industrial partners in empirical research projects;
iv. evaluation of transferability of empirical results to practice.

The iRESEARCH workshop program featured two empirical studies illustrating two contexts of industry-relevant research carried out with practitioners on board. To each paper there was a discussant assigned. This helped generate discussion and focus on important aspects of the application of empirical research techniques and particular challenges faced by the authors.

We hope you enjoyed the workshop and the review of the workshop proceedings.

Acknowledgments. We would like to thank the Program Committee members for their dedication to rigorous and timely peer review, which allowed us to highlight the very best research from the empirical EDOC community. We also thank the authors who considered iRESEARCH as the destination of their empirical papers. Finally, we would like to express our appreciation for the timely response and assistance that we received from the Organizing Committee and the staff of the EDOC 2023 conference and, in particular, to the EDOC 2023 General Chairs Dimka Karastoyanova and Marten van Sinderen, and the EDOC 2023 Workshop Chairs Tiago Prince Sales and Sybren de Kinderen.

iRESEARCH Organization

Workshop Chairs

Maya Daneva   University of Twente, The Netherlands
Faiza A. Bukhsh   University of Twente, The Netherlands

Program Committee

Jelena Zdravkovic   Stockholm University, Sweden
Pnina Soffer   University of Haifa, Israel
Hajo Reijers   Utrecht University, The Netherlands
Jeewanie J. Arachchige   University of Twente, The Netherlands
Said Assar   Institut Mines Telecom Business School,
                                  France
Oscar Pastor   Universidad Politecnica de Valencia, Spain
Hans Weigand   Tilburg University, The Netherlands
Selmin Nurcan   University of Paris, France
Stefanie Ronderle-Ma   TUM, Germany
Barbara Weber   University of St. Gallen, Switzerland
Patrício de Alencar Silva   Federal Rural University of the Semi-arid
                                  Region, Brazil

Monitoring Value Chains of Organic Beverages

Hugo D. Santos[1]([✉]) [ID], Patrício de A. Silva[1][ID], Marcos E. Cintra[2][ID],
Francisco M. Mendes Neto[1][ID], and Faiza A. Bukhsh[3][ID]

[1] Federal University of the Semi-Arid, Mossoró, Rio Grande do Norte, Brazil
`{hugo.santos,patricio.alencar,milton}@ufersa.edu.br`
[2] Federal University of Espírito Santo, São Mateus, Espírito Santo, Brazil
`mecintra@gmail.com`
[3] University of Twente, Enschede, The Netherlands
`f.a.bukhsh@utwente.nl`

Abstract. The outflow of manufactured organic products needs to prevent damage to the goods. There are specifications of models of value networks with blockchain services for monitoring transactions. This paper general objective is to provide strategic models to monitor supply chains of organic beverages. The design of this network was based on the Design Science methodology, including the process of investigating the problem, proposing an artifact to tackle it, and validating its construction. A systematic literature review was made and strategic models were proposed to monitor networks with blockchain with validation by empiric evaluation and assessment with a selected company for a single case study. To construct the models, information obtained with the literature review was used, as well as information provided by the company via meetings and surveys. In the design, the e³value editor tool of the e³value framework was used. Three models were produced based on these scenarios: regional, national and international. The models were validated and positively assessed by the participating company, which answered a survey to assess the proposal according to their needs and the feasibility of implementing that technology.

Keywords: Preventive Monitoring · Food Supply Chain · Blockchain technology · Value Networks

1 Introduction

Eating is vital for human survival, underscoring the social and environmental relevance of addressing food losses and waste. The United Nations Environment Programme estimates that food waste in Brazil reaches up to 132 lbs/person/year [9], while globally, around 40% [3].

Supply Chains (SC) represent a series of activities from suppliers to customers, encompassing manufacturing, distribution, and more [5]. The distribution stage, involving storage and transportation processes, plays a crucial role in bringing products to market [6].

T. P. Sales et al. (Eds.): EDOC 2023 Workshops, LNBIP 498, pp. 81–88, 2024.
https://doi.org/10.1007/978-3-031-54712-6_5

In the distribution stage, there are instances where little to no control or monitoring occurs during transportation, as evident in studies focusing on food production and distribution processes [3,4,8].

This research aims to develop strategic models to monitor networks with blockchain and with practical application and evaluation in collaboration with Meltech, a company chosen for its accessibility and provision of data. The study also carries significance for sustainability analysis in small companies.

The research adopts the Design Science methodology, also known as "Science of the Project" or "Science of the Artificial" [7]. Resolving the research problem relies on the application of methods that bridge the gap between a problem set and a solution set: Conceptual Questions (CQ), Technological Questions (TQ), and Practical Questions (PQ).

The primary subsets of research questions include: CQ - What modeling methods are available for monitoring value network transactions using blockchain? TQ - What technologies are necessary to create models with blockchain in a value network? and PQ - How can the developed models aid a company in deciding to implement blockchain for monitoring an organic beverage supply chain?

Next, the objectives of this work are presented, in accordance with Design Science, with indication of stakeholders objectives and objectives of research [10].

Stakeholder objectives were established following research on value networks and consultations with partners in the food supply chain, particularly Meltech. The overarching vision is to enhance transportation safety and reduce transactional bureaucracy. Ensuring operational security requires monitoring and validating data in each commercial transaction within the value network, underlining the cost-benefit assessment of adopting blockchain technology.

Beyond the stakeholders objectives, the research has scientific objectives, delimited as general objective and specific objectives. The General Objective was to provide strategic models for monitoring the supply chain of organic beverages. The specific objectives had been:

1. To study the state of the art regarding existing models in the area of value networks and blockchain by means of a systematic literature review;
2. To collect the practical requirements alongside the interested parties for the construction of proper models;
3. To formulate the models in accordance with a metamodel.

Next, the objectives of this research are described, as the methodology of Design Science, and in accordance with the research questions - CQ, TQ, PQ. There were no objectives of instrumentation and forecast defined, since the research does not include the construction of tools beyond the already the existing ones for the development of the artifact and there are no forecast objectives on its use.

Objective of Knowledge: Describe the principles for modeling the monitoring in value networks with blockchain based on the literature and in consultation with the interested parties.

Objective of Device: To formulate a set of business models related to monitoring value networks with blockchain, according to a chosen metamodel.

2   Theoretical Framework

This section introduces key concepts related to Design Science, Supply Chains, Value Networks, Ontologies, Business Modeling, the e^{3}value Framework, and Blockchain technology.

Design Science is a research methodology integrating structured processes of scientific inquiry and technological artifact development. This cyclic process involves four stages: 1 - Problem inquiry or implementation assessment; 2 - Treatment design; 3 - Treatment validation; 4 - Treatment implementation.

In the realm of **Supply Chains and Value Networks**, goods and services production and distribution hinge on roles fulfilled by organizations. These roles shape a **supply chain**, involving relationships through commercial transactions.

Transactions initiate after documentation issuance, like certifications. Beyond paperwork, transactions demand vigilance, notably in product transportation, necessitating monitoring in distribution.

Supply chains involve a network forming a **value network**. These interconnected transactions constitute a value network, with organizations exchanging valuable items to meet a consumer market's needs.

Ontologies form a foundation for construction methodologies and analysis. Principles involve ontologically understanding a business system, including internal constituents, relationships, and constraints.

Business modeling with ontologies applies to administration and corporate contexts, structured based on represented value networks.

This work adopts [1]'s ontology for organic beverage supply chains. Business modeling represents the value network with blockchain-based monitoring, using the tool within the e^{3}value framework.

Blockchain Technology is an encrypted ledger of business transactions evolving from independent processes. It is now represented through ontologies.

Blockchain models exist, including Weigand's. A business can be depicted through a model sketch, showing data cycles and information exchange in value network transactions marked by blockchain. Each transaction involves creating new smart contracts recorded in the blockchain, with actors concatenating contracts defining their roles and object sharing in the value network.

The business model illustrates a network structure with nodes representing actors in the value network.

Figure 1 shows a sketch with actors, commercial transactions, and smart contract sharing. Actors include Regulators, Suppliers, Organizations, Transporters, and Commercial Partners (Points of Sale and Independent Resellers).

Concatenation of blocks with smart contracts on the right side signifies data recording, while on the left, it denotes a data reading process for investigating and confirming process information.

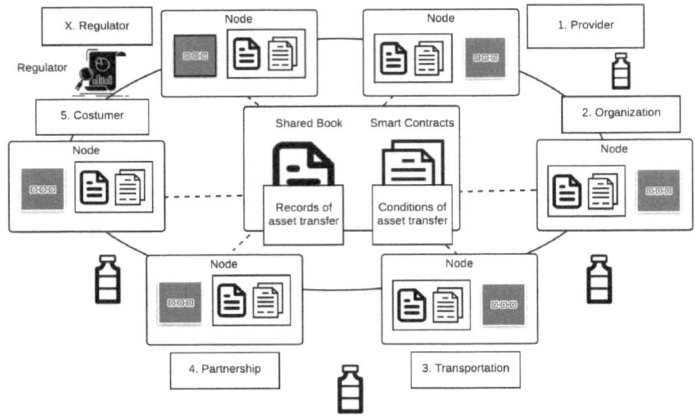

Fig. 1. Adaptation of Business Sketch with blockchain (Source: [2])

3   Modeling of Value Networks with Blockchain Services

This section details the application of the e^3value framework tor model business strategies with blockchain within value networks, specifically focusing on manufacturing companies of organic products. The blockchain technology is explored as a means to optimize input transportation and ensure transparency and integrity in the supply chain for organic products.

3.1   The e^3value Framework

The e^3value framework, an intuitive tool for modeling value networks, was employed using the e^3value editor. This editor allows users to select and connect elements of the e^3value ontology, representing relationships within the network. Additionally, it offers functions to verify commercial transactions and convert models into spreadsheets for consistency checks.

The generated spreadsheets are instrumental in assessing model consistency and profitability, providing insights into potential profits for actors in the value network scenarios. These spreadsheets serve as motivation for network actors to join the business network.

Utilizing the e^3value editor, various scenarios were created to depict different operational conditions. Three business models were developed and evaluated:

– Regional Model: Introduces a blockchain supplier with Information Technology support.
– National Model: Extends the Regional Model nationally, involving regulators and national transporters.
– International Model: Extends the National Model internationally, encompassing international regulators and transporters.

Both the e^3value editor and e^3value tools support quantitative analysis by generating necessary spreadsheets. The e^3value editor facilitates quantitative and economic analysis of models, including profitability calculations.

3.2 Technical Action Research (TAR)

The e^3value editor played a pivotal role in crafting value network models for proposing a business strategy, considering blockchain adoption. Three models were developed, each addressing specific scenarios based on literature reviews and insights from the company. The Technical Action Research (TAR) process, guided by Wieringa's protocol, involved stages, cycles, and customer engineering.

Requirements for models were derived from literature reviews and information collected through meetings and questionnaires. The TAR process included research stages and experimentation cycles. The researcher, acting as both inquirer and technology developer, addressed Meltech's need to monitor the organic beverage transportation chain through blockchain.

The customer's problem involves monitoring the transportation chain of organic beverages through blockchain technology. To collect information and assess the models, meetings with company representatives and a Requirements Survey were implemented. The survey aimed with main stakeholders, to identify and analyze actors and functions within the company's value network.

3.3 Presentation of the Business Models

The e^3value framework tool was instrumental in modeling the business networks. The first model represents Meltech's current value network for organic beverages. The value network comprised various actors, including Meltech, Consumers or Customers, and Suppliers (organic food producers and input suppliers).

Meltech's current value network involves transactions in supply, transportation, regulation, and partnership chains. This network ensured the quality, safety, and availability of organic products to consumers through well-defined transactions. These elements form Meltech's current value network model Fig. 2.

Figure 2 depicts key actors and transactions in the Meltech value network. It includes the Organization (Meltech), Consumers or Customers, and Suppliers, with Suppliers representing organic food producers and input suppliers.

Three scenarios were proposed for implementing blockchain in Meltech's value network, each focusing on monitoring the transportation of goods. The scenarios were designed for regional, national, and international expansion.

Figure 3 depicts the specifications of a regional scenario for Meltech, introducing the Information Technology Support actor to provide blockchain services for monitoring transportation.

The regional scenario involves the use of blockchain to monitor the transportation of lots, enhancing business safety and reducing fraud risk. In the national scenario (Fig. 4a), Meltech extends the regional model to the national level. Blockchain services now include regulators and national transporters.

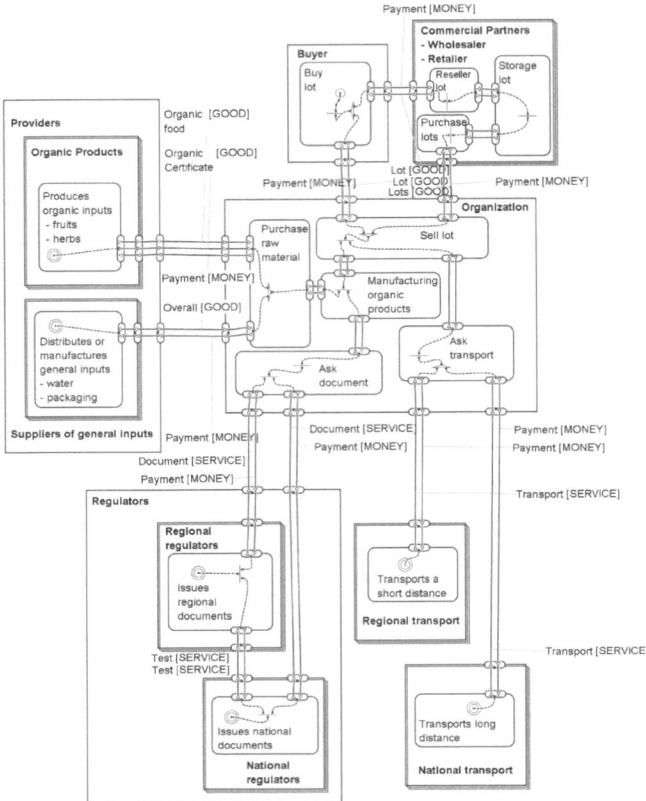

Fig. 2. Current model of the value network of organic product manufacturing

The international scenario (Fig. 4b) further extends the national model, involving international regulators and transporters.

3.4   Assessment

No inconsitencies were found in the value network models using the e³value editor tool and the generation of profitability sheets. The assessment involved a presentation and a survey. The respondents found the models suitable for visualizing the value network. The company stated that the models supported their decision-making on adopting blockchain to monitor transportation.

The positive reception of the models indicates qualitative viability for blockchain implementation, although more insights into the company's decision-making processes are needed.

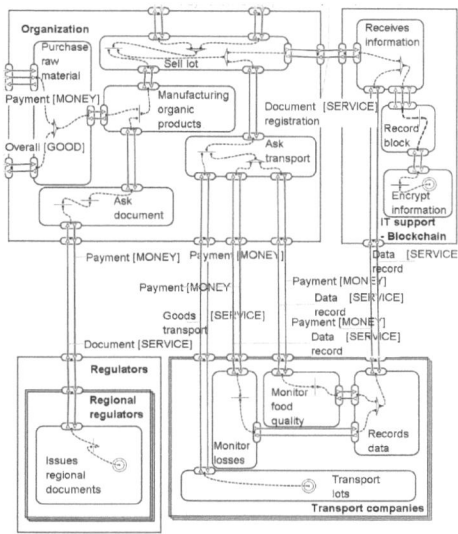

Fig. 3. Regional Model of a value network for Meltech

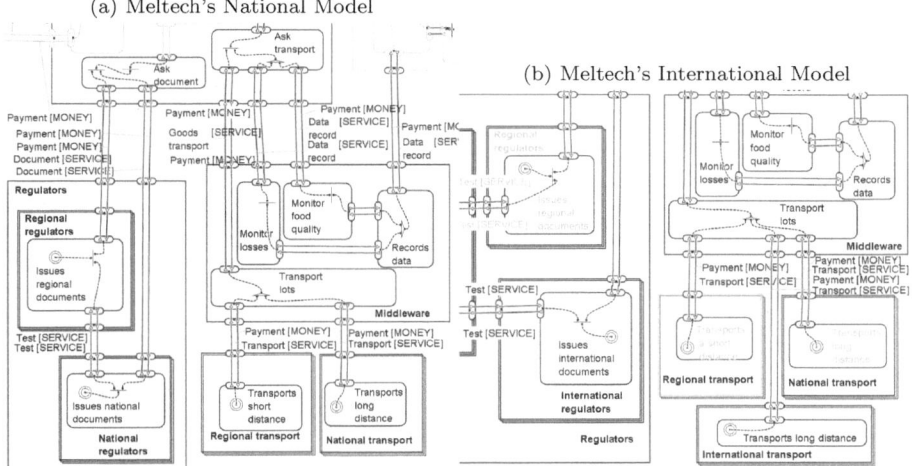

Fig. 4. National and International Models of a value network for Meltech

4   Conclusions

Our goal to develop strategic models for monitoring the organic beverage supply chain was successfully achieved with the value network scenarios integrated with blockchain-based monitoring. This monitoring mechanism facilitates real-time communication of product status between producers and customers, emphasizing product quality and overall customer satisfaction.

Three distinct models were meticulously crafted to address different scopes: regional, national, and international. Each model was developed based on the existing business model, incorporating insights from systematic literature reviews, meetings, and data collection instruments with the company. These models were vital components of a comprehensive Technical Action Research initiative, which included a survey for evaluating the proposed models [10]. Survey responses provided valuable data for model assessment, indicating potential for future implementation. However, a definitive decision from the company is still pending.

Despite limitations, including the practical challenges of single-company evaluation, the research yielded valuable insights encompassing blockchain integration into value networks, the role of blockchain service providers in transaction monitoring, unexplored facets of value network modeling, and support for food, organic products, and biotechnology companies.

As future research, we intend to expand value networks using a blockchain ontology, the development of a value/Protégé plugin, extension of Technical Action Research to add other network actors, instantiation of models with real-world data, and integration of value modeling with Data Science to gain a deeper understanding of the economic viability of these models.

References

1. Gordijn, J.: A design methodology for trust and value exchanges in business models. In: BLED 2003 Proceedings, p. 2 (2003)
2. Gupta, M.: Blockchain for Dummies. Wiley, Hoboken (2020)
3. Kayikci, Y., Subramanian, N., Dora, M., Bhatia, M.S.: Food supply chain in the era of industry 4.0: blockchain technology implementation opportunities and impediments from the perspective of people, process, performance, and technology. Prod. Plann. Control 33(2–3), 301–321 (2022)
4. Kumar, D., Kumar, M., Anandh, R.: Blockchain technology in food supply chain security. Int. J. Sci. Technol. Res. 9(1), 3446–3450 (2020)
5. Ronaghi, M.H.: A blockchain maturity model in agricultural supply chain. Inf. Process. Agric. 8(3), 398–408 (2021)
6. da Silva, G.R., da Silva, A.C.R.: Comércio eletrônico a luz do código de defesa do consumidor e-commerce the light of the consumer protection code. Direito Realidade 7(10) (2019)
7. Simon, H.A.: The Sciences of the Artificial. MIT Press, Cambridge (2019)
8. Tse, D., Zhang, B., Yang, Y., Cheng, C., Mu, H.: Blockchain application in food supply information security. In: 2017 IEEE International Conference on Industrial Engineering and Engineering Management (IEEM), pp. 1357–1361. IEEE (2017)
9. UNEP, U.N.E.P.: Food waste index report 2021. Nairobi (2021)
10. Wieringa, R.J.: What is design science? In: Wieringa, R.J. (ed.) Design Science Methodology for Information Systems and Software Engineering, pp. 3–11. Springer, Heidelberg (2014). https://doi.org/10.1007/978-3-662-43839-8_1

An Enterprise Coherence Quantification Framework for General Enterprise Architecting

Joost Bekel[1]([✉]), Roel Wagter[2], Henderik A. Proper[3], and Frank Harmsen[4]

[1] De Nederlandsche Bank (DNB - Dutch Central Bank),
Amsterdam, The Netherlands
joost.bekel@casema.nl
[2] Solventa B.V., Nieuwegein, The Netherlands
roel.wagter@solventa.nl
[3] TU Wien, Vienna, Austria
e.proper@tuwien.at
[4] Maastricht University, Maastricht, The Netherlands
f.harmsen@maastrichtuniversity.nl

Abstract. Enterprise coherence pertains to the extent to which all relevant aspects of an enterprise are connected in such a way that these connections facilitate an enterprise in obtaining/meeting its desired results. The GEA (General Enterprise Architecting) method treats enterprise coherence as something that can be governed explicitly. GEA's Enterprise Coherence Framework (ECF) is qualitative in nature. Being able to really measure enterprise coherence would greatly support the analysis of enterprise coherence. In this paper we setup a research approach for developing enterprise coherence metrics and perform a first step in working towards an Enterprise Coherence Quantification Framework (ECQF) as part of a methodology. A case from GEA training practice is used for validation of a first application of the ECQF.

Keywords: Enterprise Coherence · Enterprise Coherence Quantification Framework · GEA · Enterprise Architecture · Strategy Framework

1 Introduction

Strategies fail due to a lack of coherence and consistency [9]. Coherence between various enterprise facets is essential for success [10]. Leinwand and Mainardi [14] showed a relation between enterprise coherence and enterprise performance. Complex System Governance (e.g. [13]) teaches that -since system viability relies on design [12] - the viability of organization is threatened by lack of coherence in design. Own research shows that coherence in organizations is unsatisfactory on average, and even poor when it concerns enterprise design [21]. Measurement of the level of enterprise coherence would greatly support the analysis -and

T. P. Sales et al. (Eds.): EDOC 2023 Workshops, LNBIP 498, pp. 89–101, 2024.
https://doi.org/10.1007/978-3-031-54712-6_6

thereby- governance of enterprise coherence [21]. This paper explores a quantification framework for strategy planning frameworks, and more specifically GEA, as a step in gradually working from simple to more refined ontologies.

2   Theoretical Background

The notion of enterprise coherence was coined by Wagter [8] as part of the GEA (General Enterprise Architecting) method [8,24]. GEA defines *enterprise coherence* as *"the extent to which all relevant aspects of an enterprise are interconnected, such that these connections facilitate an enterprise in achieving its management's desired results"* [25]. Based on the GEA definition, the GEA method includes the Enterprise Coherence Framework (ECF) [8], that evolves around the notions of *Level of Purpose* and *Level of Design* and involves ten relevant aspects of coherence: Mission, Vision, Core Values, Goals, Strategies, Perspective, Core Concept, Core Model, Guiding Statement, and Relevant Relationship. The ECF with a few example perspectives is shown in Fig. 1. With an ECF in place, it is possible to address business issues with coherent solution elements [8]. The ability to quantify enterprise coherence is expected to aid GEA practitioners and scholars in their analysis [8].

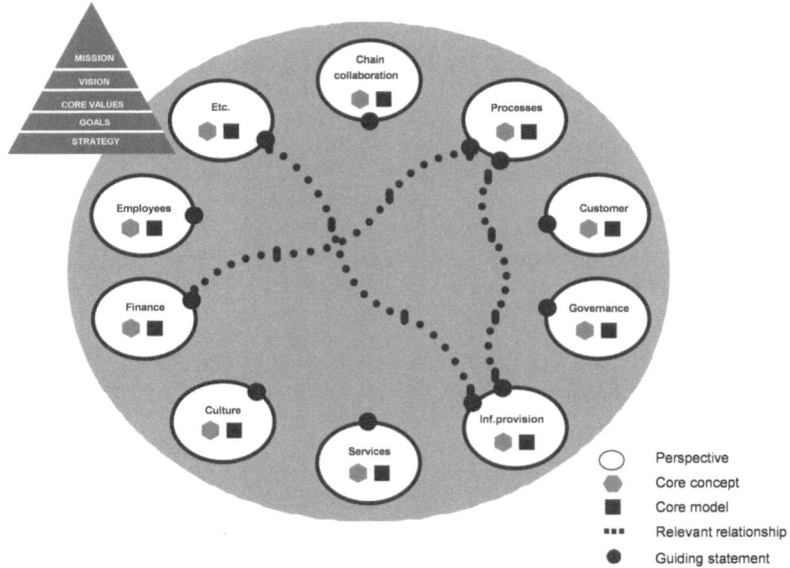

Fig. 1. The Enterprise Coherence Framework (ECF) within GEA

Understanding the interactions between the components of a system is key to understanding it on a quantitative and predictive level [18]. Even when mechanisms are unexplained, graphs and their topology allow to understand its properties [18]. Earlier research [20,22] showed multiple graph-based approaches to coherence. This makes the ability to express a strategy planning framework as a graph a key requirement.

3   Research Design and Methodology

The research to quantify enterprise coherence falls into the higher level engineering cycle [11] of enterprise coherence governance [6] as part of enterprise architecture (EA), which again facilitates organizational design that is consistent and coherent in supporting the organization's strategy and viability. The relationship between the coherence in the design of an organization and its viability [12] and the demonstrated lack of enterprise coherence governance [21] drives us to the research effort of quantifying enterprise coherence. The research positioning is as follows Fig. 2:

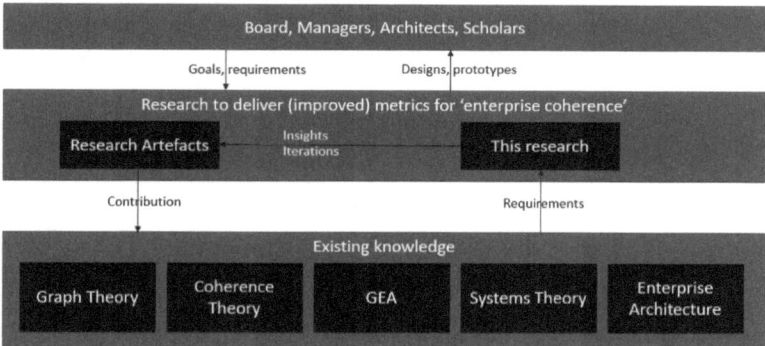

Fig. 2. Quantification of Enterprise Coherence Research positioning (cf. [11])

An important step within the GEA process is the analysis of the ECF [6]. Qualitative analysis goes hand in hand with good quantitative analysis [5]. Quantifications for the GEA ECF however are currently lacking (e.g. [25]). This alone already gives a reason for embarking on this research. Apart from GEA it may be clear that consistency and coherence between various enterprise facets are essential to implement strategic choices successfully [10]. While EA is a means to guide the design and development of the organization and its aspects [4], quantification within EA has not advanced far yet [17]. This research will also add to this area. A survey (yet unpublished research, available on request) indicates that metrics that measure the 'enterprise coherence' will be of value to a target group formed by Enterprise Architects and Senior Management of larger (over 750 employees) organizations. Within the iterative approach proposed for this research we will include validations on usefulness for the target group, e.g. by means of surveys (see Sect. 3.3). The creation of metrics will be based on knowledge from Coherence Theory, System Theory, Graph Theory, Enterprise Architecture, and -as part of the latter- GEA (see Sect. 2).

3.1 Hypothesis

The driving hypothesis is: "*A dashboard can be designed to represent enterprise coherence*".

Apart from design questions on application, usability, interoperability, maintainability, and information security, to name just a few areas, the hypothesis also gives rise to knowledge questions, e.g.:

- What are main concerns on enterprise coherence?
- How is coherence quantified in other domains and why?
- How many metrics would be required to measure enterprise coherence?
- Would it be possible to integrate multiple enterprise coherence metrics into a single index?

These questions will have to be specified and answered in the course of the research.

3.2 Research Goal

The research goal is to deliver a continuously improving information product of enterprise coherence metrics. Goals specific for the social context [11] are:

1. Allow measurement of enterprise coherence.
2. Improve prediction of enterprise performance.

Related design science research goals [11] are:

1. A (set of) enterprise coherence metric(s).
2. A method to arrive at metrics.
3. A system where measurement takes place.
4. Understanding what coherence in graphs of enterprise statements actually means.
5. Being able to predict patterns of coherence in these graphs.

   The goal has been achieved if:

- The metrics are defined, and scope and function are described, including effect and sensitivity, and -where relevant- critical values.
- The metrics express the concerns and goals of stakeholders where it regards enterprise coherence.
- The metrics are applications of, combinations of, and/or build on graph measures grounded in literature.
- A practical method for measurement is described.
- A methodology for improving and/or creation of metrics is described.
- Supporting software is available.
- Example practices of metrics and predictions for metrics are given (Fig. 3).

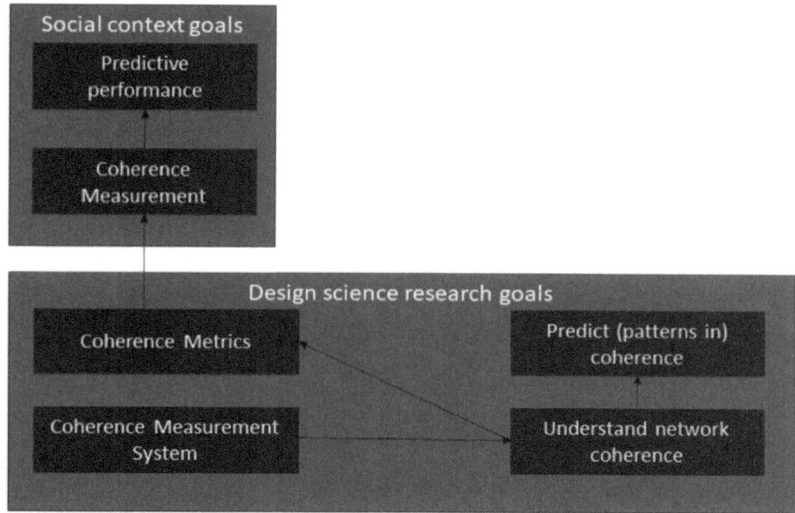

Fig. 3. Goal Structure for the Research (cf. [11])

3.3 Artefacts

We choose to develop in parallel the following artefacts:

1. A set of metrics to measure (aspects of) enterprise coherence. We will call this the Dashboard for Enterprise Coherence (DEC).
2. A graph construct that follows an ontology for enterprise coherence. We will call this graph the Enterprise Guidance Graph (EGG). The EGG starts out expressing basic ontology rules, and iteratively express a more complex ontology, with GEA's ECF ontology as destination. At that point the EGG and ECF will be fully conformant [27].
3. An architecture to import data, perform calculations, and present results in written form and in visualizations (see Fig. 4).
4. A methodology to create and improve the DEC. We will call this the DEC Methodology. As part of the DEC Methodology we will design an Enterprise Coherence Quantification Framework (ECQF) to give guardrails to the development of DEC metrics. The ECQF is elaborated on in Sect. 4.

We develop the DEC Methodology because enterprise coherence is too complex to come up with the right metrics for the DEC right away. Continuous improvement will be needed to be successful. This research will develop the artefacts until the level that others are able to build on further. We will develop a set of metrics to show proof for the methodology, and to allow first measurements to actually take place. All artefacts are subject to design cycles: the DEC Methodology will provide the design cycle for the DEC and the EGG. The architecture will have a design cycle of its own, however we will not explicit elaborate on it, because of its little importance for the research. The DEC Methodology will also have a design cycle of its own, and we will make improvements on DEC Methodology part of the research. The iterations for the various design cycles may include consultation of the target group to improve decision making.

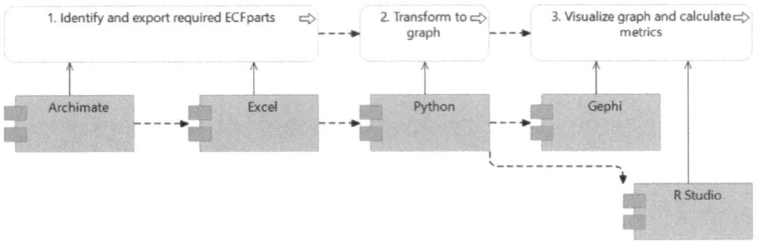

Fig. 4. Current Architecture for the DEC

3.4   Requirements

Requirements are under development. A first set of user requirements has been deducted from a survey among representatives from the target group (yet unpublished research, available on request):

- Being able to compare the effect on enterprise coherence for different architecture design decisions.
- Being able to quantify the impact of strategic change on enterprise coherence.
- Being able to quantify the fit of a solution design based on enterprise coherence.
- Being able to assess the stability of the 'guidance graph' with respect to changes.
- Being able to assess the importance of cross-domain relations.

Apart from user requirements, first sets of (mostly ontology) requirements have been deducted from coherence theory, graph theory, system theory, and GEA. It goes beyond the scope of this paper to describe them here.

4   Enterprise Coherence Quantification Framework

4.1   Enterprise Guidance Graph (EGG)

We define an Enterprise Guidance Graph generically as a set of enterprise statements that can be grouped by certain attributes, and that can have interrelationships. We define an enterprise statement for now loosely as 'a statement that gives direction to a certain aspect of the enterprise', and refer to [6] for more specific definitions for GEA. Enterprise statements and attributes represent the nodes of the EGG (see Fig. 5). Relations between these nodes represent the edges of the EGG. The relations can be directed or undirected. If it is directed it can be hierarchical or non-hierarchical. A common attribute will be expressed with an undirected relation. We define 'atomic' coherence as the relation between two guiding statements Si and Sj, with Coherence weight equal to Cij. In this way enterprise coherence could be expressed in the adjacency matrix Sij as shown in Fig. 6. The coherence relations determine the further form of the graph representation and will allow to calculate metrics on all kinds of granularity.

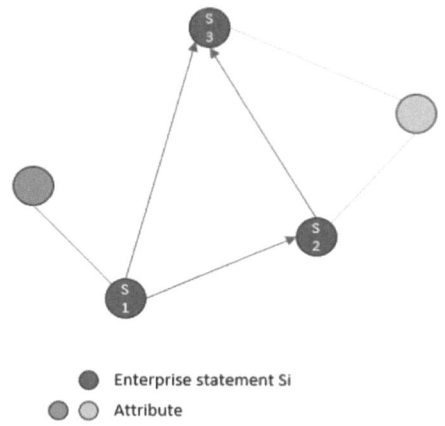

Enterprise statement Si

Attribute

Fig. 5. Example of nodes and edges in an Enterprise Guidance Graph (EGG)

ECF	S_1	S_2	S_3	...	S_n
S_1	0	C_{21}	C_{31}	...	C_{n1}
S_2	C_{12}	0	C_{32}	...	C_{n2}
S_3	C_{13}	C_{23}	0	...	C_{n3}
...	...	...	...	...	...
S_n	C_{1n}	C_{2n}	C_{3n}	C_{4n}	0

Fig. 6. Coherence Matrix (adjacency matrix for enterprise statements Si)

4.2 ECQF

Conceptually coherence can be assessed:

1. In the set of guiding statements, i.e. in the EGG.

2. Between the set of guiding statements and solutions.
3. In the set solutions.

The latter becomes visible through the first two, with an assumed positive correlation between them. To make this work, we develop both EGG and ECQF to suit both less refined ontologies as well as GEA, as to allow gradual development. Graphs are typically organized on microscopic, mesoscopic, and macroscopic level [23]. We will follow this setup. We add a layer for 'Solutions' since that is where coherence is supposed to end up. And we will add the aspect of evolution, with the value of being able to analyze and predict coherence patterns over time (Fig. 7).

Fig. 7. Enterprise Coherence Quantification Enterprise Coherence Framework ECQF

1. Microsopic level constitutes the study of individual vertices to understand their behaviour. Degree or other centrality measures are typically used [23]. For now we use the term *guiding statement* for any type of statement that directs desirable behavior (including e.g. references to used models).
2. Mesoscopic level concerns the study of modules or community structure. Modules are formed by corresponding properties of nodes described by undirected relations. Modularity is an example of a general metric for community quality and for community detection algorithms [19], and e.g. associated with limiting unnecessary complexity in systems [15]. This way GEA's 'perspective' and 'level' could be expressed.
3. Macroscopic level classifies the global structure of the graph. E.g. hierarchical structure is pervasive across complex networks with examples spanning

from neuroscience, economics, social organisations, urban systems, communications, pharmaceuticals and biology [23], and it is shown that hierarchical coherence [23] is a proxy for stability. A set of guiding statements is most often hierarchical in nature ('tree'-like), although not per se perfect, and multiple trees may exist.

4. We define a solution element as a (foreseen) (part of an) implemented solution. A solution element will be coherent with a guiding statement if it contributes to its intent. Contribution of a set of solution elements can be measured, as shown earlier [22].

5. Business practice changes guiding statements, directly or through a 'domino-effect' (see e.g. [7]. We will introduce an evolution model that allows for modeling behavior and predictions in a later stage of the research.

5   Single Case Experiment

We use a single case experiment with realistic conditions and expert opinion. This is to understand first behavior of the developed model in practice, and to weed out bad design parts early [11].

We want to be able to measure figures conform the ECQF that make sense for analytical purposes. And we expect figures to follow systemic behavior. This leads to the following hypotheses:

1. For microscopic, mesoscopic, and macroscopic level of the ECQF sensible -though maybe not ideal- measures can be found.
2. Measures show explainable results.
3. Systemic behavior can be demonstrated.

We will use these metrics in an experiment to prove that the ECQF setup is plausible. As Object of Study (OoS) we take results of a fictive case that is used in GEA trainings, about a supermarket that needs to survive several changes. Coherence calculations need to add value to coherence analysis. An ECF has been put together for this case in several steps, whereby, the normal GEA practice [25] was followed:

1. Initial Level of Purpose, with relations Mission-Vision, Mission/Vision-Core Values, Mission/Vision/Core Values-Goals, and Goals-Strategies. We will call this *LoP1*.
2. New Level of Purpose, based on discussions. We will call this *LoP2*.
3. Level of Design, including relations Goals-Objectives, Core Values-Principles, and Strategies-Policy. We will call this *LoPD1*.
4. New Level of Design, based on discussions. We will call this *LoPD2*.

We need concrete metrics to be able to validate the abilities from the previous subsection. As preliminary metrics we used measures that have been used extensively in other domains, and that have a thorough mathematical grounding. Together they cover to a broad extend the currently defined ECQF:

1. For microscopic level centrality measures we will use coherence weighted degree and PageRank [1]. The first because it allows easy interpretation due to the direct relation with coherence definition on 'atomic' level (see Sect. 4). The latter because PageRank gives a more advanced view in the relative importance of the various nodes. Although other centrality measures may be good candidates too, the broad acceptance of the proposed measures makes them acceptable first candidates.
2. For mesoscopic level community structures we will use modularity (e.g. [3]) and smallworldness [2, 26] as first measures. Modularity expresses a preferred way of coherence known from software architecture (e.g. [16]) and from other systems (e.g. [13]. Smallworldness expresses modularity and integration in a single measure. Smallworldness has also been researched extensively [26].
3. For macroscopic level hierarchical coherence we will use hierarchical incoherence [23], which we return as hierarchical coherence by subtracting from 1. Other hierarchical measures may be researched later.

Based on the fact that the events described in the previous subsection were intended to be improvements on the ECF, we expect an increase of:

1. coherence weighted degree
2. modularity
3. hierarchical coherence
4. smallworldness
5. a power law for PageRank values, due to increasing system effects along with size.

The experiment has been carried out in various sessions. Coherence calculations were done afterwards, so the outcome did not influence the decisions. The excels were filled in by the Core Team on the various events and graphs were created. The quantitative results for the measures coherence degree, modularity, hierarchical coherence, and smallworldness are shown in the tables below for the Level of Purpose, and for the combined Level of Purpose and Level of Design. We normalized all figures against the highest value to come to the radar (see Fig. 9).

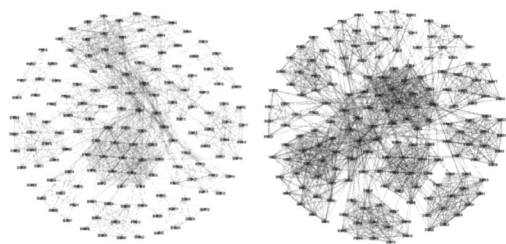

Fig. 8. Visual comparison of LoPD01 (left) and LoPD02

The results for PageRank where used to assess systemic behavior. PageRank was calculated using the directed edges only for LoPD2, i.e. the entire graph in the end situation. The results are shown graphically in Fig. 9.

Metric	LoP1	LoP2	Increase (%)
Coherence degree	8.6	11.8	37%
Modularity	0.3	0.4	46%
Hierarchical coherence	0.6	0.6	−3%
Smallworldness	1.6	1.7	6%

Metric	LoPD1	LoPD2	Increase (%)
Coherence degree	28.5	30.4	7%
Modularity	0.36	0.40	10%
Hierarchical coherence	0.01	0.11	56%
Smallworldness	0.67	0,68	2%

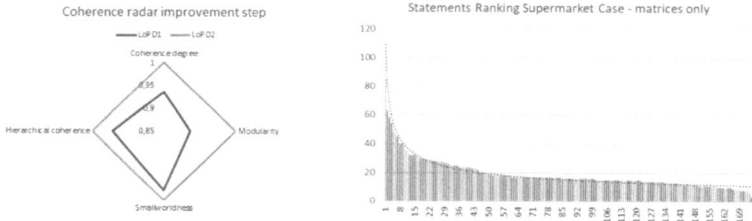

Fig. 9. *Coherence Radar for improvement* and *PageRank showing power law*

6   Conclusions and Discussion

The results for the measures coherence degree, modularity, hierarchical coherence, and smallworldness showed an increase for almost all coherence measures, in line with expectation. There was a decrease in hierarchical coherence for the level of purpose, but it was very small. Graph visualizations (see Fig. 8) show differences in concentrations in the graphs, that apparently go together with different coherence values. The results for the measure PageRank which we used to validate systemic behavior showed a clear power law. We conclude a positive indication that the used metrics show coherence improvement. An interesting additional result was that visualizations seem indicative for the quantitative results.

For the overall experiment hypotheses we conclude:

1. For microscopic, mesoscopic, and macroscopic level of 'Quantification' sensible -though maybe not ideal- measures can indeed be found.
2. Systemic behavior can indeed be demonstrated.
3. The parts *microscopic*, *mesoscopic*, and *macroscopic* of the ECQF where of use as container for the preliminary metrics.

7   Limitations and Further Study

Since this is a new field in enterprise architecture, there were clearly limitations in both preliminary model and practical application. The coherence figures were not yet comparable with other cases, which makes plausibility and significance more difficult to assess. Although the results show correlations that support our hypotheses, mechanisms are yet unexplained. In follow up research we will look at how to address this with the use of synthetic graphs. This is a threat to validity. Also, the preliminary measures should be regarded as 'minimal viable product'. Furthermore, to properly support the ECF, the ECQF should include a framework for evolution. Finally, additional real life cases are necessary to allow better comparison for insights into the behavior of the ECF graph and its metrics.

References

1. Brin, S., Page, L.: The anatomy of a large-scale hypertextual web search engine. Comput. Netw. ISDN Syst. **30**(1–7), 107–117 (1998)
2. Watts, D.J., Strogatz, S.H.: Collective dynamics of 'smallworld' networks. Nature **393**(6684), 440–442 (1998)
3. Newman, M.E.J.: Modularity and community structure in networks. Proc. Natl. Acad. Sci. **103**(23), 8577–8582 (2006)
4. A Pocket Guide to TOGAF Version 8.1.1 Enterprise Edition. The Open Group (2007)
5. Allwood, C.M.: The distinction between qualitative and quantitative research methods is problematic. Qual. Quant. **46**, 1417–1429 (2012)
6. Wagter, R.: Enterprise coherence governance. Ph.D. thesis. Radboud University, Nijmegen, The Netherlands (2013)
7. Wagter, R., Proper, H.A., Witte, D.: Enterprise coherence governance in the public sector – custodial institutions agency of the dutch ministry of security and justice. In: IEEE 15th Conference on Business Informatics, CBI 2013, Vienna, Austria, 15–18 July 2013, pp. 117–124. IEEE Computer Society Press, Los Alamitos (2013). https://doi.org/10.1109/CBI.2013.25. ISBN 978-0-7695-5072-5
8. Wagter, R.: Enterprise coherence governance. 's-Hertogenbosch: BOXPress (2013)
9. Dietz, J.L.G., Hoogervorst, J.A.P.: The unifying role of enterprise engineering. In: Magalhàes, R. (ed.) Organization Design and Engineering, pp. 11–38. Palgrave Macmillan, London (2014). https://doi.org/10.1057/9781137351579_2
10. Simon, D., Fischbach, K., Schoder, D.: Enterprise architecture management and its role in corporate strategic management. Inf. Syst. e-Bus. Manag. **12**(1), 5–42 (2014)
11. Wieringa, R.J.: Design Science Methodology for Information Systems and Software Engineering. Springer, Cham (2014). https://doi.org/10.1007/978-3-662-43839-8. ISBN 978-3-662-43838-1
12. Whitney, K., et al.: Systems theory as a foundation for governance of complex systems. Int. J. Syst. Syst. Eng. **6**(1–2), 15–32 (2015)
13. Keating, C.B., Katina, P.F.: Complex system governance development: a first generation methodology. Int. J. Syst. Syst. Eng. **7**(1–3), 43–74 (2016)

14. Leinwand, P., Mainardi, C.R.: Strategy That Works: How Winning Companies Close the Strategy-to-Execution Gap. Harvard Business Review Press, Boston (2016)
15. Potts, M., et al.: Hidden structures: using graph theory to explore complex system of systems architectures. In: International Conference on Complex Systems Design & Management (2017)
16. Rocha, H., et al.: DCL 2.0: modular and reusable specification of architectural constraints. J. Braz. Comput. Soc. **23**, 1–25 (2017)
17. Rodrigues, L.S., Amaral, L.: Stakeholder perspectives on time horizon and quantification of enterprise architectures benefits/value drivers. In: Proceedings of 32nd IBIMA Conference (2018)
18. Thurner, S., Hanel, R., Klimek, P.: Introduction to the Theory of Complex Systems. Oxford University Press, Oxford (2018)
19. Cherifi, H., et al.: On community structure in complex networks: challenges and opportunities. Appl. Netw. Sci. **4**(1), 1–35 (2019)
20. Bekel, J., Wagter, R.: Enterprise coherence metrics in enterprise decision making. In: Aveiro, D., Guizzardi, G., Pergl, R., Proper, H.A. (eds.) EEWC 2020. LNBIP, vol. 411, pp. 213–227. Springer, Cham (2021). https://doi.org/10.1007/978-3-030-74196-9_12
21. Bekel, J., Wagter, R.: Measurement of enterprise coherence by means of the GEA C-Index-a first investigation. In: 2020 IEEE 22nd Conference on Business Informatics (CBI), vol. 2, pp. 57–64. IEEE (2020)
22. Bekel, J., Wagter, R.: Quantifying Enterprise Coherence - A Design Based Comparison Of Calculation Methods (2020)
23. Moutsinas, G., et al.: Graph hierarchy: a novel framework to analyse hierarchical structures in complex networks. Sci. Rep. **11**(1), 13943 (2021)
24. Proper, H.A., Wagter, R., Bekel, J.: Enterprise coherence with GEA – a 15 year co-evolution of practice and theory. In: Serral, E., Stirna, J., Ralyté, J., Grabis, J. (eds.) PoEM 2021. LNBIP, vol. 432, pp. 3–18. Springer, Cham (2021). https://doi.org/10.1007/978-3-030-91279-6_1
25. Stovers, R., de Ruijter, J., Wagter, R.: GEA Enterprise Architecture in Practice - Better Performance by Managing Coherence. Dialoog, Zaltbommel, the Netherlands (2021). ISBN 9789461264350
26. Aprile, F., Onesto, V., Gentile, F.: The small world coefficient 4.8 ± 1 optimizes information processing in 2D neuronal networks. NPJ Syst. Biol. Appl. **8**(1), 1–11 (2022)
27. The Open Group. TOGAF Version 9.1. 10th. Van Haren Publishing, Zaltbommel, The Netherlands (2011). ISBN 978-9-087-53679-4

MIDas4CS

MIDas4CS – First Workshop on the Modelling and Implementation of Digital Twins for Complex Systems

Pedro Valderas[1], Fabrizio Fornari[2], Luís Ferreira Pires[3], Marten van Sinderen[3], and Giancarlo Guizzardi[3]

[1]Universitat Politècnica de València, Spain
pvalderas@dsic.upv.es
[2]University of Camerino, Italy
fabrizio.fornari@unicam.it
[3]Semantics, Cybersecurity & Services, University of Twente, The Netherlands
g.guizzardi@utwente.nl

The concept of Digital Twin is becoming increasingly popular since it was introduced in the scope of the Smart Industry (Industry 4.0). A Digital Twin (DT) is a digital representation of a physical twin that is a real-world entity, system, or event. It mirrors a distinctive object, process, building, or human, regardless of whether that thing is tangible or non-tangible in the real world. The DT technology provides benefits such as real-time remote monitoring and control; greater efficiency and safety; predictive maintenance and scheduling; scenario and risk assessment; better intra- and inter-team synergy and collaborations; more efficient and informed decision support systems; personalisation of products and services; and better documentation and communication.

The ultimate purpose of Digital Twins is to improve decision-making for solving real-world problems, by using the digital model to create the information necessary for decision-making and subsequently applying the decisions in the real world. Nowadays, Digital Twins are not limited to industrial applications but are spreading to other areas as well, such as, for example, the healthcare domain, in personalised medicine and clinical trials for drug development.

This workshop focuses on getting a better understanding of the techniques that can be used to model and implement Digital Twins and their applications in different domains. We aim to attract researches and industry practitioners to discuss formal definitions of Digital Twin as well as to describe applications of Digital Twins in different domains. Contributions on tooling for Digital Twins are also welcome.

The first MIDas4CS was organized as a half-day workshop in conjunction with EDOC 2023. This workshop attracted eight international submissions, and each of them was reviewed by two members of the Program Committee. From these submissions, four works were accepted as full papers for presentation at the workshop.

First, Callisto et al. presented the implementation of a Digital Twin Prototype for the industrial research project SAFE, which aimed to design and implement smart and life-saving furniture systems for schools and offices, in case of an earthquake. Next, Milosevic and van Schalkwyk discuss how socio-economic factors can be gradually transformed into a set of governance rules for building, operating, and evolving responsible digital twin solutions and ecosystems. Third, Moreria proposes a set of research directions to improve interoperability in Digital Twins, considering perspectives such as architecture of distributed systems, model-based system engineering, ontology-driven conceptual modeling, and linked data and semantic web technologies. Finally, Schultenkämper and Bäumer discuss how tracking user activity across different online social networks and the consolidation of the collected profile information is of considerable importance for the compilation of a Digital Twin.

We hope that the reader will find this selection of papers useful to keep track of the latest advances of Digital Twins.

Acknowledgments. We thank the authors for their contributions and the members of the Program Committee for their invaluable help in the reviewing phase. We also wish to thank the organizers of EDOC 2023 for their help with the organization of the workshop.

MIDas4CS 2023 Organization

Workshop Chairs

Pedro Valderas	Universitat Politècnica de València, Spain
Fabrizio Fornari	University of Camerino, Italy
Luís Ferreira Pires	University of Twente, The Netherlands
Marten van Sinderen	University of Twente, The Netherlands
Giancarlo Guizzardi	University of Twente, The Netherlands

Program Committee

Abel Armas Cervantes	University of Melbourne, Australia
Emanuele Laurenzi	FHNW, Switzerland
Barbara Re	University of Camerino, Italy
Estefanía Serral	KU Leuven, Belgium
Victoria Torres Bosch	Universitat Politècnica de València, Spain
Dimitris Karagiannis	University of Vienna, Austria
Erik Proper	Technical University of Vienna, Austria
Tony Clark	Aston University, UK
Oscar Pastor Lopez	Universidad Politécnica de Valencia, Spain
Ethan Hadar	Accenture Cybersecurity Labs, Israel
Geert Poels	Ghent University, Belgium
Hans Vangheluwe	University of Antwerp, Belgium

Design and Development of a Digital Twin Prototype for the SAFE Project

Massimo Callisto De Donato$^{(\boxtimes)}$, Flavio Corradini , Fabrizio Fornari ,
Barbara Re , and Matteo Romagnoli

School of Science and Technology, Computer Science Department,
University of Camerino, Via Madonna delle Carceri, 7, Camerino, Italy
{massimo.callisto,flavio.corradini,fabrizio.fornari,barbara.re,
matteo.romagnoli}@unicam.it

Abstract. The rapid advancements in digital technologies have paved
the way for the development and utilization of digital twins that allow
bridging the gap between physical systems and their virtual representations. This digital twin concept is gaining importance especially in the
design of complex IoT and Cyber-Physical systems. At design time a digital twin can in fact be used to represent the to-be system reflecting its
characteristics in the digital world and especially to conduct simulations
before the system is actually implemented.

This paper reports about an approach for the design and implementation of a Digital Twin Prototype for a project involving an IoT life-saving
system designed to support the rescue operation of people during a seismic event. The approach as well as the software tool can be adopted to
other IoT or Cyber-Physical systems.

Keywords: Digital Twin · Digital Twin Prototype · Internet of
Things · 3D Modelling · 3D Simulation

1 Introduction and Motivation

There has been a rapid rise of interest in the potential of Digital Twins (DTs) to
transform a vast range of Internet of Things (IoT) and Cyber-Physical System
(CPS) applications [15]. The field of DT is appearing to undergo a large increase
in attention from both industry and academia. The 2023 Gartner emerging tech
impact radar, places DTs among the most impactful emerging technologies and
trends [22]. In addition, according to a 2022 report, nearly 60% of executives
across a broad spectrum of industry plan to incorporate DTs within their operations by 2028 [19].

In academia, an increasing amount of research papers is being published every
year. We can notice works ranging from those that investigate the definition of
DT [3,8,9,20], to more extensive works that cover several aspects of the DT
topic such as modelling and enabling technologies [6,17,21], to works that focus
on DT applications to specific domains [7].

T. P. Sales et al. (Eds.): EDOC 2023 Workshops, LNBIP 498, pp. 107–122, 2024.
https://doi.org/10.1007/978-3-031-54712-6_7

In this research work we explore the implementation of a DT solution for the SAFE scenario. "S.A.F.E. - Sustainable design of Antiseismic Furniture as smart life-saving systems during an Earthquake" was an Industrial Research project[1] concluded in 2021, that aimed to design and implement smart and life-saving furniture systems in case of earthquake for school and office contexts [18]. A deployment of the SAFE "system" to an actual classroom of a school in the Marche Region of Italy is planned as part of another project called VITALITY[2].

The design and implementation in a real environment of the SAFE system is complex both in terms of components to consider (furniture, IoT sensors, ICT infrastructure), and as regards to the validation of their integrated operations. Testing operations of the entire system are particularly challenging since they require the entire system to be deployed or a small-scale physical prototype to be created facing the challenge of trying to replicate the conditions of an earthquake. It therefore becomes of extreme importance to be able to anticipate the validation of the system right from the design stages, making evaluations and behavior simulations even before the components themselves are actually installed. The definition of a DT in order to study the system before installing it in the physical environment, could bring several benefits to the SAFE scenario. Especially, we refer to the notion of Digital Twin Prototype (DTP) [9] since the corresponding physical twin of the SAFE scenario does not exists yet.

In this paper we report our experience in the design and development of a DTP for the SAFE scenario especially focusing on the process we adopted to graphically modeling and simulating the scenario. With respect to the implementation of DTs, IoT platforms are often seen as the starting point. According to [19] by 2028 the 90% of IoT platforms will be extended to support DTs. To implement our SAFE DTP we mainly relied on the ThingsBoard[3] IoT platform which we extended to support 3D modeling and visualization of a scenario, as well as 3D simulation of a scene in which multiple devices are deployed. The Things-Board extension is available at https://pros.unicam.it/digitaltwin/dtplatform. The interested reader can take inspiration from our approach as well as make use of our tool to start implementing a DTP of his own scenario.

The rest of the paper is structured as following. In Sect. 2 we report details about the SAFE project. Considering the complexity of the SAFE scenario, we focus on the PIR-based motion detection device (we call it SAFE PIR) of which we report a description of its dynamic behavior. We then discuss in Sect. 3 the process we followed to design a DTP of a SAFE classroom based on a virtual deployment of multiple SAFE PIRs. In Sect. 4 we report about the modelling of the SAFE scenario while in Sect. 5 we report about a mechanism we defined for simulating the SAFE scenario within ThingsBoard. We report in Sect. 6 a discussion on functionalities that our DTP enables as well as some limitations. Section 7 reports about related work that focus on the implementation of DTs for complex scenarios. We close the paper with Sect. 8 by drawing conclusions.

---

[1] SAFE project: http://projects.cs.unicam.it/safeproject/index.html.
[2] VITALITY project: https://vitality-spoke6.unicam.it/en/.
[3] ThingsBoard IoT platform: https://thingsboard.io/.

2   The SAFE Project

In this section we first provide an overview of the SAFE project for then focusing on the SAFE PIR device and its dynamic behavior.

2.1   Project Overview

The main objective of the SAFE project was the design and prototyping of furniture for schools and offices capable of transforming themselves into intelligent systems of passive and "life-saving" protection of people during an earthquake, integrating technical-scientific knowledge and skills as those of Industrial Design, Structural Engineering, Computer Science and Chemistry and facilitating a process of cross-fertilization. The basic idea of the project resulted from the observation of a recurring phenomenon: during an earthquake, furniture and mobile equipment become obstacles that aggravate the dangerous conditions or, on the contrary, represent a casual protection of life in the event of collapses.

The challenge of the project was to innovate the design of traditional furniture (e.g. desk, equipped wall, etc.), for schools and offices, transforming them into intelligent systems through the integration of IoT sensors (SAFE devices) and a related ICT infrastructure. The ICT infrastructure was in charge of integrating the SAFE devices data through local gateways and a dedicated instance of the ThingsBoard IoT remote platform used to provide the basic monitoring and management services. Data collected from the SAFE devices could then be used to support the localization and rescue of survivors under the rubble during an earthquake [18].

The SAFE devices consisted of battery powered wireless IoT devices, designed to be integrated in the SAFE furniture as shown in Fig. 1 and Fig. 2. The primary objective of these devices, in case of a earthquake, is to detect and communicate whether there are persons being protected by the SAFE furniture. The information then is made available to rescue teams supporting localization and rescue activities. Given the importance of detecting people under the smart furniture, the SAFE PIR device has been developed in such a way to fit within the furniture and to adapt its behavior in case of a seismic event.

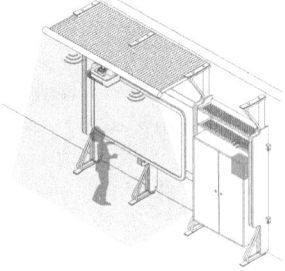

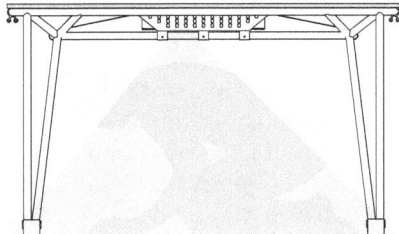

Fig. 1. SAFE Equipped Wall.   **Fig. 2.** SAFE Desk.

2.2 SAFE PIR Behavior

The SAFE PIR implements a *dynamic behavior* that changes from *Peace* Mode - the modality adopted when no seismic event is present - to *War* Mode - the modality adopted when a seismic event occurs. We describe and illustrate such a behavior by means of two BPMN models. Figure 3 reports the behavior in *Peace* Mode (i.e., before the earthquake) and Fig. 4 reports the behavior in *War* Mode (i.e., during and after the earthquake). Considering that the BPMN notation lately acquired relevance in the modelling of IoT and CPS systems [1,2,24], it came natural for us to conceptualize the PIR behavior using such a notation. The use of BPMN gives the advantage of using a notation that is easily understandable, even to non-expert users.

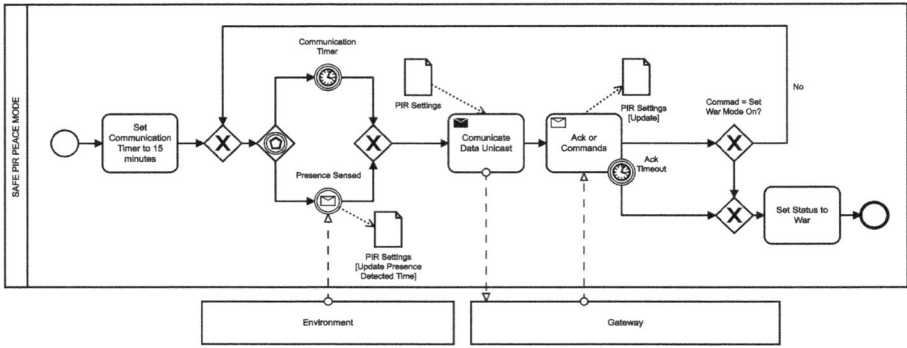

Fig. 3. PEACE Mode Behavior of the SAFE PIR represented with the BPMN notation.

Peace Mode Behavior. The default SAFE PIR's behavior is the one we indicate with *Peace Mode*. The first activity performed in Peace Mode sets the communication timer to 30 min. This timer will be used for sending regular *keep-alive messages* to ensure the communication between sensors and gateway is active, as well as for sending diagnostic information about the device (i.e., *battery status*, *device-temperature*, etc.). Next, either the *Communication Timer* expires (i.e., 30 min have passed) or a movement is detected through the arrival of a *sensing* message from the *Environment* that is represented in the model as a black box pool. The SAFE PIR sensor is triggered whenever a temperature variation is detected within its field of view. This variation can be associated with a movement of any heat-emitting object, such as people or animals.

After one of the two events occurs, the SAFE PIR activates a Unicast Communication (*Communicate Data Unicast*) for sending a message to the *Gateway*, represented in the model as a black box pool. Then, the SAFE PIR waits to receive an *Ack* message that could also include some *Commands* used to request to switch in War Mode or to set different values for Ack and communication timers. Here, three situation may occur. 1) An Ack message is received and no command has been provided. 2) An *Ack Timeout* occurs while waiting for the Ack message, this means the gateway for some reason is not reachable anymore and the *War* Mode is activated. 3) An Ack message from the gateway is received and it contains some commands the SAFE PIR will have to consider, for instance a command requesting the SAFE PIR to switch to War mode due to an earthquake.[4] After handling any of the mentioned cases, the SAFE PIR can either exit from Peace Mode or go back to wait for the Communication Timer to expire or for a presence to be sensed.

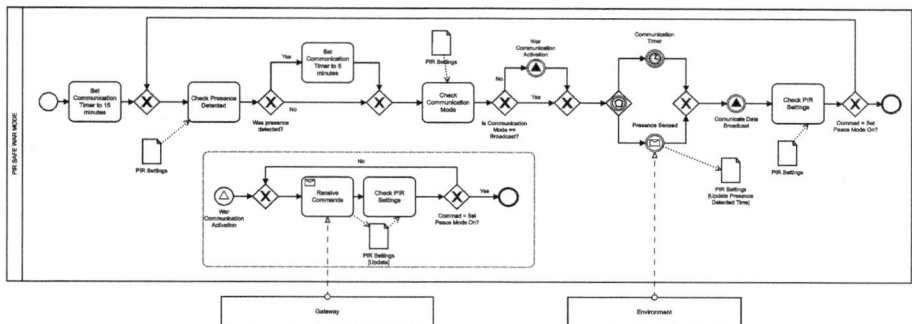

Fig. 4. WAR Mode behavior of the SAFE PIR represented with the BPMN notation.

In *War Mode*, the *Check Presence Detected* activity checks if a movement has been detected (i.e., at least one *sensing* message has been received). If it is the case, the SAFE PIR updates the communication timer (e.g., to 1 min) increasing therefore the rate of messages sent so to generate more accurate information for the rescue teams.

Then, the SAFE PIR activates, if not already activated, a broadcast communication modality. This means the transmission system is turned on to continuously listen for possible incoming commands from a gateway. In case the local gateway is not reachable anymore, a possible flying gateway (by means of a drone) could be deployed and could act as gateway for collecting sensed information from the various SAFE PIR sensors and also for requesting an update of the communication timer or a possible switch back to Peace Mode. We represented this behavior through the *War Communication Activation* signal that triggers the corresponding event subprocess.

Finally, the SAFE PIR waits for either the communication timer to expire (e.g., after 1 min) or for sensing movements from the person protected by the SAFE furniture. In both cases, a new message will be broadcasted. Then the device checks whether or not to maintain the War Mode behavior.

---

[4] The SAFE gateway implements an Earthquake Early-Warning detection system through a specific accelerometer. In case of an earthquake, the gateway sends a command to the SAFE devices requesting them to switch to War Mode.

3   The Adopted Process for a SAFE DTP

Among all the characteristics that a DT can have [3,13], for the SAFE scenario
we focused on 3D modeling and 3D simulation. We reported in Fig. 5 the process
we adopted to design and implement the SAFE DTP.

As first step, we designed the 3D model of the SAFE PIR reflecting the real
device. Then we associated the 3D model to digital representations registered
in ThingsBoard, we refer to them as *Digital Devices*. The digital devices can be
enriched with attributes, treated as key-value pairs, to describe characteristics
about the physical devices such as: *name, description, firmware version, latitude,
longitude*, etc. In addition, within an IoT platform like ThingsBoard, telemetry
data coming from the physical devices are associated to the digital ones and
made available for inspection so to allow monitoring the actual state of the
physical device and of the environment's aspects it perceives. Then we designed
the 3D model of a real classroom and we combined it with the SAFE PIR digital
devices and related 3D models, to design a 3D scene of the SAFE scenario.

After designing the 3D SAFE scenario, we focused on the steps needed to
simulate it. As first, we encoded the SAFE PIR behavior in ThingsBoard as
described in Sect. 2.2. Then, we designed and executed the SAFE simulation
using the 3D scene we previously defined with the objective to test the SAFE
PIR behavior.

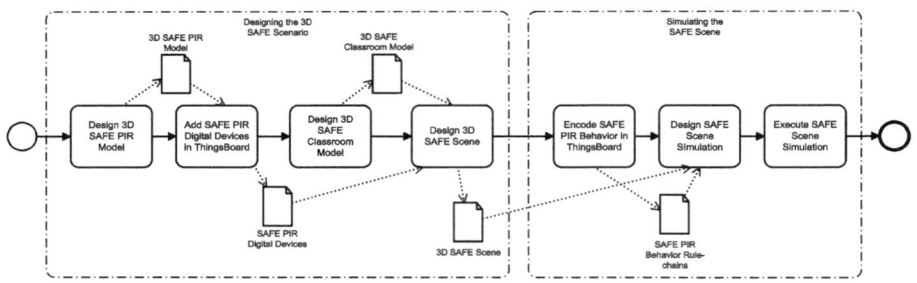

Fig. 5. Steps for implementing the SAFE Digital Twin Prototype.

In the next sections we describe in detail how we conducted the modelling
and simulation of the SAFE scenario.

4   Modelling the SAFE Scenario

For designing the 3D model of the SAFE PIR device and of the SAFE classroom we used Blender[5] a free and open-source 3D creation suite. We started our modelling activities from a real SAFE PIR device reported in Fig. 6. The SAFE PIR is composed of: a printed circuit board (PCB) with the PIR sensor, a battery pack, an antenna, and the wires that connects them. As it can be seen from Fig. 7 we faithfully designed the 3D model of the SAFE PIR device and its components.

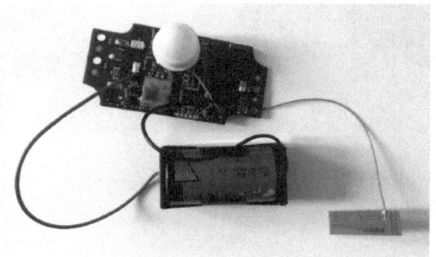

Fig. 6. Real SAFE PIR device.

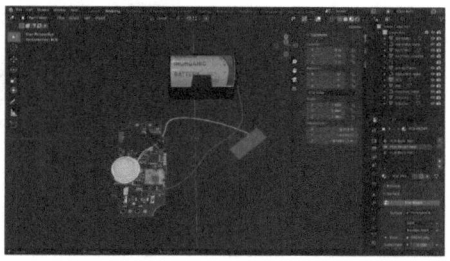

Fig. 7. SAFE PIR 3D Model in Blender.

The SAFE PIR, like any other IoT device, can be registered on the Things-Board platform leading to the definition of a digital device. To associate the 3D model to the SAFE PIR digital device we developed a widget, partially shown in Fig. 8. The widget offers a straightforward and intuitive 3D visualization of a single object. It allows users to rotate, zoom in/out, and visualize the exploded view of the object. With the simple orbit controls, users can easily manipulate the object's orientation and gain a comprehensive understanding of its spatial features as shown in Fig. 9.

Fig. 8. Adding 3D Model in Things-Board.

Fig. 9. 3D SAFE PIR in ThingsBoard.

---

[5] Blender https://www.blender.org/.

After taking care of the SAFE PIR representation, we started to model the SAFE classroom in Fig. 10 with the various components such as walls, windows, doors, desks, chairs, etc. Again, we used Blender to design the 3D model of the SAFE classroom as reported in Fig. 11.

Fig. 10. Real SAFE classroom.   **Fig. 11.** 3D SAFE Classroom in Blender.

Since the SAFE classroom is not a single IoT device, we do not associate it with a digital device in ThingsBoard. Instead, by means of a widget that we developed, we designed the 3D scene to simulate by importing the 3D model of the environment and then incorporating the 3D models of the digital devices. Specifically, we designed the SAFE 3D scene modifying the 3D classroom model by adding the 3D SAFE PIR model, as can be seen in Fig. 12, and we adjusted the scene positioning the devices under the furniture, as to reflect what will be the real scenario, see Fig. 13.

Fig. 12. SAFE Scene Design.   **Fig. 13.** SAFE Pir device 3D model.

5   Simulating the SAFE Scenario

In this section we describe how we encoded the SAFE PIR behavior in Things-Board as wells as the mechanism we proposed to simulate the SAFE scenario.

5.1   Implementing the SAFE PIR Behavior

As anticipated in Sect. 3, we encoded the SAFE PIR behavior described in Sect. 2.2 into ThingsBoard. We used the ThingsBoard *Rule Chain Editor*, that makes use of a low-code approach, as many other IoT platforms do [12], to allow users to define complex rules in terms of connected control flows where certain conditions can trigger specific actions based on the data received from devices. In Fig. 14 we report, for presentation purpose, an excerpt of the rule-chains we defined. Especially, part a) of the figure reports the root rule-chain that combines three other rule-chains: *Set CTimer & CMode*, *CTimer or Presence*, and *Communication*. Part b) of the figure reports the expanded *Set CTimer & CMode* rule-chain. We report these rule-chains as examples to illustrate how we used Thingsboard to encode the SAFE PIR's behavior.

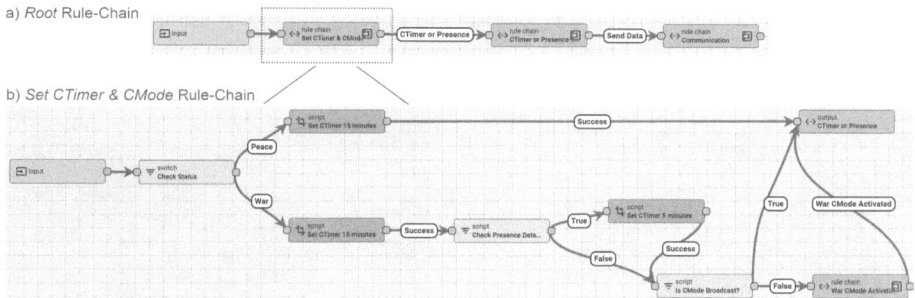

Fig. 14. SAFE PIR's behavior encoded via Thingsboard's rule-chains.

The root rule-chain starts by invoking the *Set CTimer & CMode* rule-chain that checks whether the SAFE PIR is set in Peace or in War mode. Then, it sets the communication timer to 30 min. But, if the PIR is in War mode, it also checks whether a presence is detected. In case a presence is detected then it sets the communication timer to 1 min and, in case the broadcast communication is not already active, it switches to War communication mode, i.e., broadcast, (handled by the *War CMode Activate* rule-chain). At the end of the rule-chain, the control moves to the next *CTimer or Presence* rule-chain that takes care of handling the possible upcoming events (i.e., the communication timer expiration or the sensing of a presence). The last rule-chain *Communication*, takes care of handling the Communication with a Gateway.

5.2   Simulation Mechanism

Every rule-chain defined in ThingsBoard can be executed by means of a *Rule Chain Engine*, a powerful tool mainly used for processing and analyzing data generated by IoT devices. We propose a simulation mechanism that leverages the capability of the engine to actually simulate the SAFE PIR's behavior.

Besides the concept of digital entity that we use to represent the SAFE PIR device in ThingsBoard, we introduced the concept of *Simulated Device* (SIM-PIR in Fig. 15). In our case, simulated devices are basically copies of SAFE PIR digital devices and inherit all their characteristics as well as possible associated rule-chains. The simulated devices are the ones actually used for running the simulations. We made this distinction for avoiding simulated telemetry data to override real telemetries coming from the physical world and reflected on the SAFE PIR digital devices.

Once the rule-chain and the simulated devices have been defined, we can play the role of a *Simulated Designer* and create and simulate, by means of a *simulation widget* we developed, the behavior of IoT or CPS systems in a virtual environment. For doing so we need some programming skills, especially some familiarity with the Three.js[6] and the cannon-es[7] libraries is required to adapt the *3D Scene* adding additional 3D objects and for handling the physics.

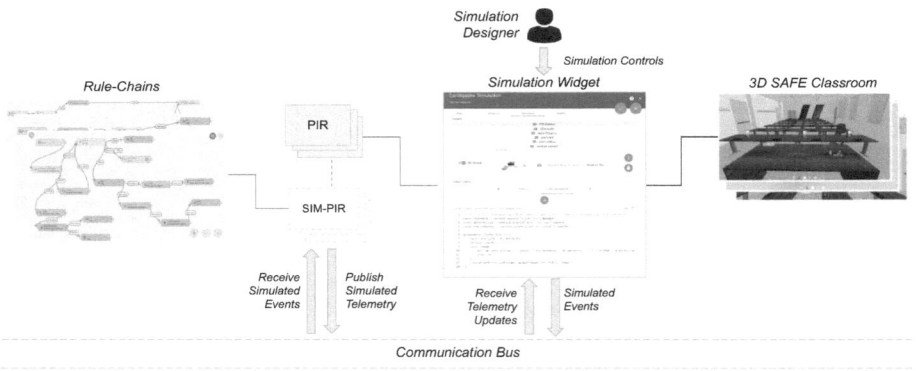

Fig. 15. A representation of the components involved in the design of a 3D simulation in ThingsBoard.

In Fig. 15 we illustrate the 3D simulation widget with the various components involved in the design and execution of a 3D simulation. The components communicate by means of a *Communication Bus* that abstracts the communication layer of ThingsBoard. Especially, when a simulation is activated by a user, simulated events in the simulated environment may occur. Such simulated

---

[6] Three.js: https://threejs.org/.
[7] Cannon-es: https://pmndrs.github.io/cannon-es/.

events are published on the communication bus and received by the corresponding simulated digital device which handles the event by updating its telemetry. If a rule-chain that predicates on that event is available, then the rule-chain fires and the simulated behavior of the simulated digital device starts. Also the execution of a rule-chain might cause the update of some telemetries associated with the simulated digital device. Such telemetries are then published on the communication bus and received by the simulation widget that will reflect those updates in the simulated virtual environment.

5.3 SAFE Simulation

We used the simulation mechanism previously described to design and execute a *3D Simulation* of the SAFE scenario. In Fig. 16 we show the initial setup of the simulation which includes the SAFE classroom with three SAFE PIR devices and two humanoids that simulate the presence of two persons in the room. The simulation has been programmed in such a way to simulate an earthquake scenario. As soon as a user starts the simulation, the classroom will start shaking, the objects will be affected by the forces applied by the earthquake and the individuals within the scene will seek out the nearest smart furniture equipped with the SAFE PIR device to take shelter under it.

A 2D icon is associated to each SAFE PIR in the 3D scene. The icon will change reflecting the PIR's behavior change from *Peace mode* to *War mode*. A white icon is used to indicate that the SAFE PIR is in peace mode, as in Fig. 16. A yellow triangle represents that the SAFE PIR is in war mode but that no presence has been detected, while a red triangle represents that the SAFE PIR is in war mode and a presence has been detected, both are shown in Fig. 17.

The detection of a presence is simulated by the collision occurring between the cone collider, that represents the SAFE PIR's coverage, and the humanoid collider. When a presence is detected, an event is published on the communication bus and the corresponding SIM-PIR will receive it and update its telemetry. In turn, this update triggers the rule-chain that predicates over that telemetry.

Fig. 16. Initial 3D simulation settings.

Fig. 17. Earthquake simulation.

6 Discussion

In this section we discuss the practical implications of the proposed SAFE DTP implemented in ThingsBoard, thanks to the extensions we developed, and we report about some limitations of the present solution.

6.1 Enabled Functionalities

The use of a DTP for the SAFE scenario enables the possibility to test the behavior of the SAFE PIR devices before actually deploying them in a real setting. By means of a platform that allows to define digital devices with attributes to reflect the real characteristics of the physical device (dimensions, components disposition, device coverage, etc.) we can use *3D modelling* to effectively describe a real-world environment and reflect such characteristics. For instance we can use the modelling to display the device coverage, see Fig. 18, and plan an optimal dispositions of the furniture to avoid device interference.

While 3D modeling allows us to faithfully represent a real scenario, *3D simulation* enables us to evaluate the run time behavior under different hypothesis. The possibility to setup 3D simulations of the SAFE classroom, allows us to test the SAFE PIR behavior at design phase, according to the desired simulated conditions. This allows us to asses whether the devices behave correctly according to the simulated condition, and before actually deploying it in the real scenario.

Moreover, when the physical SAFE devices will be deployed in the physical classroom we will be able to link digital and physical devices. This will allow, thanks to the extensions we developed, to visualize the actual data coming from the physical twin, directly within the 3D model as shown in Fig. 19, enabling therefore the possibility to conduct *3D Monitoring* of the physical environment. We will also be able to start simulations from real telemetry data.

Fig. 18. Visualized PIR's coverage.   **Fig. 19.** SAFE Pir device 3D model.

6.2   Limitations

We recognize and report in the following limitations of the presented approach.

The design of 3D models especially for non expert users may be a cumbersome activity. In several domain such as manufacturing, construction, etc., digital 3D models are already being used therefore as a possible future direction we envision the possibility to integrate the support for such models (STL, IFC, etc.) directly into the platform used for developing the DT solution.

The encoding of devices behavior by means of rule-chains may not scale well when the behavior to represent is complex, in fact the behavior we represented with two BPMN models required thirteen ThingsBoard rule-chains that we manually encoded. More complex scenarios may require the manual design of too many rule-chains. For solving this issue we envision the possibility to define a parser from BPMN models to ThingsBoard rule-chains or to directly combine a BPMN engine with ThingsBoard.

Designing a graphical simulation with our ThingsBoard extension requires some programming skills, therefore we envision the possibility to define alternative approaches to facilitate this step, i.e., a model drive approach could be defined to support this step.

At the present stage, it is possible to visualize the execution of the simulation only by means of the 3D scene and by looking at the ThingsBoard log. However it would be interesting to be able to check the graphical rule-chain and see from there which is the action the PIR is performing at a specific moment.

7   Related Work

Several research work focus on the design and development of DTs using different approaches dependent on the kind of scenario and requirements needed to be fulfilled. We report in the following a non-exhaustive list of related work that focus on implementing DTs solutions for complex scenarios.

In [11] the authors use DTs and a related IoT platform to address congestion problem caused by container trucks in port areas scenario. The decision making support system implements a Python simulation framework aided with advanced visualization modules. The behavior to simulate is conceptualized by means of BPMN models and then parsed into python modules executed by a simulator developed using Python SimPy.

In [10] the authors propose an interactive DT platform based on Unity3D to implement the simulation and visualization features for offshore wind farms tracking conditions. The simulation layer relies on Functional Mock-up Unit (FMU) and Matlab to model the wind turbine and imported though Unity FMI Add-on.

In [14] the authors propose an hospital DT model based on discrete event simulation and IoT computing devices to optimise health care services. The simulation model relies on FlexSim HealthCare as 3D simulation and modelling tool used to evaluate and visualize patients and staff flows scenarios within the simulated model run-cycles.

In [4] the authors report an approach for supporting the representation, simulation, and visualization of digital process twins of autonomous systems. The approach has been built on top of BPMN collaborations, for representing the system behavior, the MIDA tool, for simulating the system, and Gazebo for visualizing the outcomes. A demonstration scenario is implemented regarding an autonomous system for airport luggage handling.

In [5] the authors presents a novel concept of executable digital process twins to effectively enable the monitoring, analysis, and refinement of process-driven systems. They illustrate how to implement an executable digital process twin in a cooperative multi-robot scenario. The approach is supported by a tool PROWIN to implement the monitoring of the executed system from the process and the physical perspectives. The tool also allows the deployment of a refined process model into the robots, thus enabling the synchronization between the physical and the digital systems. They assess the approach by means of a BPMN-driven multi-robot system deployed in a warehouse.

In [23] a microservice architecture to support the implementation of DTs for IoT-Enhanced Business Processes is presented. This architectural solution is supported by a model-driven development approach, that allows to move from modelling to implementation of the DT for the IoT-Enhanced Business Process. A scenario concerning a CO2 Management system for a smart library is reported and used as a demonstrator.

The related work previously reported mostly rely on a composition of tools for supporting the development of DTs. This means that users need to install and configure all these tools to make them work together, which can be time-consuming and complex. Furthermore, from a developer's perspective, this requires knowledge of all the tools used and an understanding on how to extend the composition for further improvements. Differently from them, in our work we mainly focus on the usage of a single IoT platform extended to support DT aspects. In addition some works tend to be too specific for their use case, limiting their usability in different contexts. This can make it challenging to adapt the solution to different use cases or scenarios.

With respect to the implementation of DTs solutions, DT platforms have started to appear in the market such as: *Azure Digital Twins, AWS IoT Twin-Maker, iTwin Bentley, Ansys Twin Builder*, and many others. Most of those platforms are proprietary and have different characteristics and provide different supports for DTs [16]. In our case we chose to develop a DT solution extending the ThingsBoard open source IoT platform instead of using a proprietary DT platform, remaining also consistent to the ICT infrastructure designed in the SAFE project which already relied on the ThingsBoard IoT platform.

8   Conclusion

In this work, we presented the SAFE scenario and described the process and tools we adopted to implement its Digital Twin Prototype. Once the real devices will be deployed in the actual environment, we will be able to perform 3D monitoring and to run up-front simulations starting from actual telemetries of the physical devices. This can enable various analysis of the IoT or CPS system deployed as well as possible predictive maintenance operations. We also discussed some limitations of the presented approach and proposed ways to overcome them as possible future work. The approach as well as the software tool can be adopted to implement Digital Twins for other IoT or CPS scenarios.

Acknowledgements. This work has been partially supported by the European Union - NextGenerationEU - National Recovery and Resilience Plan, Mission 4 Education and Research - Component 2 From research to business - Investment 1.5, ECS_00000041-VITALITY - Innovation, digitalisation and sustainability for the diffused economy in Central Italy.

References

1. Bourr, K., Corradini, F., Pettinari, S., Re, B., Rossi, L., Tiezzi, F.: Disciplined use of BPMN for mission modeling of multi-robot systems. In: Proceedings of the Forum at Practice of Enterprise Modeling, Riga, Latvia, 24–26 November 2021, vol. 3045, pp. 1–10. CEUR Workshop Proceedings (2021)
2. Compagnucci, I., Corradini, F., Fornari, F., Polini, A., Re, B., Tiezzi, F.: A systematic literature review on IoT-aware business process modeling views, requirements and notations. Softw. Syst. Model. **22**(3), 969–1004 (2023)
3. Corradini, F., Fedeli, A., Fornari, F., Polini, A., Re, B.: DTMN a modelling notation for digital twins. In: Sales, T.P., Proper, H.A., Guizzardi, G., Montali, M., Maggi, F.M., Fonseca, C.M. (eds.) EDOC 2022. LNBIP, vol. 466, pp. 63–78. Springer, Cham (2022). https://doi.org/10.1007/978-3-031-26886-1_4
4. Corradini, F., Pettinari, S., Re, B., Rossi, L., Tiezzi, F.: An approach to support digital process twin. In: IEEE DASC/PiCom/CBDCom/CyberSciTech 2022, Falerna, Italy, 12–15 September 2022, pp. 1–4. IEEE (2022)
5. Corradini, F., Pettinari, S., Re, B., Rossi, L., Tiezzi, F.: Executable digital process twins: Towards the enhancement of process-driven systems. Big Data Cogn. Comput. **7**(3), 139 (2023)
6. Dalibor, M., Jansen, N., Rumpe, B., Schmalzing, D., Wachtmeister, L., Wimmer, M., Wortmann, A.: A cross-domain systematic mapping study on software engineering for digital twins. J. Syst. Softw. **193**, 111361 (2022)
7. Fuller, A., Fan, Z., Day, C., Barlow, C.: Digital twin: enabling technologies, challenges and open research. IEEE Access **8**, 108952–108971 (2020)
8. Grieves, M.: Intelligent digital twins and the development and management of complex systems. Digital Twin **2**(8), 1–8 (2022)
9. Grieves, M., Vickers, J.: Digital twin: mitigating unpredictable, undesirable emergent behavior in complex systems. In: Kahlen, F.-J., Flumerfelt, S., Alves, A. (eds.) Transdisciplinary Perspectives on Complex Systems, pp. 85–113. Springer, Cham (2017). https://doi.org/10.1007/978-3-319-38756-7_4
10. Hasan, A., Hu, Z., Haghshenas, A., Karlsen, A., Alaliyat, S., Cali, U.: An interactive digital twin platform for offshore wind farms' development. In: Karaarslan, E., Aydin, Ö., Cali, Ü., Challenger, M. (eds.) Digital Twin Driven Intelligent Systems and Emerging Metaverse, pp. 269–281. Springer, Singapore (2023). https://doi.org/10.1007/978-981-99-0252-1_13

11. Hofmann, W., Branding, F.: Implementation of an IoT-and cloud-based digital twin for real-time decision support in port operations. IFAC-PapersOnLine **52**(13), 2104–2109 (2019)
12. Ihirwe, F., Ruscio, D.D., Mazzini, S., Pierini, P., Pierantonio, A.: Low-code engineering for internet of things: a state of research. In: ACM/IEEE 23rd International Conference on Model Driven Engineering Languages and Systems, Canada, 18–23 October, 2020, Companion Proceedings, pp. 74:1–74:8. ACM (2020)
13. Jones, D., Snider, C., Nassehi, A., Yon, J., Hicks, B.: Characterising the digital twin: a systematic literature review. CIRP J. Manuf. Sci. Technol. **29**, 36–52 (2020)
14. Karakra, A., Fontanili, F., Lamine, E., Lamothe, J., Taweel, A.: Pervasive computing integrated discrete event simulation for a hospital digital twin. In: 15th IEEE/ACS International Conference on Computer Systems and Applications, Aqaba, Jordan, 28 October–1 November 1 2018, pp. 1–6. IEEE Computer Society (2018)
15. Larsen, P.G., Fitzgerald, J., Woodcock, J.: How do we engineer trustworthy digital twins? Res. Direct.: Cyber-Phys. Syst. 1–6 (2023)
16. Lehner, D., et al.: Digital twin platforms: requirements, capabilities, and future prospects. IEEE Softw. **39**(2), 53–61 (2022)
17. Mihai, S., et al.: Digital twins: a survey on enabling technologies, challenges, trends and future prospects. IEEE Commun. Surv. Tutor. **24**(4), 2255–2291 (2022)
18. Pietroni, L., Mascitti, J., Galloppo, D.: Life-saving furniture during an earthquake. intelligent, interconnected and interacting. AGATHÓN | Int. J. Archit. Art Design **10**, 218–229 (2021)
19. Researchandmarkets: Digital twins market by technology, twinning type, cyber to-physical solutions, use cases and applications in industry verticals 2022–2027. https://www.researchandmarkets.com/report/digital-twin
20. Semeraro, C., Lezoche, M., Panetto, H., Dassisti, M.: Digital twin paradigm: a systematic literature review. Comput. Ind. **130**, 103469 (2021)
21. Thelen, A., et al.: A comprehensive review of digital twin-part 1: modeling and twinning enabling technologies. Struct. Multidiscip. Optim. **65**(12), 354 (2022)
22. Tuong, N., Jump, A., Casey, D.: Emerging tech impact radar: 2023: gartner research excerpt. https://www.gartner.com/en/doc/emerging-technologies-and-trends-impact-radar-excerpt
23. Valderas, P.: Supporting the implementation of digital twins for IoT-enhanced BPs. In: Nurcan, S., Opdahl, A.L., Mouratidis, H., Tsohou, A. (eds.) RCIS 2023. LNBIP, vol. 476, pp. 222–238. Springer, Cham (2023). https://doi.org/10.1007/978-3-031-33080-3_14
24. Valderas, P., Torres, V., Serral, E.: Towards an interdisciplinary development of IoT-enhanced business processes. Bus. Inf. Syst. Eng. **65**(1), 25–48 (2023)

Towards Responsible Digital Twins

Zoran Milosevic[1]([⊠]) [iD] and Pieter van Schalkwyk[2,3] [iD]

[1] Deontik, Brisbane, Australia
zoran@deontik.com
[2] XMPRO, Dallas, USA
pvs@xmpro.com
[3] XMPRO, Sydney, Australia

Abstract. A digital twin is a virtual representation of real-world entities and processes, synchronized at a specified frequency and fidelity. The capability of digital twins is continually evolving from simple decision support, via decision augmentation for end users to autonomous decision automation. This evolution is enabled by increasingly sophisticated technologies used by digital twins, e.g. advanced analytics, IoT and AI. In many applications, multiple digital twins can be used to address different system functionality, and composed as required, leading to potentially quite complex technical systems. Digital twins further increasingly require explicit consideration of *socio-economic* factors, to ensure building *responsible* digital twin solutions, minimizing potential harm for the users. This paper discusses how such socio-economic factors, particularly the enterprise, legal and ethics policies and various value constraints, can be gradually transformed into a set of governance rules for building, operating and evolving responsible digital twin solutions and ecosystems. These policies include voluntary type of rules, e.g. digital ethics norms, as well as regulatory policies, which impose formal legal obligations, e.g. legislative and regulatory mechanisms. We use two application domains at two ends of the complexity spectrum, namely personalized health care and renewable energy, to illustrate our approach.

Keywords: Digital Twins · Machine Learning · Artificial Intelligence · complex system · computable policy · obligations · prohibitions · accountability · ethics

1 Background

A digital twin (DT) is a virtual representation of real-world entities and processes, synchronized at a specified frequency and fidelity [1]. DTs can be used to study, monitor, and optimize the composition and functions of their physical counterpart. This emerging field has witnessed a meteoric rise, with an impressive growth rate of 71% between 2020 and 2022 [2]. This trend is projected to continue upward, with a forecasted leap from USD 10.1 billion in 2023 to USD 110.1 billion by 2028, representing a compound annual growth rate (CAGR) of 61.3% [3].

The concept of digital twins, initially introduced within the manufacturing sector by Grieves and Vickers [4], has since evolved and permeated a broad spectrum of industries. This includes aerospace and defense, agriculture, food and beverage, architecture

T. P. Sales et al. (Eds.): EDOC 2023 Workshops, LNBIP 498, pp. 123–138, 2024.
https://doi.org/10.1007/978-3-031-54712-6_8

and construction, financial services, healthcare and life sciences, mobility and transportation, natural resources, and telecommunications, as reflected in The Digital Twin Consortium's diverse working groups [1].

The rapid growth of DTs highlights their importance in the digital transformation of various industries. This growth prompts a discussion on the responsibilities tied to their development and use. As DTs evolve from simple to complex systems, the digital transformation process becomes more intricate.

A discrete DT represents a single entity, like a robot arm in a factory. When multiple discrete DTs are combined, they form a composite DT, representing a larger system comprising various components. For instance, a production cell's DT is a composite of the DTs of the devices within the cell. This process of combining discrete DTs into composite ones illustrates how DTs can represent increasingly complex systems.

DTs improve decision-making through real-time data and context-specific information. They provide users with detailed data visualizations, aiding in informed operational decisions. With the integration of AI and advanced analytics, they can extract hidden insights from large datasets, a task challenging for manual processing. This leads to decision augmentation, providing users with prescriptive recommendations.

In the future, DTs will move beyond decision augmentation to decision automation (Fig. 1). They will make strategic decisions based on AI, analytics, and business rules, enabling 'lights-out' operations and driving an algorithmic business model [5]. As such, their responsible use will become increasingly important, with the need to identify and integrate governance policies, as responsible features of digital twins. These policies can be voluntary, e.g. digital ethics norms as well as regulatory and legislative policies, with formal legal obligations, as also suggested in [14].

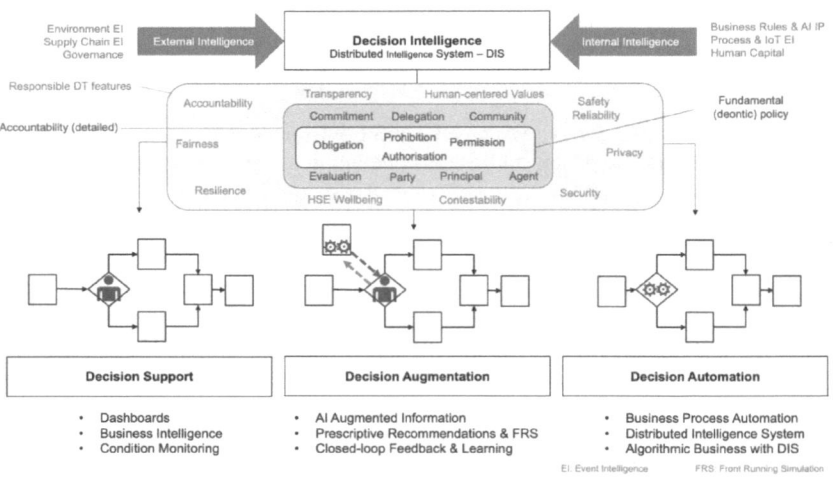

Fig. 1. From decision support to decision automation

The Digital Twin Consortium's (DTC) Digital Twin Capabilities Periodic Table [6] and Reference Architecture [7] exemplify efforts to provide technical and architectural guidance for the development and implementation of DTs. Additionally, the Industrial Digital Twin Association (IDTA), a German-led initiative under the Industrie 4.0 umbrella [8], offers specific guidance on the technological implementation of digital twins within the manufacturing sector. These initiatives collectively contribute to the evolving body of knowledge and best practices in the field of DT technology.

While instrumental in advancing DT implementation, the technology-centric approach presents a challenge because it does not adequately address the socio-economic impact of utilizing DT technology. Furthermore, it does not sufficiently consider the implications for a DT's responsible and ethical use in facilitating effective digital transformation, highlighting the need for a more comprehensive approach that integrates technological advancements with socio-economic impact and ethical considerations.

The next section delves into the challenges and problems associated with the responsible use of DTs and the potential repercussions of failing to address this issue. Section 3 introduces a Responsible Digital Twins (RDT) framework. This framework aims to address ethical and socio-economic considerations in a standards-based, machine-readable format of policy expressions, providing a comprehensive approach to DT technology's responsible and ethical use. Section 4 discusses two application domains that represent different ends of the DT complexity spectrum. These serve to illustrate the diverse applications, potential impacts of DT technology in real-world scenarios and our RDT proposal. Section 5 provides concussions and future work directions.

2   Problem

While DTs present substantial opportunities to influence the digital transformation of organizations profoundly, it is important to acknowledge that, akin to other technologies such as AI and IoT, they can be utilized for both beneficial and detrimental purposes. This dual potential extends to impacts on humans, the environment, and institutional sectors such as healthcare and finance.

Enterprise or socio-economic rules, considered as constraints on behaviour of various actors in the DT ecosystems, are crucial in developing and deploying DTs across the spectrum from simple discrete through to complex composite DT systems. These rules can be described in terms of the primitive policy concepts, i.e. obligations, permissions, prohibitions, and authorizations, also known as deontic concepts [10], which in turn, can be combined to express more complex, accountability concepts modelling enterprise, legal or legislative policies. These rules, help ensure that DTs are aligned with enterprise policy, ethical norms and legislative/regulative policies. A comprehensive approach to integrating such rules in developing and deploying DTs is important to address interoperability challenges and conflicts related to the precedence or prioritization of the business and societal impacts of certain DT use cases [9].

This paper seeks to address a specific set of challenges for expressing enterprise or deontic rules in a machine-readable format. The primary objective is to develop a methodology that is both standards-based and scalable, capable of accommodating a wide range of applications, from simple, discrete systems to large-scale, ultra-complex system-of-systems configurations. It involves navigating the complexities of translating enterprise rules into a format that can be readily interpreted by DTs, while adhering to established standards. The ultimate goal is to create a practical framework that can effectively address the increasing complexity of DT applications, accommodating socioeconomic factors, thereby enhancing their utility and impact in various sectors.

3   Solution Approach

3.1   Motivations

Digital Twins are made possible by the combination of technology such as event-based processing and analytics, modelling and simulation, machine learning, and AI, as introduced above. DTs are essentially *technical systems* but involve close interactions and synchronization with *human actors*, in many respects like the SCADA systems, used in support of industrial systems, such as power, irrigation and water systems.

Enterprise and Social Policies – Governance of the Synchronization Points
The close interactions between technical systems and actions of humans and the effect of decisions made by automated systems on humans, require careful analysis of *synchronization points* between physical and digital systems – with the aim of identifying the *enterprise or social policies* that need to be respected at these points and beyond. This would need to apply to the design, implementation, testing, operation and updates stages of DT components life-cycle, while in compliance with the organizational, regulative, legislative and policies reflecting safety and ethical standards and norms.

We propose the term 'responsible digital twins' to signify the explicit integration of these policies at DT's life cycle. Our approach is influenced by the increasing recognition of a need for supporting 'responsible AI' technologies, while adding the specifics arising from the broader set of DT technical and engineering characteristics.

We propose the following characteristics of DTs (Fig. 2), as their 'responsible' properties, where the first group below is influenced by the AI ethics principles [11, 14]:

- Human, societal and environmental wellbeing - capturing the fact that DT systems should benefit individuals, society and the environment.
- Human-centred values - emphasizing the fact that DT systems should respect human rights, diversity, and the autonomy of individuals.
- Accountability – referring to the actions of parties involved in developing and deploying DT systems, including their responsibility for any harm that is caused by their systems.
- Transparency – referring to the ability of users to understand the operation of a complex system, such as a black box AI system, how their data are used and how decisions are made; referred to as explainability in the AI context.
- Contestability - enables consumers to challenge the output of the AI algorithm when it impacts them.
- Fairness - DT systems should be fair in their treatment of all users, regardless of their race, gender, religion, or other personal characteristics.
- Privacy - DT systems should respect the privacy of users and should not collect or use personal data without their consent.

We also believe that the 'responsible' properties cover engineering principles of:

- Security - DT systems should enable precise access control over specific data, resources, and actions in your deployment, also supporting privacy property.
- Reliability and Safety – DT systems should operate in accordance with their purpose and should not pose a risk to users' physical or psychological well-being; they should function well for people across different use conditions and contexts, including ones it was not originally intended for.
- Resilience - DT should absorb disturbance and reorganize while undergoing change thus retaining the same function, structure, identity, and feedbacks; this includes adaptation to system changes as technology and society evolve.

These characteristics (in outer layer of policies in Fig. 1), are guiding principles, similar to ethics [11, 14] or the Gemini principles [15]. Note that 'trustworthiness' is sometimes used to refer to security, privacy, safety, reliability, and resilience [8].

We also note that current consumer laws define safety and quality requirements for goods or services to minimise harm for consumers, but the specifics of consumer-facing uses of AI such as generative AI have not yet been considered by a court [14].

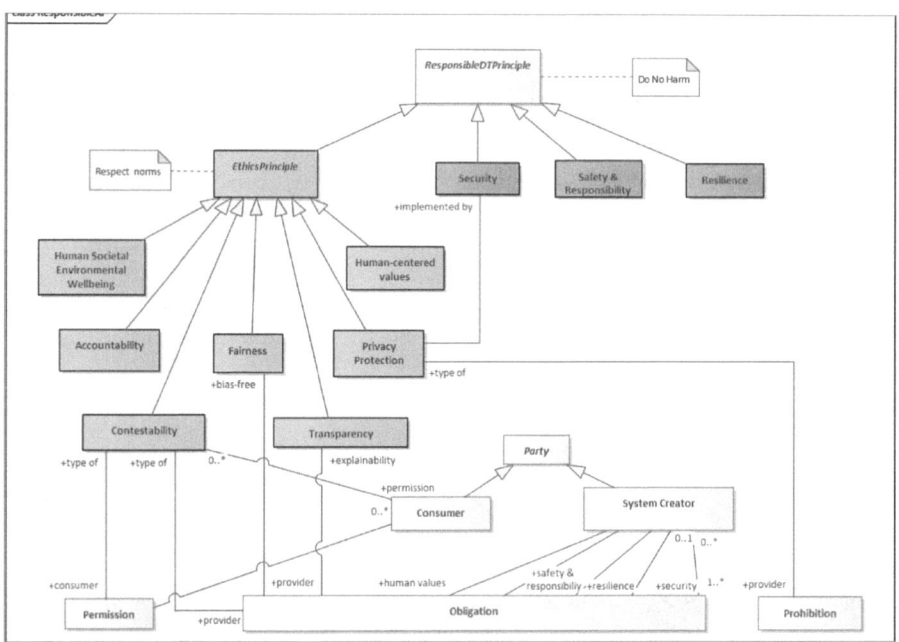

Fig. 2. Classification of DT responsible principles and mapping onto deontic policies

Operationalization of Principles

We need an approach for operationalizing high-level principles mentioned above. One option, similar to the AI responsible patterns [13], would be to develop a catalogue of reusable responsible DT patterns. They would provide reusable solutions to common problems occurring in system developments. Such approach was also used in the early interoperability framework in Australia [16] for identifying interoperability patterns.

Another approach is to express the enterprise and social policies associated with each of the responsible DT characteristics, using computable (machine readable) expression of foundational, i.e. deontic, policies of authorizations, obligations, prohibitions, permissions and their violations. This approach is introduced in [11] which describes a detailed mapping of digital ethics principles into deontic policy concepts. This was further elaborated in modelling the consent as an authorization policy [17]. This is the approach that we adopt for the operationalization of responsible DT principles, where the mapping of each of the principles can be refined into the fundamental deontic concepts (Fig. 2). The approach is presented next.

3.2 Standard-Based Specification Framework

Our solution for a computable expression of policies is based on the ISO/IEC 15414 Enterprise Language (EL) standard, from the family of Reference Model for Open Distributed Processing (RM-ODP) standards [10], augmented with related work from ontology research, in particular the conceptual modelling of legal relations [20]. The Enterprise Language standard provides precise expression and guidelines in the expression of *foundational* (deontic) policies of obligation, prohibition, permission, and authorisation, and the expression of *accountability* policies of the parties involved in the system, whether using, controlling or interacting with it. The accountability concepts are an element of responsible characteristics, and derived from deontic concepts, shown as middle layer of policies in Fig. 1. Both the foundational and accountability concepts can be used to express constraints on the actions of parties filling various roles in a system, be they humans or automated systems.

This standard thus provides foundations for computable expression of enterprise specifications for a system, which in our case is a digital twin ecosystem. This specification would typically involve defining:

- the purpose of a digital twin system in terms of behaviour of the system

  - individual components, their interactions, compositions etc.

- policies that capture further restriction on the behaviour

  - between the system and its environment, or
  - within the system itself, related to the business decisions by the system owners

- explicit description of ecosystems that can span multiple policy domains (e.g. federation) and are not owned by a single party.

This specification style places greater emphasis on the expression of correct or normal behaviour and on the chain of responsibility involved in achieving it [10]. This in turn supports the expression of business rules and behaviour that clearly describe obligations, permissions, authorisation and prohibitions (the so-called deontic concepts), as well as the accounatbility of each of the objects involved in the specification, as explained next (Note: an object can represent an IT system or a natural person).

Deontic Concepts

The EL standard includes the concepts of obligations, prohibitions and permissions, stating the constraints for actions that are obliged, prohibited or permitted. In addition, the standard provides concepts for modelling the dynamics of deontic constraints i.e. when they become applicable to the actions of parties and how they are passed among parties. These are needed for the governance, compliance and management of interactions between autonomous decision-making components and humans in a system. This is achieved by introducing a special type of enterprise object, called *deontic token*, which captures deontic assertions. The deontic tokens are held by the parties involved and holding one controls their behaviour [10]. Deontic tokens can be manipulated as objects while deontic constraints (e.g. obligation) cannot. There are three types of deontic tokens: *burden*, representing an obligation, *permit* representing permission and *embargo*, representing prohibition. In the case of a burden, an active enterprise object holding the burden must attempt to discharge it either directly by performing the specified behaviour, or indirectly by engaging some other object to take possession of the burden and performing the specified behaviour. In the case of permit, an object holding the permit is able to perform some specified piece of behaviour. In the case of embargo, the object holding the embargo is inhibited from performing the behaviour.

Another concept introduced to support modelling the dynamics of deontic constraints is *speech act*, Fig. 3. This is a special kind of action used to modify the set of tokens held by an active enterprise object. The name was chosen by analogy to the linguistic concept of speech act, which refers to something expressed by an individual that not only presents information but performs an action. Thus, a speech act intrinsically changes the state of the world in terms of the association of deontic tokens with active enterprise objects. This concept fits well with the nature of AI enabled applications, as it allows the speech act to be performed by people and AI systems, yet distinguish them when needed to establish links with ethics, legal and social norms.

Accountability Concepts

The deontic modelling framework is further extended to support traceability of obligations of parties, according to their broader responsibilities derived from ethical, social or legal norms, referred to as a set of accountability concepts [10]:

Principal is a party that has delegated something (e.g. authorisation or provision of service) to another. *Agent* is an active enterprise object that has been delegated something (e.g. authorisation, responsibility of provision of service) by, and acts for, a party.

Delegation is an action that assigns something (e.g. authorisation, responsibility of provision of service) to another object, e.g. agent.

Additional action types, capture important business events in any organisational system, and model how responsibilities evolve.

Commitment, is an action resulting in an obligation by one or more participants in the act to comply with a rule or perform a contract. This effectively means that they will be assigned a burden. Examples are commitments by clinicians to deliver safe, reliable and effective healthcare to patients.

Declaration, is as an action by which an object makes facts known in its environment and establishes a new state of affairs in it. For example, an AI system (or a party managing it) may inform the interested parties about change of some legal rule.

Evaluation, is an action that assesses the value of something. Value can be considered in terms of various variables e.g. importance, preference and usefulness, such as performance parameters to express administrative performance, or accuracy or reliability measures associated with research findings or to assess the fairness of training data.

Prescription, is an action that establishes a rule. Prescriptions provide a mechanism for changing the system's business rules at runtime, enabling its dynamic adaptation to business changes, such as creation of new policies reflecting new legislations for AI.

Authorisation, is an action indicating some empowerment, through which an enterprise object issues a required and will itself undertake a burden to facilitate the behaviour. For example, the contestability is an authorisation for the consumer to challenge AI decisions, through a permit by the AI system which has the burden to enable it.

Deontic and accountability concepts are constraints over *actions* of the parties or systems (Fig. 3), making it possible to define computable constraints over the actions, thus supporting real-time monitoring and downstream discretionary or non-discretionary enforcements. There are several policy languages for expressing such constraints, which is beyond the limits of this paper, and are for example discussed in [17].

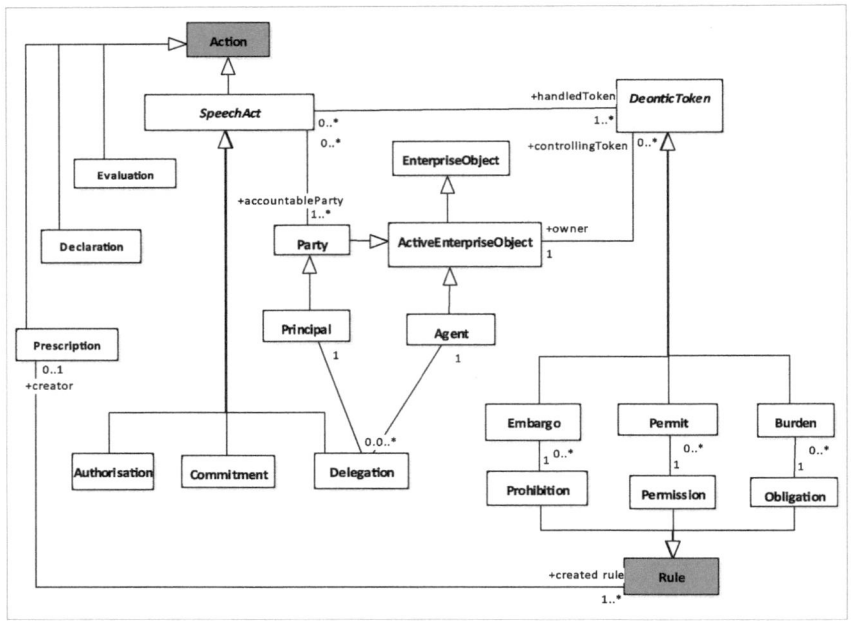

Fig. 3. ODP Enterprise Language: deontic and accountability concepts

3.3 Practitioners-Friendly

The computable policy framework provides a way of translating high-level character-istics of responsible digital twins (RDT) into a set of computable policies that can be integrated in the design, implementation and operation of DT systems.

In order to make this rather technical framework practitioner friendly, we are propos-ing a mapping framework as shown in Fig. 4. Physical entities are virtually represented by DTs that synchronise twinning information at a certain frequency and fidelity. This requires technical integration that is governed by technical architecture and integra-tion capabilities for each digital twin use case. The collection or combination of all the digital twin use cases interoperates to provide operational, tactical, and strategic decision support. The digital twin of a complex system is not a single twin, but the harmonious operation of the collection of digital twin use cases. The framework intro-duces a Business Process Logic layer that enables stakeholders to manage how these use cases interoperate by providing operational rules, optimisation and AI models, and enterprise or socio-economic rules. This framework allows stakeholders to influence business outcomes by adjusting and prioritising the different rules and models.

This solution is result of our experience in architecting and building many indus-trial, financial or health systems, reflecting the needs to support customer specific or government specific requirements.

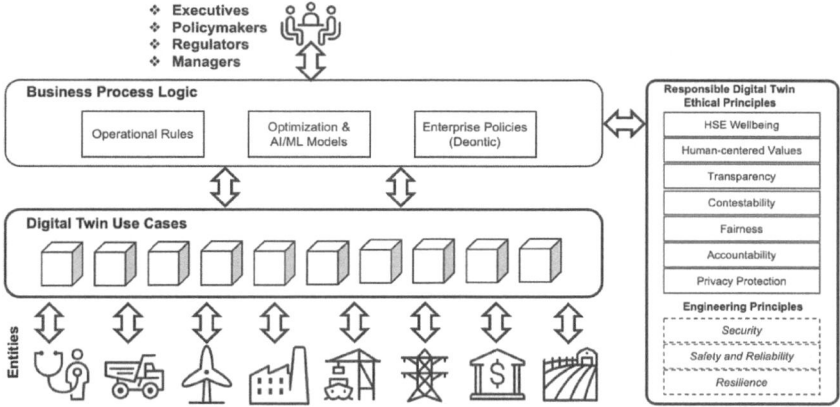

Fig. 4. Adding Responsible DT layer to a DT system

4 Two Application Domain Considerations

4.1 Digital Health – Personalized Medicine

DTs are used to address several healthcare challenges, including surgery, pharmacy, cardiology and operating theatres [18]. They can be also used in support of personalized medicine where the bi-directional data flow between a patient and its virtual replica,

(Fig. 5) allows for real-time continuous updating of the virtual model and, conversely, targeted interventions on the patient based on predictive simulations performed on DTs [19].

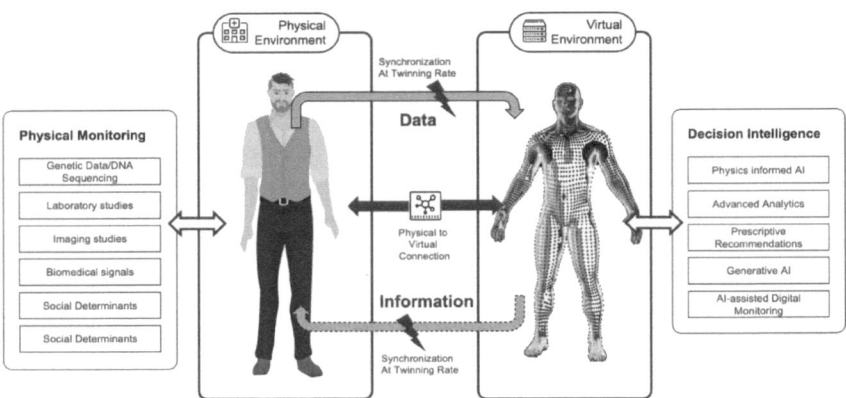

Fig. 5. Single DT for a person

There are also DT applications across more complex healthcare systems which would involve multiple DTs, focusing on different aspects of healthcare. These would be for example DTs that are used as part of large hospital information systems, aimed at improving organizations' workflow and resource management. Such DTs can reference virtual copies of individual patients which can then be integrated into higher-level representation of clinical workflows in the hospital, effectively expressing interoperability between these twins, from the application perspectives. In the case of responsible DTs, these workflows need to explicitly embed rules that govern responsible DTs, reflecting rules associated with clinical care, but also rules emanating from organizational policies or external regulatory policies as mentioned in Sect. 3. In all these settings, DT applications could improve the study and monitoring of highly complex systems characterized by many interacting components and thousands of variables that can be difficult to characterize with traditional approaches.

One interesting solution for single digital twin is their use in enabling better precision and personalized of dementia care [12]. In this case clinician first enters patient data to a mobile Decision Support System (DSS), which is linked to a server running the Machine Learning or Deep Learning Algorithm. The algorithm connects to the database containing data about past dementia cases to find one or more past cases that best match the data of the present patient. Algorithm then constructs the appropriate DTs through union of best matching cases and the DT and all related information are shown to the end-user via the mobile DSS. This helps clinician performs a more informed and precise diagnosis and treatment planning decision, after which the details and outcomes about new patient get recorded as new data for future reference.

4.2 Renewable Energy

Renewable or distributed energy resources are increasingly employing digital twins to address many use cases across these complex assets' value chains and life cycle. A prime example of this is the energy grid challenge associated with introducing renewable or distributed energy resources into power systems networks.

The electricity grid represents an ultra-large scale complex cyber-physical system that merges engineering automation and control technology with emerging digitalization capabilities, such as digital twins. These digital twins provide decision intelligence, as shown in Fig. 6 to facilitate decision support, augmentation, and automation. This integration of digital twins into complex systems underscores the transformative potential of digitalization in addressing contemporary challenges in the energy sector.

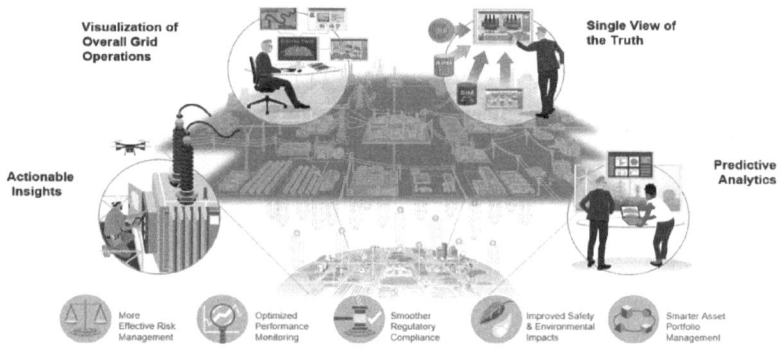

Fig. 6. Digital Twins in a Sustainable Energy Grid [21]

DTs, with their extensive applications across the value chain, establish a complex system within the renewable energy sector, including applications such as wind farms, hydroelectric power, biomass, and green hydrogen production. They facilitate process and network optimization, thereby augmenting efficiency in wind turbine operations or hydroelectric power generation. They employ predictive analytics to forecast asset performance and maintenance requirements, reducing downtime in biomass processing facilities or hydrogen production plants. They contribute to quality management and monitor Environmental, Social, and Governance (ESG) factors, endorsing sustainable operations across all renewable energy applications. They identify potential operational risks and enhance safety through scenario simulations, improving the safety protocols in wind farms or hydroelectric plants. Moreover, they optimize supply chain operations and aid in workforce management by providing real-time visibility and predictive insights, streamlining operations across the renewable energy sector.

The combination of different use cases in each of the application areas described across the overall value stream of generation, transmission, and distribution for power systems results in a complex digital twin system of systems.

The development and deployment of DTs in the renewable energy sector present an even more complex task, given the extensive continuum of decision support required across the value chain through the combination of traditional and emerging technology. The temporal scope of use cases can vary significantly, from long-term energy market optimization to near real-time operational responses. This variability necessitates consistent and coherent policy frameworks across diverse use case categories and time considerations.

Operational rules across these use cases are often encapsulated as first-order logic rules, readily expressed in a machine-readable format for digital twins. These rules facilitate decision support, decision augmentation, and in some instances, business process automation based on the model as shown in Fig. 4 that depicts adding a responsible DT layer to a DT system.

Statistical and mathematical models for simulation, optimization, and prediction, typically code-based, are also machine-readable and can be embedded within digital twin use cases. However, deontic and accountability rules, are often overlooked during the requirements-gathering phase. This oversight may lead to interoperability challenges and potential conflicts regarding the precedence or prioritization of the business and societal impacts of digital twin use cases.

Contrary to operational rules and AI/ML models, deontic and accountability rules are infrequently presented in an explicit machine-readable format. This highlights a potential area for improvement in the responsible use of DTs, as proposed by the authors, underscoring the need for a more comprehensive approach to incorporating such rules in DT decision-making processes for renewable energy use cases.

The following scenarios illustrate conflicting operational and enterprise rules:

- An operational rule may stipulate that additional battery storage is required to stabilize the national grid. However, this could lead to increased mining activities for the raw materials necessary for battery production, subsequently resulting in a rise in reportable (scope 1, 2, and 3) emissions. This outcome could conflict with a public commitment to reduce the reportable emissions on a year-by-year basis towards a 2030 goal. Such a policy statement might be communicated through press releases and investor briefings, but it is not typically presented in a machine-readable format that could inform the operational digital twin of the potential conflict, which our proposal can address.

- An AI model optimizing a renewables-based energy grid may necessitate consumer data regarding behaviour and energy utilization patterns, potentially indicating anomalies for certain users. This use case may interoperate with a revenue optimization DT use case, making anomalous event data accessible to service agents. These agents could then utilize this information to target specific individuals or organizations. However, without explicit machine-readable privacy deontic policies, such applications of DT could occur irresponsibly, without the consent of both organizational and user stakeholders. This underscores the critical need for comprehensive privacy policies in the deployment and operation of DTs, to ensure their responsible and ethical use.

- The World Economic Forum [23] underscores how recycling to conserve metals utilized in wind turbines represents one pathway toward a circular economy. The decommissioning and disposal of such assets constitute significant asset management use cases for DTs within the overall value chain, particularly towards the end of the physical asset's life cycle. Operational rules may dictate that the most cost-effective approach would be to abandon or dispose of these assets in landfills rather than invest in an active recycling policy. However, implementing such a policy could override operational decisions made through these DTs, highlighting the potential for DTs to contribute to sustainable practices in the renewable energy sector.

The digital health and renewable energy scenarios underscore the imperative for a responsible DT (RDT) framework, accommodating RDT principles, and including machine readable and standards-based policy expressions, both of which provide a comprehensive guide and support for the ethical development, deployment, and operation of DTs, as shown with the examples in Table 1 next. An RDT framework will ensure that DTs contribute positively to individuals, society, and the environment.

Table 1. Responsible DT (RDT) principles – Healthcare and Renewable examples

RDT principle	Health	Renewable
Human-centered	Dementia DT should respect human rights, diversity, and the autonomy of individuals, e.g. obtaining and recording patient consent for using their data as part of the Dementia DT system, taking into account their specific demographic data as well as their autonomy in making decisions - or relying on a delegated person who make decision on behalf of patient	The model should not be used to target specific individuals or organizations in a discriminatory way. For example, the model should not be used to target low-income households or minority communities for higher energy prices
Accountability	Developers are obliged to develop and deploy the DT system, which support patient preferences, and their changes over time; they are obliged to minimise any harm that is caused by their systems; clinicians are obliged to check the recommendation by the virtual DT and make final professional decision before they are permitted to prescribe a medication	It is important to have clear processes in place to hold those responsible for developing and deploying the AI model accountable for their actions. This could include having a board of directors or an ethics committee that oversees the development and deployment of the model

(*continued*)

Table 1. (*continued*)

RDT principle	Health	Renewable
Transparency	Dementia DT should provide mechanisms to both patients and clinicians showing how ML/AI/DSS components arrive at a decision treatment, and also state clinical risks and benefits for the person in question, taking into account their medical history, demographics, and other parameters	Model workings should be transparent to individuals and organizations. This could include providing information about the data that was used to train the model, the algorithms used to make decisions, and the potential biases that could be present in the model
Fairness	Dementia DT systems should be fair in their dementia care support to all users, regardless of their race, gender, religion, or other personal characteristics	Model should not discriminate against some groups. For example, it should not target low-income households or minority communities for higher energy prices
Privacy	Dementia DT should respect the privacy of users, and should not collect or use personal data without their consent; consent should be regarded as a combination of permission (for patients) and obligation (for clinicians' respecting patient preferences) of accessing patient health records, i.e. fine-grained data access support	The data about consumer behavior and energy utilization patterns could be sensitive and used to identify individuals or organizations. Clear privacy policies should explain how data will be collected, used, and shared. There should be mechanisms for individuals to control their privacy settings and opt out of data collection
Safety and reliability	Dementia DT should operate in accordance with their purpose, to support dementia patients and should not pose a risk to users' physical or psychological well-being	The model should not make decisions that could endanger people or property. The model should also be resistant to hacking and manipulation

5 Conclusions and Future Work

This paper presents our proposal for starting new inquiry into responsible DTs, by explicitly positioning of enterprise and social policies in the context of DT technologies. The aim is to help practitioners with designing, building, operating and evolving responsible DTs which embed computational expression of such policies, while balancing value proposition and risks. We find that there are still some legal and ethics ambiguities about the chain of responsibilities involving humans and automated decision makers, and it is the level of risks that can determine best governance mechanisms for responsible

DTs, as also discussed in [14]. We argue that the concept of responsible DTs may have been overlooked so far due to the focus on technical issues such as interoperability and composability. We believe that our proposal for computational expression of policies, implementing socioeconomic constraints for responsible DT principles, can create interest by developers involved in building tools for DT solutions and provide valuable guidelines to practitioners helping end-users on this specific digital transformation journey. We are also hoping that the deontic-based formalism used in our approach, and based on the ODP Enterprise Language, can provide a new perspective on the formalization of architecture principles in general [24], and RDT principles in particular.

In future, we are planning to develop detailed proof of concept prototypes involving end users in renewable energy, digital health, but also manufacturing, finance, supply chain. These would need to include expressive and machine-readably policy language to operationalize the RDT principles, which we presented elsewhere [11, 17], but the elaboration of which was beyond the space limitations of this paper. Such a policy language could be implemented by a separate DT instance, further allowing simulation of complex policy interactions, to detect policy conflicts. This in turn could support real-time monitoring and enforcement of actions of parties according to their legal, ethical or professional policies.

Another area of investigation would be how to model various value functions to capture business and social objectives, and use them to resolve conflicts of policies when composing DTs across complex systems. This would help in addressing ethics dilemmas and provide further support to humans when dealing with conflicting policies, including how to implement complexities associated with monitoring of obligations and prohibitions in case of trade-offs between the compliant behaviour and cost of violations, as discussed in [22].

Another topic is to bring in elements of legal concepts and their relationships, captured through respective ontologies as discussed in [20]. For example, the concept of rights, signifies permission of some actors, but puts an obligation on others, on opposing side of the relationship, and these 'correlatives' may provide more tighter accountability expressions over our accountability modeling concepts. Further, the concept of liability, such as one discussed in [23], can be related to an obligation of a party who is expected to perform some action, which it fails to perform (i.e. violation), but may also have links to the concept of power.

References

1. Digital Twin Consortium. Working Groups (2023). https://www.digitaltwinconsortium.org/workinggroups.htm
2. IoT Analytics. Decoding Digital Twins: Exploring the 6 main applications and their benefits (2023). https://iot-analytics.com/6-main-digital-twin-applications-and-their-benefits/
3. Markets and Markets. Digital Twin Market by Application, Industry, Enterprise, and Geography – Global Forecast to 2028 (2023). https://www.marketsandmarkets.com/Market-Reports/digital-twin-market-225269522.html
4. Grieves, M., Vickers, J.: Digital twin: mitigating unpredictable, undesirable emergent behavior in complex systems. In: Kahlen, F.-J., Flumerfelt, S., Alves, A. (eds.) Transdisciplinary Perspectives on Complex Systems, pp. 85–113. Springer, Cham (2017). https://doi.org/10.1007/978-3-319-38756-7_4

5. XMPro. Why Decision Intelligence with Digital Twins is Kinda Like DCS for Automation and Control (2023). https://xmpro.com/why-decision-intelligence-with-digital-twins-is-kinda-like-dcs-for-automation-and-control/
6. Digital Twin Consortium. Capabilities Periodic Table (2022). https://www.digitaltwinconsortium.org/initiatives/capabilities-periodic-table/
7. Digital Twin Consortium. Platform Stack Architectural Framework: An Introductory Guide Form (2023). https://www.digitaltwinconsortium.org/platform-stack-architectural-fram-for mework-an-introductory-guide-form/
8. IDTA. Submodels (2023). https://industrialdigitaltwin.org/en/content-hub/submodels
9. McKinsey. Digital twins and the enterprise metaverse (2022). https://www.mckinsey.com/capabilities/mckinsey-digital/our-insights/digital-twins-the-foundation-of-the-enterprise-metaverse
10. ISO/IEC 15414, Information technology: Open distributed processing, Reference model – Enterprise Language, 3rd edn. (2015)
11. Milosevic, Z.: Ethics in digital health: a deontic accountability framework. In: 2019 IEEE 23rd International Enterprise Distributed Object Computing Conference (EDOC), Paris, France, pp. 105-111 (2019). https://doi.org/10.1109/EDOC.2019.00022
12. Wickramasinghe, N., et al.: Digital twins to enable better precision and personalized dementia care. JAMIA Open 5(3), ooac072 (2022). https://doi.org/10.1093/jamiaopen/ooac072
13. Responsible AI Pattern Catalogue, CSIRO/Data61. https://research.csiro.au/ss/science/projects/responsible-ai-pattern-catalogue/
14. Safe and responsible AI in Australia, Discussion paper, June 2023, Australian Government, Department of Industry, Science and Resources
15. Gemini Principles, University of Cambridge (2022). https://www.cdbb.cam.ac.uk/DFTG/GeminiPrinciples
16. Interoperability Framework 2.0. https://developer.digitalhealth.gov.au/resources/interoperability-framework-v2-0
17. Milosevic, Z., Pyefinch, F.: Computable consent – from regulatory, legislative, and organizational policies to security policies. In: Almeida, J.P.A., Karastoyanova, D., Guizzardi, G., Montali, M., Maggi, F.M., Fonseca, C.M. (eds.) EDOC 2022. LNCS, vol. 13585, pp. 3–18. Springer, Cham (2022). https://doi.org/10.1007/978-3-031-17604-3_1
18. Hassanzadeh, H., Boyle, J., Khanna, S.: Digital twins in healthcare: an operating theatre flow modelling case study. In: Digital Health Institute Summit. AIDH, Brisbane (2022). Csiro: EP2022-2887. http://hdl.handle.net/102.100.100/444330?index=1
19. Digital Twins: The New Frontier for Personalized Medicine? Appl. Sci. 13(13), 7940 (2023). https://www.mdpi.com/2076-3417/13/13/7940
20. Griffo, C., Almeida, J.P.A., Guizzardi, G.: Conceptual modeling of legal relations. In: Trujillo, J., et al. (eds.) ER 2018. Lecture Notes in Computer Science, vol. 11157, pp. 169–183. Springer, Cham (2018). https://doi.org/10.1007/978-3-030-00847-5_14
21. Bentley. Digital Twins for a Sustainable Grid (2022). https://blog.bentley.com/digital-twins-for-a-sustainable-grid/
22. Linington, P.F., Milosevic, Z., Tanaka, A., Vallecillo, A.: Building Enterprise Systems with ODP, An Introduction to Open Distributed Processing. Chapman & Hall/CRC Press (2011)
23. Report on the safety and liability implications of Artificial Intelligence, the Internet of Things and robotics. EUR-Lex (2020). https://eur-lex.europa.eu/legal-content/EN/TXT/?uri=CELEX:52020DC0064
24. Greefhorst, D., Proper, H.A.: Architecture Principles - The Cornerstones of Enterprise Architecture. The Enterprise Engineering Series. Springer, Heidelberg (2011). https://doi.org/10.1007/978-3-642-20279-7. ISBN 978-3-642-20278-0

The Role of Interoperability for Digital Twins

João Luiz Rebelo Moreira[✉]

University of Twente - Semantics, Cybersecurity & Services (SCS) group,
AE Enschede, 7500 Enschede, The Netherlands
j.luizrebelomoreira@utwente.nl

Abstract. The concept of Digital Twin (DT) has gained popularity as a digital representation of physical entities that interact with their real-world counterparts in (near) real-time through sensors and actuators. DTs can be applied across different sectors, offering benefits like simulation, remote monitoring, and predictive maintenance, which are relevant capabilities of smart systems. However, achieving the full potential of DTs requires addressing interoperability challenges posed by the complex networks of devices and systems that play different roles in DTs. This paper presents a research agenda aimed at enhancing DT interoperability grounded in four perspectives, which reflect knowledge fields in computer/information science, i.e., architecture of distributed systems, model-based system engineering, ontology-driven conceptual modeling, and linked data with semantic web. This paper highlights how leveraging on existing standards, such as modelling languages and ontologies, is important for improved DT interoperability. This becomes increasingly relevant for driving research directions related to ongoing initiatives such as the International Data Spaces and the Digital Product Passport.

Keywords: Digital twin · interoperability · ontology · modeling language

1 Introduction

A Digital Twin (DT) is a digital version of a physical entity, system, or event (tangible or intangible) that can interact (sense and actuate) with the "real-world" version through the Internet-of-Things (IoT) technologies and, therefore, is a smart distributed system [1]. A DT can support decision-making through digital models for real-world problem-solving, and can be used for different purposes, such as simulation, real-time remote monitoring, predictive maintenance, risk assessment, personalized products and services. DTs are expanding beyond smart manufacturing to diverse domains like smart city, healthcare, agriculture, civil engineering, among others. Artificial Intelligence (AI) plays a crucial role in enhancing the capabilities and functionality of DTs across these various domains, contributing to DT development, operation, and analysis.

T. P. Sales et al. (Eds.): EDOC 2023 Workshops, LNBIP 498, pp. 139–157, 2024.
https://doi.org/10.1007/978-3-031-54712-6_9

Within smart systems, machinery and devices are interconnected, generating data throughout process execution. Extracted insights from this data aid in comprehending organizational occurrences and accelerating process optimization. This creates new opportunities in the whole business value chain, once lead times can be shortened and work can be performed more efficiently. Nonetheless, these interconnected networks of automated devices (sensors and actuators), and systems pose interoperability issues that are fundamental for the DTs [2].

The relation between the concepts of DT and interoperability is becoming an increasingly popular research topic. The result of a simple search for the terms in *Science Direct* shows that they were mentioned by 16 papers in 2017, 43 in 2018, jumping to 137 in 2019, 203 in 2020, 303 in 2021, and 512 in 2022. Several of these are about interoperability solutions for DTs, including literature reviews in domains like civil infrastructures [2], manufacturing [3], and smart cities [4]. Most of these reviews highlight the relevance of interoperability for successful DTs, and call for further research in interoperability and data integration for improved DTs. This research becomes even more relevant with ongoing initiatives such as (i) standardization of ontologies for Smart Systems; (ii) Digital Product Passport (DPP) [5] for implementing DTs of any products, which will be implemented from 2026 with renewable batteries[1]; and (iii) the International Data Spaces (IDS), which aims at establishing a secure and trustworthy data ecosystem for enabling international data sharing and collaboration [6].

This paper proposes a research agenda to address interoperability issues in DTs from different perspectives that reflect important fields of knowledge in computer/information science, namely architecture of distributed systems, model-based system engineering, ontology-driven conceptual modeling, and linked data with semantic web technologies. We discuss how these perspectives are relevant for improved interoperability when developing DTs, and propose a set of research directions, which are presented according to the design science methodology [7].

This paper is structured as follows. Section 2 motivates the research on DT interoperability. Section 3 covers the conceptual framework for the research agenda, structured according to the four aforementioned perspectives (fields of knowledge). Section 4 presents relevant initiatives for DTs. Section 5 presents relevant research directions that cover theoretical foundations for digital threads. Section 6 presents relevant applied research directions in the ongoing initiatives of semantic-based standardization, IDS and DPP. Section 7 concludes this paper.

2   Digital Twin Interoperability

Interoperability refers to the capability of multiple systems or components to exchange and effectively utilize shared information. Therefore, interoperability defines the way of interconnection between sensors, devices, manufacturing systems, and people, including exchange of products and materials among facilities. In particular, semantic interoperability is the most challenging because it is about the "interpretation of shared data in an unambiguously way, ensuring

---

[1] https://ec.europa.eu/commission/presscorner/detail/en/qanda_20_2311.

that the understanding of the information is the same for senders and receivers". Establishing automatic semantic interoperability for seamless systems' integration is an arduous task [8].

The core function of a DT relies on merging the virtual model with sensor data that are collected with support of IoT technologies. DT data are formalized in diverse ways, gathered from various sensors and must be integrated with other data that rely on different languages and their serialization syntax. These can vary according to the different domains and purposes, such as the Building Information Modeling (BIM) language for the construction industry [9] and the Fast Healthcare Interoperability Resources (FHIR) for healthcare [10]. This complexity elevates integration and interoperability challenges at both syntactical and semantic aspects, and in all interoperability levels: legal, organizational, semantic and technical, according to the European Interoperability Framework.

We have been working with the concepts of *digital thread*, *digital model* and *digital shadow* within the DT research [1], which involves various representations of a target system adapted for specific purposes. These representations can include digital models for static analysis or simulation of different system versions. Advances in IoT technology enable the creation of digital shadows, using real-time data for visualization. DTs take this further through a bidirectional connection to the real system, utilizing real-time data to mimic and influence the actual behavior of the system, facilitating analysis, prediction, and rapid corrective actions by integrating models from the digital thread with sensor data and system actuators. In this context, the specification artifacts covered by the architecture of distributed systems play an important role for digital threads, since they prescribe the structural and behavioral elements of the systems, such as components, data sources, and services.

3 Research Disciplines for Digital Twins

This section introduces the conceptual framework for the research agenda.

3.1 Architecture of Distributed Systems

A DT is a distributed system and requires proper **Architecture of Information System** to describe its main components, helping organizations to unify distributed IT systems, align with goals, and boost inter-organizational collaboration. This approach manages the complexity of several information systems, ensuring efficient IT support, and avoiding data silos. These characteristics are relevant for architectural patterns to address business needs within enterprise architecture (EA). In this context, middleware systems play an important role to enable the interaction among software applications via standardized communication (like RPC and messaging) to avoid point-to-point integrations that impact maintenance, performance, reliability, safety, and scalability.

This layered approach promotes modularity and easy modification, which are principles of **Service Oriented Architecture (SOA)**. SOA is a design discipline that structures software applications as a collection of services, allowing components to interact and collaborate over a network. It promotes loose coupling, reusability, and flexibility in building complex systems by encapsulating functionalities into services that can be easily accessed and combined. There are a number of as-a-service models ("XaaS") based on SOA principles, such as SaaS (for Software), iPaaS (for integration Platform) and FaaS (for function). Web Service technologies enable SOA by providing standardized protocols and formats, like SOAP and REST for communication between distributed services through Application Programming Interfaces (APIs). For example, the Open-TripModel (OTM)[2] is an open API that offers access to travel-related services and information, fostering interoperability within the logistic domain. The OTM API is an example of SOA by providing a structured interface for accessing travel-related services and their data through standardized protocols and endpoints, documented through OpenAPI Specification (OAS), so these services can be accessed and integrated independently, showcasing the key principles of loose coupling and modularity that are inherent to SOA.

Recently, the microservices architectural style has taken attention as a specialization of SOA by breaking down applications into "smaller" and independently deployable services [11]. Each microservice is responsible for a specific business capability, operating as a standalone unit with its own database and communication mechanisms, enabling organizations to evolve services more independently. Often Domain Driven Design (DDD) is used for the design of microservice architectures, supporting the modelling of business domains, often through UML class diagrams, leveraging on the concept of encapsulation around business capabilities, guiding the identification of bounded contexts and aggregates, which can ensure that microservices are designed around distinct and cohesive domain concepts.

The ArchiMate standard[3] is often used to design EA of distributed systems based on SOA due to its emphasis on the notion of services and their relations in different levels (business, application and technology). For example, the European Interoperability Reference Architecture (EIRA), a standardized framework to enhance interoperability across European public administrations - under development within the Interoperable Europe initiative[4] - is represented with ArchiMate. EIRA models provide a visual representation to illustrate structural and behavioral aspects so public organizations can implement interoperability standards effectively. Besides ArchiMate, other approaches are used to design distributed systems, most of them modeling languages. In EA research field, the topic of applying multiple modelling languages for different purposes in system engineering has been discussed for many years now (e.g., the Zachman framework) and has a relevant role in Model-Based System Engineering.

---

[2] https://www.opentripmodel.org/.
[3] https://pubs.opengroup.org/architecture/archimate3-doc/.
[4] https://joinup.ec.europa.eu/interoperable-europe.

3.2 Model-Based System Engineering

Model-Based System Engineering (MBSE) in the context of systems engineering involves employing visual models to describe, analyze, and design complex systems. An example of an MBSE approach is the Systems Modeling Language (SysML)[5], which is as a standardized notation to create graphical representations of system components, interactions, and behaviors. By utilizing SysML, engineers can enhance their understanding of system architecture, requirements, and interactions, improving interoperability through a standardized modeling language that facilitates seamless communication and collaboration. In this context, MBSE and Product Lifecycle Management (PLM) are interconnected approaches that enhance the development and management of complex products. MBSE uses system models to define, analyze, and optimize system requirements and designs, while PLM provides a framework to manage the entire lifecycle of a product, from concept and design to manufacturing, operation, and eventual retirement, with MBSE models often serving as valuable inputs and references throughout this lifecycle.

In the context of Software Engineering, Model-Driven Development (MDD) employs models as primary development artifacts, with implementations often generated automatically from these models. Model-Driven Architecture (MDA) is a subset of MDD, following the Object Management Group's (OMG) standards, while Model-Driven Software Engineering (MDSE) is a broader concept that encompasses complete software engineering processes, including tasks like model-based evolution and reverse engineering [12]. In general, MBSE plays a crucial role in enhancing interoperability among complex systems, by ensuring that all stakeholders can effectively contribute, comprehend, and align their efforts towards a coherent and interoperable system architecture. In the particular context of MDSE, we highlight the relevance of the so-called "model transformations" as Model-Driven Interoperability (MDI) solutions to define bridges between systems, aligning their metamodels through transformations while separating syntactic and semantic mappings. This approach employs projectors, acting as software for syntactic mapping, to transform models between formats. By abstracting and simplifying reality, models enable efficient analysis of domain-specific perspectives, and projectors, acting as parsers, facilitate transformations using general-purpose languages or model-to-text transformation languages.

We have been working in a particular modeling language to improve the interoperability of situation descriptions coined as Situation Modeling Language (SML) [8]. The SML is a DSL designed to model situations and events within specific contexts. SML was designed with support of ontological foundations, particularly the Unified Foundational Ontology (UFO) [13], which provides a rigorous framework for defining the foundational concepts and relationships, ensuring a solid semantic basis for representing situations and events accurately across diverse domains. This ontological approach enhances the precision, consistency, and interoperability of SML models, making it a powerful tool for capturing complex real-world scenarios and facilitating domain-specific analysis.

---

[5] https://www.omg.org/spec/SysML.

There are a number of modeling languages that are relevant for developing DTs, and some DT-specific languages and platforms are offered by vendors like Microsoft Azure, Amazon Web Services (AWS) and Eclipse, respectively Digital Twin Definition Language (DTDL), Eclipse's Vertolang, and AWS IoT TwinMaker. A recent research [14] compared the metamodel of these languages with object orientation (OO) principles as an initial step toward elucidating the essence of DT modeling. It concluded that these DT platforms rely on well-known OO principles, but also extend general-purpose concepts with features like quantities and units, besides additional constraints on performance considerations. DTDL shows a particular feature on allowing the use of domain-specific ontologies in OWL through JSON for Linked Data (JSON-LD) standard.

3.3   Linked Data and Semantic Web Technologies

The concepts of **Linked Data and Semantic Web (LDSW)** technologies enable enhanced data integration, sharing, and interpretation across diverse contexts. Linked Data principles emphasize structuring information in a standardized way, interconnecting data sources through semantic relationships, and using Uniform Resource Identifiers (URIs) for uniquely identifying resources. Linked Data fosters a web of data, enriching traditional web pages with meaningful relationships and enabling machines to better understand and process information. Semantic Web technologies, including RDF, SPARQL, and OWL, provide the foundation for formalizing, querying, and reasoning about data semantics, paving the way for more advanced applications like intelligent data analysis, knowledge graphs, and improved information discovery.

The Findable, Accessible, Interoperable, and Reusable (FAIR) data principles were conceived from the LDSW research as good practices on data management and stewardship to amplify the effectiveness of data management and reuse. The FAIR data principles prescribe good practices for enhancing data quality and accessibility that can be addressed by semantic web tools by enabling precise data representation, standardized vocabularies, and structured relationships that foster semantic interoperability and meaning. The utilization of semantic web technologies facilitate the integration of FAIR-compliant data into a linked and coherent network, unlocking the potential for more informed decision-making, advanced analytics, and knowledge discovery [15].

Besides the Interoperability principles of FAIR we also highlight the Reusable principles R1.2 regarding "detailed provenance" and R1.3 regarding "domain-relevant community standards", which are good practices that also contribute to semantic interoperability. In this context, some standardization efforts are currently applying LDSW technologies to address interoperability, such as the European semantic standard for IoT by the European Telecommunication Standardization Institute (ETSI), coined as Smart Appliances REFerence (SAREF) ontology[6], W3C standards like PROV (for provenance)[7], and domain-specific standards like the HL7 Fast Healthcare Interoperability Resources (FHIR) RDF[8].

The SAREF standard has gained traction as a standardized framework for enhancing the interoperability of smart appliances and IoT devices, being applied in several domains beyond consumer electronics, such as smart cities and industrial automation. Ongoing efforts involve extending SAREF to incorporate more advanced semantics and address the evolving requirements of diverse industries, fostering a more comprehensive and adaptable foundation for achieving seamless device integration and sustainable IoT ecosystems.

Among the various FAIR initiatives, we highlight the concept of FAIR Data Point (FDP)[9] as metadata repository that can store information about data sets in a way that the FAIR principles can be realized and data can be retrieved without requiring APIs, enabling anyone to publish their data on the web. The FDP system focuses on metadata for Findability and Reusability, and providing a uniform open method of Access. Its implementation includes three components: an API specification based on semantic metadata standards (e.g., W3C DCAT) and REST principles, a metadata registration service with an authentication system, and a web front-end client for adding, editing, and querying metadata information, aiming to enhance the interoperability and accessibility of data on the web. FDP is a relevant component of the FAIR-in-a-box [16], which also covers the RDF Mapping Language (RML)[10], which is a MDSE approach to map and implement the transformations from heterogeneous data structures and formats to RDF data sets, including relational databases and common data syntax serializations like CSV, XML, and JSON.

3.4 Ontology-Driven Conceptual Modeling

Studies suggest semantic modeling and ontologies are fundamental for data integration and interoperability in DT models [9]. Semantic modeling utilizes web-based methods to map data streams, active sensing data, and relational data into a dynamic structure of elements. Conversely, ontologies offer a formal representation of shared domain concepts. Exploring semantic data modeling giving appropriate support to sensor data, and data formalized with specific-domain standards (e.g., BIM models), and data from other systems is essential for standardizing DT data, enhancing integration and interoperability.

The concept of ontology traces back to Aristotle's theories of metaphysics, encompassing the study of fundamental categories of being and their relationships. The goal of an ontology is to represent entities, relationships, properties, and rules of a domain, addressing construct ambiguity through formal representation and automated reasoning. Ontology deals with the relationships between

---

[6] https://saref.etsi.org/core/v3.1.1/.
[7] https://www.w3.org/TR/prov-o/.
[8] https://www.hl7.org/fhir/rdf.html.
[9] https://www.fairdatapoint.org/.
[10] https://rml.io/specs/rml/.

the conceptual level, language symbols, and real-world phenomena, known as the semiotic triangle, which is a model to address problems like overloaded terminology and ambiguity in concepts, and manifestation of constructs often referring to only one interpretation. A well-defined foundational ontology categorizes fundamental concepts and relations that are usually formalized through axioms. A well-founded core or domain ontology is an ontology that is coherently grounded in a foundational ontology. This process enhances semantic interoperability while avoiding wrong representations.

We have been working with the UFO and its role in the **Ontology-Driven Conceptual Modeling (ODCM)** approach [17]. ODCM leverages traditional conceptual modelling enhanced by the ontological theories inherited in UFO, allowing the representation of reference ontologies as conceptual models described with OntoUML and operational ontologies as OWL, with gUFO[11]. ODCM is based on ontological theories in the philosophical sense, covering axiomatic theories of categories and their connections, and involves the development of languages, methodologies, and tools for the conceptual modeling discipline. ODCM relies on UFO, which is an ontological system that accurately reflects the conceptual meta-categories employed by humans to formulate their conceptualizations of reality. UFO integrates theories from Formal Ontology with Philosophy, Cognitive Science, Linguistics, and Philosophical Logics, encompassing several micro-theories that address fundamental conceptual modeling notions such as types, objects, properties, relations, and events [13].

UFO is a theoretical framework while OntoUML is the ontological language based on UFO and designed as a UML class diagram profile. An open-source OntoUML/UFO Catalog is available with an expressive number of ontologies, conceived to allow collaborative and empirical research in ODCM[12]. gUFO is the ontology (or "semantic model") based on UFO and designed as OWL. There are other "operational ontologies" based on UFO implemented according to other specific technologies, such as relational database system (through SQL statements) and Data Warehousing cubes (through multidimensional modeling) [18]. A complete toolset to support OntoUML/UFO is available and leverages on existing software systems, in particular the Visual Paradigm through a plug-in that enables users to design OntoUML models, visually verify and validate them and automatically generate gUFO/OWL ontologies[13] through MDSE transformations.

ODCM stands out for its potential on improving the "real" semantics of these operational ontologies (no matter the specific technology) from the conceptual phase of Software Engineering. In particular, if the aimed software is a LDSW application (based on standards like RDF and OWL) then following an Ontology Engineering methodology is recommended. There are a number of Ontology Engineering methods, and we have been using the Systematic Approach for Building Ontologies (SABiO) for over a decade now [19]. SABiO

---

[11] https://nemo-ufes.github.io/gufo/.
[12] https://github.com/OntoUML/ontouml-models.
[13] https://github.com/OntoUML/ontouml-vp-plugin.

is designed to facilitate the systematic construction of ontologies and emphasizes efficiency and clarity improvement, providing a step-by-step framework that guides designers (or "ontologists") through the life-cycle, from conceptualization (through ODCM) to implementation, similar to Software Engineering methodologies. Because of the use of ODCM, SABiO ensures that ontologies are developed coherently and align with established standards, such as the aforementioned from LDSW (e.g., RDF, OWL). Through systematic practices and leveraging its structured methodology, SABiO can enhance the interoperability of ontologies, contributing to improved knowledge representation.

One particular research direction that we have been working in applying ODCM that is quite relevant for DTs is on Explanibale AI (XAI), where we applied the ontological analysis approach over a Machine Learning (ML) ontology (MLSchema) [19]. ML-based AI applications show promise in diverse fields, but require large, high-quality training data sets, which are often manually labeled, time-consuming, and error-prone. Researchers suggest leveraging DTs to accelerate ML training by generating and labeling synthetic data sets through simulation, supplemented by real-world data for validation. Several DT initiatives incorporate AI to enhance decision-making and coordination. We have developed the first UFO-based ontology crossing the bridge to the XAI world, implementing and validating the approach with popular tools on explainable ML, like LIME and Jupyter Notebook.

4   Relevant Initiatives for Digital Twins

This section covers three relevant initiatives for the proposed research agenda.

4.1   Semantic-Based Standards for Smart Systems

These technologies facilitate seamless integration through improved interoperability across diverse platforms and applications, which is a core requirement of an Industry 4.0 architecture. An Industry 4.0 architecture is characterized by the extensive use of the IoT standards and technologies, supporting the interconnection of devices to collect vast amounts of data, which are processed and analyzed using AI and big data analytic technologies to make real-time decisions and optimize processes. An Industry 4.0 architecture also emphasizes cyber-physical systems, where physical processes are closely integrated with digital systems, enabling automation and control. SOA plays a major role in Industry 4.0 architecture by ensuring interoperability, modularity, and scalability. It is worthwhile to mention that the Industry 5.0 concept is a further enhancement of the Industry 4.0 concept that emphasizes the collaboration between humans and machines in a sustainable way, integrating human skills and creativity with advanced technologies to create more flexible and adaptive manufacturing systems. While Industry 4.0 is more machine-centric, emphasizing automation and machine-to-machine communication, Industry 5.0 is more human-centered, aiming to balance between automation and human intervention.

We have been working in several research directions across the aforementioned disciplines, and here we highlight the main ongoing initiatives. In the context of the aforementioned disciplines, we have been working in the "SEmantic Model-driven development for IoT Interoperability of emergenCy serviceS" (SEMIoTICS) framework, which can be used to develop interoperable IoT-based Early Warning Systems (IoT-EWS) for different application domains, enabling an IoT-EWS to act as a cloud-based semantic broker for emergency decision support. SEMIoTICS is leveraged by the adoption of ontology-driven conceptual modelling and is based on the ontological analysis of the Situation Aware theory, taking into account the FAIR data principles, in which the role of using standards is emphasized. SEMIoTICS framework was validated in a case study that covered the detection of health issues and accidents with truck drivers, resulting in the extension of the European semantic standard for IoT, the SAREF ontology, with the representation of ECG data, coined as SAREF4health [8]. This extension focused in the concept of time series, which was latter adopted by the standard as the extension of SAREF for e-Health and Aging Well (SAREF4ehaw)[14]. In the health domain, it is relevant to highlight the role of FHIR as the evolution of the HL7 standards, which RDF version is also under improvements with the participation of W3C members.

4.2   International Data Spaces

A relevant ongoing initiative is the International Data Space (IDS). The International Data Spaces (IDS), led by the International Data Spaces Association (IDSA), aims at establishing a secure and trustworthy data ecosystem for enabling data sharing and collaboration. The IDSA is a global network of organizations that collaboratively work towards the development and implementation of IDS. IDS promotes the use of decentralized architectures, standardized data models, and secure data exchange protocols to ensure data sovereignty, privacy, and trust. By adhering to the principles of data sovereignty and secure data exchange, the IDS framework facilitates seamless and controlled sharing of data across different organizations, sectors, and countries.

We've been working in collaboration with IDSA, addressing research needs related to IDS. Recently, an IDS Connector Store was developed [6] as a broker system to facilitate the discovery and selection of IDS Connectors, data sources, as well as participants active in a data space. This led to the definition of an IDS architecture (in ArchiMate) that covers the main IDS goals, which is being adopted by the EIRA. This architecture is extensible for the definition of specific elements of the IDS ecosystem, such as for the Clearing House process, which involves service termination, data policy conciliation, and contract settlement; and the Interoperability Simulator, an approach that enables the measurement of associated costs of data interoperability scenarios, being able to simulate data exchange, and assess the information gap between the data consumer's requirements and the data provided.

---

[14] https://saref.etsi.org/saref4ehaw/.

4.3   Digital Product Passports

Meanwhile, the European Commission (EC) is putting forward the concept of Digital Product Passport (DPP) as a means to enhance transparency and promote circularity by sharing product information throughout the entire product lifecycle. The main idea of the DPP is to enable the implementation a DT of any product, tracking all associated information of the product, from the idea to the consumer and the end of life. The first list of product groups (renewable batteries) shall comply with the DPP specification from 2026. The DPP will contribute to decoupling economic growth from resource extraction, waste generation, and carbon emissions, thereby making a significant positive impact for sustainability. The DPP is a groundbreaking circularity approach, but aspects such as scope, technology infrastructure, and data governance are still under development [5]. Interoperability is a fundamental concept for DPP, since interoperability and sustainability are interconnected concepts, which is highlighted by the Industry 5.0 concept, in particular within manufacturing and supply chain contexts. Sustainable supply chain operations depend on the interoperability of activities and processes, and without interoperability, supply chains cannot be truly sustainable. Some research highlights that proper interoperability reduces costs and boosts productivity, contributing to the economic aspect of sustainability [20].

5   Research Directions in Digital Threads

The main goal of this research agenda is to improve the technical interoperability of DTs with emphasis on the syntactic and semantic aspects. This section highlights open issues on foundations of digital threads through four directions: the development of a well-founded DT core ontology, the application of well-founded domain ontologies for DTs, the systematic use of multiple modeling languages as specification artefacts, and the general problem of ontology reuse.

5.1   Well-Founded Digital Twin Core Ontology

An open issue is the lack of a reference (core) ontology grounded in a foundational ontology (such as UFO) of the DT concept, exploiting the main structural and behavioral aspects, and therefore, describing precisely what is (and what is not) an DT. Since IoT is a fundamental concept of DTs, this core ontology should leverage on the many existing IoT ontologies, and in particular the ones that are standardized, such as SAREF. Our previous research showed that a complete ontological analysis of SAREF is required to improve its semantics [8]. Grounding SAREF in UFO can be performed through gUFO and executed through the systematized approach on inferring ontological categories from OWL [21]. Besides grounding SAREF in gUFO, it is relevant to provide ontology alignments with the current version of SAREF and its extensions, as well as covering other standardized IoT ontologies such as SSN/SOSA, making sure to cover the foundational elements such as actuators (*saref:Actuator*) and their costs through profiles (*saref:Profile*). These alignments can be implemented as semantic translations and their validation should cover their semantic completeness in different application domains.

Developing this well-founded DT core ontology becomes even more challenging as AI plays a role in the concept of DT, which implies a need on defining what is (artificial or non-artificial) intelligence, which is a well-known challenge in computer science. This ontology would have a clear connection to the XAI ontology that we have been working on [19]. An interesting direction to approach the diverse explainability dimensions is to leverage on the recent work on the ontological analysis of explanations [22,23], which introduces the concept of "ontological unpacking" based on the ODCM approach.

Since perdurant notions such as situation and event are core aspects of the perceived reality, their formalization in UFO has a potential impact on the well-founded DT core ontology. To achieve this, a deeper ontological analysis on theoretical foundations and formalization of situation awareness theory are required. For example, the use of the Situoid theory along with an epidemiological causality model (e.g., the Bradford Hill Criteria) can be relevant for representing causation relationships between situations and events, which can be leveraged by the work on scene representations in UFO [24].

5.2   Ontology-Driven Digital Twins

In the domain of smart healthcare, we are currently investigating how to provide a systematic way of improving IoT interoperability for e-Health in scenarios where different ontologies are used. In particular, we are extending SAREF4ehaw with medical terms from the SNOMED CT ontology [25]. As output of this research, we identified that the SAREF4ehaw ontology requires further work, as empirically validating it against other ontologies such as the FHIR RDF, which is quite relevant towards higher semantic interoperability within e-Health. Besides validating, new ontology alignments between SAREF4ehaw and FHIR RDF standards are required, evaluating them in scenarios where these semantic artefacts play different roles. Furthermore, an ontological analysis of FHIR standard based on UFO, perhaps grounding the FHIR RDF version in gUFO/OWL (similar to SAREF) can improve FHIR semantic expressivity and correctness, besides helping to identify the mappings for the semantic translations' rules [26].

In general, this kind of approach can actually be applied over the main domain-specific standards that have a close relation to IoT, as the FIWARE Smart Data Models[15], and even if the standard is not based on RDF/OWL. For example, for the logistics domain, an ontological analysis of the OTM can result in improved interoperability for logistics systems. The semantic mappings and their respective translations can be realized with RML, which enables the development of transformation mappings from the JSON model of the OTM API to the OTM operational ontology in gUFO/OWL. Within this context, align-

---

[15] https://www.fiware.org/smart-data-models/.

ments of OTM with other traditional data models, such as EDIFACT[16], is quite relevant to demonstrate how data exchange can happen with legacy systems.

5.3 Multiple Modeling Languages as Specification Artefacts

Besides domain specific standards, the ontological analysis approach is also relevant for improving the interoperability of general purpose modelling languages used in well-established fields like Enterprise Architecture (e.g., through ArchiMate), Business Process (e.g., BPMN), Business Modelling (e.g., through e3-value), System Engineering (eg., through SysML), Data Warehousing (e.g., through MDX), and domain specific ones (but still general within the domain), such as in Construction Engineering (e.g., through BIM). All these modeling languages have their specific purposes for representing systems' characteristics, and therefore, play a pivotal role as modeling languages of the artefacts that compose digital threads. Using multiple languages in a systematic and consistent way for the specification of information systems is an old challenge, which is still open in the MBSE field, and is even challenging within MDSE, i.e., for automatic generating the technology-specific implementation artefacts. Research has shown that this consistency among modelling languages can be supported through the ODCM approach where a foundational ontology (in particular UFO) serves as a "single-source of truth".

The SEMIoTICS framework guides the use of three specific languages for IoT-EWS specification: OntoUML for context modeling, SML for situation identification modeling, and BPMN for situation reaction modeling. These are agnostic from the implementation technology. Models represented with these three languages can then be used to generate operational languages through MDSE transformations, like gUFO/OWL, Java ESPER (event processing language), and jBPM (business processes automation) respectively. The implementation of architectural decisions can also be automated, for example from the EA, DDD and OAS models, which can than be transformed into microservices (REST endpoints) that expose the data interfaces with JSON-LD serialization of gUFO/OWL. Future work comprises the improvement and further validation of SML by implementing and comparing new MDSE transformations for different Complex Event Procesing (CEP) technologies, such as cloud- and fog-based stream analytics. In particular, we identified the need of developing transformations for the SIMPLE platform, covering patterns adopted in the Scene approach [24], such as aggregation functions and boolean operators for composing comparative relations.

5.4 General Problem of Ontology Reuse

Ontology reuse is a quite relevant topic within the field of ontology engineering and still represents a significant challenge. Inefficient ontology reuse results in redundant efforts, as ontology engineers are forced sometimes to reinvent the

---

[16] https://unece.org/trade/uncefact/introducing-unedifact.

wheel, expending valuable time and resources. This leads to a waste of intellectual capital and financial investments, hindering technological progress. Among the main issues, ontologies are often domain-specific, and developed to capture knowledge within a particular context or industry. This specificity means that reusing an ontology from one domain in another may require extensive modifications, potentially rendering the reuse effort inefficient and time-consuming. The failure to address the challenges of ontology reuse not only impedes technological advancements but also has far-reaching societal and economic repercussions by inhibiting efficient knowledge sharing and stifling innovation.

Ontologies are typically created by different individuals or groups with varying points of view, leading to disparities in structure, naming conventions, and modeling choices. These inconsistencies make seamless integration and reuse across ontologies a complex task. In addition, evolving technologies and changing domain-specific requirements can either render existing ontologies obsolete or require new versions, necessitating continuous updates and adaptations for reuse, further complicating ontology management and governance. Although several research and innovation initiatives fostered the standardization of ontological frameworks and the definition of good practices, the lack of a proper ontology reuse methodology still causes misunderstandings and miscommunications within and across industries, potentially compromising interoperability and integration. A promising approach is likewise the proposed for grounding SAREF in gUFO/OWL within the well-founded DT core ontology, which can be (semi) automatically inferred from OWL.

6 Applied Research in Data Spaces and Sustainability

In this section we highlight relevant research directions related to DTs.

6.1 Architectural Patterns for Data Spaces

Previous research already showed how applying ontological analysis is relevant to improve the semantics of ArchiMate, either via patterns or extensions, such as on capabilities [27], trust [28], security [29], services [30] and contracts [31]. These aspects also reflect requirements from IDS and DPP specifications, and applying the proposed ArchiMate patterns and extensions is a research that can help validating and improving them, as well as improving the specifications of the IDS architecture. For example, we are working with the IDS clearing house architecture, which involves service termination, a phase that is not covered by the ArchiMate patterns on service lifecycle [30]. For service modeling, it seems quite relevant to analyse the matamodel behind DDD, which is used for modelling microservices' architectures and is implemented as a UML profile. Since ArchiMate is often used to design IT landscapes based on SOA principles, an important research is the integration between ArchiMate and DDD, whether concepts of DDD could be incorporated (or merged) within ArchiMate and/or MDSE transformations could support their interoperability. In this context, understanding how ontologies can support the definition of the granularity level of microservices, in addition to DDD, is a topic that requires further investigation.

Within IDS context, our current work with the Interoperability Simulator and the Data Exchange component (for data transfer) still miss the use of ontologies and semantic web technologies, which can be addressed by ontology matching techniques such as semantic translations. We have been working with a methodology for developing semantic translations that is time-consuming for numerous TBox elements, since it is descriptive and depends on experts. Therefore, future work should balance quality improvement with automation on automatic development of semantic translations. Additionally, comparing the SPARQL approach and IPSM approach may be exploited with other methods like ShEx and SHACL. Exploiting other ontology matching techniques besides semantics translations is also a relevant direction in this research.

Finally, we also identified an open issue with IDS architecture on representing how to measure the economic feasibility of IDS adoption through different business models, and mechanisms for transparent and fair cost-gain sharing. We see a relevant connection between the concepts of a data space (IDS) and a product passport (IDS), where both call for using standards and open platforms such as SAREF, the FIWARE IoT platform along with its Smart Data Models, the OTM API for logistics, and other domain-specific open models.

6.2 Data Provenance for Product Passports

We identified a clear connection of our work on product provenance for value networks [32] with the DPP requirements on tracking product information throughout the whole product lifecycle. This raises interesting research questions on how to enable PLM platforms to implement the DPP requirements, and how to model value exchange of digital product provenance in value networks, using and improving languages like e3-value and ArchiMate with support of reference ontologies. A related research direction is the ontological analysis of open and proprietary data models of PLM platform, investigating data interfaces of REST endpoints of API-based PLM platforms like Contact Software[17]. We believe that developing digital threads of smart products can benefit from the alignment of PLM practices with Application Lifecycle Management (ALM).

Reproducibility is highly relevant in PLM as it ensures that processes and results can be accurately replicated over time. This is crucial for maintaining product quality, consistency, and compliance throughout various stages of the lifecycle, contributing to efficient production, improved decision-making, and regulatory adherence. Workflow and protocol systems play a pivotal role in enhancing reproducibility by providing structured and standardized procedures. We identified in our previous work on FAIR protocols and workflows [33] the

---

[17] https://www.contact-software.com/.

need of improving the interoperability of such systems by performing ontological analysis and integrating tools like Protocols.io and MyExperiment.org. In addition, the integration between such workflow systems with data management plans and research data repositories showed to be challenging, requiring further research. Reproducibility of workflows is important for DTs to ensure consistent and reliable simulations, allowing for accurate modeling, analysis, and prediction of real-world systems and behaviors.

7 Conclusion

This paper proposes a research agenda that aims to enhance DT interoperability by addressing theoretical foundations and practical research aspects. The research agenda is based on a conceptual framework that combines theories and approaches from four computer (and information) science disciplines: architecture of distributed systems, model-based system engineering, ontology-driven conceptual modeling, and linked data with semantic web technologies. We argue that these disciplines contribute to different levels and aspects of interoperability and can be combined to address open issues in DT research. We also discuss three relevant initiatives for DTs: (i) Standardization of ontologies for Smart Systems; (ii) International Data Spaces; and (iii) Digital Product Passports.

We propose a set of six research directions classified as (a) foundations for digital threads, and (b) applied research. Within foundations, we discuss the relevance of developing a well-founded DT core ontology, improving DTs with well-founded domain ontologies, systematically using multiple modeling languages as specification artefacts, and the general problem of ontology reuse. Within applied research, we discuss the possibilities on architectural patterns for Data Spaces, and data provenance for Product Passports. These directions cover topics like Explainable AI, situation awareness theories, IoT interoperability, and modelling languages for Enterprise Architecture (e.g., ArchiMate, DDD) and System Engineering (e.g., SysML). Lastly, the relevance of reproducibility in PLM is emphasized, and the integration of workflow and protocol systems to enhance reproducibility in DTs is explored, with an emphasis on their importance in ensuring consistent and reliable simulations for accurate modeling and prediction of real-world systems. In general, we argue that the semantics of a foundational ontology should be used for improved DT interoperability.

References

1. Pessoa, M.V.P., Pires, L.F., Moreira, J.L.R., Wu, C.: Model-based digital threads for socio-technical systems. In: Marques, G., Gonzalez-Briones, A., Molina Lopez, J.M. (eds.) Machine Learning for Smart Environments/Cities. Intelligent Systems Reference Library, vol. 121, pp. 27–52. Springer, Cham (2022). ISBN 978-3-030-97516-6. https://doi.org/10.1007/978-3-030-97516-6_2
2. Naderi, H., Shojaei, A.: Digital twinning of civil infrastructures: current state of model architectures, interoperability solutions, and future prospects. Autom. Constr. **149** (2023). ISSN 0926–5805. https://doi.org/10.1016/j.autcon.2023.104785

3. Böttjer, T., et al.: A review of unit level digital twin applications in the manufacturing industry. CIRP J. Manuf. Sci. Technol. **45**, 162–189 (2023). ISSN 1755–5817. https://doi.org/10.1016/j.cirpj.2023.06.011

4. Jeddoub, I., Nys, G.A., Hajji, R., Billen, R.: Digital twins for cities: analyzing the gap between concepts and current implementations with a specific focus on data integration. Int. J. Appl. Earth Obs. Geoinf. **122** (2023). ISSN 1569–8432. https://doi.org/10.1016/j.jag.2023.103440

5. Walden, J., Steinbrecher, A., Marinkovic, M.: Digital product passports as enabler of the circular economy. Chem. Ing. Tech. **93**(11), 1717–1727 (2021). https://doi.org/10.1002/cite.202100121

6. Firdausy, D.R., de Alencar Silva, P., van Sinderen, M., Iacob, M.E.: A data connector store for international data spaces. In: Sellami, M., Ceravolo, P., Reijers, H.A., Gaaloul, W., Panetto, H. (eds.) Cooperative Information Systems. CoopIS 2022. LNCS, vol. 13591, pp. 242–258. Springer, Cham (2022). ISBN 978-3-031-17834-4. https://doi.org/10.1007/978-3-031-17834-4_14

7. Wieringa, R.J.: The Design Cycle, pp. 27–34. Springer, Berlin, Heidelberg (2014). ISBN 978-3-662-43839-8. https://doi.org/10.1007/978-3-662-43839-8_3

8. Moreira, J., Pires, L.F., Van Sinderen, M., Daniele, L., Girod-Genet, M.: Saref4health: towards IoT standard-based ontology-driven cardiac e-health systems. Appl. Ontol. **15**(3), 385–410 (2020). ISSN 1570–5838. https://doi.org/10.3233/AO-200232

9. Tuhaise, V.V., Tah, J.H.M., Abanda, F.H.: Technologies for digital twin applications in construction. Autom. Constr. **152**, 104931 (2023). ISSN 0926–5805. https://doi.org/10.1016/j.autcon.2023.104931

10. Gaebel, J., Keller, J., Schneider, D., Lindenmeyer, A., Neumuth, T., Franke, S.: The digital twin: modular model-based approach to personalized medicine. Curr. Dir. Biomed. Eng. **7**(2), 223–226 (2021). https://doi.org/10.1515/cdbme-2021-2057

11. Richardson, C.: Benefits and drawbacks of the microservice architecture. Manning Publications (2017). ISBN 978-1617294549

12. Brambilla, M., Cabot, J., Wimmer, M.: MDSE Principles. In: Model-Driven Software Engineering in Practice. SLSE. Springer, Cham (2017). ISBN 978-3-031-02549-5. https://doi.org/10.1007/978-3-031-02549-5_2

13. Guizzardi, G., Botti Benevides, A., Fonseca, C.M., Porello, D., Almeida, J.P.A., Prince Sales, T.: UFO: unified foundational ontology. Appl. Ontol. **17**(1), 167–210 (2022). https://doi.org/10.3233/AO-210256

14. Pfeiffer, J., Lehner, D., Wortmann, A., Wimmer, M.: Modeling capabilities of digital twin platforms - old wine in new bottles? J. Object Technol. **21**(3), 3:1–14 (2022). ISSN 1660–1769. https://doi.org/10.5381/jot.2022.21.3.a10. The 18th European Conference on Modelling Foundations and Applications (ECMFA 2022)

15. Guizzardi, G.: Ontology, ontologies and the I of FAIR. Data Intell. **2**(1–2), 181–191 (2020). ISSN 2641–435X. https://doi.org/10.1162/dint_a_00040

16. Benhamed, O.M., et al.: The FAIR data point: interfaces and tooling. Data Intell. **5**(1), 184–201 (2023). ISSN 2641–435X. https://doi.org/10.1162/dint_a_00161

17. Sales, T.P., et al.: A fair catalog of ontology-driven conceptual models. Data Knowl. Eng. (2023). ISSN 0169–023X. https://doi.org/10.1016/j.datak.2023.102210

18. Moreira, J., Cordeiro, K., Campos, M.L., Borges, M.: Ontowarehousing – multidimensional design supported by a foundational ontology: a temporal perspective. In: Bellatreche, L., Mohania, M.K. (eds.) Data Warehousing and Knowledge Discovery. DaWaK 2014. LNCS, vol. 8646, pp. 35–44. Springer, Cham (2014). ISBN 978-3-319-10160-6. https://doi.org/10.1007/978-3-319-10160-6_4

19. Nakagawa, P.I., Pires, L.F., Moreira, J.L.R., Bonino da Silva Santos, L.O., Bukhsh, F.: Semantic description of explainable machine learning workflows for improving trust. Appl. Sci. **11**(22) (2021). ISSN 2076-3417. https://doi.org/10.3390/app112210804. https://www.mdpi.com/2076-3417/11/22/10804

20. Yadav, G., Kumar, A., Luthra, S., Garza-Reyes, J.A., Kumar, V., Batista, L.: A framework to achieve sustainability in manufacturing organisations of developing economies using industry 4.0 technologies' enablers. Comput. Ind. (2020). ISSN 0166-3615. https://doi.org/10.1016/j.compind.2020.103280

21. Barcelos, P.P.F., et al.: Inferring ontological categories of owl classes using foundational rules. In: 13th International Conference on Formal Ontology in Information Systems (FOIS 2023) (2023)

22. Guizzardi, G., Guarino, N.: Semantics, ontology and explanation. CoRR, abs/2304.11124 (2023). https://doi.org/10.48550/arXiv.2304.11124

23. Romanenko, E., Calvanese, D., Guizzardi, G.: Towards pragmatic explanations for domain ontologies. In: Corcho, O., Hollink, L., Kutz, O., Troquard, N., Ekaputra, F.J. (eds.) Knowledge Engineering and Knowledge Management. EKAW 2022. LNCS, vol. 13514, pp. 201–208. Springer, Cham (2022). ISBN 978-3-031-17105-5. https://doi.org/10.1007/978-3-031-17105-5_15

24. Almeida, J.P.A., Costa, P.D., Guizzardi, G.: Towards an ontology of scenes and situations. In: Rogova, G.L., Lebiere, C., Gundersen, O.E., Salfinger, A., Baclawski, K. (eds.), IEEE Conference on Cognitive and Computational Aspects of Situation Management, CogSIMA 2018, Boston, MA, USA, 11–14 June 2018, pp. 29–35. IEEE (2018). https://doi.org/10.1109/COGSIMA.2018.8423994

25. de Souza, P.L., et al.: Ontology-driven IoT system for monitoring hypertension. In: Proceedings of the 25th International Conference on Enterprise Information Systems - Volume 1: ICEIS, pp. 757–767. INSTICC, SciTePress (2023). ISBN 978-989-758-648-4. https://doi.org/10.5220/0011989100003467

26. Trojahn, C., Vieira, R., Schmidt, D., Pease, A., Guizzardi, G.: Foundational ontologies meet ontology matching: a survey. Semant. Web **13**(4), 685–704 (2022). https://doi.org/10.3233/SW-210447

27. Azevedo, C.L., Iacob, M.E., Almeida, J.P.A., van Sinderen, M., Pires, L.F., Guizzardi, G.: Modeling resources and capabilities in enterprise architecture: a well-founded ontology-based proposal for archimate. Inf. Syst. **54**, 235–262 (2015). https://doi.org/10.1016/j.is.2015.04.008

28. Amaral, G., Sales, T.P., Guizzardi, G., Almeida, J.P.A., Porello, D.: Modeling trust in enterprise architecture: a pattern language for ArchiMate. In: Grabis, J., Bork, D. (eds.) The Practice of Enterprise Modeling. PoEM 2020. LNBIP, vol. 400, pp. 73–89. Springer, Cham (2020). https://doi.org/10.1007/978-3-030-63479-7_7

29. Oliveira, I., Sales, T.P., Almeida, J.P.A., Baratella, R., Fumagalli, M., Guizzardi, G.: Ontological analysis and redesign of security modeling in ArchiMate. In: Barn, B.S., Sandkuhl, K. (eds.) The Practice of Enterprise Modeling. PoEM 2022. LNBIP, vol. 456, pp. 82–98. Springer, Cham (2022). https://doi.org/10.1007/978-3-031-21488-2_6

30. Nardi, J.C., et al.: Service commitments and capabilities across the archimate architectural layers. In: 2016 IEEE 20th International Enterprise Distributed Object Computing Workshop (EDOCW), pp. 1–10 (2016). https://doi.org/10.1109/EDOCW.2016.7584386

31. Griffo, C., Almeida, J.P.A., Guizzardi, G., Nardi, J.C.: Service contract modeling in enterprise architecture: an ontology-based approach. Inf. Syst. **101**, 101454 (2021). https://doi.org/10.1016/j.is.2019.101454

32. Saraiva, L., Silva, P., Castro, A., Ribeiro, C., Moreira, J.: Ontology of product provenance for value networks. In: Nurcan, S., Opdahl, A.L., Mouratidis, H., Tsohou, A. (eds.) Research Challenges in Information Science: Information Science and the Connected World. RCIS 2023. LNBIP, vol. 476, pp. 577–584. Springer, Cham (2023). ISBN 978-3-031-33080-3. https://doi.org/10.1007/978-3-031-33080-3_40

33. Celebi, R., et al.: Towards FAIR protocols and workflows: the openpredict use case. PeerJ Comput. Sci. **6**, e281 (2020). https://doi.org/10.7717/peerj-cs.281

From Digital Tracks to Digital Twins: On the Path to Cross-Platform Profile Linking

Sergej Schultenkämper[1(✉)], Frederik S. Bäumer[1], Benjamin Bellgrau[2], Yeong Su Lee[2], and Michaela Geierhos[2]

[1] Bielefeld University of Applied Sciences and Arts, Bielefeld, Germany
{sergej.schultenkaemper,frederik.baeumer}@hsbi.de
[2] University of the Bundeswehr Munich, Research Institute CODE, Neubiberg, Germany
{benjamin.bellgrau,yeongsu.lee,michaela.geierhos}@unibw.de

Abstract. In recent years, many studies have focused on correlating the profiles of real users across different social media. On the one hand, this provides a better overview of the user's social behavior; on the other hand, it can be used to warn of possible abuse through identity theft or cyberbullying. We try to make the threat on the Web predictable for the individual user by creating digital twins. To do this, it is important to use different data sources and to merge overlapping data across platforms. In this paper, we show that YouTube is a suitable entry point into the online social network for making connections between platforms, tracking user activity across platforms, and finally merging the collected profile information into an overall picture, the digital twin.

Keywords: Profile Matching · Identity Linkage · Social Media

1 Introduction

In 2023, the average number of social media platforms that Internet users aged 16 to 64 actively use per month worldwide is 6.7, according to DataReportal [9]. Different online social networks (OSNs) have their own characteristics and services. As a result, users use their platforms to share different types of information with each other. For example, Instagram is used for uploading photos and videos, while Facebook is a platform for communication and information sharing between friends. As a result, the information available and the description of each user differs from one social network to another. By linking users in different OSNs, it is possible to create very comprehensive profiles of users, reconstructing their overall profile and behavior, as well as their preferences, activities and network of friends. In the area of cybercrime, such as cyberbullying or the spread of fake news, the digital footprint can be used to track and target such users and create digital twins (DTs) [7].

T. P. Sales et al. (Eds.): EDOC 2023 Workshops, LNBIP 498, pp. 158–171, 2024.
https://doi.org/10.1007/978-3-031-54712-6_10

In order to develop preventive methods to detect digital traces, it is necessary to answer the following key question: How can an account in one OSN x be correlated with an account in another OSN y? However, there are three main challenges: (1) heterogeneity of data in different social media, (2) low data quality, and (3) lack of information in one or another social media [21]. Since there are so many different OSNs, another challenge is to select the relevant platforms and weight the available information. All these considerations are part of the ADRIAN (Authority-Dependent Risk Identification and Analysis in online Networks) project, which is dedicated to the research and development of AI-based methods for detecting potential threats to individuals based on online datasets [7].

The paper shows which platforms can be used to create DTs and what data is available. In addition, we will analyze the connectivity between the OSNs and show which network is suitable to be used as an entry point. For this purpose, we discuss related work in Sect. 2. We then describe the concept and the research objective in Sect. 3.1, before giving an overview of the collected data in Sect. 3.2 and presenting our analysis in Sect. 3.3. Finally, we discuss our findings in Sect. 4 and draw our conclusions in Sect. 5.

2 Related Work

In this section, we discuss the notion of DTs in the context of cyber threats and present related work on social engineering and user profile matching.

2.1 Digital Twins in the Context of Cyber Threats

DT is an ambiguous term and is used in different areas of research and practice. It can be found in the fields of mechanical engineering, medicine and computer science [3,7].

For us, there are three relevant levels of integration for DTs [3]: (a) *Digital Model*, (b) *Digital Shadow*, and (c) *Digital Twin*. A Digital Model is the basic representation of a physical object or system in the virtual world, without any automatic flow of information between the virtual and physical worlds. Changes to the physical object must be manually updated in the digital model. A Digital Shadow goes further and involves a unidirectional automatic flow of information from the physical world to the virtual world. Sensors measure information from the physical model and transmit signals to the virtual model. A full DT exists when the virtual and physical environments communicate bidirectionally, with information flowing automatically between both environments. This allows the DT to accurately reflect the current state and evolution of its physical counterpart. However, the situation is different when looking at sociotechnical systems. They include both human and machine components, making it relevant to explore the notion of a Human DT [11]. Despite its growing importance, there is no consensus on a standard definition or understanding of this concept [12]. The digital data available about individuals is often referred to as *Digital Footprint* or *Digital Representation*, with the two terms often used interchangeably. These terms refer to data left by users on the Internet, often unknowingly and without clear identification or association with the individual. To differentiate the concepts of *Digital Footprint*, *Digital Shadow*, and *Digital Twin*, several aspects can be considered, such as identifiability, active or passive data collection, individualized or aggregated evaluation, real-time or later analysis, decision-making authority, and comprehensive representation [11]. The Human DT aims to store and analyze relevant characteristics of an individual for a specific situation. This may include demographic or physiological data, skill or activity profiles, or health status [11].

In the ADRIAN project, we understand the term DT as the digital representation of a real person instantiated by information available on the Web [5,7]. In this context, the DT can never reflect the full complexity of a real person, but reproduces characteristics that, alone or in combination with other characteristics, may pose a threat to the real person [4]. In this way, the DT makes it possible to model and measure a person's vulnerability. The modeling of DTs is based on established and freely available Semantic Web standards such as Schema.org and FOAF (Friend of a Friend). This makes it easy to connect and extend DTs.

2.2   Social Engineering: Criminal Exploitation of Available Data

This section explores the field of social engineering, focusing on how data extracted from social media platforms can be manipulated for such purposes. Recent research underscores the urgency for increased awareness and security in social media interactions by highlighting a range of methods and tools that demonstrate the ease with which sensitive information can be collected.

An important study is the Robin Sage Experiment [23], which created a fictitious social media persona to demonstrate the ease of gathering confidential information from military and government contacts. This experiment highlighted the alarming vulnerabilities inherent in social networks. Another notable development [16] was the automation of social engineering through bots. The bots were designed to build trust with potential victims on social networking sites, and then trick them into clicking on malicious links or revealing sensitive information. The evolving nature of online threats is underscored by the sophistication of these bots.

In addition, in the area of targeted attacks, Seymour and Tully [24] explored the use of data science to create personalized spear phishing attacks on Twitter. Their research demonstrated the ability to efficiently distribute large volumes of phishing messages, underscoring the growing risks of personalized cyberattacks. This shows that even large amounts of data are not a challenge to process, but rather a treasure trove of information. This is also shown by Labuschagne et al.'s study [18], who analyzed user comments for social engineering purposes. Using language analysis tools, attackers can identify emotional states and character traits, facilitating the creation of emotionally resonant and manipulative messages. This highlights how psychological profiling can be weaponized in social engineering. Lastly, speaking of large amounts of data, the exploitation of geolocation data in social networks poses significant privacy risks [13]. The creation of detailed movement profiles from geolocation features in social networks demonstrates the depth of personal information that can be mined from these platforms.

The research highlights the need for enhanced privacy and security measures to be implemented on social media platforms. Vigilant and informed user behavior, as well as robust security protocols from social media companies, are required due to the sophistication and variety of social engineering techniques that leverage social media data. Our strategies for mitigating the risks of social engineering must evolve as well.

2.3   Matching User Profiles Across Social Media

The approaches presented so far for profile matching in social media are mainly based on public user profile information and observable user behavior.

OSN users disclose a range of personal information in their profiles that can be used to uniquely identify specific individuals. These attributes are usually openly available and can be retrieved through the platform's APIs [1].

Traditional string matching methods are used to match this data. These include three main approaches: (i) phonetic encoding, (ii) pattern matching, and (iii) token-based comparisons [26]. Most studies focus on user names. Thus, only user and display names in different social media were compared to match the profiles of a user [20]. It has been shown that accuracy drops drastically when there is only a small difference in display names on different OSNs [2]. Another approach is based on the observation that most users have certain patterns in how they generate their display names. Therefore, the degree of similarity between the two names is calculated [28]. Other works consider additional features besides usernames.

For example, content information such as the timing of posts or profile/status updates, places visited, etc. [14] can be used to infer user behavior and movements, in addition to analyzing the language and writing style used in posts as a starting point for recognition. For profile matching, Xing et al. [29] developed a two-stage scoring method based on the information entropy to assign a weight to each attribute. Furthermore, Halimi et al. [15] calculated the similarity between location, gender, activities, interests, and also profile photos. With the help of face recognition, profile pictures can also be used for profile matching [25].

Graph-based approaches look at the underlying graph structure of social media. In addition, they analyze a user's network and merge it using similarity measures. Therefore, a user's friend relationships in different OSNs are analyzed and profile matching is performed using user characteristics as well as profile pictures and friend relationships [8,17,19,21,22,27]. While Kasbekar et al. [17] used the graph structure of OSNs as well as features such as username and profile picture to detect friend relationships, Müngen et al. [22] addressed the network alignment and similarity problem using both user profile features and their relationships with other users. Bennacer et al. [6] take advantage of the fact that some users have already linked their profiles on the social media platforms they use. In their approach, both the network topology and the personal information (attributes) disclosed in the profiles are used for matching. Based on the existing cross-links, initial profile pairs can be identified. The equally weighted profile attributes (first name, last name, username) are then compared to match profiles across platforms with a high precision of 94%. Based on the matches found, the algorithm then uses the new hits to iteratively find more pairs of profiles.

3   Backtracking of the Digital Traces

Individual pieces of information that can be found on the Web make it possible to create DTs. The question is where to start searching for information. This question has to be answered on the one hand by the expected information quality and on the other hand by the digital traces that lead to new data sources. In the following, we discuss the procedure of creating DTs (cf. Sect. 3.1) and show which starting points are suitable for information search (cf. Sect. 3.3), based on a performed data collection (cf. Sect. 3.2).

3.1   Creating a Digital Twin

As mentioned above, the average OSN user has more than one account on multiple platforms. A threat to users arises when information from different platforms is combined to create a more complete picture of the real person than the scattered pieces of information, and was never intended by the users of the platforms. Keeping individual accounts on OSNs separate and avoiding any overlap of stored information, especially usernames, content, and email addresses, is one way to protect against such information aggregation. However, the reality is different: In order to get traffic to different social media profiles, users link the profiles together, which makes it relatively easy to merge the profiles.

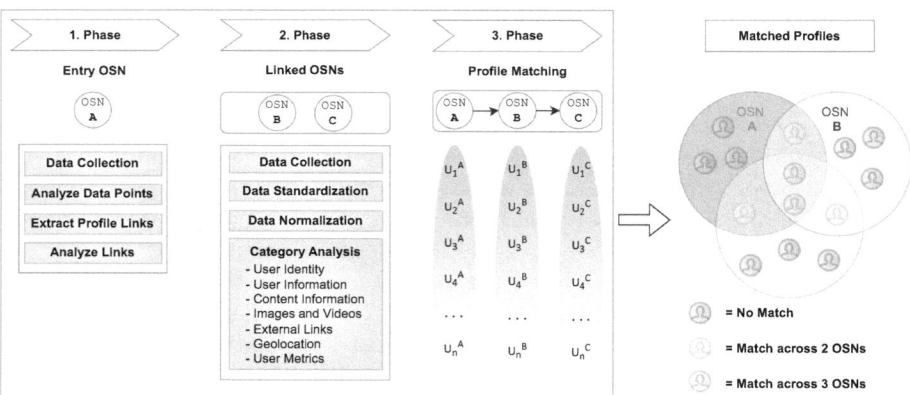

Fig. 1. ADRIAN's profile merging pipeline.

In the ADRIAN project, the cross-platform profile linking consists of three phases: processing of (1) an entry OSN and (2) linked OSNs, as well as (3) profile matching (cf. Fig. 1). The first phase is dedicated to the acquisition of the entry network, i.e., a platform that is predestined as an entry point due to defined characteristics, such as many or particularly high-quality links. This involves collecting and storing a user's individual data points, such as name or profile ID, as well as searching for and analyzing additional links. In this step, an initial network of profiles is created. The second phase is to incorporate the information from the tracked links. In contrast to the first phase, it is necessary to weight the information according to its quality and to identify inconsistencies. In addition, the information must be standardized. Currently, the information is being adapted to the format of the OSN entry. In the third phase, the profiles are merged. This happens when there is enough evidence that it is the same user on two or more platforms. This is done by comparing the identified aspects.

It becomes clear that the decision of which portal to acquire first has an impact on how successful the information search will be, although it can be argued that one could simply search all OSNs in all directions. However, due to the large number of OSNs, links, and profiles, this is not feasible in a reasonable amount of time. Therefore, when collecting information for DT compilation using this pipeline, the following question arises again: How can an account in one OSN x be correlated with an account in another OSN y? Below, we break this question down into the following sub-questions: Which OSNs are a good starting point for linking profiles? How can links between profiles on OSNs be verified?

To answer these questions, it is necessary to collect and analyze data from the OSNs. In this work, we focus on the major OSNs YouTube, Twitter, Instagram, and Facebook. In the context of the ADRIAN project, social sports platforms and business networks are also of great interest [7]. The former reveal high quality location information about shared running routes, while the latter put detailed biographical data online in a semi-structured form.

3.2 Dataset Creation and Description

To investigate how users engage on different OSNs and how they link profiles, we conducted data collection over three months (12/2021 – 02/2022) in several countries. The list of countries includes Germany, the Netherlands, France, the United Kingdom, and the United States. An analysis of the data points on each platform showed that the most links were found on YouTube. Therefore, YouTube was chosen as the entry point for our data collection.

For this purpose, the top 100 videos in each country were saved daily, including titles and descriptions. YouTube is particularly well suited as an entry point, as users have plenty of space in the video descriptions to place links to other OSNs, and it is common practice to do so. Popular accounts in particular use this opportunity to point to additional channels for content distribution and donation opportunities. To give you an idea, we will take a closer look at YouTube and Twitter (cf. Table 1). The Twitter profiles can be associated with the YouTube accounts via user-defined links. Table 1 shows that the YouTube data contains

Table 1. Descriptive statistics for the YouTube and Twitter datasets.

YouTube	#	Twitter	#
Total Videos	4,605	Total Tweets	345,748
Total Channels	2,841	Total Users	842
Total Links	32,464	Total Links	467,834
Total Videos with Link	4,108	Total Tweets with Link	345,748
Videos per Channel (min)	1	Tweets per User (min)	1
Videos per Channel (mean)	1.62	Tweets per User (mean)	411.12
Videos per Channel (max)	39	Tweets per User (max)	87,343
Links per Video (min)	0	Links per Tweet (min)	1
Links per Video (mean)	6.94	Links per Tweet (mean)	1.35
Links per Video (max)	88	Links per Tweet (max)	8
Links per Channel (min)	1	Links per User (min)	1
Links per Channel (mean)	11.43	Links per User (mean)	607.58
Links per Channel (max)	513	Links per User (max)	174,356

on average 10 times fewer videos per channel than the Twitter data contains tweets per user. It is also noticeable that a YouTube video contains about five times as many links as a tweet. This is due to the limited length of a tweet (280 characters, at the time we collected the data). There are also more links per user than links per channel because the Twitter data was collected only from the 842 users linked from the YouTube data. The next step is to analyze the links in video descriptions and tweet texts.

Table 2. YouTube (left) and Twitter (right) data for a given domain.

Target URL	# of links	% of links	Target URL	# of links	% of links
YouTube	4,647	14.31	Twitter	277,058	59.22
Bit	4,285	13.20	Screammov	87,054	18.61
Instagram	4,258	13.20	Trib	20,772	4.44
Twitter	2,334	7.19	Independent	11,061	2.36
Amazon	1,441	4.44	Bit	7,634	1.63
Facebook	1,415	2.78	TheGuardian	5,904	1.27
TikTok	903	2.78	LiverpoolEcho	4,881	1.04
Twitch	826	2.54	WioNews	4,567	0.98
Discord	540	1.66	FoxNews	2,983	0.64
Lnk	447	1.38	YouTube	2,925	0.63

Table 2 shows the domain distribution for links from YouTube videos and tweets. Most of the links in the YouTube videos lead to Instagram, Twitter and Facebook. This correlates with the OSNs that are relevant for our use case. Therefore, we analyze these three platforms in more detail. In this context, it is important to determine how many links to the different OSNs are included in all videos or per channel. It is clear that most links are to other OSNs. However, there is a difference in the linking behavior between the platforms: While YouTube mainly links to other profiles, Twitter also links to content, especially news sites. This can be explained by the fact that video descriptions are meta information about videos, while tweets are the primary content that can also link to other sources. The domains "Bit" and "Goo" are URL shortening services that hide other links. One reason for using these services is the character limit that exists on most platforms. In Table 3, the domain distribution for the resolved Bit and Goo URLs for YouTube and Twitter is shown.

Table 3. Resolved URLs for Bit/Goo domains from YouTube (left) and Twitter (right).

Target URL	# of links	% of links	Target URL	# of links	% of links
YouTube	2,414	54.04	20Minutes	3,609	47.13
Instagram	356	7.97	BeINSports	709	9.29
Twitter	215	4.81	RTVoost	529	6.91
Facebook	164	3.67	WhatCulture	342	4.47
Twitch	59	1.32	SwanseaCity	248	3.24
RStyle	58	1.30	YouTube	235	3.07
SkySports	40	0.90	RFEF	207	2.70
Spotify	33	0.74	Patriots	128	1.67
Spox	31	0.69	Ligue1	96	1.25
Google	30	0.67	Andertons	67	0.88

For YouTube, 4,467 of the 4,666 Bit and Goo URLs could be resolved. Of the remaining 199, the URL was unreachable. Our analysis of these URLs shows that 70.31% also have social media platforms behind them. For Twitter, 7,038 of the 7,658 URLs were resolved, and among the top 10 URLs, only YouTube was represented as a social media platform. Instagram has the most links, followed by Twitter and Facebook. Even with a number between 2 and 10 links, Instagram achieves the highest number. It is also important to determine how many links overlap. A YouTube channel that contains links to all three platforms is particularly relevant for creating a cross-platform profile. Of the 2,841 YouTube channels examined, 768 descriptions link to all three platforms.

These users, who are present on all platforms, are of particular interest to us because many data sources enable a broad and high-quality compilation of the DT. In addition to the aggregation of profile information, the content created also plays a role. For this reason, we also include the user content of the respective OSNs in the further analysis.

3.3 Overlap Analysis for Cross-Platform Profile Linking

Based on the related work, a review of the platforms' programming interfaces, and the collected data presented above, the questions raised in Sect. 3.1 can be answered. Before answering the question of how to merge social media profiles, it is important to clarify where most users place their links. As the data overview in Sect. 3.2 shows, YouTube is very well suited as an entry OSN here, since many links to other platforms can be placed in the video descriptions. Our analysis of YouTube channel links shows that in 674 cases, more than one profile is linked to another OSN. Of course, not all users on the Web also have a channel on YouTube, so an analysis of the other OSNs is also necessary. However, due to the sheer size of the platforms, it is essential to define an entry point. Nevertheless, the links given on the profiles are only potential profiles of a person. It must be clarified whether they are profiles of one and the same person.

Matching profiles based on usernames alone is not always a viable approach because users often have different usernames because their username is already taken or they do not want to be recognized. Therefore, other indicators are needed to verify that the user profile belongs to the same person. For this reason, we additionally analyzed the data points within the profiles on the OSNs that are suitable for profile matching to verify that they belong to the same individual. To this end, we collected multiple profiles from YouTube, Instagram, Facebook, and Twitter and analyzed the different data points within these profiles to classify them into different categories (cf. Table 4).

The extracted data points form the basis for correlating social media profiles to initialize DTs. First, we need to find out in which aspects the profiles are similar and therefore correlate all the collected data points. We group them into several categories for further work, as many different methods are needed to achieve this. The first category we are interested in is the association between usernames and real names. As marked in Table 4, the channel title or username is present on all OSNs. For Instagram and Twitter, we also have the name, but while some users use their real name here, others use their display name. The next category deals mainly with textual information about the channel or user profile. The most important item here is whether the profile is private, to determine how much data can be accessed. In general, the most interesting points are the description and whether the profile belongs to an organization (ORG) or a person (PER). The content provided by the channel or user is also important. Most of the relevant data points can be found in published content. The data points here are very diverse because the content is different. Typically, tweets and Facebook posts are text with images or videos, and YouTube and Instagram are usually images or videos with text. In addition, many insights can be gained, such as the source of the post, the tags, and even if the content is considered sensitive. Furthermore, images and videos are a key factor for the comparison of user profiles on different OSNs. Cross-platform profile linking can be done using

Table 4. Example of relevant data points for cross-platform profile linking.

Category	Data Point	YouTube	Instagram	Twitter	Facebook
Channel/User Identity	Channel ID / User ID	✓	✓	✓	✓
	Title / Username	✓	✓	✓	✓
	Name	✗	✓	✓	✓
Channel/User Information	Description	✓	✓	✓	✓
	Created (Timestamp)	✓	✗	✓	✗
	Private	✓	✓	✓	✓
	Verified	✗	✓	✓	✗
	Categories	✓	✗	✗	✓
	Type (ORG or PER)	✗	✗	✗	✓
Content Information Information	Post Id	✓	✓	✓	✓
	Created (Timestamp)	✓	✓	✓	✓
	Title/Caption	✓	✓	✗	✗
	Text	✓	✗	✓	✓
	Source	✗	✗	✓	✗
	Language	✓	✗	✓	✗
	Sensitive Content	✓	✗	✓	✗
	Context Annotations	✗	✗	✓	✗
	Tags / Hashtags	✓	✓	✓	✗
	View Count	✓	✗	✗	✗
	Like Count	✓	✓	✓	✓
	Quote Count	✗	✗	✓	✗
	Type (Video or Image)	✓	✓	✗	✗
	Keywords	✓	✗	✓	✗
Links to Image or Video	Channel/User Image	✓	✓	✓	✓
	Images URL	✗	✓	✓	✓
	Videos URL	✓	✓	✓	✓
External Links	External Profile URL	✗	✓	✓	✓
	External Post URL	✗	✗	✓	✗
	Facebook Link	✗	✓	✗	✗
Geolocation Information	Channel/User Location	✗	✗	✓	✗
	Location Entities	✗	✗	✓	✗
	Datailed Location	✗	✓	✓	✓
	Country	✓	✗	✓	✗
	Coordinates	✗	✗	✓	✗
	Bounding Box	✗	✗	✓	✗
Channel/User Metrics	Follower Count	✓	✓	✓	✓
	Following Count	✗	✓	✓	✓
	Content Count	✓	✓	✓	✗
	View Count	✓	✗	✗	✗

template matching and its histogram, for example. The external links posted by a profile can lead directly to another OSN and are an important point. They have been considered and analyzed in detail in this work. While platforms like Twitter, Instagram, and Facebook include these links as a data point, YouTube requires these links to be extracted from the textual content. As for geolocation data, textual information can be found on all OSNs. Twitter stands out because it offers many different projections, such as latitude and longitude coordinates, a bounding box showing the area, or even identifying locations by extracting entities from posts. The final category is metrics related to the channel or user. Here, all platforms typically offer metrics such as the number of followers or following. These can be used to determine the reach and activity of users. In addition, some platforms allow you to extract followers to create and analyze a network.

4   Discussion

We want to discuss our pipeline using a concrete real-world example: a random YouTube user who maintains multiple links in his video descriptions (cf. Fig. 2). The YouTube channel contains a link to Facebook and Twitter profiles. On Facebook, for example, we can determine whether the profile belongs to an individual or an organization. This is important because the compilation for the DT is initially focused on people. In addition, the Twitter account contains a link to another social media platform such as LinkedIn, an OSN for professional networking and career development, but no link to link-sharing sites such as LinkTree, which can be an additional source [10]. Here, the user provides additional information such as name, photo, location, and professional history.

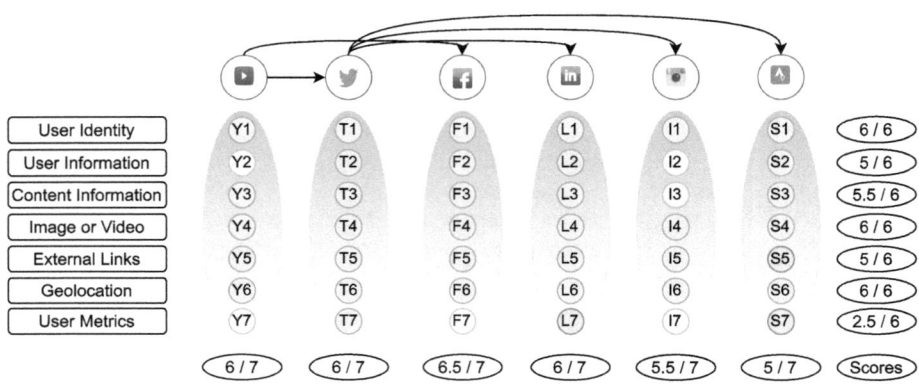

Fig. 2. Different user profiles in OSNs: a real-world example.

The user is also active on Twitter, posting sports activities that lead directly to Strava, an OSN for tracking physical activity that includes social networking features. Since the source of his tweets is Instagram, the user also has another social media account that is in use. To Instagram, he posts photos that contain lots of private information. He even uses Strava to share all of his running routes, including geographic data. In most of the cases, these routes start from the same place, most likely from his house.

This example illustrates the potential risks associated with consolidating different profiles across OSNs. This process not only allows validating information, but also filling information gaps, resulting in higher overall DT quality. However, merging data from different OSNs, as seen in the case of a user's activities on Twitter, Instagram, and Strava, significantly increases the risks of social engineering and data breaches. Similar to the studies discussed above, this consolidation of online profiles can become a goldmine for attackers using social engineering tactics. For example, the Robin Sage experiment demonstrated the ease with which confidential information could be gathered from a fictitious persona and showed how attackers could use similar methods by analyzing the integrated information from different social media profiles. Furthermore, automated bots like those studied by Huber et al. [16] could exploit social media profile interconnectedness to build trust and gather personal information. The emotional and psychological profiling techniques discussed by Labuschagne et al. [18] could also be more effectively applied with the rich data available from multiple social media platforms, allowing attackers to create more manipulative and targeted messages. Finally, the exploitation of geolocation data, as highlighted by Gan and Jenkins [13], is a major concern in this context. The sharing of walking routes and geographic information can lead to the creation of detailed movement profiles, posing serious privacy and security risks.

5   Conclusion

Matching different profiles allows us to answer the following question: To what extent do the categories in which users are active on different platforms overlap? We therefore presented an approach to correlate profiles across OSNs, in particular YouTube and Twitter, based on those individuals who disclose links to their different profiles.

As shown, YouTube is a good entry point for data collection because there are many links to other OSNs in the video descriptions. This makes it possible to identify a user across multiple OSNs and compare individual characteristics. This makes it possible to create a high quality DT and derive the threat to the user and warn them. However, there are concerns: for example, we are only able to observe a very small portion of the Web at a time and do not include smaller Web resources such as blogs, personal or employer Web sites in our observations. In addition, the persistence of the data we collect is severely limited: Content on the Web is highly volatile and changes rapidly. Responding to this is challenging. Another reason is that we do not want to keep the data longer than it exists in the real world.

Acknowledgements. This research is funded by dtec.bw – Digitalization and Technology Research Center of the Bundeswehr. dtec.bw is funded by the European Union – NextGenerationEU.

References

1. Agarwal, A., Toshniwal, D.: SmPFT: social media based profile fusion technique for data enrichment. Comput. Netw. **158**, 123–131 (2019). https://doi.org/10.1016/j.comnet.2019.04.015
2. Ahmad, W., Ali, R.: User identification across multiple online social networks using cross link attribute and network relationship. J. Interdiscip. Math. **23** (2020). https://doi.org/10.1080/09720502.2020.1721713
3. Barricelli, B.R., Casiraghi, E., Fogli, D.: A survey on digital twin: definitions, characteristics, applications, and design implications. IEEE Access **7**, 167653–167671 (2019). https://doi.org/10.1109/ACCESS.2019.2953499
4. Bäumer, F.S., Grote, N., Kersting, J., Geierhos, M.: Privacy matters: detecting nocuous patient data exposure in online physician reviews. In: Damasevicius, R., Mikasyte, V. (eds.) Information and Software Technologies. ICIST 2017. CCIS, vol. 756, pp. 77–89. Springer, Cham (2017). https://doi.org/10.1007/978-3-319-67642-5_7
5. Bäumer, F.S., Kersting, J., Orlikowski, M., Geierhos, M.: Towards a multi-stage approach to detect privacy breaches in physician reviews. In: SEMANTICS Posters & Demos (2018)
6. Bennacer, N., Nana Jipmo, C., Penta, A., Quercini, G.: Matching user profiles across social networks. In: Jarke, M., et al. (eds.) Advanced Information Systems Engineering. CAiSE 2014. LNCS, vol. 8484, pp. 424–438. Springer, Cham (2014). https://doi.org/10.1007/978-3-319-07881-6_29
7. Bäumer, F.S., Denisov, S., Su Lee, Y., Geierhos, M.: Towards authority-dependent risk identification and analysis in online networks. In: Halimi, A., Ayday, E. (eds.) Proceedings of the IST-190 Research Symposium (RSY) on AI, ML and BD for Hybrid Military Operations (AI4HMO) (2021)
8. Cai, C., Li, L., Chen, W., Zeng, D.D.: Capturing deep dynamic information for mapping users across social networks. In: 2019 IEEE International Conference on Intelligence and Security Informatics, ISI 2019 (2019). https://doi.org/10.1109/ISI.2019.8823341
9. Data Portal: (October 2023). https://datareportal.com/reports/digital-2023-october-global-statshot. Accessed 18 Nov 2023
10. Denisov, S., Bäumer, F.S.: The only link you will ever need: how social media reference landing pages speed up profile matching. In: Lopata, A., Gudoniene, D., Butkiene, R. (eds.) Information and Software Technologies. ICIST 2022. CCIS, vol. 1665, pp. 136–147. Springer, Cham (2022). https://doi.org/10.1007/978-3-031-16302-9-10
11. Engels, G.: Der digitale Fußabdruck, Schatten oder Zwilling von Maschinen und Menschen. Gruppe. Interaktion. Organisation. Zeitschrift für Angewandte Organisationspsychologie (GIO) **51**(3), 363–370 (2020). https://doi.org/10.1007/s11612-020-00527-9
12. Feher, K.: Digital identity and the online self: footprint strategies – an exploratory and comparative research study. J. Inf. Sci. **47**(2), 192–205 (2019). https://doi.org/10.1177/0165551519879702
13. Gan, D., Jenkins, L.R.: Social networking privacy-Who's stalking you? Future Internet **7**(1), 67–93 (2015)
14. Goga, O., Lei, H., Parthasarathi, S.H.K., Friedland, G., Sommer, R., Teixeira, R.: Exploiting innocuous activity for correlating users across sites. In: Proceedings of the 22nd International Conference on World Wide Web, pp. 447–458. WWW '13,

Association for Computing Machinery, New York, NY, USA (2013). https://doi. org/10.1145/2488388.2488428

15. Halimi, A., Ayday, E.: Efficient quantification of profile matching risk in social networks using belief propagation. In: Chen, L., Li, N., Liang, K., Schneider, S. (eds.) Computer Security – ESORICS 2020. ESORICS 2020. LNCS, vol. 12308, pp. 110–130. Springer, Cham (2020). https://doi.org/10.1007/978-3-030-58951-6_6

16. Huber, M., Kowalski, S., Nohlberg, M., Tjoa, S.: Towards automating social engineering using social networking sites. In: 2009 International Conference on Computational Science and Engineering, vol. 3, pp. 117–124. IEEE (2009)

17. Kasbekar, P., Potika, K., Pollett, C.: Find me if you can: aligning users in different social networks. In: Proceedings - 2020 IEEE 6th International Conference on Big Data Computing Service and Applications, BigDataService 2020, pp. 46–53 (2020). https://doi.org/10.1109/BigDataService49289.2020.00015

18. Labuschagne, A., Eloff, M., Veerasamy, N.: The dark side of web 2.0. In: Hercheui, M.D., Whitehouse, D., McIver, W., Phahlamohlaka, J. (eds.) ICT Critical Infrastructures and Society. HCC 2012. IFIPAICT, LNCS, vol. 386, pp. 237–249. Springer, Berlin, Heidelberg (2012). https://doi.org/10.1007/978-3-642-33332-3_22

19. Li, Y., Ji, W., Gao, X., Deng, Y., Dong, W., Li, D.: Matching user accounts with spatio-temporal awareness across social networks. Inf. Sci. **570** (2021)

20. Li, Y., Peng, Y., Zhang, Z., Yin, H., Xu, Q.: Matching user accounts across social networks based on username and display name. World Wide Web **22**(3), 1075–1097 (2019). https://doi.org/10.1007/s11280-018-0571-4

21. Mbarek, A., Jamoussi, S., BenHamadou, A.: Tuser3: a profile matching based algorithm across three heterogeneous social networks. In: Yang, X., Wang, C.D., Islam, M.S., Zhang, Z. (eds.) Advanced Data Mining and Applications. ADMA 2020. LNCS, vol.12447, pp. 191–206. Springer, Cham (2020). https://doi.org/10.1007/978-3-030-65390-3_16

22. Müngen, A.A., Gündoğan, E., Kaya, M.: Identifying multiple social network accounts belonging to the same users. Soc. Netw. Anal. Min. **11**(1), 29 (2021)

23. Ryan, T., Mauch, G.: Getting in bed with Robin Sage. In: Black Hat Conference, pp. 1–8 (2010)

24. Seymour, J., Tully, P.: Weaponizing data science for social engineering: automated E2E spear phishing on Twitter. Black Hat USA **37**, 1–39 (2016)

25. Sokhin, T., Butakov, N., Nasonov, D.: User profiles matching for different social networks based on faces identification. Hybrid Artif. Intell. Syst. 551–562 (2019). https://doi.org/10.1007/978-3-030-29859-3_47

26. Soltani, R., Abhari, A.: Identity matching in social media platforms. In: SPECTS, pp. 64–70. IEEE (2013)

27. Wang, L., Hu, K., Zhang, Y., Cao, S.: Factor graph model based user profile matching across social networks. IEEE Access **7**, 152429–152442 (2019)

28. Xing, L., Deng, K., Wu, H., Xie, P., Gao, J.: Behavioral habits-based user identification across social networks. Symmetry **11**, 1134 (2019)

29. Xing, L., Deng, K., Wu, H., Xie, P., Zhang, M., Wu, Q.: Exploiting two-level information entropy across social networks for user identification. Wirel. Commun. Mob. Comput. **2021**, 1–15 (2021)

SoEA4EE

SoEA4EE – 15th Workshop on Service-Oriented Enterprise Architecture for Enterprise Engineering

Selmin Nurcan[1,2] and Rainer Schmidt[3]

[1]Centre de Recherche en Informatique
selmin.nurcan@univ-paris1.fr
[2]Management School of Sorbonne, University Paris 1 Panthéon-Sorbonne, Paris, France
[3]Munich University of Applied Sciences, Munich, Germany
rainer.schmidt@hm.edu

1 Position Statement

Since its foundation in 2009 [1], the SoEA4EE workshop complements well-established topics of the EDOC conferences such as service-oriented architectures and enterprise service architectures by addressing the coupling of business processes and services and the alignment of business and IT. The SoEA4EE workshop also includes topics such as Business Process Management, Enterprise Service Architectures, Analytics, Big Data, Networked Enterprise Solutions, and their connections.

According to [2], smart companies define how they (will) do business (using an operating model) and design processes and infrastructure critical to their current and future operations using enterprise architecture (EA). Enterprise Engineering (EE) is the application of engineering principles to the design of enterprise architectures. It enables deriving the EA from the enterprise goals and strategy and aligning it with the enterprise resources. EA [2] maps the enterprise goals and strategy to the enterprise's resources (actors, assets, IT supports) and supports the evolution of this mapping.

There are different paradigms for creating enterprise architectures. In the SoEA4EE series, the one that is considered as the most promising is to encapsulate the functionalities of IT resources as services. By this means, it is possible to clearly describe the contributions of IT both in terms of functionality and quality and to define a service-oriented enterprise architecture (SoEA).

Two special journal issues [3, 4] have been published in the International Journal of Information Systems in the Service Sector (IJISSS), the first with invited papers from SoEA4EE 2010, 2011, and 2012, the second with invited papers from SoEA4EE 2013, 2014 and 2015. The extended papers went again into a systematic review process and accepted papers were included in those special issues. A third special issue is in progress.

2 Goal and Objectives

The goal of the workshop is to develop concepts and methods to assist the engineering and management of service-oriented enterprise architectures and the software systems supporting them. Five themes of research were pursued during SoEA4EE 2023:

1. Digital Enterprises, Industry 4.0, and Platforms in the Computing Continuum
2. SoEA and the Influence of Artificial Intelligence, Social Information Systems, and Big Data in Enterprise Engineering
3. Alignment of the Enterprise Goals and Strategy with the SoEA
4. Design of SoEA
5. Governance of SoEA

Acknowledgments. We wish to thank all authors for having shared their work with us, as well as the members of the SoEA4EE 2023 Program Committee and the organizers of EDOC 2023 for their help with the organization of the workshop.

References

1. Nurcan, S., Schmidt, R.: Service-oriented enterprise-architecture for enterprise engineering introduction. In: 2009 13th Enterprise Distributed Object Computing Conference Workshops, pp. 247–253 (2009). https://doi.org/10.1109/EDOCW.2009.5331988
2. Ross, J.W., Weill, P., Robertson, D.: Enterprise Architecture as Strategy: Creating a Foundation for Business Execution. Harvard Business School Press, Brighton (2006)
3. Nurcan, S., Schmidt, R.: Special issue selected papers from the SoEA4EE 2010, 2011, and 2012 on "service-oriented enterprise architecture on enterprise engineering". Int. J. Inf. Syst. Serv. Sector (IJISSS) **7**(1) (2015)
4. Nurcan, S.: Special issue selected papers from the SoEA4EE workshops 2013, 2014, and 2015 on "service-oriented enterprise architecture on enterprise engineering". Int. J. Inf. Syst. Serv. Sector (IJISSS) **10**(3) (2018)

SoEA4EE Organization

Workshop Chairs

Rainer Schmidt   Munich University of Applied Sciences, Germany

Selmin Nurcan   University Paris 1 Panthéon-Sorbonne, France

Program Committee

Said Assar	Institut Mines-Télécom Business School, France
Colin Atkinson	University of Mannheim, Germany
Khalid Benali	LORIA, Nancy, France
François Charoy	Université de Lorraine – LORIA, France
Ulrik Franke	RISE, Sweden
Jānis Grabis	Riga Technical University, Latvia
Sung-Kook Han	Won Kwang University, South Korea
Maria-Eugenia Iacob	University of Twente, The Netherlands
Michael Möhring	Hochschule Reutlingen, Germany
Jolita Ralyté	University of Geneva, Switzerland
Ulrike Steffens	Hamburg University of Applied Sciences, Germany
Irene Vanderfeesten	KU Leuven, Belgium
Alfred Zimmermann	Hochschule Reutlingen, Germany

Paving the Path Towards Platform Engineering Using a Comprehensive Reference Model

Ruben van de Kamp[1,2(✉)], Kees Bakker[2], and Zhiming Zhao[1,3]

[1] Multiscale Networked Systems, University of Amsterdam,
1098XH Amsterdam, The Netherlands
ruvdkamp@gmail.com, z.zhao@uva.nl
[2] Wehkamp, 8021 EV Zwolle, The Netherlands
{ruvdkamp,kbakker}@wehkamp.nl
[3] LifeWatch Virtual Lab and Innovation Center (VLIC),
1098XH Amsterdam, The Netherlands

Abstract. Amidst the growing popularity of platform engineering, promising improved productivity and enhanced developer experience through an engineering platform, e.g., an Internal Developer Platform (IDP), this paper addresses the prevalent challenge of a lack of a shared understanding in the field and the complications in defining effective, customized strategies. Introducing a definitive Platform Engineering Reference Model (PE-RM) based on the Reference Model for Open Distributed Processing (RM-ODP) framework to provide a common understanding. This model offers a structured framework for software organizations to create tailored platform engineering strategies and realize the full potential of platform engineering. By facilitating a shared vocabulary and providing a roadmap for implementation, this paper aims to mitigate prevailing complexities and accelerate the adoption and effectiveness of platform engineering across organizations, showcasing the added value.

Keywords: Platform engineering · Reference model · System modeling · Cloud infrastructure · Development Lifecycle

1 Introduction

The digital age has initiated substantial transformations across all industries, making digitalization an imperative for survival in today's volatile market landscape [3]. This transition has amplified the importance of software development and deployment, with methodologies like DevOps and Agile acting as instrumental drivers of this digital revolution [7,18]. Agile, advocating adaptability and customer collaboration, and DevOps, fostering cooperation between development and operations teams, enhancing the efficiency and quality of software delivery [2,15].

T. P. Sales et al. (Eds.): EDOC 2023 Workshops, LNBIP 498, pp. 177–193, 2024.
https://doi.org/10.1007/978-3-031-54712-6_11

Amid increasing technological complexity, platform engineering is emerging as a promising discipline.[1] It focuses on altering the engineering culture and creating an engineering platform, e.g., an Internal Developer Platform (IDP), to offer self-service capabilities for software development teams in the cloud-native era [10,20]. Yet, interpretation variations tied to personal perspectives and organizational contexts could render the definition ambiguous.

Platform engineering adoption faces challenges such as inconsistencies in understanding across different stakeholders and the interchangeable use of terminology such as "Internal Developer Platform" and "DevOps", which could create communication hurdles and compromise the efficiency of technological strategies.[2] Moreover, clear guidelines about the separation of accountability between different types of teams are essential. Further addressing the team types differentiated by team topologies [22]. Hence, standardizing the platform engineering terminology is critical to establishing a shared understanding.

Another significant challenge involves crafting a tailored platform engineering strategy, which requires extensive knowledge of the organization's processes and culture. It also necessitates comprehending how implementing platform engineering could alter these facets. The complexity in this paradigm shift to platform engineering extends to organizational changes, architectural design, technology selection, and operational management [4].[3] To address these challenges, the paper focuses on the following research questions:

- How to model platform engineering in the context of a software company?
- How to define a customized platform engineering design tailored to a specific organization?
- How to effectively construct a technical platform engineering implementation?

To answer these RQs, we proposed a reference model for platform engineering grounded and validated in a case study and experiments. This Platform Engineering Reference Model (PE-RM) seeks to clarify the nature and scope of platform engineering, bridging comprehension gaps among various stakeholders. Further validated and applied in a case study that proposes both a conceptual design and technical implementation guided by the PE-RM as a guideline and example to showcase the added value of platform engineering.

The paper is based on work done in the thesis [14] and unfolds as follows. Section 2 discusses related work. Section 3 presents the Platform Engineering Reference Model. Section 4 offers a case study in which a conceptual design and technical implementation with experiments are conducted. Section 5 discusses the achievements and lessons learned. Finally, Sect. 6 presents the conclusion and future work.

---

[1] https://platformengineering.org/blog/what-is-platform-engineering.

[2] https://www.gartner.com/en/articles/what-is-platform-engineering.

[3] https://thenewstack.io/platform-engineering/platform-engineering-challenges-and-solutions.

2   Related Work

Three streams of related work are relevant to this paper: publications detailing system proposals inclusive of platform engineering characteristics, industrial articles and whitepapers on platform engineering, and publications presenting reference models to depict methodologies and architectures. Extensive research has been conducted on the multifaceted nature of platforms and their diverse applications, yielding various definitions [12]. The first use of the concept of platform was the "product platform", and it was defined as specific modular product architectures that help develop product families [13,16]. Platforms can be categorized in different ways, one of which is innovation platforms and transaction platforms [5]. The concept of an innovation platform lies closest to the platform engineering philosophy. Governance within the platform's technological system is established through technological interfaces and standards, leveraging modularity [1]. This underscores the pivotal role of the platform designer, functioning as an architect to ensure the seamless integration of different platform components-an aspect synonymous with the role of platform engineering. A seminal study delves into platform-based product development in enterprise application development, emphasizing its crucial role in enhancing efficiency and flexibility [24]. The authors highlight the significance of increased academic research in this domain and advocate for closer collaboration between academia and industry. However, in contrast to the Platform Engineering Reference Model (PE-RM), this study does not provide a comprehensive roadmap for implementing platform engineering within an organization.

Next, regarding articles pushed from the industry related to platform engineering, the most prominent is the IDP reference model proposed by Humanitec [11]. Since platform engineering heavily relies on an engineering platform e.g., Internal Developer Platform (IDP), Humanitec proposes a reference architecture for such IDP. The IDP architecture provides insight into its possible realization with specific tools and the significance of its components. However, this reference architecture delves into specific tool choices, which reduces the applicability of this architecture since this can depend on individual preferences and pre-existing toolsets. Together with the organizational aspect and a general integration for platform engineering the PE-RM provides a more comprehensive model.

As this research adopts an ontology-based approach to propose a reference model, we provide related work concerning approaches of this type. Various reference models exist for similar methodologies, such as the DevOps Reference Architecture (DRA) is an architecture proposed to deploy IoT into the cloud [8]. This DRA consists of four different models: DRA contextual model, conceptual model, logical model, and physical model. Lastly, research into a software architecture framework for quality-aware DevOps has been conducted [6]. The authors state that many stakeholders are involved in DevOps but do not have a direct relation to the product but account for the product's organizational stability. The primary distinction between these reference models and the PE-RM lies in their scope of application. While DevOps and Agile are primarily geared toward enhancing team-level processes and collaboration, platform engineering aims to drive improvements across the entire organization.

In summary, while extensive research has delved into various platforms and their unique characteristics, there exists a noticeable scarcity of literature specifically addressing platform engineering as a distinct methodology. The limited available literature presents diverse viewpoints, underscoring a lack of consensus on the subject. This underlines the limited support in identifying and elucidating what platform engineering necessitates and its potential applications. The current reference architecture for platform engineering appears to be inadequate, and since platform engineering is different from other methodologies, the existing reference models are insufficient for platform engineering. Therefore, this paper offers significant value by providing a comprehensive reference model of platform engineering, integrating both technical and organizational aspects. The Reference Model for Open Distributed Processing (RM-ODP) is used to facilitate the creation of this reference model. The RM-ODP is a conceptual framework for designing and describing distributed systems [17,21]. Moreover, the RM-ODP has been used to model complex IT systems, e.g., the reference model for environmental research infrastructure [9,19].

3   Platform Engineering Reference Model

This section introduces the Platform Engineering Reference Model (PE-RM). Based on the existing related work, a general understanding of platform engineering is needed and will be achieved by creating a multi-viewpoint reference model. It is an ensemble of viewpoints that illustrate the principal objects within each viewpoint, their organization by the platform engineering lifecycles, and their correlations with objects defined in other viewpoints. The viewpoints suggested by the PE-RM aim to be as loosely coupled as possible to enable parallel design and development efforts across the organization. The PE-RM outlines five viewpoints (Fig. 1), and the following subsections explain the methodology and elaborate on these viewpoints.

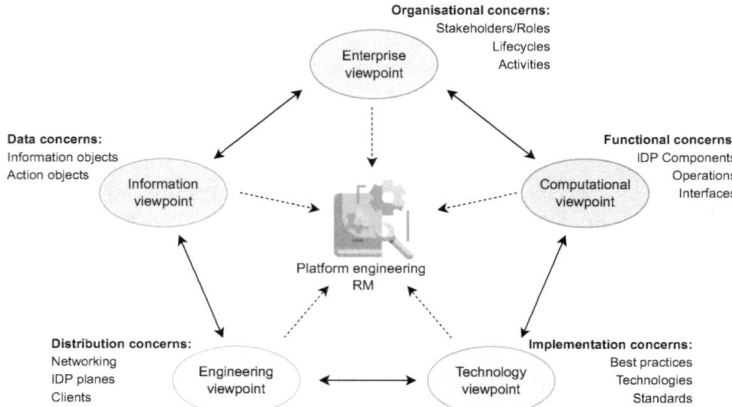

Fig. 1. The five viewpoints of the Platform Engineering RM.

3.1   Methodology

An iterative approach was used to acquire a comprehensive understanding of platform engineering, which started by conducting a series of interviews with numerous experts, each from diverse professional backgrounds and roles. The organization investigated already manifested aspects of platform engineering, and a need for greater standardization of terminology was apparent to enhance its applicability in this and other organizations. Therefore, we interviewed industry experts outside the organization for a more holistic understanding. Consequently, the RM-ODP framework was leveraged to express the platform engineering terminology, refining its interpretation and application.

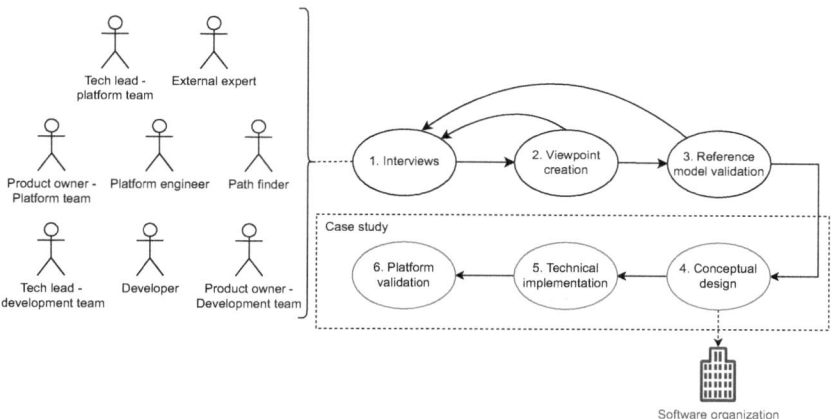

Fig. 2. Visualisation for Methodology of the Platform Engineering Reference Model.

The first step in developing this reference model involved interviewing eight software engineering experts with varied roles and backgrounds within and outside the organization (see Fig. 2). Their perceptions guided the formation of the viewpoints in the second step. Its validity was assessed via additional interviews and comparison with related work in step three. The primary validation of the reference model was done in the case study consisting of a conceptual design, technical implementation, and experiments to help showcase the added value and applicability of the PE-RM. Notably, the methodology adopted an iterative approach, necessitating continuous refinement of the reference model in light of fresh insights and varied perspectives. This recursive cycle of refining greatly enhanced the model's maturity and reliability.

3.2   Enterprise Viewpoint

The enterprise viewpoint focuses on the organizational context of the domain in which the designed systems are intended to operate. This viewpoint concentrates on the lifecycle, stakeholders (roles), and activities that the adoption of platform engineering will introduce. The enterprise viewpoint is intended to cover the process changes and how this impact different lifecycles, teams, and their responsibilities. With these concepts, the following lifecycles are introduced:

– *Platform engineering lifecycle* is the lifecycle in which the engineering platform will be introduced and maintained by a newly created platform team. It includes phases that help the platform team create a platform that fulfills the needs of the development teams and improves the platform.
– *Application lifecycle* is the lifecycle in which the development teams create business value while using the engineering platform to increase productivity and developer experience. With platform engineering, the continuous development lifecycle will not be affected.

With these lifecycles, new roles have to be introduced and assigned. The roles can be divided into two categories: *active* and *passive* roles. See Table 1.

Table 1. Part of platform engineering roles and stakeholders.

Active role	Mission	Typical behavior
Platform team	Build and support an engineering platform to increase the productivity of development teams	Maintain the platform. Support the development teams
Enterprise architects	Investige (platform) improvements and improve overall software processes	Investigate software processes. Kickstart platform engineering adoption
Development teams	Use the platform to increase productivity when creating business value	Develop applications. Utilize platform
Development guilds	Groups of developers with the same expertise responsible for best practice adoption	Maintain golden paths. Explore best practices
Passive role	Mission	Typical behavior
Engineering platform	Improve the application lifecycle by offering self-service capabilities	Offers self-service capabilities
Cloud platform	The platform where applications and services are running in production	Running applications to deliver a working system

Each role engages differently in the platform engineering and application lifecycles, with the platform team more focused on the former and development teams on the latter. As stakeholders of the engineering platform, development teams can request new features, prompting the platform engineering lifecycle. Typically, if a tool is used and maintained separately by different development teams, it will become part of the platform team's responsibility.

3.3   Information Viewpoint

The information viewpoint specification enables the clear and concise representation of the information objects consumed and produced by the phases in the platform engineering and application lifecycles introduced in the enterprise viewpoint. Providing a standard model, that can be referenced throughout a complete design specification, assures that the same interpretation of information is applied at all levels, including the activities related to these objects. The PE-RM information viewpoint aims to achieve a shared model for the design activity, given that it can cover a federation of tools and integration of legacy systems.

The main modeling concepts of the information viewpoint are *information objects* and *action objects*, which are explained in Table 2 and 3. From the information viewpoint, the emphasis is on the data, their evolution, and the activities which enable that evolution. The action objects are based on the stakeholders and roles introduced from the enterprise viewpoint. Based on the lifecycles defined in the enterprise viewpoint, the information and action objects will also have relationships since action objects cannot modify all information objects.

One of the key information objects that are introduced is the golden path. The term "golden path" refers to a set of best practices, tools, libraries, and architecture choices supported by the organization and maintained by development guilds. By adhering to the golden path, development teams can more effectively build, test, and deploy applications with greater consistency, reliability, and speed[4].

Table 2. Part of the platform engineering lifecycle information and action objects.

Information object	Description
Architecture design	Displays the tools used separated into different planes
Roadmap	A planning of the platform to track the development progress
Backlog	A list of functionalities, based on the roadmap and architecture, readable for the platform team
Deliverable	The functionalities created by the platform team, which could be different based on the type of functionality
Release	A bundle of new platform features deployed at a fixed time
Platform version	The version of the platform, including an announcement, documentation, and change logs
Golden paths	Step-by-step tutorials to execute a task utilizing the platform
Service catalog	Centralized system that keeps track of ownership and metadata for all the software (components)
Action object	Description
Enterprise architect	Helps with the architecture design of the platform and roadmap based on new feature requests and observations
Product owner platform team	Responsible for the platform roadmap and backlog with incoming feature requests
Platform team	Responsible for the platform by building deliverables, releases, and deploying new platform versions
Development Guild	Responsible for the golden paths

Table 3. Part of the application lifecycle information and action objects.

Information object	Description
Architecture	The design of the application domain to deliver business value
Application domain	The resources and applications needed to deliver business value, based on the architecture
Resources	The application domain resources provisioned by the platform
Application	The code created and maintained by the development team
Platform feature request	The requests made by the development teams for the need for specific tools and support in the platform
Action object	Description
Development team	Maintains and provisions the architectural design of the application domain and can request platform features

3.4   Computational Viewpoint

The computational viewpoint specification models the components that provide different functionalities for processing data assets and allows the lifecycle to continue to other phases. The computational viewpoint is concerned with developing the high-level design of the processes and applications supporting the platform's self-service capabilities and activities done during the lifecycles. The viewpoint expresses models in terms of functional components of the engineering platform and how different parts will interact with typed interfaces by performing a sequence of activities. The computational viewpoint specifications refer to specific parts of the information viewpoint. Table 4 presents different operations.

Table 4. Part of the platform engineering operations.

Operation	Description
Utilize golden paths	Development teams using golden paths to adopt best practices and use the engineering platform
Maintain golden paths	Development guilds maintaining golden paths based on platform support and best practices
Provision application domain	Based on the architecture, provisioning the application domain, including all necessary services
Deploy applications	Development teams deploying their application using the engineering platform

The main modeling concepts of the Computational Viewpoint are the different platform components, their passive and active interfaces, and the relevant configuration in which objects are integrated to provide their services. Depending on the context and organization, these operations can be different. The computational viewpoint operations can be translated into golden paths, which can be used to execute these sequences, emphasizing the importance of golden paths.

3.5   Engineering Viewpoint

The primary goal of the engineering viewpoint is to represent the distribution of components among different software systems and tools. The engineering viewpoint tackles the problem of diversity in platform structure and gives the prescriptions for supporting the necessary abstract computational interactions in various situations, explained in the computational viewpoint. The engineering viewpoint is also concerned with providing the management with guarantees (transparency). These assurances are understood to manifest in planes that enable an engineering platform to substantiate the platform engineering discipline. It will help identify the various improvements that must be made as an organization to fully adopt platform engineering with a simplified overview and separation of concerns. Given that most organizations will already possess an engineering setup, it can be enhanced by reshaping it according to the model offered from the engineering perspective.

The main modeling concepts of the engineering viewpoint are engineering objects, containers, and channels. However, to ensure that the platform engineering is correctly acknowledged, the engineering platform has been separated into different planes based on the IDP reference architecture of Humanitec [11].[5] The resource plane can be seen as the foundation for the platform and applications. The engineering platform can be separated into two features: construct applications and enable applications to run in production, where the latter is not explicitly modeled in this diagram (Fig. 3).

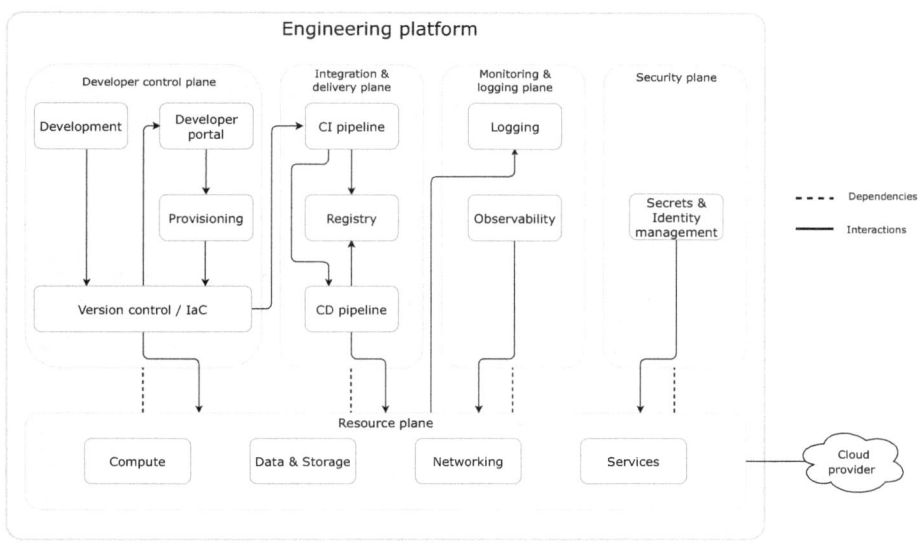

Fig. 3. Planes and components of the engineering platform.

---

[5] https://humanitec.com/reference-architectures.

3.6   Technology Viewpoint

Technology viewpoint specifications represent the concrete dependencies between design and implementation. The technology viewpoint is concerned with managing real-world constraints, such as existing application platforms, tools, or restrictions based on requirements and budget. The adoption of platform engineering will rarely have the luxury of being a greenfield project [23]. Therefore this viewpoint brings together information about the existing infrastructure and technology stack. It is concerned with the selection of universal standards to be used in the system and the allocation and configuration of resources. It represents the software components and techniques of the implemented system based on the engineering viewpoint specifications. In Table 5, the diagram represents the platform components and the best practices/standards.

Table 5. Part of the best practices of the engineering platform components.

Plane	Component	Description	Best practices
Developer control plane	IDE	The local development environment.	IDE & Backlog management
	Developer Portal	Frontend for developers to interact with the platform.	Developer portal & ChatBot
	Provisioning service	Engine to provision application domains and ensure governance is in place.	Microservice
	Version control/IaC	Location to store code.	Git & IaC
Integration & Delivery plane	CI pipeline	Pipeline to build code and push artifacts to the registry	Containerization
	Registry	Location to store releasable artifacts like docker containers and packages.	Repositories
	CD pipeline	Pipeline to update the environment with the artifacts, triggered by CI or manually.	Containerization
Monitoring & Logging plane	Observability	Gathering and showing metrics (dashboards, alerts)	Metrics Scraper & Elastic storage
	Logging	Storing, and querying logs created by the application running in production.	Elastic storage & Querying tool
Security plane	Secrets & identity management	Secrets that will be injected as soon as the application is deployed.	Role management & secret manager
Resource plane	Compute	The resources used to run the application based on given configurations	Docker & Kubernetes
	Data & storage	The resources that can store data and other artifacts like images or files.	Databases & file storage
	Networking	Handles the networking tasks like load balancing and reachability.	Load balancer & gateways
	Services	Services that are needed to make the application domain work	Example: message broker

This viewpoint also has an essential role in the management of testing conformance to the overall specification, because it specifies the information required from implementers to support this testing. The main modeling concepts of the technology viewpoint are *components*, *standards*, and in our case, *best practices*. Since the engineering platform is a central collection of tools, services, and automated workflows, which can differ for each organization and environment, this viewpoint does not focus on state-of-the-art tools, unlike the Humanitec IDP reference architecture [11].

4   Case Study

Several research activities were conducted to implement and validate the proposed Platform Engineering Reference Model in a software organization and context. We initially assess the viability of generating a conceptual design using the reference model within an organizational context to verify its utility in platform engineering design. This is followed by creating a basic proof-of-concept, derived from the conceptual design, for an engineering platform to test its technical relevance. Finally, we undertake experiments to evaluate the implementation's effectiveness and added value. The case study for the conceptual design is carried out in a Dutch online retailer.

4.1   Conceptual Design

This case study utilized the PE-RM to design platform engineering for a software-based Dutch online retailer. The analysis illuminated the organization's current practices, highlighting areas for improvement. A significant finding was the communication gap between the platform and development teams, affecting productivity and development processes. This insight emphasized the need for improved organizational cooperation, leading to the suggestion of development guilds, platform versioning, and the introduction of golden paths for standardized application provisioning. These golden paths ensure not only consistent application onboarding but also reduce cognitive load on developers.

The computational viewpoint indicated that golden paths could refine operational processes, simplifying operations and boosting software quality. Based on the performance analysis, there is a significant improvement that can be made with the adoption of golden paths and standardization. From the engineering and technology viewpoint, integrating tools like the Backstage developer portal would bolster platform engineering capabilities, fostering better communication and service discoverability. The PE-RM's application in the study showcased its capability to offer tailored platform engineering solutions. The study reinforced that successful platform engineering is not just about new tools but aligning them with organizational needs. Embracing a developer portal will streamline integration and adoption, laying a foundation for efficient platform engineering, serving as a blueprint for other organizations.

4.2 Technical Implementation

Derived from the observations and opportunities gathered in the conceptual design, we did a separate technical implementation as proof of concept. The architectural design for the engineering platform is illustrated in Fig. 4. Guided by the PE-RM's engineering and technology viewpoints, this design highlights the platform's components, their functions, and associated design choices, underscoring the value of an engineering platform.

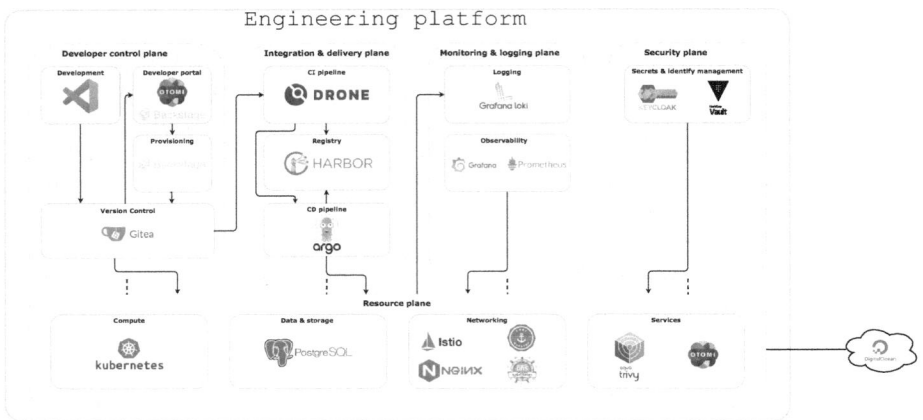

Fig. 4. Technical implementation: engineering platform infrastructure design.

The prototype's primary goal is to demonstrate key platform engineering features, rather than tool choices. To achieve this, we used Otomi[6], an opensource Platform as a Service system. The framework integrates multiple tools tailored to fit our needs. Additionally, we've customized it to add new functions, including integration with tools like Backstage.

This technical execution focuses on two crucial areas of the application lifecycle that demonstrate platform engineering's significance: (1) application domain provisioning and (2) observability and logging. For domain provisioning, we've introduced golden paths that guide development teams in setting up the application domain, as shown in Fig. 5. These paths handle application provisioning, pipelines, metrics exposure, and deployment configurations. For observability and logging, utilizing these golden paths ensures alignment with the platform's default logging and metric tools. There are ready-made dashboards, offering precise and default metrics across all applications. If an application logs messages, these are automatically collected, enhancing visibility. Thus, the platform offers self-service features that refine development teams' application lifecycles.

---

[6] https://otomi.io.

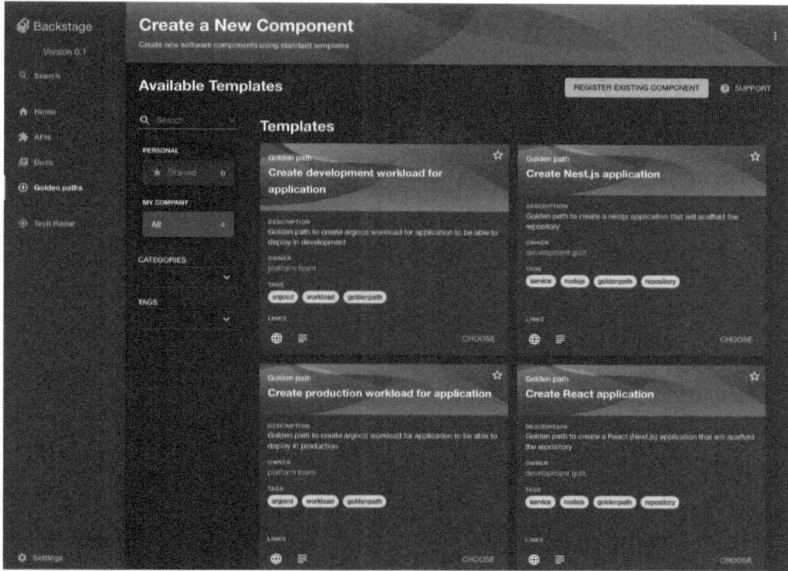

Fig. 5. Technical implementation: golden paths.

4.3   Experiments

Several experiments were conducted to validate and highlight the value of the technical implementation. To measure the engineering platform's usability and productivity, we conducted a study assessing software developers' perceived productivity enhancements. We also showcased a demo and distributed a questionnaire to platform experts for their feedback. Ten participants, ranging from students to senior developers, were involved in the productivity and usability study. These participants performed different tasks and afterward completed a questionnaire. Additionally, five platform experts, including engineers, architects, and tech leads, participated in another study to gather a diverse set of feedback.

Two key performance metrics emerged from the productivity analysis in the conceptual design: application onboarding time and developer onboarding time. The application onboarding time is the time it takes to create a new application and get it into production with all the requirements. The developer onboarding time is the time it takes for a developer to deploy their first application into production. Before the study, participants estimated an average of 7 h to onboard an application. However, the results showed a significant reduction in onboarding time when using an engineering platform (Fig. 6).

Usability feedback was generally positive. The platform's ease of use averaged a rating of 4 out of 5, with participants experiencing that 90% of the work was managed by the platform. Moreover, we observed that the most likable features are Backstage and golden paths, as it support developers onboard new applications, including configurations and standardization. From the platform

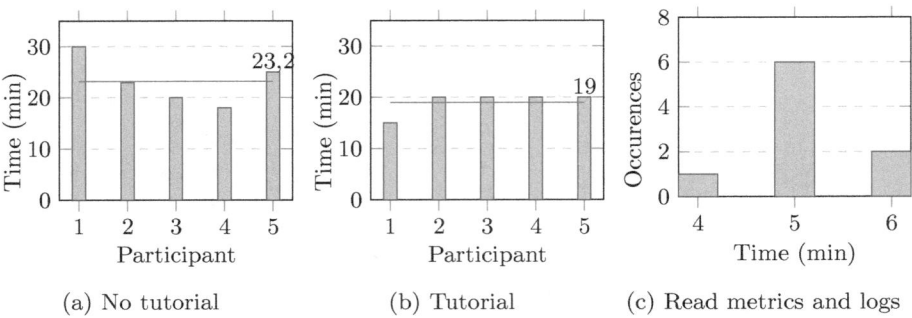

Fig. 6. Experimentation results.

perspective, feedback underlined the implementation as exemplary but noted potential integration challenges with existing systems due to Otomi. Nevertheless, all experts acknowledged its value and recommended this technical approach.

5   Discussion

During this research, we have achieved several milestones in relation to platform engineering. First, we have modeled platform engineering within a comprehensive reference model by deploying a multi-viewpoint approach. This method allowed us to dissect and explore platform engineering from various angles, resulting in a rich and detailed model that captures the inherent complexities of this discipline. Second, we delved into the complexity of implementing platform engineering by conducting a case study in which we created a conceptual design and technical implementation guided by the PE-RM. This technical implementation is further validated by experiments gaining insight into the added value of platform engineering by evaluating the productivity of developers. Third, we validated our reference model, demonstrating its utility and validity. Our validation confirmed that the model is theoretically sound and practically applicable, making it a valuable tool for organizations. The experiments exposed the added value of a drastically reduced onboarding time. Together, these achievements underscore the potential and value of the reference model as a guideline for organizations seeking to adopt platform engineering.

Regardless, challenges arise due to the lack of scientific research in this area, making systematic reviews difficult. Additional empirical data collection and analysis are critical to further support the model's validity. The experiments are focused on a select number of metrics, which do not cover all the aspects of platform engineering integration. The context-dependent nature of platform engineering may limit the model's broad applicability, as implementations could vary significantly across organizations. The environment in which a platform is introduced could also play an important role, where we focussed on a cloud environment and not on an on-premises environment. While the model is deemed beneficial for numerous organizations, it may not align seamlessly with all contexts, representing a recognized limitation. To strengthen and increase the relevance of the proposed model, further, diverse validation efforts, both quantitative and qualitative, across different organizational types are recommended. This could help to investigate the trade-off that must be made between the costs that integrating platform engineering entails versus what it delivers, which is currently not covered in this research.

6   Conclusion and Future Work

To conclude, in this paper, an understanding of platform engineering is presented through a reference model based on the RM-ODP framework. The validation and implementation of this reference model within a software organization are demonstrated, including a conceptual design and technical implementation. The proposed reference model will be a helpful tool for organizations to adopt platform engineering efficiently. While our findings are based on a single case study, we assume that this reference model applies to different types of organizations.

Future work involves three fronts: explore the integration of platform engineering across different organizational styles, enabling the model's customization for broader contexts and thus enhancing its applicability and utility; implement platform engineering to gather more empirical data on the effects of platform engineering integration in the long term, including a broader range of productivity metrics; and investigate the trade-off between the investment of integrating platform engineering and the benefits it brings to the organization.

Acknowledgements. This research is partially funded by the EU Horizon program under grant agreements 101094227 (BlueCloud 2026 project) and 860627 (CLARIFY project) and partially supported by LifeWatch ERIC and Dutch NWO LTER-LIFE project.

References

1. Baldwin, C.Y.: Design Rules, volume 2: How Technology Shapes Organizations. Harvard Business School Research Paper Series, pp. 19–042 (2018)
2. Beck, K., Beedle, M., Bennekum, V., et al.: The agile manifesto (2001)
3. Bharadwaj, A., Sawy, O.A.E., Pavlou, P.A., Venkatraman, N.: Digital business strategy: toward a next generation of insights. MIS Q. **37**(2), 471–482 (2013). https://doi.org/10.25300/misq/2013/37:2.3
4. Campbell, M.: Platform engineering challenges: small teams, build versus buy, and building the wrong thing. InfoQ (2023)
5. Cusumano, M.A., Gawer, A., Yoffie, D.B.: The Business of Platforms: Strategy in the Age of Digital Competition, Innovation, and Power, vol. 320. Harper Business New York (2019)
6. Di Nitto, E., Jamshidi, P., Guerriero, M., Spais, I., Tamburri, D.A.: A software architecture framework for quality-aware DevOps. In: QUDOS 2016, pp. 12–17. Association for Computing Machinery (2016). https://doi.org/10.1145/2945408.2945411

7. Dingsøyr, T., Nerur, S., Balijepally, V., Moe, N.B.: A decade of agile methodologies: towards explaining agile software development. J. Syst. Softw. **85**(6), 1213–1221 (2012). https://doi.org/10.1016/j.jss.2012.02.033

8. Ghantous, G.B., Gill, A.Q.: DevOps reference architecture for multi-cloud IoT applications. In: 2018 IEEE 20th Conference on Business Informatics (CBI), vol. 01, pp. 158–167 (2018). https://doi.org/10.1109/CBI.2018.00026

9. de la Hidalga, A.N., Hardisty, A., Martin, P., Magagna, B., Zhao, Z.: The ENVRI reference model. In: Zhao, Z., Hellström, M. (eds.) Towards Interoperable Research Infrastructures for Environmental and Earth Sciences. Lecture Notes in Computer Science, vol. 12003, pp. 61–81. Springer, Cham (2020). https://doi.org/10.1007/978-3-030-52829-4_4

10. Humanitec: State of platform engineering report. Technical report, Humanitec (2022)

11. Humanitec: Reference architecture for an enterprise-grade internal developer platform built with humanitec on AWS. Technical report, Humanitec (2023)

12. Jacobides, M.G., Cennamo, C., Gawer, A.: Externalities and complementarities in platforms and ecosystems: from structural solutions to endogenous failures. Res. Policy **53**(1), 104906 (2024). https://doi.org/10.1016/j.respol.2023.104906

13. Jiao, J., Simpson, T.W., Siddique, Z.: Product family design and platform-based product development: a state-of-the-art review. J. Intell. Manuf. **18**, 5–29 (2007). https://doi.org/10.1007/s10845-007-0003-2

14. van de Kamp, R., Bakker, K., Zhao, Z.: Paving the path towards platform engineering using a comprehensive reference model. Ph.D. thesis, University of Amsterdam (2023). https://doi.org/10.5281/zenodo.8379087

15. Kim, G., Humble, J., Debois, P., Willis, J., Forsgren, N.: The DevOps handbook: how to create world-class agility, reliability, & security in technology organizations. IT Revolution (2021)

16. Krishnan, V., Gupta, S.: Appropriateness and impact of platform-based product development. Manag. Sci. **47**(1), 52–68 (2001). https://doi.org/10.1287/mnsc.47.1.52.10665

17. Linington, P.F., Milosevic, Z., Tanaka, A., Vallecillo, A.: Building enterprise systems with ODP - an introduction to open distributed processing. In: Chapman and Hall/CRC Innovations in Software Engineering and Software Development (2011)

18. Lwakatare, L.E., Kuvaja, P., Oivo, M.: Dimensions of DevOps. In: Lassenius, C., Dingsøyr, T., Paasivaara, M. (eds.) Agile Processes in Software Engineering and Extreme Programming, pp. 212–217. Springer, Cham (2015). https://doi.org/10.1007/978-3-319-18612-2_19

19. Martin, P., Magagna, B., Liao, X., Zhao, Z.: Semantic linking of research infrastructure metadata. In: Zhao, Z., Hellström, M. (eds.) Towards Interoperable Research Infrastructures for Environmental and Earth Sciences. LNCS, vol. 12003, pp. 226–246. Springer, Cham (2020). https://doi.org/10.1007/978-3-030-52829-4_13

20. Nigel Kersten, K.M., Michael Stahnke, C.O.: State of DevOps report. Puppet (2021)

21. Raymond, K.: Reference model of open distributed processing (RM-ODP): introduction. In: Raymond, K., Armstrong, L. (eds.) Open Distributed Processing. IFIPAICT, pp. 3–14. Springer, Boston (1995). https://doi.org/10.1007/978-0-387-34882-7_1

22. Skelton, M., Pais, M.: Team topologies: organizing business and technology teams for fast flow. It Revolution (2019)

23. Sousa, C.D.: Brownfield redevelopment versus greenfield development: a private sector perspective on the costs and risks associated with brownfield redevelopment in the greater Toronto area. J. Environ. Plann. Manag. **43**(6), 831–853 (2000). https://doi.org/10.1080/09640560020001719

24. Zhou, J., Ji, Y., Zhao, D., Liu, J.: Platform engineering in enterprise application development. In: 2010 International Conference on E-Business and E-Government, pp. 112–115 (2010). https://doi.org/10.1109/ICEE.2010.36

Towards a Knowledge Base of Terms on Enterprise Architecture Debt

Ada Slupczynski[1] and Simon Hacks[2(✉)]

[1] RWTH Aachen University, Aachen, Germany
slupczynski@swc.rwth-aachen.de
[2] Stockholm University, Stockholm, Sweden
simon.hacks@dsv.su.se

Abstract. The term Enterprise Architecture (EA) Debt has been coined to grasp the difference between the actual state of the EA and its hypothetical, optimal state. Since its first definition in 2019, different theses have been conducted on the topic, and different articles have been published working on and with the term EA Debt. Consequently, using different terms has evolved to describe different phenomena within the domain. Due to the different authors involved in this development, perceiving these terms might differ. To avoid misunderstandings and to ease common understanding of the domain, we propose an ontology for the domain of EA Debt. We rely on a lightweight methodology for rapid ontology engineering (UPON light) and the Unified Foundational Ontology (UFO) to engineer our ontology.

Keywords: Enterprise Architecture Debt · Ontology · Knowledge Base

1 Introduction

Digital transformation comes with opportunities and challenges, such as business-IT alignment [47] (BITA). A holistic view is required to achieve BITA that helps understand the impact of products, employees, and business models [39]. One solution that provides a holistic view is Enterprise Architecture (EA) [33], which provides methods and tools to align business with IT, operationalize the business strategy, and can drive innovations [34]. EA provides transparency utilizing business-related views, application landscapes, and information technology sketches [33,53].

EA has often been established in many large organizations, and related research elaborates on various frameworks, methods, and tools [29,32]. Organizations' EAs usually reflect this evolution through an organically grown architecture with many artifacts and systems implemented. Simultaneously, the general perception of EA is bureaucratic, document-centric, and hampering agility due to its focus on long-term effects [10,52]. However, there might be significant discrepancies between long-term EA objectives and individual projects, causing

T. P. Sales et al. (Eds.): EDOC 2023 Workshops, LNBIP 498, pp. 194–210, 2024.
https://doi.org/10.1007/978-3-031-54712-6_12

conflicts due to a misalignment between EA plans and business needs. These conflicts could be: (1) Complex application landscapes with legacy systems and redundancies; (2) Outdated or incomplete EA artifacts and documentation; or (3) Procedures and organizational units in EA management that hamper IT innovations.

These conflicts are caused by past decisions that might have been justified at the corresponding time. Still, due to organizational change, these changes might not be reflected in the application landscape. To cope with this challenge, Hacks et al. proposed the term EA Debt to describe those results from past decisions that hamper changes in the organization [22]. Like technical debt, EA Debt represents obstacles moving from the current EA (as-is) towards a desired to-be-landscape. In contrast to technical debt, EA Debt provides a more holistic view, not just encompassing technical systems but also processes, organizational units, and regulations.

Since the first definition of EA Debt in 2019 [22], different works have been conducted within the domain. Naturally, different terms have evolved to describe different phenomena within the domain, and due to the different authors involved, the perception of terms might differ. To avoid misunderstandings and to ease common understanding of the domain, this work has the Research Objective to **develop an ontology for the domain of EA Debt**.

The rest of this work is structured as follows: Next, we go into more detail about the concept of EA Debt and present the research already conducted in the field. Then, we explain the research method we followed to build our ontology, followed by a demonstration of the ontology on an example from previous EA Debt research. Before we conclude the work and discuss the ontology's implications, we present related work on ontologies in EA and technical debt.

2   Background

The digitalization of organizations is accompanied by agile methods, which is a challenge for EA, as the time to define proper target architectures becomes reduced [49]. This is caused by product owners preferring short-term business value over sustainable architectural solutions. At the same time, approaches that ease long-term architectural solutions are scarce [19,50].

To address this challenge, Hacks et al. [22] extend the concept of Technical Debts, which describes past technical shortcuts that hamper IT developments [12,37], to the EA domain by suggesting a more holistic view on the organization. Concretely, Hacks et al. [22] originally defined EA Debt as "a metric that depicts the deviation of the currently present state of an enterprise from a hypothetical ideal state". Such a deviation can result from (1) decisions that are expedient in the short term but cause future changes to be more costly or (2) from a deviation in the actual EA that might have arisen due to changes in the valuation. The latter arises when an original decision aligns with the optimal EA, but a recent change in the strategy leads to another optimal EA, while the first hampers implementing better solutions immediately.

Research conducted in the field of EA Debt can be separated into two streams [2]: On the one hand, research related to the technical aspects of EA Debt. On the other hand, research elaborates on the socio-technical aspects of EA Debt.

Most of the research is related to technical aspects of EA Debts. Salentin and Hacks [41] defined the term EA Smell and published the first set of EA Smells together with a prototype that could identify some of the smells in ArchiMate models. Lehmann et al. [35] and Tieu and Hacks [48] continued in this line of research by finding other smells based on known anti-patterns and software architecture smells. Smajevic et al. [46] developed tool support to identify EA Smells in an automatized way in EA models.

Given a set of EA Debts, Yeong et al. [55] provide a method to prioritize which EA Debt to solve next. They adapt portfolio theory and utility functions to prioritize different EA Debts based on an organization's preferences. Having this prioritization, refactoring is necessary, presented by Liss et al. [38] to guide the removal of the respective debts. Slupczynski et al. [44] propose a process for evaluating the prudence and recklessness of enterprise architecture debts.

The technical proposals are framed by research on the socio-technical aspects. For instance, Alexander et al. propose a process to manage EA Debts [2]. It is suggested first to identify and collect EA Debts, assess and prioritize, and finally, remove or monitor actively. Here, the work of Jung et al. [28] provides a workshop format to identify EA Debts and EA Smells that cannot be detected solely relying on EA models. This was further developed by Daoudi et al. [13] to be more time efficient and also to consider when an EA Debt has a negative influence on an organization.

Finally, Hacks and Jung [23] conducted a first experiment to evaluate if the concept of EA Debt leads to a better EA. Therefore, they taught a group of students the concept. Afterward, the students were supposed to model a fictitious organization, and experts compared these models to models from student groups that did not know the concept. However, a positive effect could not be found in the experiment.

3   Method

To build our ontology to reason about the domain of EA Debt, we rely on the Unified Process for Ontology building (UPON) lite [14], which is a simplified version of UPON [15]. UPON lite is designed to enable domain experts with no deeper knowledge of ontology engineering to develop their ontology. As the authors of the article can be considered domain experts for EA Debt due to their involvement in a substantial amount of articles in the field and missing experience in the development of ontologies, UPON lite is deemed a well-suited solution to accomplish the overall goal of unifying the different terms in the domain.

UPON lite comprises six steps (cf. Fig. 1). In the following, we give a short recap on the single steps and how we realized them to build our ontology:

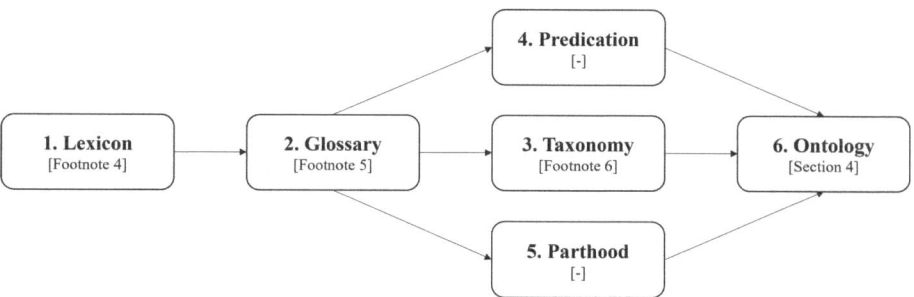

Fig. 1. Steps to Build an Ontology according to UPON lite [14]

1. **Lexicon:** In the first step, a lexicon of all terms in the domain is created. This lexicon is a flat list of undifferentiated terms that also includes synonyms.
   To create such a lexicon, we considered all papers citing the original paper [22] suggesting the definition of EA Debt. We only excluded papers not in English or not available for download and added two papers in the publishing process [13,23]. Next, we identified 1150 keywords in all papers via Yet Another Keyword Extractor (YAKE) [11][1] and removed all duplicates and non-relevant keywords (e.g., author names). The resulting lexicon comprises 117 entries and can be found in github[2].
2. **Glossary:** The second step aims to unify the lexicon by identifying synonyms and providing a textual description of the single terms. Moreover, more semantics can be added to the terms, e.g., by relying on established foundations like the Unified Foundational Ontology (UFO) [21] or the Object, Process, Actor Modeling Language (OPAL) [16].
   Accordingly, we identified synonyms and provided a textual description of 56 terms. Additionally, we first classified the terms according to UFO [21] as it is an established approach in our community and provides good tool support with its integration into Visual Paradigm. The glossary can be found in github[3].
3. **Taxonomy:** The third step focuses on defining a taxonomy of the terms within the glossary. I.e., one establishes a hierarchical "is a" order among the terms. Moreover, this step also evaluates the previous two steps in which unnecessary terms are removed, and missing terms can be added.
   Structuring the terms into a taxonomy, we identified 33 top-level concepts, 20 first-level specifications, and three second-level specifications. The resulting taxonomy can be found in github[4].

---

[1] We used the following parameters: $NGRAM = 3, Keywords\_Number = 50, Deduplication\_Threshold = 0.5$.
[2] https://github.com/simonhacks/ead_ontology/blob/main/Keywords.xlsx.
[3] https://github.com/simonhacks/ead_ontology/blob/main/Definitions.xlsx.
[4] https://github.com/simonhacks/ead_ontology/blob/main/Taxonomy.xlsx.

4. **Predication:** The fourth step determines the relevant attributes of the different concepts in an ontology. Generally, three types of properties are differentiated: atomic properties (AP), complex properties (CP), and reference properties (RP).

   Due to our focus on defining terms and often missing information about the concrete properties of certain concepts, we decided to neglect this step for now.

5. **Parthood:** In the fifth step, the concepts are analyzed towards their architectural structure. In other words, PART-OF relations among these concepts are identified and documented.

   We identified 22 PART-OF relations between the terms. We also added 24 terms, which we recognized were complementary to existing terms. Finally, we clustered the different terms into 5 clusters that refer to the main concepts in the domain of EA Debt.

6. **Ontology:** Finally, the ontology is constructed based on the findings from the previous steps. Additionally, domain-specific relations and constraints, such as cardinalities, are added, and the ontology is documented in a formal language.

   We documented the ontology within Visual Paradigm following UFO [21]. The resulting ontology is presented in Sect. 4 along with its basic concepts. The ontology is available on github[5].

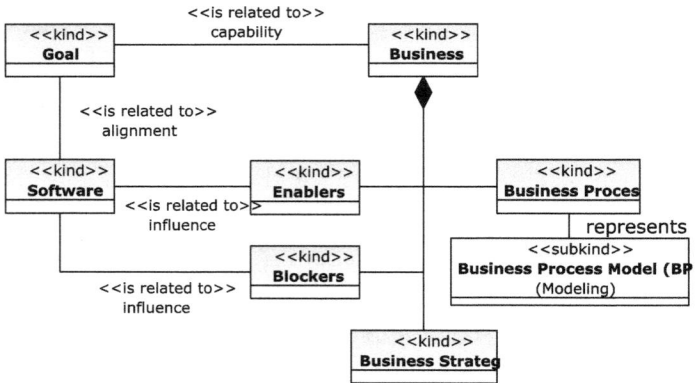

Fig. 2. Business domain ontology

4   Ontology

The ontology was split into five diagrams, representing five domains, namely Enterprise Architecture (EA), Technical Debt (TD), Software Engineering (SE),

---

[5] https://github.com/simonhacks/ead_ontology/blob/main/ead-ontology.vpp.

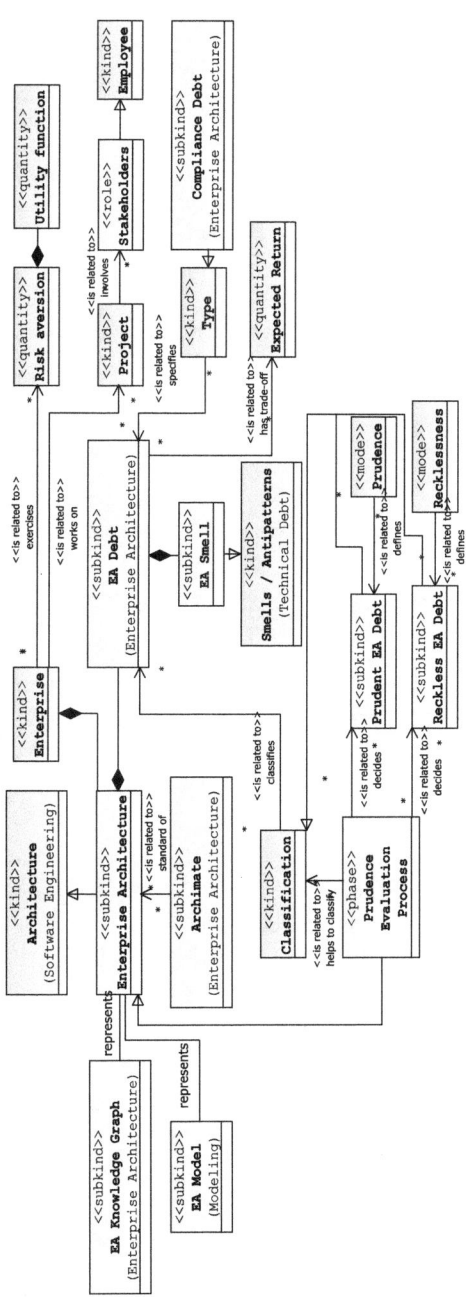

Fig. 3. EA domain ontology

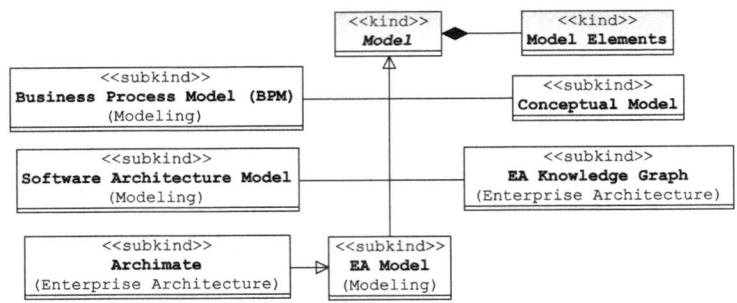

Fig. 4. Modeling domain ontology

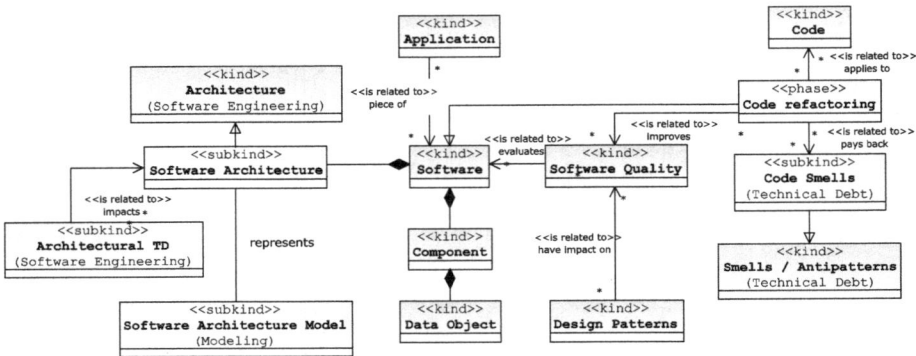

Fig. 5. SE domain ontology

and smaller Business and Modelling domains. In each diagram, keywords and their relations are presented, ordered hierarchically to improve readability. Each keyword is colored to indicate its UFO classification. Due to the page limitation, the roles and features of ontology classes, relationships, and attributes are explained and available on github[6].

Enterprise Architecture. The first domain is EA [54], which is the most relevant to our study. It is tightly related to other domains, spanning the Business, Data, Application, and Technical layers. As presented in Fig. 3, the EA domain focuses on representing information, and EA Debt [22] is at the center of focus. During the work on the ontology, we observed some points worth considering: Although

---

[6] https://github.com/simonhacks/ead_ontology.

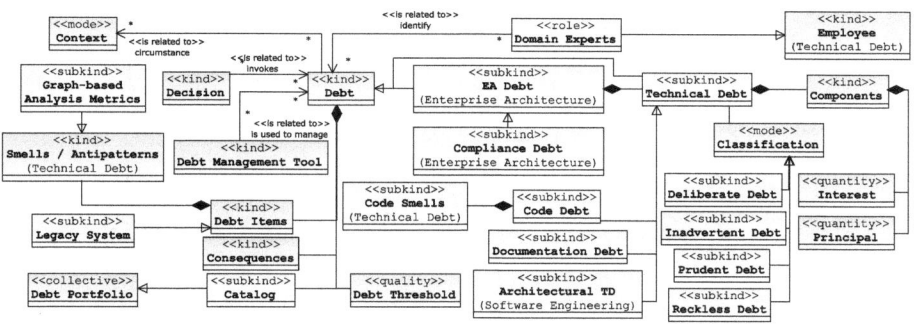

Fig. 6. TD domain ontology

Architecture is a big part of EA, in the identified keywords, this is not reflected. In the publications, there is no focus on architecture and projects, but instead on financing (as seen by the emphasis on debt [43] and risk aversion [55]), as well as conveying knowledge (as seen by the focus on representation [20] and stakeholders [31, 45]).

Notably, we recognized a change in the used definition of EA Debt, no longer including the aspect of being a metric, thus defining it as: *"the deviation of the currently present state of an enterprise from a hypothetical ideal state."* (e.g., [23]). This is mainly motivated to better differentiate between cause (debt) and symptom (smell), initially manifested in a single definition. As this eases the understanding of the concept, we also follow this differentiation. Furthermore, a discussion arose around the phrase "hypothetical ideal state" as it is impossible to determine. One suggestion is to use "planned future state" instead. However, we do not think this properly reflects the idea beyond EA Debt as a planned future state does not need to be flawless and thus still can incorporate EA Debts that are consciously taken but should be documented.

Given how young the field of EA Debts is, one can only expect the ontology to change and grow with time. This is rightfully so, as with each piece of information, there will be more clarity about the definitions and relations of the terms.

Technical Debt. The second domain (cf. Figure 6) concerns TD. TD is an inseparable part of EA Debts. It involves the debt committed on the Technical and Application layer. It is tightly related to the product and has been studied longer than EA Debts. Even though the two are inseparable, based on the identified keywords, there is a gap in their consideration in papers related to EA Debts. We observed that only one of two metrics is discussed, leaving the review of the principal insufficient. Similarly, considering the TD classification proposed

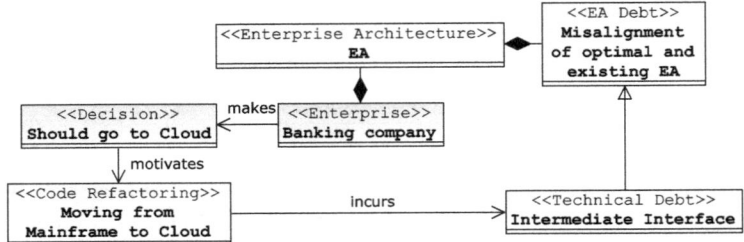

Fig. 7. Instantiation of the Ontology for an Intermediate Interface.

by Fowler [17], only inadvertent debt got enough attention to appear as one of the identified keywords. This might indicate a lack of research into other debt classes.

As the concepts of TD and EA Debt are related to Financial Debt, one can observe that many keywords on the diagram are from the financial sector.

Software Engineering. As the area of SE has been studied longer, it was easier to identify the underlying relations between the identified keywords. As seen in Fig. 5, the diagram presents a small part of a SE ontology composed of keywords often appearing in the context of EA Debts. However, it still provides valuable information. It is related to TD through Refactoring [18], which pays back the TD made visible through Code Smells. It is also associated with EA through the consideration of Architecture. The limited review of Architecture in the context of EA Debt indicates that SE is closer to TD than EA. This is further supported by the definition of EA, which focuses more on Business and Data, leaving the Technical aspects compared to TD.

Business. The Business domain (cf. Figure 2) focuses on the process and aspects enabling or blocking it. Relevant business information can be modeled to support stakeholders in evaluating the business processes [51]. However, business seems to be a supporting domain as it does not result in many relevant keywords.

Modeling. Modeling is a supporting domain for the entire ontology and is shown in Fig. 4. It represents the functionality needed to assess the state of other domains, especially business, EA, and SA.

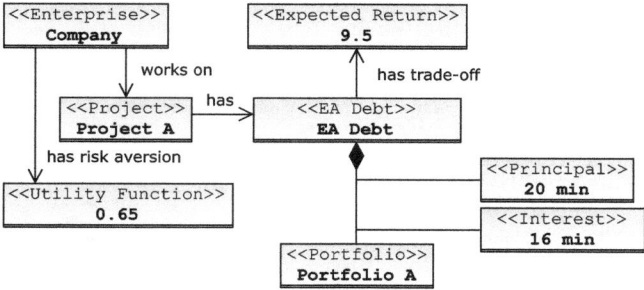

Fig. 8. Instantiation of the Ontology for Calculating the Optimal Portfolio.

5 Demonstration

We create concrete instances based on previously reported cases to showcase the developed ontology. More concretely, we illustrate one case from the first publication [22], one case elaborating on the prioritization of EA Debts [55], and one case introducing the concepts of prudence [44]. We opted for these cases as they cover many aspects captured in the ontology.

The first case [22] takes place in a company in the banking domain, which is step-by-step moving its applications from the mainframe to the cloud. Two applications that depend on each other should go to the cloud. However, due to delays, one of the applications cannot be moved to the cloud at the same time as the other application. Therefore, an intermediate interface between the cloud and the mainframe needs to be implemented that is not part of the envisioned optimal EA and, thus, causes an EA Debt. The instantiation of this example can be found in Fig. 7.

The second case [55] illustrates how a company can decide which project to conduct to find the optimal amount of EA Debt according to their risk aversion. Therefore, five project options are envisioned with their respective portfolio risk and expected return. To explain the computation of these parameters, one project is presented in more detail, with four different EA Debts. The principal, the interest, and the interest growth rate are given for each EA Debt. Additionally, the covariance between the EA Debts is provided to calculate the portfolio risk and the expected return. The instantiation of this example can be found in Fig. 8.

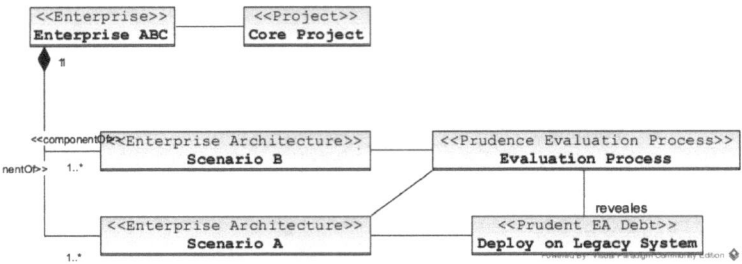

Fig. 9. Instantiation of the Ontology for Prudence in EA Debt.

The third case [44] presents a toy example where an enterprise faced with complex maintenance of a core functionality project decides to work on reducing TD through refactorings and enforcing architecture guidelines. The conflict between on the one hand time and budget constraints and on the other hand the importance of new functionality forces the enterprise to evaluate the prudence and recklessness of two potential scenarios using the Prudence Evaluation Process (PEP). In the first scenario, the guidelines are violated by deploying on the legacy system, saving time and resources. The second scenario is where policies are followed by deploying the modern system while spending more time and resources on integration with the core functionality. The instantiation of this example can be found in Fig. 9.

6 Related Work

One stream of research that links ontologies and EA uses ontologies to describe EA itself. As such, Kang et al. [30] describe an ontology that provides more detailed semantics about EA and facilitates communication around the different stakeholders. Therefore, they define three different ontologies. One ontology to explain business terms, one for the elements of the EA, and finally, the different concepts are linked via relationships. Al Hadidi and Baghdadi [1] propose an ontology to model the interaction between different organization types. They focus on loosely coupled enterprises that join forces to provide new services and temporary cooperations to access new markets. Similarly, Janulevičius et al. [27] suggest an ontology to reflect on the security properties of cloud computing in EA. Mainly, they focus on security controls for the essential documents and integrating the ontology into EA modeling.

Another direction of research elaborates on linking EA models with concrete ontologies. For example, Hinkelmann et al. [25,26] use EA models to have a graphical organization representation and integrate them with machine-readable enterprise ontologies. Therefore, they map the EA modeling notation to a respective ontology that provides additional information to make the graphical representation machine-readable. Another angle is taken by Bakhshandeh et al. [9] and Antunes et al. [5,6], who use ontologies to integrate ArchiMate with different other modeling languages that are better suited for specific domains. Moreover, their integration of ArchiMate and ontologies allows a better analysis of the model.

A third facet of related research uses ontologies to enrich existing EA modeling approaches with new concepts. Azevedo et al. [7,8] perform an ontological analysis on the concepts of resources, capabilities, and competencies and extend ArchiMate to be able to cope with these concepts in the domain of portfolio management. Other approaches enrich ArchiMate to allow risk analysis [40] based on the Common Ontology of Value and Risk, perform value modeling [42] illustrated on the case study of a low-cost airline, or incorporate trust [4] demonstrated on a COVID-19 data repository.

Finally, there is research that elaborates on ontologies for Technical Debt. However, research in this direction is scarce. We could only identify three works that use ontologies to structure knowledge around Technical Debt or use it for its analysis. Firstly, Alves et al. [3] propose a first step to an ontology of terms of Technical Debt. Secondly, an ontology has been proposed for a more concrete instance of Technical Debt, i.e., Requirements Debt [36]. And finally, Händler and Neumann [24] suggest an ontology for refactoring in game design, which is used in a teaching case.

7   Conclusion

In this work, we have presented a first step to an ontology describing the domain of EA Debts. To achieve this, we analyzed the existing publications in the field, identified the most relevant keywords, and arranged them in the ontology. Moreover, we added further concepts that were missing. Those concepts seem to be understudied in the domain as they are usually considered in the domain of Technical Debt but do not appear in research related to EA Debt. Thus, this draws an opportunity for future research.

From a methodological point of view, we recognized a lack of tool support for extracting keywords from articles. We were forced to perform significant manual work to enable the analysis, as the articles are often solely provided in semi-structured format (PDF).

Finally, this is the first attempt to structure the knowledge in the domain of EA Debt. This is a continuous effort; the ontology needs to be updated as the field develops. Moreover, we plan to perform other actions to improve the ontology, e.g., by interviewing researchers and practitioners to grasp concepts not documented in scientific articles.

References

1. Al Hadidi, F., Baghdadi, Y.: Ontology for enterprise interactions: extended and virtual enterprises. In: Baghdadi, Y., Harfouche, A. (eds.) ICT for a Better Life and a Better World. LNISO, vol. 30, pp. 365–379. Springer, Cham (2019). https://doi.org/10.1007/978-3-030-10737-6_24
2. Alexander, P., Hacks, S., Jung, J., Lichter, H., Steffens, U., Uludağ, Ö.: A framework for managing enterprise architecture debts - outline and research directions. In: CEUR Workshop Proceedings, vol. 2628 (2020)
3. Alves, N.S., Ribeiro, L.F., Caires, V., Mendes, T.S., Spínola, R.O.: Towards an ontology of terms on technical debt. In: 2014 Sixth International Workshop on Managing Technical Debt, pp. 1–7 (2014). https://doi.org/10.1109/MTD.2014.9
4. Amaral, G., Sales, T.P., Guizzardi, G., Almeida, J.P.A., Porello, D.: Modeling trust in enterprise architecture: a pattern language for ArchiMate. In: Grabis, J., Bork, D. (eds.) PoEM 2020. LNBIP, vol. 400, pp. 73–89. Springer, Cham (2020). https://doi.org/10.1007/978-3-030-63479-7_6
5. Antunes, G., Bakhshandeh, M., Mayer, R., Borbinha, J., Caetano, A.: Using ontologies for enterprise architecture integration and analysis. Complex Syst. Inform. Model. Q. **1**, 1–23 (2014)
6. Antunes, G., Bakhshandeh, M., Mayer, R., Borbinha, J., Caetano, A.: Using ontologies for enterprise architecture analysis. In: 2013 17th IEEE International Enterprise Distributed Object Computing Conference Workshops, pp. 361–368 (2013). https://doi.org/10.1109/EDOCW.2013.47
7. Azevedo, C.L., Iacob, M.E., Almeida, J.P.A., van Sinderen, M., Pires, L.F., Guizzardi, G.: An ontology-based well-founded proposal for modeling resources and capabilities in archimate. In: 2013 17th IEEE International Enterprise Distributed Object Computing Conference, pp. 39–48 (2013). https://doi.org/10.1109/EDOC.2013.14
8. Azevedo, C.L., Iacob, M.E., Almeida, J.P.A., van Sinderen, M., Pires, L.F., Guizzardi, G.: Modeling resources and capabilities in enterprise architecture: a well-founded ontology-based proposal for ArchiMate. Inf. Syst. **54**, 235–262 (2015). https://doi.org/10.1016/j.is.2015.04.008

9. Bakhshandeh, M., Antunes, G., Mayer, R., Borbinha, J., Caetano, A.: A modular ontology for the enterprise architecture domain. In: 2013 17th IEEE International Enterprise Distributed Object Computing Conference Workshops, pp. 5–12 (2013). https://doi.org/10.1109/EDOCW.2013.8
10. Bente, S., Bombosch, U., Langade, S.: Collaborative Enterprise Architecture: Enriching EA with Lean, Agile, and Enterprise 2.0 Practices. Morgan Kaufmann (2012)
11. Campos, R., Mangaravite, V., Pasquali, A., Jorge, A.M., Nunes, C., Jatowt, A.: YAKE! Collection-independent automatic keyword extractor. In: Pasi, G., Piwowarski, B., Azzopardi, L., Hanbury, A. (eds.) ECIR 2018. LNCS, vol. 10772, pp. 806–810. Springer, Cham (2018). https://doi.org/10.1007/978-3-319-76941-7_80
12. Cunningham, W.: The WyCash portfolio management system. ACM SIGPLAN OOPS Messenger **4**(2), 29–30 (1993). https://doi.org/10.1145/157710.157715
13. Daoudi, S., Larsson, M., Hacks, S., Jung, J.: Discovering and assessing enterprise architecture debts. Complex Syst. Inform. Model. Q. (2023)
14. De Nicola, A., Missikoff, M.: A lightweight methodology for rapid ontology engineering. Commun. ACM **59**(3), 79–86 (2016). https://doi.org/10.1145/2818359
15. De Nicola, A., Missikoff, M., Navigli, R.: A software engineering approach to ontology building. Inf. Syst. **34**(2), 258–275 (2009)
16. D'Antonio, F., Missikoff, M., Taglino, F.: Formalizing the OPAL eBusiness ontology design patterns with owl. In: Gonçalves, R.J., Müller, J.P., Mertins, K., Zelm, M. (eds.) Enterprise Interoperability II, pp. 345–356. Springer, London (2007). https://doi.org/10.1007/978-1-84628-858-6_38
17. Fowler, M.: Technical debt quadrant (2009). https://martinfowler.com/bliki/TechnicalDebtQuadrant.html
18. Fowler, M.: Refactoring: improving the design of existing code. In: 11th European Conference, Jyväskylä, Finland (1997)
19. Gampfer, F., Jürgens, A., Müller, M., Buchkremer, R.: Past, current and future trends in enterprise architecture-a view beyond the horizon. Comput. Ind. **100**, 70–84 (2018)
20. Glaser, P.L., Ali, S.J., Sallinger, E., Bork, D.: Model-based construction of enterprise architecture knowledge graphs. In: Almeida, J.P.A., Karastoyanova, D., Guizzardi, G., Montali, M., Maggi, F.M., Fonseca, C.M. (eds.) EDOC 2022. LNCS, vol. 13585, pp. 57–73. Springer, Heidelberg (2022). https://doi.org/10.1007/978-3-031-17604-3_4
21. Guizzardi, G., Botti Benevides, A., Fonseca, C.M., Porello, D., Almeida, J.P.A., Prince Sales, T.: UFO: unified foundational ontology. Appl. Ontol. **17**(1), 167–210 (2022)
22. Hacks, S., Hofert, H., Salentin, J., Yeong, Y.C., Lichter, H.: Towards the definition of enterprise architecture debts. In: 2019 IEEE 23rd EDOCW, pp. 9–16. IEEE (2019)
23. Hacks, S., Jung, J.: A first validation of the enterprise architecture debts concept. In: van der Aa, H., Bork, D., Proper, H.A., Schmidt, R. (eds.) BPMDS EMMSAD 2023. LNBIP, vol. 479, pp. 17–226. Springer, Cham (2023). https://doi.org/10.1007/978-3-031-34241-7_15

24. Haendler, T., Neumann, G.: Ontology-based analysis of game designs for software refactoring. In: CSEDU (1), pp. 24–35 (2019)
25. Hinkelmann, K., Gerber, A., Karagiannis, D., Thoenssen, B., van der Merwe, A., Woitsch, R.: A new paradigm for the continuous alignment of business and it: combining enterprise architecture modelling and enterprise ontology. Comput. Ind. **79**, 77–86 (2016). https://doi.org/10.1016/j.compind.2015.07.009. Special Issue on Future Perspectives On Next Generation Enterprise Information Systems
26. Hinkelmann, K., Maise, M., Thönssen, B.: Connecting enterprise architecture and information objects using an enterprise ontology. In: Proceedings of the First International Conference on Enterprise Systems: ES 2013, pp. 1–11 (2013). https://doi.org/10.1109/ES.2013.6690088
27. Janulevičius, J., Marozas, L., Čenys, A., Goranin, N., Ramanauskaitė, S.: Enterprise architecture modeling based on cloud computing security ontology as a reference model. In: 2017 Open Conference of Electrical, Electronic and Information Sciences (eStream), pp. 1–6 (2017). https://doi.org/10.1109/eStream.2017.7950320
28. Jung, J., Hacks, S., De Gooijer, T., Kinnunen, M., Rehring, K.: Revealing common enterprise architecture debts: conceptualization and critical reflection on a workshop format industry experience report. In: Proceedings - IEEE International Enterprise Distributed Object Computing Workshop, EDOCW, pp. 271–278 (2021). https://doi.org/10.1109/EDOCW52865.2021.00058
29. Kaisler, S., Armour, F.: 15 years of enterprise architecting at HICSS: revisiting the Critical Problems. In: Proceedings of the 50th Hawaii International Conference on System Sciences 2017, pp. 4807–4816 (2017)
30. Kang, D., Lee, J., Choi, S., Kim, K.: An ontology-based enterprise architecture. Expert Syst. Appl. **37**(2), 1456–1464 (2010). https://doi.org/10.1016/j.eswa.2009.06.073
31. Kanji, S., Alexander, P., Lichter, H.: Reporting framework for enterprise architecture debts. Master's thesis (2022)
32. Kotusev, S.: Enterprise architecture: what did we study? Int. J. Coop. Inf. Syst. **26**(4) (2017)
33. Lankhorst, M.: Enterprise Architecture at Work. Springer, Heidelberg (2009)
34. Lapalme, J.: Three schools of thought on enterprise architecture. IT Prof. **14**(6), 37–43 (2012)
35. Lehmann, B.D., Alexander, P., Lichter, H., Hacks, S.: Towards the identification of process anti-patterns in enterprise architecture models. In: 8th International Workshop on Quantitative Approaches to Software Quality in conjunction with the 27th Asia-Pacific Software Engineering Conference (APSEC 2020), vol. 2767, pp. 47–54 (2020)
36. Lenarduzzi, V., Fucci, D.: Towards a holistic definition of requirements debt. In: 2019 ACM/IEEE International Symposium on Empirical Software Engineering and Measurement (ESEM), pp. 1–5 (2019). https://doi.org/10.1109/ESEM.2019.8870159
37. Li, Z., Avgeriou, P., Liang, P.: A systematic mapping study on technical debt and its management. J. Syst. Softw. **101**, 193–220 (2015). https://doi.org/10.1016/j.jss.2014.12.027

38. Liss, L., Kämmerling, H., Alexander, P., Lichter, H.: Towards a catalog of refactoring solutions for enterprise architecture smells. In: Joint Proceedings of SEED 2021 & QuASoQ 2021 Co-located with 28th Asia Pacific Software Engineering Conference 2021, Taipei [Virtual], 6 December 2021, vol. 3062, pp. 60–69 (2021)
39. Morakanyane, R., Grace, A., O'Reilly, P.: Conceptualizing digital transformation in business organizations: a systematic review of literature. In: 30th Bled eConference: Digital Transformation - From Connecting Things to Transforming our Lives, BLED 2017, pp. 427–444 (2017)
40. Prince Sales, T., Almeida, J.P.A., Santini, S., Baião, F., Guizzardi, G.: Ontological analysis and redesign of risk modeling in ArchiMate. In: 2018 IEEE 22nd International Enterprise Distributed Object Computing Conference (EDOC), pp. 154–163 (2018). https://doi.org/10.1109/EDOC.2018.00028
41. Salentin, J., Hacks, S.: Towards a catalog of enterprise architecture smells. In: WI2020 Community Tracks, pp. 276–290. GITO Verlag (2020)
42. Sales, T.P., Roelens, B., Poels, G., Guizzardi, G., Guarino, N., Mylopoulos, J.: A pattern language for value modeling in ArchiMate. In: Giorgini, P., Weber, B. (eds.) CAiSE 2019. LNCS, vol. 11483, pp. 230–245. Springer, Cham (2019). https://doi.org/10.1007/978-3-030-21290-2_15
43. Schütz, J., Gómez, J.M.: Towards collaborative technical debt management in systems of systems. In: Proceedings of the 3rd International Conference on Technical Debt, TechDebt 2020, pp. 87–91. Association for Computing Machinery, New York (2020). https://doi.org/10.1145/3387906.3388620
44. Slupczynski., A., Alexander., P., Lichter., H.: A process for evaluating the prudence of enterprise architecture debts. In: Proceedings of the 25th International Conference on Enterprise Information Systems - Volume 2: ICEIS, pp. 623–630. INSTICC, SciTePress (2023). https://doi.org/10.5220/0011971400003467
45. Slupczynski, A.M.: Towards a framework for evaluating the prudence of enterprise architecture debts. Masterarbeit, RWTH Aachen University, Aachen (2022). https://doi.org/10.18154/RWTH-2022-01253, https://publications.rwth-aachen.de/record/840789. veröffentlicht auf dem Publikationsserver der RWTH Aachen University 2022; Masterarbeit, RWTH Aachen University, 2021
46. Smajevic, M., Hacks, S., Bork, D.: Using knowledge graphs to detect enterprise architecture smells. In: Serral, E., Stirna, J., Ralyté, J., Grabis, J. (eds.) PoEM 2021. LNBIP, vol. 432, pp. 48–63. Springer, Cham (2021). https://doi.org/10.1007/978-3-030-91279-6_4
47. Tabrizi, B., Lam, E., Girard, K., Irvin, V.: Digital transformation is not about technology. Harv. Bus. Rev. 2–7 (2019)
48. Tieu, B., Hacks, S.: Determining enterprise architecture smells from software architecture smells. In: 2021 IEEE 23rd Conference on Business Informatics (CBI), vol. 02, pp. 134–142 (2021). https://doi.org/10.1109/CBI52690.2021.10064
49. Uludağ, Ö., Kleehaus, M., Xu, X., Matthes, F.: Investigating the role of architects in scaling agile frameworks. In: 2017 IEEE 21st International Enterprise Distributed Object Computing Conference (EDOC), pp. 123–132. IEEE (2017)
50. Uludag, Ö., Reiter, N., Matthes, F.: What to expect from enterprise architects in large-scale agile development? A multiple-case study. In: 25th AMCIS (2019)

51. Weske, M.: Business Process Management-concepts, Languages, Architectures. Springer, Berlin (2007). https://doi.org/10.1007/978-3-540-73522-9
52. Wierda, G.: Chess and the Art of Enterprise Architecure. R&A (2015)
53. Wierda, G.: Mastering ArchiMate, 2 edn. R&A (2017)
54. Winter, R., Fischer, R.: Essential layers, artifacts, and dependencies of enterprise architecture. In: 2006 10th IEEE International Enterprise Distributed Object Computing Conference Workshops (EDOCW 2006), p. 30. IEEE (2006)
55. Yeong, Y., Hacks, S., Lichter, H.: Prioritization of EA debts facilitating portfolio theory. In: CEUR Workshop Proceedings, vol. 2511 (2019)

A Quantitative Assessment Method for Microservices Granularity to Improve Maintainability

Famke Driessen[2]([✉]), Luís Ferreira Pires[1][iD], João Luiz Rebelo Moreira[1][iD], Paul Verhoeven[2], and Sander van den Bosch[2]

[1] Semantics, Cybersecurity and Services group, University of Twente, PO Box 127, 7500 AE Enschede, The Netherlands
{l.ferreirapires,j.l.rebelomoreira}@utwente.nl
[2] Deloitte Consulting, P.O. Box 58110, 1040 HC Amsterdam, The Netherlands
{fdriessen,paverhoeven,svandenbosch}@deloitte.nl
https://www.utwente.nl/en/eemcs/scs/

Abstract. The popularity of microservices has increased over the past decade due to their potential benefits for distributed enterprise applications. Developing and maintaining a microservices architecture (MSA) is challenging, amongst others because the size (granularity) of the microservices has an impact on most system properties, such as, e.g., maintainability, performance, and scalability. Currently, architects determine the granularity of the microservices by identifying bounded contexts or business capabilities, which is mainly based on their experience. This paper presents a quantitative assessment method to evaluate the granularity of the microservices for improved system maintainability. The method is based on a set of metrics that are relevant for maintainability, namely change coupling, structural coupling, weighted service interface count, lines of code, service interface data cohesion, and change frequency. By evaluating these metrics, focusing on coupling, cohesion, and size, the method can assess refactors of an architecture in which microservices are merged or decomposed. We validated our method with three open source microservice-based projects with different sizes and structures. Our method can substantiate the design decisions concerning the granularity of microservices, identifying services that are candidates for merging and decomposition towards maintainability evolution, with clear benefits particularly for enterprise applications.

Keywords: microservices architecture · granularity · maintainability · service coupling · service cohesion · change coupling

1 Introduction

The popularity of microservices for the development of enterprise applications has increased tremendously over the past decade. Microservices are acclaimed to

T. P. Sales et al. (Eds.): EDOC 2023 Workshops, LNBIP 498, pp. 211–226, 2024.
https://doi.org/10.1007/978-3-031-54712-6_13

bring a wide range of benefits over monolithic applications (monoliths), such as language agnosticism, improved scalability and maintainability. However, adopting a microservices architecture (MSA) can be challenging. For instance, guaranteeing data consistency in MSA with multiple databases may require significant effort [15]. Transactions in coarse-grained systems are encapsulated in a single service, which facilitates handling data consistency. However, if the granularity level of a coarse-grained system enforces tightly-coupled services, this can significantly reduce the maintainability and scalability of a system. Hence, one of the main challenges in MSAs is the definition of an appropriate level of granularity for the microservices [14].

Maintainability is strongly influenced by the granularity of the microservices [5]. It is generally expected that the maintainability of an application improves when an MSA is adopted, because different development teams can be assigned to specific microservices and work in parallel [16]. However, if the granularity of the microservices architecture is not properly designed, dependencies among microservices can result in a maintenance nightmare. This tight coupling can enforce change propagation, which requires developers to update multiple services as a consequence of changes in one service. Since maintainability is a challenge in MSA [5], we investigated the assessment of microservices granularity from a maintenance perspective. Domain-Driven Design (DDD) [9] is an approach that can be used to define the granularity of the microservices at design-time by determining boundaries (the scope) of the services. However, DDD does not offer concrete decision support, since it only outlines how bounded contexts can be identified for each domain concept [22], relying on (expensive) experienced architects to get appropriate results, which are still prone to subjectivity.

This paper presents a method to assess the granularity of microservices with respect to maintainability. The method is based on metrics that are relevant for maintainability, namely change coupling, structural coupling, weighted service interface count, lines of code, service interface data cohesion, and change frequency. By evaluating these metrics, our method can assess refactors of a microservices architecture according to maintainability requirements. To automate the execution of this method and capture these metrics, we reused available tools and developed features to extract relevant information from code repositories. We validated our method with three open source projects of different sizes and structures, and this paper discusses two of them. Our results show that the design decisions identified by our method are mostly in accordance with the maintainability evolution as perceived by the experts involved in the investigated projects, which indicates that our method can be potentially used as a component in a design decision support tool especially for enterprise applications.

This paper is further structured as follows: Sect. 2 discusses related work, Sect. 3 describes our research approach, Sect. 4 defines the metrics to assess the granularity of microservices from a maintenance perspective used in our method, Sect. 5 introduces our assessment method, Sect. 6 describes the validation of our method and Sect. 7 gives our final remarks.

2   Related Work

Inherent to the popularity of microservices is the intensive research on this topic. However, we found only a few publications that focus directly on assessing the granularity of microservices. A method to collect coupling metrics at runtime with focus on monitoring the evolution of maintainability in an MSA is introduced in [3]. Although their results are promising, as the evolution in metrics seems to correspond with the architectural evolution of the system, their method does not assess cohesion and requires a test suite covering the complete system, which decreases the accessibility of their method as such a test suite is not always at hand. Our research addresses these limitations by introducing metrics that capture cohesion as well as coupling and size, providing a different perspective for evaluating maintainability in relation to granularity.

A method based on Model-Driven Engineering techniques is introduced in [8], which provides insight into the evolution of different quality attributes of an MSA in reaction to architectural changes. An obstacle to using their approach is that a model of the architecture is required. Although there are techniques to automatically recover architectures from MSAs [2,10,11], these techniques require specific input data that is not always available. In contrast, our work focuses primarily on maintainability and uses metrics that can be automatically obtained from the software and version control data. Our research complements existing works by offering a different method that uses a larger metric suite and improves the understanding and evaluation of microservice architecture quality.

3   Approach

This section discusses the problem context, our research steps and the selection of cases to develop and validate the method.

3.1   Problem Definition

Currently, practitioners identify service boundaries (and therefore their granularity) primarily based on their experience and insight without making use of any frameworks or tools, except for DDD [9,22]. However, DDD fails to offer concrete decision support, leaving room for subjectivity, and we can never be sure that sufficient experience for determining microservice boundaries is available in each MSA-based project. Furthermore, it is not possible to define some generic optimal granularity values that apply in all circumstances, since varying system requirements often require different levels of granularity. For example, while finer-grained services are locally less complex, the whole application may become less flexible if these services are tightly coupled. Hence, a method to support granularity decisions cannot be agnostic with respect to system requirements, i.e., it should consider granularity from the perspective of some specific requirement.

Design decision support for the definition of microservices' granularity is a relevant open issue for both practice and research [21], which calls for the development of a method that supports the definition of granularity for improved maintainability based on assessment of microservices. The goal of this research has been to develop such a method, which should be able to reduce the need for experience in making choices on microservice granularity.

3.2 Research Steps

Our research approach consisted of seven steps: Literature review, Requirement elicitation, Instrumentation, Case selection, Data collection, Data analysis and Validation. With a systematic literature review we identified a set of maintainability metrics that are applicable to MSA. We then selected metrics that complement each other, aiming to cover maintainability aspects in our assessment method.

Based on the maintainability metrics, we formulated two sets of requirements: (1) for the software projects we used as cases; and (2) for the instrumentation we selected. We identified 3 cases, selected 4 tools and developed a script for calculating change frequency and for data cleaning. Subsequently, we performed data collection from the selected cases. The preparation of the data (extracting and cleaning) was an essential step in our research. The compatibility of the tools with the selected cases is not always a given: it was not possible to derive certain metrics for some cases while for others some case-specific adjustments to the instrumentation were made. For some metrics, manual interventions were inevitable and additional steps that had to be taken were project-specific.

In the data analysis step, we analysed the different metrics obtained during our assessment, calculating the metrics per refactor type. Expert opinion was used to validate whether the findings of our assessment method corresponded with reality, where the experts were architects or developers involved in the real refactor(s) of the cases. During these semi-structured interviews, the experts were asked about the team's intentions for a refactor, i.e., which system property they tried to improve by that refactoring, and the aftermath, i.e., the extent to which the refactor can be considered successful. Finally, the findings of our assessment method were compared to the statements of the interviewees for each case. The validity of our assessment method depended on whether it could reflect the same evolution in maintainability as experienced by the experts.

3.3 Cases Selection

We selected three freely available cases, which are MSA-based open source application projects. An important requirement is that in each project different code releases were properly stored in a version control system (Git), so that we could access this code before and after each code refactor. In addition, each application should be implemented to address real-life business needs, i.e., it should not be a sample application for demonstration purposes. Each project should also provide refactor(s) in which the granularity of the application was affected.

To be able to draw conclusions on the generalisability of our method, we covered the following additional requirements: (i) a smaller application consisting of less than 3 services; (ii) a large application consisting of more than 10 services; (iii) an MSA using orchestration; (iv) an MSA based on choreography; (v) a system using synchronous API calls; (vi) a system communicating asynchronously via events (Pub-Sub message brokers); (vii) an open-source project and; (viii) a project developed in an enterprise context. In this way, we aimed at capturing development experience in terms of the architectural reasons for rearranging microservices in each of these refactors.

4   Maintainability Metrics

This section discusses the metrics and heuristics that we selected to assess maintainability in MSAs, based on [6].

4.1   Size Metrics

Lines of code (LOC) refer to the number of lines of code of the service implementation, from which blank lines and comments are excluded. This is a popular but controversial metric, as it is influenced by the verbosity of the programming languages [6]. However, we considered LOC due to its direct relation to complexity. Since the freedom of choosing a programming language (polyglot programming) is one of the claimed benefits of microservices, other complexity metrics such as, e.g., cyclomatic complexity are hard to measure as the required tooling is language-dependent. However, a strong correlation exists between LOC and cyclomatic complexity [12].

Since LOC may not be ideal to assess an MSA with microservices implemented with different programming languages, we complemented it with *Weighted service interface count* (WSIC), which is a size metric proposed in [13] that considers the number of operations exposed in the interface of a service. Intuitively, it can be an appropriate indication for maintainability, as a higher number of operations implies a more complex service, and higher complexity for the system as a whole, since more operations directly require larger implementation and testing efforts. This metric can be weighted in different ways to account for the number and complexity of the parameters of each operation, but in the absence of validated weighting methods, we used the default weight of 1. Thresholds to interpret WSIC values are given in [7].

4.2   Coupling Metrics

Two software modules s_1 and s_2 are structurally coupled if there are code or structural dependencies between them. In the context of MSA, such a structural dependency can be, e.g., in the form of service calls or a producer-consumer relation. A definition of *structural coupling* (SC) specifically for microservices is given in formula (1), based on [18].

$$StructuralCoupling(s_1, s_2) = 1 - \frac{1}{degree(s_1, s_2)} * LWF * GWF \qquad (1)$$

This definition is based on the *local weighting factor* (LWF) and the *global weighting factor* (GWF), defined by formulas (2) and (3), respectively.

$$LocalWeightingFactor(s_1, s_2) = \frac{1 + outdegree(s_1, s_2)}{1 + degree(s_1, s_2)} \qquad (2)$$

$$GlobalWeightingFactor(s_1, s_2) = \frac{degree(s_1, s_2)}{max(degree(all\_services))} \qquad (3)$$

LWF considers the degree and the out-degree from service s_1 to service s_2, where the degree represents the total number of structural dependencies between s_1 and s_2, and the $out\_degree(s_1, s_2)$ the number of dependencies among the total degree that is directed from s_1 to s_2. GWF weighs the degree between two services with the highest degree between a service pair of the application, considering all combinations of services in the application as possible pairs. SC is a normalised metric, and a value close to 1 indicates high structural coupling. Since this metric has been validated in 17 open-source projects, we considered it in our method as originally intended [18].

Change coupling (CC) between two software artefacts, also known as *logical coupling*, is defined as "the implicit and evolutionary dependency of two software artefacts that have been observed to frequently change together during the evolution of a software system" [17]. "Changing together" can be defined in many alternative ways, and the most appropriate definition depends on the purpose of the analysis. In our method we consider all revisions in the version control data of a service that were committed within an interval of a day as a logical change set, and artefacts that change simultaneously in a large number of change sets as change-coupled. This metric can uncover relations between software artefacts that are not explicitly present in the code of a system. This makes the metric appealing to apply to MSAs, as it is able to reveal hidden dependencies regardless of hindrances such as REST calls and event buses, which obstruct code-based analyses from discovering these relations [20]. Furthermore, this metric is programming language-agnostic, since it can be directly derived from the version control history [17].

4.3   Cohesion Metrics

Change frequency (CF) is another metric that can be extracted from version control data. In MSAs, this metric corresponds to the number of times a service is modified (i.e., the number of commits) per time unit. A high CF of a service with respect to other services in the system is not a direct indication for low maintainability, but in combination with size metrics CF can help pinpoint low-cohesive services that are candidates for refactoring [20]. This is because large services with a relatively high change frequency could be covering multiple bounded contexts, and the developer should make an informed decision on whether to split these services. To allow for comparisons between different CFs, we consistently calculate CF by dividing the absolute number of changes by the number of months the changes were accumulated over.

Service interface data cohesion (SIDC) is another metric appropriate for MSAs as it is measured on an interface level. SIDC captures the equality between the parameter types of operations in an interface [4], so that if all operations defined in an interface use a common parameter data type, then the corresponding service is considered highly cohesive [6]. SIDC is defined in formula (4) for an interface I of a service S as the sum of operations with common data types (OC) divided by the total number of distinct operations (OD) assuming that this number is not zero, normalising the metric to values between 0 and 1 [4,6].

$$SIDS(S) = \frac{OC(I_S)}{OD(I_S)} \qquad (4)$$

Thresholds for the interpretation of SIDC values were defined in [7], which were calculated using a benchmark-based approach.

5   Assessment Method

Our assessment method consists of two steps, namely *data preparation*, in which the metrics values are collected and prepared for analysis, and *data interpretation*, in which each metric value is interpreted with regard to maintainability in different refactor contexts. This section discusses which versions of a system to analyse to properly capture the evolution of maintainability, gives guidelines to perform data preparation by prescribing tools and data cleaning steps, and presents the framework for metrics interpretation that is used to assess the maintainability of the MSAs.

5.1   Capturing Experience

Surveys show that approximately 90% of software projects use a version control system [1], which enables the retrieval of previous versions of an application. In our approach, version control systems allow us to apply our assessment to different versions of an application and learn about the evolution of maintainability in reaction to changes. For validation purposes we focused on refactors that affected the granularity of the system, analysing system versions before and after such a refactor to gain insight into how the changes in granularity influenced maintainability. This allows one to capture experience by learning from the past.

To accurately capture the impact of a refactor on maintainability, we need to make an informed decision regarding which versions of the application to analyse. We need to ensure that the refactor of interest is the only refactor implemented between the two analysed versions, to isolate and measure the effect on maintainability of only the refactor under analysis, since if we analyse versions between which multiple refactors had been carried out then we would end up measuring the combined impact of these multiple refactors. Refactors are not always implemented in atomic commits, but can entail a transition period. The assessment should be conducted both before and immediately after such a transition period, excluding the transition itself. This ensures that the entire impact of the refactor is accurately captured.

5.2 Data Preparation Guidelines

Our assessment method provides guidelines for data preparation and cleaning. Although we selected some specific tools, alternative instrumentation can be used as long as the necessary metric values can be obtained.

MicroDepGraph (https://github.com/clowee/MicroDepGraph) is used to capture the dependencies between microservices from the Dockerfile file (docker-compose.yml), and is used to calculate structural coupling. Dockerfile is commonly used to define the entire service composition of a system [19]. Since the tool focuses on Docker configurations, it has low applicability in event-driven architectures (EDA) in which services produce and consume events for and from a message broker. EDA adhere to the loose coupling principle, in the sense that services are agnostic of which services consume their events and of which services produced the events they consume. In case of an EDA, an alternative approach is to manually calculate the structural coupling. A condition is that documentation on the dependencies between the services is available and complete.

Code-Maat (https://github.com/adamtornhill/code-maat) is an open-source tool for mining version control and is able to perform code age analysis, ownership analysis and change coupling analysis. Code-Maat implements change-coupling analysis and allows the specification of temporal windows, in which all commits should be considered to be part of the same logical change set. Temporal windows should be selected based on the behaviour of the developer(s) of an application. The version control data should be extracted for each service of interest, and bot commits and commits affecting more than 100 files should be deleted, since they negatively affect the accuracy of the change coupling analysis. In case a service of interest is renamed or refactored during the selected time interval, our labelling scripts should be used to label this new service(s) as part of the service of interest.

We implemented our own tool to calculate change frequency (CF) of a service. The implementation is straightforward: the version control history of a service S is analysed and we count the number of commits (C) performed within the time interval under analysis. C is subsequently divided over the number of months (M) the time interval spanned to determine the CF. CF should be calculated over the same cleaned version control logs as used for the CC calculations.

cloc (https://github.com/AlDanial/cloc) is an open-source tool for measuring the Lines of code (LOC) of a service. cloc is able to recognize a wide range of programming languages and can differentiate between comment lines, code lines and blank lines for each of these languages. cloc was used to calculate the average LOC of all services in an application to identify services with a size substantially larger than the average, which might be candidates for refactoring.

Using the `git reset` command, we were able to revert to older versions of a system and measure the LOC of these versions.

RAMA-CLI (https://github.com/restful-ma/rama-cli) is a command-line tool to calculate maintainability metrics related to size, complexity and cohesion from interface specifications. The tool can parse three types of RESTful API specification languages and the metrics of our interest are service interface data cohesion (SIDC) and weighted service interface count (WSIC). As RAMA-CLI has been designed specifically for the analysis of RESTful APIs, the tool is not directly applicable to EDA, since services can produce and consume events in parallel and do not expose endpoints to each other, but to the message broker through the topics of the events. It is advisable to verify whether a specification represents a single service or multiple services, such as in the API gateway pattern, and whether it belongs to an actual microservice or to components of the message broker. In the latter cases, assessing such a specification cannot provide an accurate indication of maintainability.

5.3   Metric Interpretation Framework

This framework describes how each metric value should be interpreted with regard to maintainability in different refactor contexts, i.e., a merge (M1, M2) and a decomposition (D1, D2). For the hybrid refactors we studied all presented interpretation guidelines are relevant, as hybrid refactors (H1, H2) encompass both a merge and a decomposition.

6   Validation

To validate our assessment method, we first applied it to each selected case, by assessing pre-refactor and post-refactor versions of the systems, reverting to older versions using the version control system used in each project. After obtaining the information related to each refactor (pre-refactor and post-refactor metrics), we applied the interpretation framework presented in Table 1 to assess the maintainability of the resulting architectures. Here we only describe the refactors studied in two of the cases, but for a complete account of these assessments we refer our GitHub project site[1]. **MX**, **DX** and **HX** denote a merge refactor, a decomposition refactor and a hybrid refactor, respectively.

6.1   Case 1: Metadata

Metadata is a microservice-based metadata-driven user interface (UI) generator. It is an open-source project, developed by a single developer. It allows its users to specify UI metadata via REST endpoints, as well as via GraphQL queries. The architecture of Metadata encompasses four microservices (`metadata-rest`,

---

[1] https://github.com/famkedriessen/quantitative-assessment-method-for-microservices-granularity.

Table 1. Interpretation of metric values in different refactor contexts.

Metric	Merge	Decomposition
CC	pre: if the CC value between two services is 0.66 or more, this is regarded as evidence in favour of merging these services.	post: the decomposition of service A into services B and C is considered beneficial if the CC value between service B and C is 0.33 or lower.
SC	pre: no thresholds found in the literature, so we expect the average SC to decrease as the number of entities that contribute to coupling decreases. A merge is expected to be beneficial if the SC is higher than the average.	post: no thresholds found in the literature, so if the resulting services have an under-average SC, the merge is expected to be beneficial.
WSIC	pre: merging services A and B is not expected to be beneficial if the WSIC of either service A or B falls within the lower 50% intervals as proposed by [7], i.e., if the WSIC is higher than 15.	pre: considering the thresholds calculated by [7], we regard WSICs higher than 15 as supporting evidence for decomposing a service. post: services resulting from a decomposition are expected to have lower WSICs than their ancestor.
SIDC	pre: merging services A and B is not expected to be beneficial if the SIDC of either service A or B falls within the lower 50% intervals as proposed by [7], i.e., if the SIDC is lower than 0.64.	pre: considering the thresholds of [7], we regard SIDC values lower than 0.64 as supporting evidence for decomposing a service. post: services resulting from a decomposition are expected to have higher SIDCs than their ancestor.
LOC	pre: merging services A and B is not expected to be beneficial if the LOC value of either service A or B is higher than the average LOC value of all services in the system.	pre: a LOC value of a service higher than the average of the services in the system indicates that the decomposition can be beneficial. post: services resulting from a decomposition are expected to have lower LOC values than their ancestor.
CF	pre: merging services A and B is not expected to be beneficial if the CF of either service A or B is higher than the average CF of the services in the system.	pre: a decomposition is considered beneficial if the CF of this service is higher than the average CF of the services in the system. post: services resulting from a decomposition are expected to have lower CFs than their ancestor.

`metadata-engine`, `metadata-graphql` and `metadata-deploy`), while other modules are provided as binaries instead of services so that the user does not have to deploy yet another microservice.

The following refactors of this case have been considered:

D1. In this refactor, to increase the separation of concerns and in line with the single responsibility principle, the developer decided to decompose the `ref-impl` service, generating the `metadata-deploy` service and shifting some functionality to the service provider. By doing this, functionality related to data management was separated from the operations performed on the data.

H1. The application contains one REST-related service and one GraphQL-related service, which have a lot of functionality in common. Besides the REST and GraphQL-specific code, the operations available to both services are similar since in the end they implement the same features but using a different type of API. The developer pointed out the common functionality of the services to be a candidate for extraction into a separate service, as currently, the developer is required to make duplicate modifications in both services to maintain consistency. We included this hybrid refactor in our study, although it is not implemented yet, as we wanted to investigate to what extent our method could identify these services as candidates for refactoring.

6.2   Case 2: Loan Eligibility Checker

This case is an industrial project in which a bank wanted to automate the loan eligibility check for small and medium-sized enterprises (SMEs). This system has primarily been implemented in Java and has been developed by a team consisting of over 40 engineers. The architecture of the system covers 13 services, among them: service `PSD2-service` that allows multiple banks to connect through an API Gateway (each bank as a service) that serves the `journey-API` service as well as services `authentication-service` and `transaction-processing`. A message broker (Kafka) is used to enable event exchange with services `journey-rule-engine`, `riskmodels`, `email-service`, as well as `termsheet-service`, which interacts with service `file-upload-service`. The refactors that took place to improve maintainability during the life cycle of the project are the following:

M1. The `journey-API` and the `journey-rule-engine` services both keep track of the state of the customer journey. As they form the bridge between the front-end and the back-end of the system, the two services need to be in the same state for each process instance. To achieve this, they need to have the same data at their disposal, so complex state-carrying events are constantly being exchanged by the two services. According to the engineers, merging these services would directly increase the maintainability of the system, as changes to the state-carrying events would not require modifications in two services anymore. Although this refactor is acknowledged by the team to be beneficial, it is planned but not implemented yet.

M2. Due to a company-wide policy which initially prescribed a strict separation between business logic and the corresponding APIs, the system contains a group of three services that together form one bounded context: a service in which the business logic was implemented, a service that implemented the API of the business logic service and a service that contained the configurations to communicate with the API gateway of the system. The engineer pointed these services out as a textbook example of a bounded context divided over multiple services.

D2. By introducing the `journey-rule-engine`, a central point in the system was introduced from where all services were reachable. It was a convenient place to add new features, as the service handles the entire workflow. As a result the service grew over time. This became problematic when the bank wanted to reuse certain functionality that was now mixed into the `journey-rule-engine` in other applications. Using the same rule engine for multiple journeys would become too complex, so the team was forced to extract the new functionality from the rule engine into separate services.

H2. Employee journeys are initiated by employees of the bank and are orchestrated by the `employee-rule-engine` and their API gateway is implemented by the `employee-api-service`. These services are similar to the `rule-engine` and `journey-API`, but are tailored towards the employee journeys. The services have been partially merged, to make the constant exchange of complex state events between the two services obsolete. The merge is partial as the `employee-rule-engine` and `employee-api-service` are involved in multiple employee journeys, and the merge is only done for one specific journey. This means that the `employee-api-service`, `employee-rule-engine` and this new service in which the two are partially merged (`review-flow-engine`) co-exist after the refactor.

6.3   Results

We validated our assessment method by investigating the alignment between the assessment observations and the evolution in maintainability as perceived by the case experts. Table 2 gives an overview of this alignment, where for each refactor it indicates whether the assessed metric was in line (M), conflicted (C) or could not be determined or interpreted (NA) with respect to the experiences of the expert. In some of the assessments, some metrics play a role both in identifying refactor candidates as well as in reflecting the evolution in maintainability. These entries, such as CC in the assessment of H2, contain two outcomes (M/C in this case). The first outcome refers to the ability of the metric to identify the involved services as refactor candidates in the pre-refactor assessment, which was successful in this case, while the second one refers to the alignment of the metric with the increase in maintainability as experienced by the case expert, which conflicted in this example.

Table 2. Matching between the assessment results of our method and the experiences of the 3 case-experts

	CC	LOC	CF	SIDC	WSIC	SC
M1	M	C	C	C	C	NA
M2	M	M	M	C	M	NA
D1	M	M	C/M	M/C	C/C	M
D2	M	M/M	M/M	NA	NA	NA
H1	M	NA	NA	M	C	NA
H2	M/C	M/C	M/C	M/C	M/C	NA

We observed that CC is able to identify candidates for merging (M1, M2, H1, H2) and for reflecting the perceived maintainability evolution (D1, D2). We discussed possible causes for conflicts with the case experts since these causes can be valuable to learn the applicability and limitations of our assessment method.

SC shows low applicability. This metrics could not be measured during the assessment of the loan eligibility checker, as this system implements an event-driven architecture. In these architectures, services are agnostic with respect to the services with which they exchange data, so the actual inter-service dependencies cannot be extracted from the Dockerfiles used to calculate SC.

The interface-based metrics (WSIC and SIDC) frequently conflicted with the experiences of the expert for two reasons: (1) an interface does not map one-to-one to the functionality of a service, which sometimes caused a misalignment between our assessment and the expert's experience (e.g., in the API gateway pattern) and (2) an interface is not always updated in parallel to a refactor.

LOC and CF were both well-aligned with the experiences of the case experts. Conflicts mainly arose because some deprecated code was not removed from a service (influencing the accuracy of LOC) and because of the "newness" of a service. For example, in H2 the new service post-refactor had a higher CF than the pre-refactor services, which the case expert expected to decrease over time since a new service has more bugs that need to be fixed. This was inquired after with the case expert. We expect this to also be the cause of the conflict between the CC assessment and the experts experience for H2, where the services that had just been refactored showed high change coupling, which the expert expects to be the aftermath of refactoring.

7   Conclusions

This paper presented a quantitative method to assess the granularity of microservices in an MSA with respect to maintainability. We applied the method to selected projects to evaluate the impact of granularity on maintainability before and after refactors were performed. We compared the results of our assessment method with expert observations. Our assessments were aligned with the experts' experiences in many cases, indicating that our quantitative assessment method often matches their intuitive understanding. Exceptions were particularly for metrics measured over a short interval or compared to system averages based on a small number of services. These factors should be considered when evaluating the usability of our assessment method in future studies.

Availability of suitable cases is a limitation that needs to be addressed. Finding cases was challenging as there are only a few open-source microservice-based projects available. A data set of projects implementing an MSA is presented in [19], but most of them are sample projects that demonstrate a design pattern or the use of a framework. Additional complicating factors were the inclusion criteria imposed by our validation strategy, which required contact with a case expert and implemented refactors in the history of the system that affected granularity.

A potential threat to the validity of our research is the lack of evidence demonstrating the correlation between grouping change sets based on temporal windows and the actual change sets in multi-repository microservice-based projects. Empirical validation of this correlation would be valuable, considering that many MSA projects use multiple repositories, which hinders change coupling analysis at the commit level.

Automatic identification of dependencies between microservices in existing systems is a relevant topic for future work. Currently available support (e.g., MicroDepGraph) can derive dependencies based on Docker dependencies, but their applicability is limited, especially in EDA.

Our approach allows for the assessment of existing systems. At design-time however, only SC, WSIC and SIDC can be determined. It would be valuable to investigate the value of this smaller metric set in determining an appropriate granularity for green field applications. Finally, for our assessment method to ultimately lay the basis for a decision support tool for microservice granularity, future research should focus on empirically validating our findings on larger data sets (i.e., more projects and more refactors).

References

1. Aboalkheir, A.: Ultimate list of Version Control Systems statistics, trends (2023). https://abdalslam.com/version-control-systems-statistics. Accessed 15 Aug 2023
2. Alshuqayran, N., Ali, N., Evans, R.: Towards micro service architecture recovery: an empirical study. In: 2018 IEEE International Conference on Software Architecture (ICSA), pp. 47–4709 (2018). https://doi.org/10.1109/ICSA.2018.00014
3. Apolinário, D.R., de França, B.B.: A method for monitoring the coupling evolution of microservice-based architectures. J. Braz. Comput. Soc. **27**, 1–35 (2021). https://doi.org/10.1186/s13173-021-00120-y
4. Athanasopoulos, D., Zarras, A.V., Miskos, G., Issarny, V., Vassiliadis, P.: Cohesion-driven decomposition of service interfaces without access to source code. IEEE Trans. Serv. Comput. **8**(4), 550–562 (2015). https://doi.org/10.1109/TSC.2014.2310195

5. Bogner, J., Schlinger, S., Wagner, S., Zimmermann, A.: A modular approach to calculate service-based maintainability metrics from runtime data of microservices. In: Franch, X., Männistö, T., Martínez-Fernández, S. (eds.) PROFES 2019. LNCS, vol. 11915, pp. 489–496. Springer, Cham (2019). https://doi.org/10.1007/978-3-030-35333-9_34

6. Bogner, J., Wagner, S., Zimmermann, A.: Automatically measuring the maintainability of service- and microservice-based systems - a literature review. In: Proceedings of the 27th International Workshop on Software Measurement and 12th International Conference on Software Process and Product Measurement, IWSM-Mensura 2017, pp. 107–115. ACM (2017). https://doi.org/10.1145/3143434.3143443

7. Bogner, J., Wagner, S., Zimmermann, A.: Collecting service-based maintainability metrics from RESTful API descriptions: static analysis and threshold derivation. In: Muccini, H., et al. (eds.) ECSA 2020. CCIS, vol. 1269, pp. 215–227. Springer, Cham (2020). https://doi.org/10.1007/978-3-030-59155-7_16

8. Cardarelli, M., Salle, A.D., Iovino, L., Malavolta, I., Francesco, P.D., Lago, P.: An extensible data-driven approach for evaluating the quality of microservice architectures. In: Proceedings of the 34th ACM/SIGAPP Symposium on Applied Computing, pp. 1225–1234. ACM (2019). https://doi.org/10.1145/3297280.3297400

9. Evans, E.: Domain-Driven Design: Tackling Complexity in the Heart of Software. Addison-Wesley (2004)

10. Granchelli, G., Cardarelli, M., Di Francesco, P., Malavolta, I., Iovino, L., Di Salle, A.: MicroART: a software architecture recovery tool for maintaining microservice-based systems. In: 2017 IEEE International Conference on Software Architecture Workshops (ICSAW), pp. 298–302 (2017). https://doi.org/10.1109/ICSAW.2017.9

11. Granchelli, G., Cardarelli, M., Di Francesco, P., Malavolta, I., Iovino, L., Di Salle, A.: Towards recovering the software architecture of microservice-based systems. In: 2017 IEEE International Conference on Software Architecture Workshops (ICSAW), pp. 46–53 (2017). https://doi.org/10.1109/ICSAW.2017.48

12. Heitlager, I., Kuipers, T., Visser, J.: A practical model for measuring maintainability. In: Proceedings of the 6th International Conference on Quality of Information and Communications Technology, pp. 30–39 (2007)

13. Hirzalla, M., Cleland-Huang, J., Arsanjani, A.: A metrics suite for evaluating flexibility and complexity in service oriented architectures. In: Feuerlicht, G., Lamersdorf, W. (eds.) ICSOC 2008. LNCS, vol. 5472, pp. 41–52. Springer, Heidelberg (2009). https://doi.org/10.1007/978-3-642-01247-1_5

14. Homay, A., de Sousa, M., Zoitl, A., Wollschlaeger, M.: Service granularity in industrial automation and control systems. In: 25th IEEE International Conference on Emerging Technologies and Factory Automation, vol. 1, pp. 132–139 (2020)

15. IBM Market Development & Insights Team: Microservices in the enterprise, 2021: Real benefits, worth the challenges (2021). https://www.ibm.com/downloads/cas/OQG4AJAM

16. Li, Y., Wang, C.Z., Li, Y.C., Su, J., Chen, C.H.: Granularity decision of microservice splitting in view of maintainability and its innovation effect in government data sharing. Discrete Dynamics in Nature and Society 2020 (2020). https://doi.org/10.1155/2020/1057902

17. Oliva, G.A., Gerosa, M.A.: Chapter 11 - Change coupling between software artifacts: learning from past changes. In: Bird, C., Menzies, T., Zimmermann, T. (eds.) The Art and Science of Analyzing Software Data, pp. 285–323. Morgan Kaufmann, Boston (2015)

18. Panichella, S., Rahman, M.I., Taibi, D.: Structural coupling for microservices. In: Proceedings of the 11th International Conference on Cloud Computing and Services Science (CLOSER 2021), pp. 280–287. SCITEPRESS (2021). https://doi.org/10.5220/0010481902800287

19. Rahman, M.I., Panichella, S., Taibi, D.: A curated dataset of microservices-based systems. In: Joint Proceedings of the Summer School on Software Maintenance and Evolution. CEUR-WS 2520 (2019)

20. Tornhill, A.: Your Code as a Crime Scene. Pragmatic Bookshelf (2015)

21. Vera-Rivera, F.H., Gaona, C., Astudillo, H.: Defining and measuring microservice granularity-a literature overview. PeerJ Comput. Sci. **7**, e695 (2021). https://doi.org/10.7717/peerj-cs.695

22. Zimmermann, O.: Microservices tenets: agile approach to service development and deployment. Comput. Sci. - Res. Dev. **32**, 301–310 (2017). https://doi.org/10.1007/s00450-016-0337-0

A Digitalization Phase Model for IT Consulting Services
Definition and Evaluation of DITCOS-DPM

Meikel Bode$^{(\boxtimes)}$ ⓘ, Maya Daneva ⓘ, and Marten J. van Sinderen ⓘ

Department of Semantics, Cybersecurity and Services, University of Twente,
Drienerlolaan 5, 7522 NB Enschede, The Netherlands
{m.bode,m.daneva,m.j.vansinderen}@utwente.nl
https://www.utwente.nl/en/eemcs/scs

Abstract. In recent years, many companies recognized the importance of digitalization in IT consulting. Partly fueled by the Covid-19 crisis, the demand for digitalized IT consulting services became obvious as IT consulting firms were increasingly asked by their clients to digitally provide their service portfolio. While this created new business opportunities, it also revealed the lack of appropriate means to describe and deliver standardized, modular IT consulting services that can nevertheless be customized and delivered through digital channels. To date, there is no accepted and standardized approach that enables an IT consulting firm to drive the digitalization of its own service portfolio in a structured way.

This paper proposes a new incremental approach, the DITCOS Digitalization Phase Model, that enables IT consulting firms to (i) digitally codify their services over three defined phases using the DITCOS-DN description notation, (ii) dynamically transform the resulting service model into an executable BPMN 2.0 workflow based on user tasks, and (iii) automate the delivery of parts of the service models by dynamically transforming them into BPMN 2.0 workflows based on user and system tasks.

Using the action design research methodology, we designed, implemented, and evaluated our approach with the help of IT consulting practitioners on a digital IT consulting platform prototype.

Keywords: digital transformation · digitalization approach · digital service augmentation · service automation · IT consulting · service description · virtualization · consulting platform · service model execution · action design research · prototyping

1 Introduction

1.1 IT Consulting Digitalization

IT consulting (ITC) is part of the service sector. ITC is about advising organizations and individuals on how to digitalize their business processes and business models. Historically, ITC has been considered a people-centered business, which

© The Author(s), under exclusive license to Springer Nature Switzerland AG 2024
T. P. Sales et al. (Eds.): EDOC 2023 Workshops, LNBIP 498, pp. 227–243, 2024.
https://doi.org/10.1007/978-3-031-54712-6_14

is primarily based on interpersonal trust and the interaction between advisors and clients to arrive collaboratively at a solution [11].

To date, it is evident that the ITC domain has not – or only very little, been digitalized yet [6,12]. Mostly digital aids have been added over time, such as VoIP, digital presentation techniques and, most recently, tools supporting online collaboration. However, the actual ITC consulting process, and thus the core of the ITC business, has remained analogue to a large extend [6,12].

For the purpose of this work, we use the terms 'digitization', 'digitalization', and 'digital transformation' as defined by Gartner [8], as this suits well to the three phases of our proposed model. The first means to convert physical-world resources to a digital representation, whereas the second refers to the ability of using these new representations by software systems, and the third is about establishing new business processes, business models, or customer experiences by incorporating the aforementioned concepts.

During the Covid-19 pandemic, it became apparent that the ITC was ill prepared to deliver its own service portfolio digitally. This can partly be explained by the little research until now to support this area on the path to digitalization [12]. So far, as per a 2022 systematic mapping study [1], there are few artifacts, such as Werth's eConsulting Store [16] that are usable in practice. Whatever artifacts have been proposed, these are often specifically designed for a particular use case and can not easily be transferred to other settings [13,16].

Currently, while absorbing the lessons from the Covid-19 pandemic, ITC firms found themselves pressured to shift their service provisioning to the digital space or at least to better support their service provision digitally. To adequately achieve this, they need different means, such as digital representations of their real-world services as well as software systems to provide this kind of digital services to their customers. Whereas many IT consultancies realize that they must start 'somewhere' their digitalization journey and gain experience with the digitalization of their service portfolios, in many cases these consultancies have no idea where and how to start, and which method or procedure to follow. This situation is complicated further by the diverse and complex nature of the overall service portfolio of IT consultancies. In fact, ITC services or projects are very often extremely customer-specific, not standardized, not based on defined service modules, nor easily reproducible.

1.2 Research Goal, Method, and Contribution

This context opens a research opportunity to meet the ITC industry needs for an easy-to-follow methodology that would support and guide ITC companies on their digitalization journey. Until now there are no accepted common solutions, nor common methods for the holistic support of ITC regarding the general digitalization of its own service portfolio [12]. Our goal is to reach the best combination of manual and automated workflow in the ITC domain, what we consider to be the best symbiosis of people and systems. To reach this goal we formulate the following research question: *How must a transformation approach look like that helps ITC practitioners to digitally transform their existing real-world ITC service portfolio incrementally?*

In our earlier work [2,4], we found that the digital transformation process of ITC services should follow an incremental approach. Drawing upon this, in the present paper we suggest a generic phase model that supports both: (i) an incremental conversion of already existing classical analogue real-world ITC services to their respective digital representations and (ii) the creation of new digital ITC service offerings.

While we believe that such a generic phase model is required, it needs to be developed and continuously evaluated based on practical use cases. This is important because our goal is to not only digitally transform one single real-world ITC service, but to provide a generic and reusable solution that solves a class of problems, such as the digital transformation of complex ITC service portfolios of different ITC firms.

To reach our goal we decided to apply *Action Design Research* [15] (ADR) as we strive to develop an approach that helps ITC practitioners to digitally transform their real-world ITC service portfolios. ADR is the combination of Design Science [9] and Action Research [15]. The ADR approach follows the process of *problem formulation* covered in Subsect. 1.2, *building* IT artifacts covered in Sect. 3, its *intervention* (i.e., implementation) in a practice context (ITC), and its *evaluation*, both covered in Sect. 4.

This work makes both academic and practice-relevant contributions. First, we provide a new digitalization phase model, DITCOS-DPM (DITCOS stands for Digital IT Consulting [2,5]), which is the first to support service engineers in ITC companies starting digital transformation initiatives, by means of a structured guide to the digitalization of real-world ITC services. From a scientific point of view, this novel phase model could serve as the foundation for future research in the fields of information systems research, consulting research, and service science. Second, we provide the 'enabling artifact' for DITCOS-DPM in form of an ITC platform prototype, which is relevant for other researchers and practitioners [12]. From researchers' perspective, our prototype helps to better understand the ways in which tools for digital ITC should be structured and organized to form a cohesive whole that adds value to ITC practice. From practitioners' perspectives, our prototype helps IT consultancies to incrementally develop an early understanding of how digital ITC could work out and to gain experience and learn about the possible main advantages, drawbacks, and risks [1].

The remaining of this paper is structured as follows: Sect. 2 explains how we build on the results of previous research; Sect. 3 describes the central contribution of this paper, namely the design of DITCOS-DPM (ADR building phase), Sect. 4 describes how this design was applied and evaluated in a practical context (ADR intervention and evaluation phases), and Sect. 5 presents our conclusions and suggestions for future work.

2   Background and Foundation

Our recently published systematic mapping study of the state-of-the-art of ITC literature [1], revealed scarcity in terms of proposed and empirically evaluated artifacts that could be used in support of digital transformation activities in ITC companies. This study acknowledged that in a practical context it is important that ITC companies must evolve into a digital organization and to do this, they have to deal with the digitalization of their service portfolio. The mapping study concluded that there is no dedicated process or procedure model for this purpose to date. What companies should do is to start small and urgently gather initial experience that can then be drawn upon and learned from in subsequent scale-up efforts [1]. These results are also supported by [12].

We also performed focus group research with practitioners [4], which explicated the needs and the requirements for support that companies embarking on digital ITC initiatives might have. A central requirement that emerged from the focus group study was the definition of a *generic description language for digital IT consulting*. Accordingly, we developed such a language in two steps [2]. First, we defined the 'Digital ITC Services Ontology' (DITCOS-O) that comprehensively describes the domain of ITC in the context of digital consulting. Subsequently, we derived the 'Digital ITC Services Description Notation' (DITCOS-DN) to conceptually capture real-world ITC services and codify them digitally. Our proposed digitalization phase model builds upon the results of these previous studies and specifically adopts DITCOS-O and DITCOS-DN as a conceptual and language foundation. We will henceforth refer to it as the 'Digital ITC Services Digitalization Phase Model' (DITCOS-DPM). In order to be able to use DITCOS-DPM, we also need an 'enabling artifact' in the form of a digital ITC platform prototype (DITCOS-Platform) that supports the modeling, storing, instantiation, customization, and execution of DITCOS-DN-based ITC service models. In this work, we use a platform prototype that is based on prior work [3,5], but we only refer to the features and components that are relevant to evaluate our ITC digitalization phase model. With our platform approach we follow Nissen who suggests it as one possible future for ITC [12].

3   Building Our Phase Model Artifact

To initiate the digital transformation of real-world ITC services we argue that they first must be modeled in a standardized *computer readable notation* that can represent their inherent ITC domain concepts. For this purpose, we propose a *digital transformation model consisting of three phases* (Fig. 1), which we call DITCOS-DPM (DPM), based on the DITCOS-DN notation [2] to guide researchers and ITC practitioners. The phases DPM-I, DPM-II, and DPM-III represent a cyclic and incremental approach to either transfer real-world ITC services to their digital representations or design new ITC services directly based on DITCOS-DN. In Fig. 2 we depict the interplay of the phases and the components of the digital IT consulting platform. Due to space limits Fig. 2 fulfills

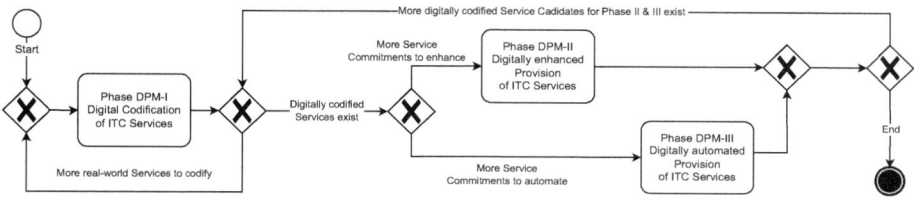

Fig. 1. Application Process of the DITCOS-DPM Phase Model

three purposes: (i) it shows the main components of our prototype, such as the *service repository* (SR), the *digital service runtime* (DSR), and the *BPMN 2.0 engine*, (ii) it shows which prototype component supports which DPM phase (DPM phase name above the components), and (iii) it depicts the instantiation of a DITCOS-DN service model description and its transition through the architecture indicated as step numbers (green circles). We implemented the DSR as suggested in [3] based on Spring Boot for the backend, REACT for the frontend, Keycloak for user authentication and authorization, and PostgreSQL as database. Additionally, for service model execution we integrated the Camunda BPMN 2.0 engine into the prototype. Based on the concerns, goals and requirements identified in the mapping study [1], the focus group study [4] as being relevant for the digital transformation process of ITC services, and based on the long year ITC professional experience of the first author, we projected some desirable outcomes of each of the phases. These can be found in Table 1, Table 3 and Table 4, without any claim to completeness.

3.1   Phase DPM-I: Digital Codification of ITC Services

This phase is to digitally codify (i.e., model) analogue real-world services using DITCOS-DN (digitize). It supports the relevant concepts [2] that real-world ITC services have in common and that serve as the basis for correct modeling. Examples of those concepts are *service commitment* (SC) which represents promises made by the IT consultancy given to the client, *business role* (BR) which describes what is necessary to fulfill a SC, and *resource* (RES) which represents generated/consumed inputs and outputs of services. Additional core concepts are *atomic service* (AS) which is built upon the aforementioned concepts and *complex service* (CS), which represents the ability to (re)combine and relate other existing ASs and CSs to flexibly design new service models to provide service offerings as required (Table 2). The implementation of phase DPM-I requires a corresponding *service repository* (SR) (Fig. 2), which is a component of the digital ITC platform prototype that persistently stores models of real-world ITC services codified using DITCOS-DN. The left part of Fig. 2 shows the activities and involved components in this phase. Table 1 lists the expected outcomes of the phase.

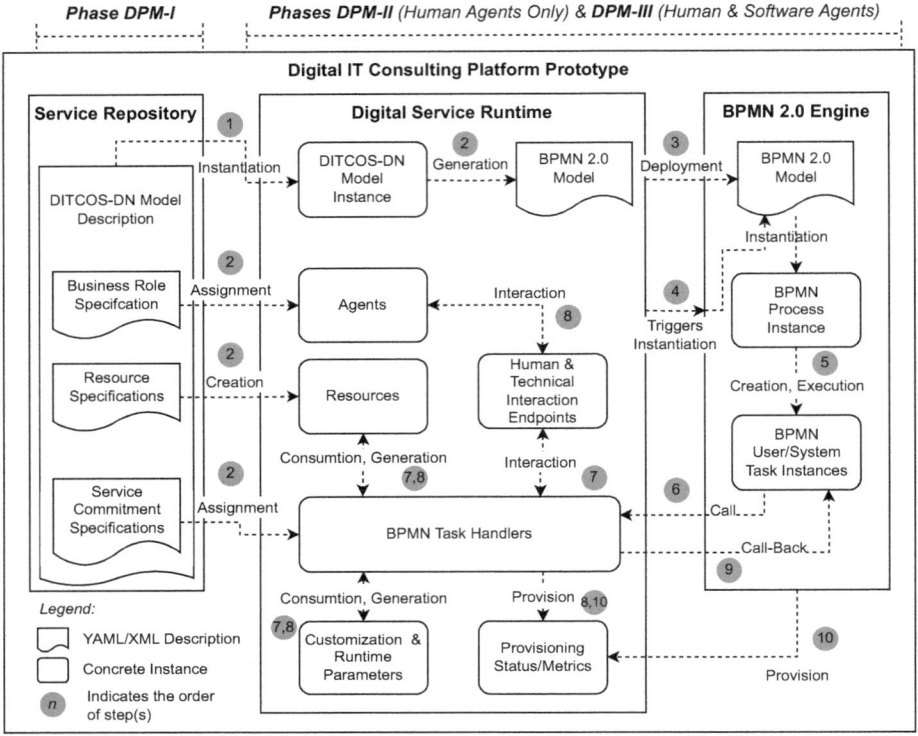

Fig. 2. Interplay of the Digitalization Phases and Components of the Digital IT Consulting Platform Prototype (Color figure online)

3.2 Phase DPM-II: Digitally Augmented Provision of ITC Services

This phase is concerned with using DITCOS-DN service models as input into a BPMN execution engine, to assure the digitally enhanced provisioning of ITC services. Once the ITC service models are transformed into DITCOS-DN models (i.e., they are computer-readable), the latter are dynamically transformed into BPMN 2.0 process models by the DSR. This is possible because the DITCOS-DN concepts can be mapped to BPMN 2.0 concepts (Table 2). The resulting customer-specific BPMN 2.0 process models could then be deployed to a BPMN engine for later execution (digitalization). Such an execution accomplishes a synchronization of real-world and digital-space aspects of the service flow, which we consider as a *digitally augmented* service provisioning. As the BPMN 2.0 process models can be automatically generated from their DITCOS-DN models on-demand by the DSR, every defined DITCOS-DN service model can be augmented in this way. The DSR locally creates a *customized service model instance* based on the DITCOS-DN description. During instantiation, the DSR can suggest or automatically assigns *concrete human agents* (business partners), such as consultants or a client organization's staff members who possess the required *capabilities* according to the underlying *business role specifications*. These human

Table 1. Expected Outcomes of DPM-I

ID: Name/Description
O1-1: *Standardization* [4, 7, 10] Digitization of services should standardize the process flows and activities. DITCOS-DN itself does not do the standardization of real-world services itself, but it supports the service engineer by providing a standardized notation for ITC services. We argue that the first step to ITC service standardization is to transform them to a defined and structured digital representation
O1-2: *Modularization* [1, 4, 7] When digitally modeled and standardized, DITCOS-DN based services can be analyzed by the service engineer and be decomposed into reusable modules. We argue that standardized service modules are an important step towards digital ITC service provision, service recombination, and automation
O1-3: *Recombination* [1, 4, 7, 10] Once standardized service modules exist, the service engineer can easily recombine those modules to new higher-order ITC service model offerings. We argue that this leads to higher efficiency and more flexible ITC service offerings
O1-4: *Know-how Transfer* [1, 4, 10] Tacit and implicit knowledge and know-how related to services and service delivery should be incorporated into digital service representations. We argue that the digital codification of real-world ITC service offerings leads to better conservation of IT consultancy owned knowledge and know-how that was prior to this, mainly available in the heads of consultants
O1-5: *Transparency* [1, 4, 14] Storing digital DITCOS-DN based ITC services offerings provides better transparency of the IT consulting portfolio through a central service repository to the consulting firm as well as their clients. Additionally, incorporated stakeholders will gain transparency of the service provisioning process due to continuous monitoring
O1-6: *Repeatability* [1, 4, 10] Digital DITCOS-DN based ITC services are easy to repeat because their structure (modules), process flow (combination), input, output and required roles are now digitally codified. Thus, theoretically, a digital ITC platform could easily 'replay' or repeat the exact same provisioning flow
O1-7: *Service Quality* [1, 4, 14] Service science literature argues that standardization and repeatability lead to a better service quality due to standardized and therefore repeatable service offerings

agents then execute their assigned *BPMN UserTasks*. Additionally, the DSR can automatically create or prepare *concrete resources* as defined by the underlying resource specifications to take these kinds of initializing tasks away from human agents.

Finally, during instantiation the DSR also provides the required *interaction endpoints* for the assigned agents, to receive information about tasks (e.g., reminders) or to provide inputs (e.g., upload data) to the service commitments, which are represented by *BPMN UserTasks* and realized in the DSR by specific *BPMN TaskHandlers*. *BPMN TaskHandlers* are central components provided by the DSR to interact with the BPMN execution engine. They take the role of a proxy that provides several important features. The BPMN TaskHandler represents a certain *service commitment*. SCs are mapped by their *kind* attribute to specific BPMN TaskHandlers classes. The middle part of Fig. 2 shows the activities and involved components in this phase. According to our previous work we think that the positive effects described in Table 3 can be achieved by conducting phase DPM-II.

Table 2. Mapping of DITCOS-DN to BPMN 2.0 Concepts

DITCOS-DN	BPMN 2.0	Description
Service (S)	Process, Subprocess	Represents the abstract service concept
Atomic Service (AS)	Process, Subprocess	Represents a concrete real-world service modeled using DITCOS-DN. An AS is based on SCs. An AS represents the smallest saleable/purchaseable unit from IT consultancy/client perspective
Complex Service (CS)	Process, Subprocess	Represents a concrete real-world service as the combination of other services, either others ASs and/or other CSs. The CS concept supports the definition of service dependencies in the form 'service b' *dependsOn* 'service a'
Service Commitment (SC)	User Task (manual, hybrid), Service Task (automated)	Represents a concrete promise of the ITC consultancy given to its client. A SC is always embedded in an AS. It consumes, generates, or updates resources. SCs require one or more business roles to be provided
Capability (CB)	No equivalent	Represents a capability specified by an business role required to fulfill the intended role behavior in the sense of 'must be able to do advanced Python programming'
Business Role (BR)	Pool, Lane	Represents a role in a collaboration of agents
Resource (RS)	Data Object, Data Store	Represents input and output resources required or generated/updated by service commitments
S.dependsOn, SC.dependsOn	Parallel Gateway ('AND')	Represents modeled dependencies of CS and AS within another CS or the SC defined in an AS

3.3   Phase DPM-III: Digitally Automated Provision of ITC Services

Once a DITCOS-DN service model is transformed into an executable BPMN 2.0 process model (representing service commitments with UserTasks), the ITC company can progress this service model to DPM-III. It has to consider which tasks currently assigned to a human agent can also be performed without human interaction. This can be based on the experience of consultants of the ITC company or based on the collected service provisioning metrics data (e.g., start time or end time). Hence, the objective is to identify SCs as candidates for automation. Selected candidates are transformed by changing their task type from BPMN UserTask to the BPMN ServiceTask (Table 2). The digital ITC platform does not require a human agent to fulfill the SC of a ServiceTask during service provisioning, but a software agent instead. Indeed, the BPMN ServiceTask requires an appropriate service handler that can perform the action necessary to provide the service promise given to the client. The service handler replaces a human agent by being a proxy for a software system that is used to call an external service of a software agent. The right part of Fig. 2 shows the activities and involved components during this phase. It has the same expected outcomes as DPM-II, plus one extra concerned with the orchestration of software agents, as indicated in Subsect. 3.3.

Table 3. Expected Outcomes of DPM-II (in addition to those of DPM-I)

ID: Name/Description
O2-1: *Human Agent Orchestration* [1,4,7] DITCOS-DN service models define business role specifications by enumerating capabilities (e.g., 'Advanced Python Programming Knowledge' or 'SAP Analytics Cloud Consulting Experience') which an assigned agent must possess to be able to fulfill a role. If the platform would have access to both the workforce skill matrix and to the capacitiy planning of employees, then it would be possible to automatically suggest or even assign certain agents to service commitments represented by BPMN tasks
O2-2: *Provisioning Metrics* [1,4] When DITCOS-DN models are transformed into executable BPMN 2.0 process models, the consulting company would gain access to important process metrics, such as the real execution time of certain service commitments compared to the upfront estimated execution time. Additionally, the consultancy would better understand which of its service commitments are provided and how frequently. This would help to identify candidate tasks worthwhile digitalizing further in DPM-III
O2-3: *Augmented Service Provisioning* [1,4] Compared to DPM-I results, the service provisioning process would be interactive. The digital ITC platform could actively approach incorporated agents to inform them about status changes, to remind them of performing certain activities, or to provide certain input required for the service process to progress properly. This would be possible through any digital channel which offer an API, such as E-Mail, WhatsApp, Slack, or MS Teams

Table 4. Expected Outcomes of DPM-III (in addition to those of DPM-II)

ID: Name/Description
O3-1: *Software Agent Orchestration* [1,4] Some service commitments can be considered for automation, meaning that their execution can be performed by a software agent without the need for human interaction. We could think of numerous additional software agents, that could be orchestrated by the digital ITC platform. By adding appropriate service commitment kinds and corresponding service handlers, we could communicate with every software system that offers API-support

3.4   Guided Application Scenario for the DITCOS-DPM Artifact

This section presents a realistic application scenario of DITCOS-DPM. It can be used as a structured guide by practitioners. Let's assume that an IT consultancy starts applying the phase model by trying to identify services that are already standardized to have an easy start. By standardized we mean that the service delivery process already has some codification, such as concepts, process descriptions, best-practices, checklists, presentations, input forms, or role descriptions that are used in each delivery instance. We note that while this would help to accelerate the digitalization process in phase DPM-I, it is not a prerequisite for using our phase model. If these kinds of inputs are not available for an existing service offering, then for the ITC company a more intense and longer modeling process would be necessary.

We have illustrated the overall process of DITCOS-DPM in Fig. 1. In the following paragraphs we suggest concrete activities regarding how to apply each DPM phase. It is important to understand that in the course of the modeling process purely DITCOS-DN constructs are used. The BPMN processes shown in the following sections are only used for visualization and are generated dynamically in the background by the DSR at runtime if required.

Applying DPM-I. A service engineer first digitally codifies a candidate service. By codification we mean that the relevant concepts are identified, e.g., the SCs, the BRs, and the RESs required during service provisioning. Then the service engineer identifies which SCs can be perceived as a particular module and whether the SCs need to be fulfilled in a particular order, as they may have dependencies on each other. The service modules are then mapped to ASs.

Once all ASs are in place, the service engineer might decide to combine them into CSs. The CSs could then be combined with other CSs or ASs. Using DITCOS-DN to model all these decisions finally results in a digital representation of the real-world service. Figure 3 depicts an example of a resulting AS consisting out of four SCs now documented as manual tasks (hand icon). The following two sec-

Fig. 3. AS with SCs based on *manual tasks* only after DPM-I

tions will illustrate how this example changes after each phase. These examples are a precursor to the results of the later evaluation of the methodology in the context of its practical application (Sect. 4). Due to space limitation, however, we are already using these results as a generic example here. We note that we consider DPM-I to be not only the starting point for the digitalization of existing real-world services. Rather, new services can of course be modeled based on DITCOS-DN right from the beginning. In our view, this will be easier and more feasible, the further the codification of existing real services progresses, due to the availability in the service repository of those ASs and CSs that have already been modeled and, hence, can be quickly reused as building blocks and combined to new service offerings.

Applying DPM-II. A DPM-II state for a service offering can be reached either by reworking existing DITCOS-DN-based service models, or by assigning SCs kinds which refer to a BPMN TaskHandler that supports the specific activities associated with the SC. From phase DPM-II perspective, the most simplistic BPMN TaskHandler provides an interaction endpoint that only requests status feedback from the assigned human agent. The human agent simply confirms that the action specified by the SC has been executed as required. Additional information such as status code and status message could be also collected.

From BPMN perspective the TaskHandler marks the corresponding BPMN task as *confirmed* and the BPMN engine progresses to the subsequent task of the process flow. This behavior continues until all tasks have reached their confirmed status and the process ends. Referring to the example AS, Fig. 4 depicts the AS after applying DPM-II. It now uses the *human task* type (person icon) for all activities and requires an appropriate task

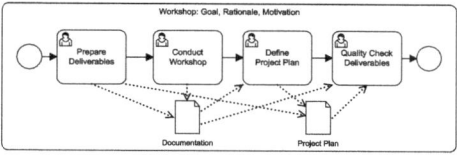

Fig. 4. AS with SCs based on *human tasks* only after DPM-II

handler. The prototype supports this behavior through a dedicated BPMN TaskHandler called *SimpleHumanAgentTaskHandler*. Through a mapping of SC kinds to handler classes, the DSR knows which BPMN TaskHandler must be assigned to the dynamically generated BPMN process model to trigger the desired behavior.

Applying DPM-III. For a DITCOS-DN service model to reach state DPM-III, additional and more specialized BPMN TaskHandlers are required, have to be implemented, and added to the digital ITC platform. Their purpose is to interact with software agents, which represent software systems providing an API. Every BPMN TaskHandler intended to interact with an API has to be implemented upfront.

Figure 5 shows a possible synthesis of *human tasks* (person icon) and *system tasks* (gear icon) representing the given example AS after applying DPM-III. The prototype supports this behavior through a dedicated BPMN

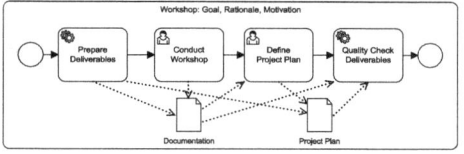

Fig. 5. AS with SCs based on *human* and *system tasks* after DPM-III

TaskHandler for REST-based web services called *RESTSystemTaskHandler* for outbound connectivity.

4   Practical Intervention and Evaluation of DITCOS-DPM

In the following sections, we evaluate the applicability of DITCOS-DPM by applying it in the practical context of a medium-sized German IT consulting company. We want to understand whether the expected outcomes of the DPM phases (Sects. 3.1–3.3) either can be confirmed, remain inconclusive, or can be rejected. The next sections have the following structure. In Subsect. 4.1 we first briefly introduce the service of study and explain why we choose it. In Subsects.

4.2–4.4 we describe how we practically applied DPM to it (ADR intervention phase), and finally in Subsect. 4.5 we describe our corresponding evaluation (ADR evaluation phase).

4.1   Service of Study: Development Method for Modern Business IT

We choose to transform an existing, already partly standardized service offering that aims at the transformation of legacy IT landscapes to modern, potentially cloud-based, and highly integrated replacements. The service offering *Development Method for Modern Business IT* (DMMB) defines four steps which are executed sequentially. We changed the name of the original service offering as this internal to the ITC firm. Each DMMB step defines several sub-steps which consist of shared deliverables, business roles, activities, and a sequence for the activities and phases. The following sections describe the application of each phase of our proposed model. Due to the complexity of the overall DMMB service offering, we present only one single AS of it. This AS was already introduced in the Figs. 3, 4, and 5. It was used earlier to describe the general scenario of applying our approach.

4.2   Applying DPM-I: Digital Codification of DMMB

The practitioners provided an elaborate set of documents that was used in several instantiations of the DMMB real-world service offering. They already tried to improve the provisioning process by implementing appropriate tooling into Microsoft (MS) Teams in the form of sequential checklists to keep track of the progress made. Especially important is the creation and continuous update of deliverables in form of result documents, such as technical concepts, checklists, and project plans. For every new instantiation of DMMB, the practitioners created a new MS Teams channel, copied documents to their target locations, and adjusted them to customer specifics. Today, all activities related to DMMB are *fully manual* and all business roles are fulfilled by human agents exclusively.

Due to the already high level of standardization of DMMB, we perceived it to be the perfect candidate evaluating DPM-I. Moreover, the fact that DMMB was applied frequently in client settings, means that it is a well-known and understood service offering from consultants' perspective. This is extremely helpful compared to service offerings that are infrequently requested by clients and only few consultants have been exposed to them. In cooperation with the practitioners we modeled the DMMB service offering based on the provided materials (i.e., process description, checklists, project plans). We required 16 CS to structure the DMMB steps and sub-steps. The modeling was straightforward and only took approximately one working day with the support of two practitioners. The whole service offering was successfully translated to DITCOS-DN. Due to its complexity, it is not possible to present the full model here. Instead, we only consider the result for one single AS of the overall DMMB service offering with four SCs initially modeled as manual tasks (hand icon) (Fig. 3). Figure 6 gives an impression of the DITCOS-Platform during the modeling process.

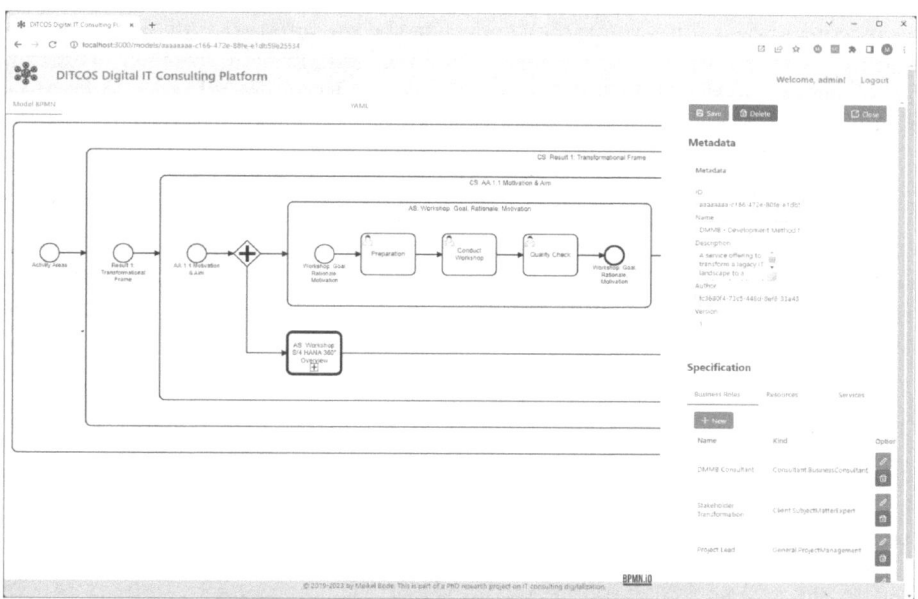

Fig. 6. Using the DITCOS-Platform prototype to digitally codify the DMMB service offering. The left side represents the dynamically rendered BPMN 2.0 model generated from the underlying DITCOS-DN codification. The right side shows the DITCOS-DN service metadata and specification related contents.

4.3 Applying DPM-II: Digital Augmentation of DMMB

After the digital codification (DPM-I) of the DMMB service, it was very easy to apply DPM-II. Digital augmentation is realized by assigning a SC kind that is linked to the SimpleHumanTaskHandler (Subsect. 3.2) to the SCs and by changing the SC execution type from *manually* (hand icon) to *hybrid* (person icon) which results in a different execution behavior (Fig. 4). The DSR automatically generates an executable BPMN 2.0 model from the DITCOS-DN service model that gets automatically deployed to the BPMN execution runtime on the service provisioning start event. The progress of the DMMB service model will then be continuously tracked by the digital ITC platform. It informs the assigned human agents to carry out the role specific behavior and requests the status of the human processing of every task continuously with the help of corresponding interaction endpoints.

4.4 Applying DPM-III: Digital Automation of DMMB

Next, we analyzed the result of DPM-II and found two candidate SCs to get further digitally transformed, namely *prepare deliverables* and *quality check deliverables* (Fig. 4). Both SCs require several activities to be performed which are common to all service instances. We were able to replace them with *service tasks* (gear icon) and so fully automate them. For the *prepare deliverables* SC we created a new task handler *SimpleDocumentPreparerTaskHandler*, which scans the *RESs* defined by the DITCOS-DN service model. Every RES that is linked to a template document is copied to the digital service instance workspace in case the RES has not been created yet. For the SC *quality check deliverables* we created another task handler, *SimpleQualityCheckTaskHandler*. It can evaluate simple rules, such as checking the existence of a document at a certain place or whether a file has been changed. When the system task gets executed by the BPMN 2.0 engine these rules get evaluated and on positive outcome the workflow proceeds. Otherwise, the workflow cannot proceed, and the resulting error situation must be resolved manually.

4.5   Evaluation

DPM-I. During the application of DITCOS-DPM to DMMB, we observed that the process definition which the practitioners used, and which only existed as Power Point and Word documents, was not consistent and in fact it was contradictory described. Due to the structured way of the modeling steps, the graphical editing support encouraged the practitioners to reflect on and re-think the DMMB service. So, DITCOS-DN helped to identify logical errors in the service provisioning flow already at this early stage. Another interesting learning was that modeling the service offerings directly supports the practitioners' needs to rearrange parts of the DMMB service offering for certain clients. We can cite one of the practitioners to indicate the current practice and nature of the DMMB service offering: "*We always offer 'the' DMMB to our clients, but it is never identically structured and delivered in the same way for all clients!*". Hence, having standardized service modules in form of basic ASs or even higher order CSs makes the daily work of the consultants easier, as they gain more flexibility. The fulfillment of the expected outcomes (O1-1–O1-7) formulated in Table 1 is as follows. *Standardization* could be reached, as the service attributes now follow the same structure due to utilizing the given DITCOS-DN constructs, such as AS or SC (Table 2). *Modularization* and *recombination* can also be confirmed, as services now exist in form of recombineable CS and AS [2]. *Know-how Transfer* through incorporating tacit knowledge into the corresponding DITCOS-DN based service model could be generally confirmed, too. However, the degree of know-how transfer could not be measured. It remains open how effective the documentation will be in the future. The same is true for the outcomes *transparency*, *repeatability*, and *service quality*, as this can only be finally proven after multiple executions of the digitalized DMMB service offering.

DPM-II. Compared to DPM-I, the results of DPM-II initially seem to be less impressive. Whereas DPM-I represents a visible big step by digitally codifying analogue services and thus giving the consultancy firm significantly more transparency about its service portfolio, DPM-II seems to have less visible effects. However, the DPM-II related change of the SC kind and its system supported execution type has significant impact for the consultancy too, as this allows the orchestration of human agents and tracking the progress of the service provisioning process. One important learning we made is, that the digital ITC platform prototype itself requires certain maturity to fully support DPM-II augmented service provisioning. For example, it is only possible to realize advantages in the context of human agent orchestration if the prototype is aware of the human workforce (e.g., consultants), its capabilities, and its availability. This raises different kind of questions related to data protection and regulation. Existing regulations, such as GDPR, may have influence on a later productive use of such a platform we propose [5]. In addition, it became apparent that completeness of the data is important. All relevant human agents must be known to the platform. Their skills must be completely maintained to allow a matching of the right consultant to the specific requirements of a particular business role. This means that data completeness and quality is key to the success of a digital ITC platform. Otherwise, human orchestration requires a generic human agent that always matches as a fallback, if no other human agent can be identified that is capable of fulfilling the requested role. The fulfillment of the expected outcomes (O2-1 – O2-3) formulated in Table 3 is as follows. *Human agent orchestration* generally works if the necessary data is complete and has the required quality (e.g., skills maintained). Collecting the *provisioning metrics* is a question of measuring continuously the events happening during the course of the service provisioning process. We realized this by hooking into the program code of our DSR and the task handlers. For every event we persist a log record containing the date and time of its occurrence, its type (e.g., CREATED, ERROR, DONE), the belonging service instance id, the id of the responsible agent, and an optional textual description. *Augmented service provisioning* could be confirmed too. As a DPM-II level service model instance constantly requires input from human agents during its provisioning, this solely takes the provisioning to a new level. The human agents incorporated in the service provisioning are constantly requested to provide status information related to the progress and this creates a considerable increase in process awareness and transparency for all incorporated stakeholders.

DPM-III. Evolving from DPM-II to DPM-III takes considerably more effort because, this requires analysis of the service offering to develop a clear understanding of those SCs that are candidates for automation. In turn, automation requires dedicated task handlers to fulfill the activities SCs consists of, such as copy a file between locations, call an API of a third-party system, or conduct a quality check on service outputs. The main learning from this phase is, that the consultancy should try to identify SCs activities and standardize them, so they can be implemented as generic as possible as task handlers. In this way, they would become reusable across different service offerings. Another learning relates to the inputs and outputs that human and software agents, respectively, provide to the services and receive from them. This must also be implemented in a way that allows a generic definition of digital interaction points (e.g., digital forms) to collect the inputs in case of human agents, and defined data formats in case of software agents. As part of our prototype, we realized this only rudimentary and we implemented them specifically for the required input. In practice this would not be possible as it would require too much effort and would therefore be ineffective. The fulfillment of the expected outcome (O3-1) formulated in Table 4 is as follows. *Software agent orchestration* works as expected and can be confirmed. An important learning is that the service depends potentially on factors, such as the availability of third-party software systems. This factor may be out of reach of the consultancy and therefore may cause error situations which could not be handled easily. An example is the access to an external file storage, that is required during service provisioning. The question that arises is how such technical error situations might disrupt the overall service provisioning process?

5   Conclusions and Future Work

With this work we contributed a new phase model DITCOS-DPM to support the IT consulting domain to conduct the digitialization of real-world service to digital representations. With DITCOS-DPM IT consultancies now have a means to approach the digitalization of their domain in an incremental, structured, and guided way. Beside DITCOS-DPM we created the technical DITCOS-Platform artifact required to support the digital modeling of those real-world services, to digitally augment them, and to identify services which are candidates to further digitalization to reach the best possible synthesis of human and system interaction during the service provisioning process. Our cooperation with ITC practitioners led to relevant learnings related to required future improvements of our current digital ITC platform prototype, such as the complete data requirement related to human actors who should fulfill BRs, that BPMN TaskHandlers must be designed and implemented for all third-party APIs which should be connected to the platform, or that DPM already supports the service engineering process at an early stage as it provides flexibility to recombine service model elements very flexible and gain new insights. With this work, we exemplified the application of DITCOS-DPM on a single real-world service offering example, namely *Development Method for Modern Business IT* (DMMB). The digital ITC DITCOS-Platform prototype contained only the necessary components to perform our very first evaluation of the digitalized DMMB. Clearly, the positive experience we had is only indicative at best and not generalizable as it is usually the case in very first evaluation studies [15]. Future research therefore needs to address these limitations and open the platform to a wider range of real-world services. In addition, a more generic set of BPMN TaskHandlers needs to be provided to support more types of service automation and better understand the digitalized delivery of DITCOS-DN-based service models.

References

1. Bode, M., et al.: Characterising the digital transformation of IT consulting services - results from a systematic mapping study. IET Softw. **16**(5), 455–477 (2022)
2. Bode, M., et al.: Describing digital IT consulting services: the DITCOS ontology proposal and its evaluation. In: IEEE 24th CBI, Amsterdam, The Netherlands (2022)
3. Bode, M., et al.: Digital IT consulting service provisioning a practice-driven platform architecture proposal. In: IEEE 25th EDOCW, Gold Coast, Australia, pp. 251–260 (2021)
4. Bode, M., et al.: Requirements for digital IT consulting services and their provision through digital consulting platforms - results from a focus group study. In: IEEE 23rd CBI, Bolzano, Italy, pp. 111–120 (2021)
5. Bode, M., et al.: Visual description of digital IT consulting services using DITCOS-DN: proposal and evaluation of a graphical editor. In: Sales, T.P., et al. (eds.) EDOC 2022. LNBIP, vol. 466, pp. 113–128. Springer, Cham (2023). https://doi.org/10.1007/978-3-031-26886-1_7
6. Christensen, C.M., et al.: Consulting on the cusp of disruption. Hardw. Bus. Rev. **91**(10), 106–114 (2013)
7. de Reuver, M., et al.: The digital platform: a research agenda. J. Inf. Technol. **33**(2), 124–135 (2018)
8. Gartner. Online Glossary (2023)
9. Hevner, A.R., et al.: Design science in information systems research. MIS Q. **28**(1), 75–105 (2004)
10. Lubarski, A., et al.: Modular professional services: conceptual goodness and research themes. In: Americas Conference on Information Systems, Boston, p. 10 (2017)
11. Mauerer, C.: The development of interpersonal trust between the consultant and client in the course of the consulting process. In: Nissen, V. (ed.) Advances in Consulting Research, pp. 273–298. Springer, Cham (2019). https://doi.org/10.1007/978-3-319-95999-3_13
12. Nissen, V.: Digital transformation of the consulting industry - introduction and overview. In: Nissen, V. (ed.) Digital Transformation of the Consulting Industry, pp. 1–58. Springer, Cham (2018). https://doi.org/10.1007/978-3-319-70491-3_1
13. Nissen, V., Kuhl, J., Kräft, H., Seifert, H., Reiter, J., Eidmann, J.: Creating a digital consulting solution for project management assessments at Dr. Kuhl Unternehmensberatung: development and initial demonstration of a fully automated asset-based consulting approach. In: Urbach, N., Röglinger, M. (eds.) Digitalization Cases, pp. 225–247. Springer, Cham (2019). https://doi.org/10.1007/978-3-319-95273-4_12
14. Parasuraman, A., et al.: A conceptual model of service quality and its implications for future research. J. Mark. **49**(4), 41–50 (1985)
15. Sein, M.K., et al.: Action design research. MIS Q. **35**(1), 37 (2011)
16. Werth, D., et al.: Self-service consulting: conceiving customer-operated digital IT consulting services. In: ACIS, San Diego (2016)

EDOC Forum

Monitoring Business Process Compliance Across Multiple Executions with Stream Processing

Chukri Soueidi[1], Yliès Falcone[1], and Sylvain Hallé[2(✉)]

[1] Laboratoire d'informatique de Grenoble, Université Grenoble Alpes, Grenoble, France
[2] Laboratoire d'informatique formelle, Université du Québec à Chicoutimi, Chicoutimi, Canada
`shalle@uqac.ca`

Abstract. Compliance checking is the operation that consists of assessing whether every execution trace of a business process satisfies a given correctness condition. The paper introduces the notion of hyperquery, which is a calculation that involves multiple traces from a log at the same time. A particular case of hyperquery is a hypercompliance condition, which is a correctness requirement that involves the whole log instead of individual process instances. A formalization of hyperqueries is presented, along with a number of elementary operations to express hyperqueries on arbitrary logs. An implementation of these concepts in an event stream processing engine allows users to concretely evaluate hyperqueries in real time.

1 Introduction

In the world of Business Process Management (BPM), the term *compliance* denotes the adherence to a set of established constraints (rules) or norms. *Compliance checking* is a technique used at various stages of a business process life cycle: design time, run time, and post-execution to ensure that business processes adhere to such predefined constraints [23]. While ideally desired at design-time, the existence of a complete formally defined process model for compliance checks cannot be always assumed, hence compliance checking is often performed at run-time and referred to as compliance *monitoring*.

Several formalisms have been employed for modeling and representing business constraints, including event calculus (EC) [25], temporal logic [2], and deontic logic [18]. Moreover, in a real-world business scenario, process instances often share resources and are seldom executed in isolation. Service-level agreements (SLA), for example are sometimes expressed not on individual cases, but as aggregated measures over a set of cases. Such constraints are known in the field as *instance-spanning* constraints (ISC) [14] and add another layer of complexity to compliance checking. Compliance checking on ISC has received less attention in literature.

To tackle these challenges, this paper utilizes Complex Event Processing (CEP). CEP is employed to address the inflexibility of formalisms by providing

© The Author(s), under exclusive license to Springer Nature Switzerland AG 2024
T. P. Sales et al. (Eds.): EDOC 2023 Workshops, LNBIP 498, pp. 247–264, 2024.
https://doi.org/10.1007/978-3-031-54712-6_15

a generic querying language over streams of events. To this end, this paper introduces the concept of a *hyperquery*. A hyperquery is a stream processing calculation involving multiple traces from a log concurrently. A special case of a hyperquery is a hypercompliance condition, which is a correctness requirement encompassing the entire log rather than individual process instance; this notion generalizes several approaches considering ISC. This paper provides examples of hyperqueries for different representative scenarios, and presents a formalization of hyperqueries along with elementary operations to express them on any logs. We implemented these concepts in an event stream processing engine, BeepBeep [21] which enable users to evaluate hyperqueries in real-time.

The rest of this paper is structured as follows. Section 2 gives an overview of compliance and hypercompliance and mentions existing solutions for compliance checking. Section 3 presents a formalization for hypercompliance. Section 4 presents the building blocks that allows user to express hyperqueries. Section 5 presents our implementation and evaluation on collection of real world and synthetic scenarios. Finally, Sect. 6 concludes the paper and discusses future work.

2   Business Process Compliance and Hypercompliance

To illustrate the problem addressed by this paper, consider a simplified school admission process, represented in the BPMN diagram of Fig. 1. The process starts with the submission of an application by the student. Upon submission, an admission officer is assigned to review the application. If additional documents are needed, they are requested. An interview is then scheduled. On the interview day, the interview is conducted and subsequently evaluated. If the applicant is successful, an acceptance letter is sent; otherwise, a rejection letter is sent.

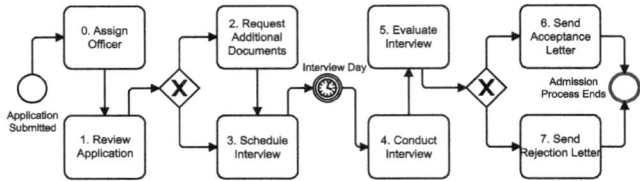

Fig. 1. BPMN representation of the school admission process.

In a typical admissions period, several instances of this process can be started every day (one for each student presenting an application); the duration of each instance is variable and can span several days, and each instance is also free to progress independently of each other. As a result, an external observer noting the activities executed for each application as they occur would see an interleaved sequence of "events" belonging to multiple instances.

The normal operation of the registration process depends on a number of conditions that can be expressed over the sequence of activities recorded by this hypothetical observer. Some of them involve each application taken in isolation, such as:

C1 *Due process:* Checks that the sequence of activities in each application is a valid execution of the BPMN diagram.

C2 *Interview rejection:* Ensures that every application process ends with a rejection letter if the interview was judged unsatisfactory.

C3 *Four-eyes principle:* Asserts that the application review and the interview must be performed by two different employees.

Some other conditions can also be expressed on the process as a whole, by looking at all its executions. For example:

H1 *Cap on applications under review:* Ensures no more than k applications are *under review* simultaneously, preventing application overload and facilitating effective management of the admissions period.

H2 *Consistency in rejections:* States that if an application is rejected for the reason of a low grade x, then all applications with grades below x should also be rejected, ensuring fairness and consistency in the process.

H3 *Threshold acceptance ratio:* Dictates that a minimum of x percent of applications must reach a positive outcome. This threshold can ensure a regular inflow of students.

H4 *Fair task distribution:* Validates an even allocation of applications across employees. This check aims to avoid overloading any individual.

H5 *"Evil employee" deterrence:* Ensures no employee rejects all assigned applications. Upholding this condition can help identify any potential prejudices in the assessment process and guarantee fairness for all candidates.

H6 *Employee capacity limit:* Restricts the number of applicants assigned to an employee at a given time to n. This promotes a sustainable workload per staff member.

Adequate management of this business process requires looking for potential violations of these various conditions, ideally in an automated fashion. Moreover, it is desirable that these eventual violations be reported when they occur—as opposed, for example, to a postmortem examination of process runs after the admissions period is over.

The scenario described above can be framed as a case of *compliance checking*, which is a technique used in Business Process Management (BPM) to ensure that business processes adhere to predefined rules or regulations. When used at run-time, compliance checking is often referred to as compliance *monitoring*, while at post-execution, it is referred to as compliance *auditing*. In the context of this work, existing approaches for checking compliance can be separated in two categories, depending on whether they consider conditions on a single instance of a process, or conditions on multiple instances.

2.1 Single-Instance Compliance

Most of the research so far has focused on constraints that target *single* instances of a process—in other words, constraints that can be checked on each execution separately. These correspond to conditions C1–C3 of our running example; and several surveys on this topic have been published [23, 26, 34].

Early compliance monitoring techniques operated on MXML logs before XES. We mention [2] where given an event log and an LTL property, an LTL Checker verifies whether the observed behavior matches the expected behavior. In [9], a framework was proposed for performing compliance checking of process execution traces with respect to business rules that are mapped to Logic Programming, using Prolog. [26] proposed a framework for Compliance Monitoring Functionalities (CMF) that enables systematic comparison of existing and new approaches for monitoring compliance rules over business processes during runtime. In [28], a novel runtime verification framework was proposed, based on linear temporal logic and colored automata, continuously verifying compliance against a predefined constraint model. On its side, reactive event calculus [10] is a formulation of event calculus suited for the incremental evaluation of properties over event streams. Research in [18] focused on the compliance of business processes with business contracts, presenting a logic-based formalism for describing both the semantics of the contract and the compliance checking procedure. Meanwhile, the work presented in [5] offered a visual approach for specifying compliance rules using a language known as BPMN-Q.

Compliance can also be ascertained using process mining: past logs of the execution of a business process are used to derive a model of the system, and subsequent executions of this process are then compared to this model; a deviation from the model may indicate a violation of a compliance requirement [16]. Finally, one can also verify that a business process is such that all its possible executions are compliant with respect to a condition, a problem that can be seen as a form of model checking. For example, [4] translated compliance rules into temporal logic formulæ for model checkers to verify whether a process model complies with the requested rule, addressing the state-space explosion problem through a set of reduction rules. [17] modeled legal documents and presented an approach to check the compliance of a legally annotated process model with rules expressed in LegalRuleML.

2.2   Instance-Spanning Compliance

The previous approaches have in common that they consider compliance as an "individual" property of a business process execution: each trace is compliant or not with respect to a specification, a model or a set of constraints. Even approaches calculating aggregate metrics from a set of executions are still composed of individual decisions on the compliance of each single execution with respect to a reference. This is the case, for example, with the notion of *degree* of compliance [27] and *level* of compliance [34], which are compliance metrics aggregated from the individual compliance calculated on multiple instances.

In contrast, fewer works have targeted compliance checking for *instance-spanning constraints*, which are constraints that extend across multiple instances of one or several process types [14], such as conditions H1–H6 of our motivating example. These conditions have first been considered in the context of information system security, where they are called *hyperproperties* [12]. In the field of business process management, research on these constraints offer means to define these constraints or target specific usage scenarios in various domains such as healthcare [24], cargo bundling transport processes [37], and security [8]. A collection of examples of such constraints can be found in [31]. Formally, while a classical property defines a set of executions (those that are considered valid), a hyperproperty defines a set of *sets* of executions. In the following, we shall call compliance to a hyperproperty *hypercompliance*.

While there exists a plethora of formal notations for defining properties (e.g. finite-state automata, temporal logic, μ-calculus), fewer have been proposed to define hyperproperties. One notable proponent is HyperLTL, which extends Linear Temporal Logic (LTL) with quantifiers over execution traces, and can express a subset of all possible hyperproperties [11]. A HyperLTL formula is of the form $Q_1\overline{\sigma}_1 : Q_2\overline{\sigma}_2 : \cdots Q_n\overline{\sigma}_n : \varphi$, where Q_i is either a universal or an existential quantifier, $\overline{\sigma}_i$ is a quantified variable standing for a trace, and φ is a classical LTL formula whose ground terms are atomic symbols from any of the $\overline{\sigma}_i$.

Finkbeiner *et al.* [15] distinguish between three scenarios for the runtime evaluation of a HyperLTL expression. First is the "parallel" model, where a *fixed* number of executions is considered, with each of them producing exactly *one* event at each step. There are also two variants of the "sequential" model, where system executions are processed one after the other. In the *unbounded* variant, the number of executions to consider is unknown and may in fact grow forever, which is not the case for the *bounded* variant. They provide algorithms for the evaluation of HyperLTL formulæ in each case.

Similarly, HyperLDL$_f$ is an extension of Linear Dynamic Logic (LDL$_f$), enabling the expression of hyper-properties that relate multiple process execution traces at once [13]. On this language, the authors consider the model checking problem, which is stated as deciding whether the set of traces accepted by a deterministic finite automaton satisfies a HyperLDL$_f$ property. In [25] a rule-based monitoring approach based on Event Calculus and the Rete algorithm is presented.

Other approaches considering instance-spanning constraints include a predictive model based on supervised machine learning, accounting for both intra and inter-case dependencies using datasets from a hospital emergency department and a manufacturing process [35]. More recently, [3] followed a database-oriented technique for compliance monitoring of instance spanning constraints. The approach requires the user to express a constraint as a quadruplet of SQL queries representing the various states in which it can be for each instance (currently/permanently satisfied/violated). As with many approaches using SQL for event-based data, explicit comparisons between event timestamps must be used to express temporal relationships equivalent to, e.g. LTL operators. The approach also currently handles Boolean constraints, but not more general instance-spanning calculations.

The evaluation of instance-spanning constraints can also be framed in the more general framework of *process querying*, which is concerned with models and methods to filter and transform representations of business processes [30]. Among the multiple available techniques, a subset concentrates on executing queries on event data, i.e. the sequence of events produced by the executions of a process [1].

3   Formalizing Hypercompliance

The presentation of related works reveals gaps in existing solutions that make them ill-suited to handle the motivating example of Sect. 2.

Obviously, single-instance solutions (Sect. 2.1) cannot evaluate conditions H1–H6 that correlate multiple executions. On the front of hyperproperties (Sect. 2.2), our business process scenario fits none of the three cases handled by Finkbeiner *et al.* [15]: new instances of the process can be started at any moment, their number is theoretically unbounded, and the events they produce can be arbitrarily interleaved. What is more, some of the hypercompliance conditions of our running example involve aggregations and other constructs that are beyond the expressiveness of existing languages such as Event Calculus [25], HyperLTL [11] and HyperLDL$_f$ [13] (which, in the latter case, is considered for model checking and not monitoring). It is also unclear how some of these queries could be handled in the SQL-based approach of [3], especially for calculations involving complex sequential relationships between events.

Our proposed approach takes a different direction, and suggests the use of arbitrary event-stream processing calculations as the basis for expressing hypercompliance conditions. It calls for a more general theoretical framework, in which arbitrary *instance-spanning* computations could be incrementally evaluated over interleaved executions of a given business process. In this section, we start by laying the foundations on which these operations will be carried.

3.1   Streams and Processors

Let Σ be a set of arbitrary *events*, sometimes called the "alphabet". A sequence $\overline{\sigma} \in \Sigma^*$ is called a *stream*. We denote by $\overline{\sigma} \cdot \overline{\sigma}'$ the concatenation of $\overline{\sigma}$ and $\overline{\sigma}'$. The empty stream is given the symbol ϵ. We say that $\overline{\sigma}$ is a prefix of $\overline{\sigma}'$, and note it $\overline{\sigma} \preceq \overline{\sigma}'$, if there exists $\overline{\sigma}''$ such that $\overline{\sigma}' = \overline{\sigma} \cdot \overline{\sigma}''$. In addition, $\overline{\sigma}$ is a *strict* prefix if $\overline{\sigma}'' \neq \epsilon$; this is noted $\overline{\sigma} \prec \overline{\sigma}'$.

A stream vector over alphabets $\Sigma_1, \ldots, \Sigma_n$ is an n-uple $\langle \overline{\sigma}_1, \ldots, \overline{\sigma}_n \rangle$, with $\overline{\sigma}_i \in \Sigma_i^*$ for $i \in [1, n]$. A stream vector $\vec{v} = \langle \overline{\sigma}_1, \ldots, \overline{\sigma}_n \rangle$ is a prefix of another vector $\vec{v}' = \langle \overline{\sigma}_1', \ldots, \overline{\sigma}_n' \rangle$, noted $\vec{v} \preceq \vec{v}'$, if $\overline{\sigma}_i \preceq \overline{\sigma}_i'$ for $i \in [1, n]$. Given two sets of stream vectors $\mathcal{V}$ and $\mathcal{V}'$, we call a *processor* any function $\pi : \mathcal{V} \rightarrow \mathcal{V}'$ respecting the progressing condition, which is that for every $\vec{v}_1, \vec{v}_2 \in \mathcal{V}$, $\vec{v}_1 \preceq \vec{v}_2$ implies that $\pi(\vec{v}_1) \preceq \pi(\vec{v}_2)$.

Intuitively, a processor is a function that transforms a stream vector into another stream vector; the cardinality of the input and output vector are respectively called the input and output *arity* of the processor. The progressing condition restricts the way in which input and output are related; more precisely, if feeding π with an input vector $\vec{v}_1$ results in an output $\vec{v}_1'$, then appending zero or more events to streams in $\vec{v}_1$ results in the vector $\vec{v}_1''$ to which zero or more events are appended. In other words, a processor that outputs events for a given input cannot "take them back" when extending that input with further events; it can only append further events to its existing output.

A processor is called *synchronous* if it satisfies the condition that, for every pair of vectors $\vec{v} = \langle \overline{\sigma}_1, \ldots, \overline{\sigma}_m \rangle$, $\vec{v}' = \langle \overline{\sigma}_1', \ldots, \overline{\sigma}_m' \rangle$ such that $\vec{v} \preceq \vec{v}'$, $\pi(\vec{v}) \neq \pi(\vec{v}')$ implies that $\vec{v} \prec \vec{v}'$. Combined with the progressing condition stated above, this entails that for such a processor to append new events to its output, at least one new event must be appended to each stream in the input vector. This condition is vacuously satisfied for any processor ingesting stream vectors of input arity 1. These definitions provide a uniform formal framework in which a wide range of existing notations can be handled, such as Moore machines, Petri nets or temporal logic.

3.2 Logs and Hyperprocessors

Let I be a set of trace *identifiers*. A *log* is denoted as a function $\lambda : I \to \Sigma^*$, which associates to some trace identifiers a specific trace. We denote by Λ the set of such logs. We say that the log *contains* a trace for identifier i if $\lambda(i) \neq \epsilon$. The size of the log, noted $|\lambda|$, is the number of traces it contains, i.e. $|\lambda| \triangleq |\{i \in I : \lambda(i) \neq \epsilon\}|$. We denote by $\varnothing$ the unique log of size 0. A log is finite if it contains a finite number of traces. Conceptually, each trace represent one execution of some system or process, and the log is the collection of these executions. In the following, we shall use the words "trace", "execution" or "case" as synonyms. We override the symbol $\preceq$ and note by $\lambda \preceq \lambda'$ the fact that a log is an extension of another. Formally, this is expressed by the fact that for every $i \in I$, $\lambda(i) \preceq \lambda'(i)$. Intuitively, a log extends another one if it appends events to already defined traces, or if it introduces a new association between an identifier and a trace.

A *hyperquery* is a function $q : \Lambda \to C$, which given a log $\lambda \in \Lambda$, performs an arbitrary calculation on this log and returns a result $q(\lambda) \in C$. A hyperproperty, as defined in existing literature [12], can be seen as the particular case where $C = \{\top, \bot\}$. Given a hyperquery q, evaluating it on a prerecorded log is a straightforward task. However, in a context where the contents of the log is captured live (for example, as instances of a process are still active and generating new events), one is rather interested in a periodical evaluation of the hyperquery. In such a case, calculating q from scratch on each version of the log would result in a considerable waste of computing resources. It would make much more sense to consider the current log as an update of the previous one, and update the value of q accordingly.

To this end, we override the symbol $\cdot$ to represent the *update* of a log. If λ and λ' are two logs, the update of λ by λ', noted $\lambda \cdot \lambda'$, is the log λ'' defined as $\lambda''(i) \triangleq \lambda(i) \cdot \lambda'(i)$ for all $i \in I$. A log update appends new events to zero or more traces. An update is called *unitary* if it adds a single new event to a single trace. A finite log λ of size n can be represented as the explicit enumeration of traces associated to each identifier: $\{i_1 \mapsto \overline{\sigma}_1, \ldots, i_n \mapsto \overline{\sigma}_n\}$. It also admits an alternative representation as a sequence of successive log updates starting from the empty log: $\lambda = \varnothing \cdot \lambda_1 \cdot \ldots \cdot \lambda_m$. For example, suppose that $I = \{0,1\}$ and $\Sigma = \{a, b, c\}$; then the log $\lambda = \{0 \mapsto ab, 1 \mapsto c\}$ can be expressed as a sequence of updates in various ways, one of them being: $\varnothing \cdot \{0 \mapsto a\} \cdot \{1 \mapsto c\} \cdot \{0 \mapsto b\}$.

Given a hyperquery $q : \Lambda \rightarrow C$, a *hyperprocessor* for q is a processor $\pi_q : \Lambda^* \rightarrow C^*$ ingesting a stream of log updates $\lambda_1, \ldots, \lambda_m$, and satisfying the condition that if $\pi_q(\lambda_1, \ldots, \lambda_m) = \overline{\sigma}$, the last event of $\overline{\sigma}$ is equal to $q(\lambda_1 \cdot \ldots \cdot \lambda_m)$. Thus, a hyperprocessor receives updates, and upon each update, is such that its latest output corresponds to the value of q on the log obtained by the sequence of updates observed so far (starting from the empty log). In other words, the hyperprocessor π_q performs the incremental evaluation and update of the hyperquery q.

4   Building Blocks for Hyperprocessors

The previous definitions provided the formal notation for expressing hyperqueries and hyperprocessors. However, we still do not have an algorithm for the efficient, and above all incremental, evaluation of a given hyper-query q. On the one hand, a hyperprocessor π_q that simply re-evaluates q from scratch after each log update satisfies the definition and is simple to implement, but is obviously suboptimal. On the other hand, it is unrealistic to expect end users to directly implement a hyperprocessor specific to each hyperquery they wish to evaluate. The approach we follow is to introduce a number of "building blocks", i.e. a set of basic hyperprocessors performing elementary operations on streams of log updates, which can then be composed to create complex hyperqueries.

4.1   Operators on Log Updates

A particular case of hyperprocessor is one where $C = \Lambda$. Such a hyperprocessor transforms a stream of log updates into another one. Primary uses of such hyperprocessors are for preprocessing or "maintenance" operations.

Sample. A common operation is to retain only a subset of an existing log, by retaining a fraction of the existing traces; this process is called *sampling* [33].

A primitive form of sampling can be implemented by merely evaluating a function $f : \Sigma \rightarrow \{\top, \bot\}$ which decides which events are let through based on a condition evaluated on the *first* event of each process instance. Given such a function f, the sampling hyperquery is the function defined as:

$$q_\pi(\lambda) = \{i \mapsto \overline{\sigma} : f(\overline{\sigma}[0]) = \top\}$$

This query evaluates a condition on the first event of each process instance. If the condition evaluates to true ($\top$), then all events of this instance are let through. On the contrary, if the condition evaluates to false ($\bot$), then all log updates for this process instance will be discarded (resulting in that instance being absent from the output log).

The XES log format associates each process instance with a number of attributes that qualify the instance as a whole. Conceptually, one can assume that these attributes are contained within the first (or every) event of each instance, and thus apply sampling based on these attributes. For instance, one could sample a log by excluding cases coming from a particular city, or lighten the log by excluding all case where the (numerical) ID does not end in a particular number (a form of statistical sampling).

Filter. A refinement of this strategy consists of pushing updates for streams in a log that satisfy a *stateful* condition. You may need to retain updates for this stream until the condition is satisfied. Given a monitor $\pi : \Sigma^* \to \{\top, ?, \bot\}^*$, the filtering hyperquery is the function defined as:

$$q_\pi(\lambda) = \{i \mapsto \overline{\sigma} : \pi(\overline{\sigma})[-1] = \top\}$$

Given a log, this hyperquery returns a new log that retains only the mappings $i \mapsto \overline{\sigma}$ that are such that π produces a true verdict when run on $\overline{\sigma}$.

Note that this query is parameterized by a processor π, which may need to receive multiple events before producing a conclusive verdict. As long as it is not the case, the corresponding trace is absent from the output log. Consider for example the monitor π defined as $\pi(\overline{\sigma} \cdot x) = \pi(\overline{\sigma}) \cdot \top$ if $\overline{\sigma} \cdot x$ contains an a, and $\pi(\overline{\sigma}) \cdot ?$ otherwise. This monitor produces the true verdict on any trace that contains an a somewhere. On the log $\{0 \mapsto bcdc, 1 \mapsto b\}$, q_π returns the empty log, as none of the traces satisfy the condition. However, on the log $\{0 \mapsto bcdca, 1 \mapsto b\}$, q_π returns $\{0 \mapsto bcdca\}$, as trace 0 satisfies the condition. Note that in this case, the whole trace appears at once.

This definition has implications for the implementation of the corresponding hyperprocessor. When a new trace is added to the output log, the hyperprocessor needs to output the sequence of unitary log updates corresponding to this trace in a single burst.

4.2   Log Combinations

The previous operators provide functionalities that transform a stream of log updates and apply modifications to the content of the log itself. A second set of operators applies a calculation to traces in a log, and combines the result obtained for each instance.

Quantification. The first combination is quantification, which evaluates a condition that must apply either on all traces in a log (universal), or for one trace in the log (existential). Quantifiers can be nested, which makes it possible to express conditions that involve several traces at the same time. Formally, a quantified hyperquery is defined as follows:

$$q_{\pi'}^{Q_1 \ldots Q_n}(\lambda) \triangleq \bigotimes_{\overline{\sigma}_1 \in \lambda} \cdots \bigotimes_{\overline{\sigma}_n \in \lambda} \pi(\langle \overline{\sigma}_1, \ldots \overline{\sigma}_n \rangle)$$

where each Q_i is either $\forall$ or $\exists$, π' is a $n{:}1$ processor and $\bigotimes_i$ is $\wedge$ if $Q_i = \forall$, and $\vee$ if $Q_i = \exists$. The notation $\overline{\sigma} \in \lambda$ means that there exists an identifier $i \in I$ such that $\lambda(i) = \overline{\sigma}$. For example, the condition that all traces in a log have the same length could be expressed as the hyperquery $q_{\pi'}^{\forall\forall}$, where π' is the processor such that $\pi'(\overline{\sigma}_1, \overline{\sigma}_2)[-1] = \top$ if $|\overline{\sigma}_1| = |\overline{\sigma}_2|$, and $\bot$ otherwise.

Quantification can be seen as a generalization of HyperLTL: indeed, contrary to this logic, the condition π' is not limited to temporal logic operators over atomic propositions, but can incorporate any arbitrary stateful calculation. For example, the condition "all traces end with the same number of a events" can be expressed using quantification, but not using HyperLTL since temporal logic does not allow counting.

Aggregation. Finkbeiner *et al.* [15] show that, without additional hypotheses on the property, a monitor for HyperLTL must retain all the events of all the traces seen so far, which limits the applicability of such an operation. To alleviate this issue, we introduce an alternate form of operation on a log which is called aggregation, defined as follows:

$$q_{\pi_T}^{\pi_A}(\lambda) \triangleq \pi_A \left(\bigodot_{\overline{\sigma} \in \lambda} \pi_T(\overline{\sigma})[-1] \right) [-1]$$

where π_T and π_A are both $1{:}1$ processors, and $\bigodot$ represents the iterated concatenation of elements to form a trace. Intuitively, an instance of π_T is run separately on each trace $\overline{\sigma} \in \lambda$; the last event of each output stream is concatenated to form a new stream, and π_A is evaluated on that stream. The last event of the output is the value of $q_{\pi_T}^{\pi_A}$ associated to the log λ.

One can see the aggregation operator as a form of "middle ground" between a compliance condition (which does not correlate traces to other traces), and the general quantification operation (which compares every trace to every other). It turns out that many hyperproperties which, when expressed in HyperLTL, require quantifiers, can actually be reformulated (and more efficiently evaluated) as aggregations. For example, take the property stipulating that all traces end with the same number of a events; contrary to the quantified formulation, which performs a calculation on each *pair* of traces in a log and is thus quadratic in the number of cases, the aggregated formulation combines values calculated on each trace *separately* and is therefore linear in the number of cases.

4.3   Qualified Conditions

When considering a single execution of a process, one can express conditions that can either be satisfied or violated. In contrast, a particular feature brought by the study of hypercompliance is the fact that the conditions they express may allow "partial" satisfaction. For example, one may want to evaluate a hyperquery only when a log reaches a certain size, or only on traces of some minimum length. At other moments, it may be reasonable to tolerate a log that deviates from a compliant state to some degree. In those situations, it is useful to see hypercompliance as formed of two separate elements: a strict, black-or-white condition, to which a mitigating factor is attached.

Weakening. A first way of qualifying hypercompliance is to express a condition that needs to be satisfied for its verdict to be considered relevant. For example, it is probably inappropriate to raise an alarm when the constraint "90% of traces end in a success" is violated on a log that contains a single case. In such a situation, one would typically add a condition that indicates when it makes sense to evaluate the policy, for example by asserting that there must be a minimum number k of completed cases in the log. We call this process the *weakening* of a constraint.

Weakening can be applied at the level of individual traces, or at the level of the whole log. The first case is handled by encasing a calculation on each trace with a *filter* hyperprocessor, as already defined in Sect. 4.1. Thus, only cases satisfying a specific condition will enter in the evaluation of the policy. The latter case can also be expressed simply, by considering both the constraint and its weakening condition as two hyperqueries q_P and q_W; the version of q_P weakened by q_W is thus the hyperquery q defined as $q(\lambda) \triangleq q_W(\lambda) \rightarrow q_P(\lambda)$. By the semantics of Boolean implication, $q(\lambda)$ produces $\top$ if the weakening hyperquery is not satisfied. The key point is that this implication is made explicit by separating the condition from the policy itself; in the example above, the policy *is* violated, but the weakening condition tells us to *disregard* its verdict.

Dampening. A second possibility is to tolerate temporary violations of a constraint, a concept that we call *dampening*. Dampened conditions are particularly appropriate for expressing service-level agreements (SLAs), for example by stating that "the system is never offline for more than five minutes", or that "95% of customer claims are processed under two days". In the following we introduce two types of dampening.

The *temporal* dampening operator considers a window of n successive evaluations of the constraint, and returns a passing verdict if at most $m < n$ of these evaluations are negative. If $\overline{\lambda}$ is a sequence of (unitary) log updates and π' is a processor, we note by $\#_{\pi'}^n(\overline{\lambda})$ the value $|\{\overline{\lambda}' \preceq \overline{\lambda} : |\overline{\lambda}| - |\overline{\lambda}'| \leq n \wedge \pi'(\overline{\lambda}')[-1] \neq \bot\}|$; this function determines how many of the longest n prefixes of $\overline{\lambda}$ are such that the constraint is not violated. Temporal dampening can then be defined as:

$$\pi_{\pi'}(\overline{\lambda} \cdot \lambda) \triangleq \begin{cases} \pi_{\pi'}(\overline{\lambda}) \cdot ? & \text{if } |\overline{\lambda} \cdot \lambda| < n \\ \pi_{\pi'}(\overline{\lambda}) \cdot \top & \text{if } \#_{\pi'}^n(\overline{\lambda} \cdot \lambda) \geq n - m \\ \pi_{\pi'}(\overline{\lambda}) \cdot \bot & \text{otherwise} \end{cases}$$

While temporal dampening allows some negative verdicts to be disregarded, *case* dampening allows some cases in a log to be disregarded. For a log λ, denote by $\lambda \backslash \{i_1, \ldots, i_n\}$ the log λ' such that $\lambda'(i) = \epsilon$ if $i \in \{i_1, \ldots, i_n\}$, and $\lambda'(i) = \lambda(i)$ otherwise. In other words, the operation erases specific traces from the log. If q is a hyperquery, the case dampening of this query can then be defined as

$$q^{-m}(\lambda) = \begin{cases} \top & \text{if there exists } I' \subseteq I \text{ with } |I'| \leq m \text{ such that } q(\lambda \setminus I') = \top \\ \bot & \text{otherwise} \end{cases}$$

The dampened version q^{-m} of q is satisfied for a log λ if it is possible to create a log λ' that satisfies q by removing at most m traces from λ. An advantage of this definition is that it can also be applied to policies that do not express a Boolean condition over individual traces. For example, in the constraint "the average trace length is less than k", none of the traces is in itself a success or a violation, yet the policy can be dampened by excluding the longest m traces of a log. Variants of this dampening operator can be obtained by changing the condition $|I'| \leq m$, for example by replacing it with a fraction of all logs.

Note that, in the previous example, dampening is different from replacing k by an interval, which does not alter the original condition in the same way. It is also worth noting that a constraint may involve a combination of these operations. Thus, one could say that the average trace length is less than k, by allowing at most m of them to be disregarded (dampening), and by considering only logs with a sufficient number m' of traces (weakening).

5   Implementation and Evaluation

The hyperprocessors presented so far have been described at the theoretical level. The question remains whether these processors can be used in practice, and how well they scale on logs of realistic size. In this section, we report on our efforts to concretely implement the hyperprocessors presented earlier, and to experimentally measure their efficiency under various conditions.

5.1   A Toolbox for Hyperqueries

As the basis of our implementation, we use an actual open source event stream processing engine, called BeepBeep [21]. BeepBeep offers a collection of simple computation units called `Processors`, which correspond exactly to the definition we gave of this concept in Sect. 3.1. Processors can then be connected to form pipelines. Over the years, BeepBeep has been involved in multiple case studies related to business processes, such as the tracking of packages in the Physical Internet [6] and the detection of trend deviations in process logs [32].

BeepBeep already provides a wealth of processors to perform computations over traces of events of various kinds, many of which can be leveraged in the expression of hyperqueries. On top of this infrastructure, we designed an extension providing support for hyperprocessors[1]. Specifically, all the operators

---

[1] https://github.com/liflab/hypercompliance.

described in Sect. 4 have been implemented as a new type of object, which can interact and be mixed with any of the existing BeepBeep processors. The end result is a "toolbox" allowing users to express and evaluate hyperqueries in a flexible and expressive manner: complex hyperqueries can be written in few lines of code, either natively in Java, or even more concisely using the Groovy scripting language. Figure 2 shows the pictorial representation of the processors introduced in the previous section.

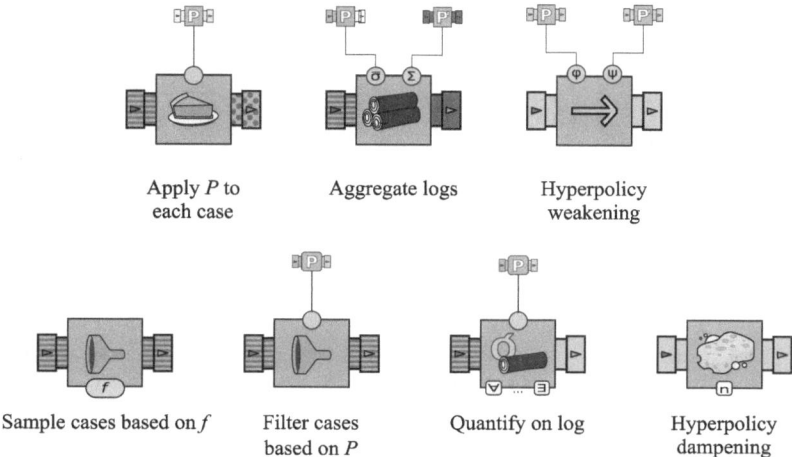

Fig. 2. Graphical representation of the hyperprocessors presented in this paper.

A range of examples of hyperqueries are implemented and available in the online repository; unfortunately they cannot be shown here due to lack of space. In particular, it is worth noting that this toolbox is expressive enough to account for all the hyperqueries presented in this paper, including properties H1–H6 of the running example of Sect. 2. Faithful to the principle of composition which is the heart of BeepBeep, these hyperqueries are carried out by the instantiation and the connection of elementary calculation units in the form of a pipeline.

5.2   Empirical Assessment

To demonstrate the effectiveness of our approach, we ran a number of experiments measuring the time required to process a hyperquery, and the memory consumed during the operation. These experiments are contained in an instance of the LabPal experimental environment [20], which makes it possible to bundle all the necessary code, libraries and input data within a single self-contained executable file. A downloadable lab instance containing the experiments of this paper is publicly available [22].

Synthetic Logs. A first set of experiments is made of generated logs for the school admission process of Sect. 2, on which the hyperqueries H1–H6 are evaluated. To this end, we implemented the school admission process with Activiti, a lightweight open-source workflow and BPMN engine. The engine allows us to model and execute multiple instances of the process. These executions are then logged into a XES log file. We utilized Synthia [29], a data structure generator, to generate choices for tasks and decisions in the process.

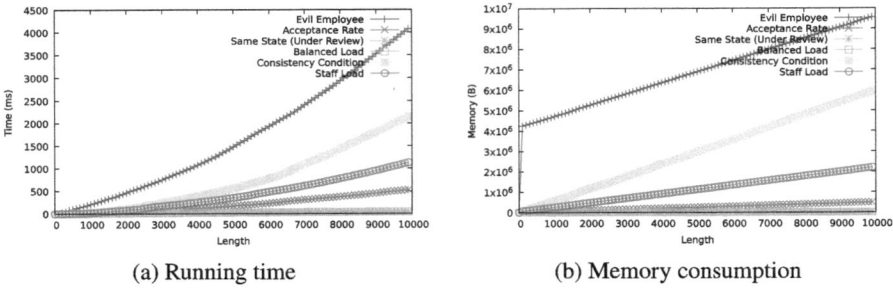

(a) Running time   (b) Memory consumption

Fig. 3. Experimental results for the school admission scenario.

Figure 3 shows the cumulative running time and instantaneous memory usage for each of the hyperqueries H1–H6, on a generated log containing approximately 10,000 updates. One can observe that total running time remains under 5 s, although the processing time per event tends to slightly increase as the log updates accumulate. Memory consumption increases linearly for all hyperqueries, but in all cases remains far lower than the size of the log itself; in other words, each pipeline of hyperprocessors does better than merely storing all events seen so far. The most complex hyperquery, both for time and memory, is *Evil Employee* (H5); this is expected, as this query contains two nested aggregations: a first for the outcomes of each application of an employee, and the other to combine the results of each employee.

Real-World Logs. In order to determine if this good performance extends to real-world logs, we also evaluated hyperqueries on a sample of XES files from various sources:

- *WABO*: an environmental permit application process in the Netherlands [7]
- *CAP*: a loan application process, from the 2018 BPI Challenge [7]
- *Hospital*: medical procedures in a Dutch hospital, from the 2011 BPI Challenge [36]

The largest of these logs contains over 275,000 events. We selected hyperqueries that could be evaluated on each scenario, regardless of the nature and meaning of the events in the log. *Concurrent instances* evaluates the number of process instances that are active at any point in the log, while *Average length* calculates the mean length of all instances. *Mean time interval* counts the average time difference between two successive events across all instances; *Same next* extracts all activities that always have the same successor in every process instance; *Directly follows* associates to each activity the set of its successors occurring in any instance. As one can observe, some of them are not hyperproperties, but genuine hyper*queries*, as they produce a result that is not a simple pass/fail verdict.

Table 1. Throughput and memory consumption for various real-world logs.

Scenario	Events	Cases	Hyperquery	Throughput (Hz)	Max memory (B)
Hospital	151434	1143	Concurrent instances	901392	8059
			Directly follows	277351	3660379
			Mean time interval	1130104	5615
			Average length	369351	522071
			Same next	304084	5401821
CAP	275287	13087	Concurrent instances	920692	12863
			Directly follows	79700	39075895
			Mean time interval	1228959	5615
			Average length	7995	5991691
			Same next	87698	38400801
WABO	39881	937	Concurrent instances	1375206	8055
			Directly follows	419800	1873161
			Mean time interval	1172970	5615
			Average length	162117	278085
			Same next	302128	2669627

Due to lack of space, the results can only be presented in aggregate form in Table 1. One can observe a throughput (expressed in Hz) that often ranges in the hundreds of thousands of events per second. Some queries are more affected by the number of distinct cases in a log, such as *Average length* running considerably slower on the CAP log, which contains more cases. The highest memory usage also occurs on this log, and reaches close to 40 MB for the *Directly follows* hyperquery. This is expected, as this log contains a large number of activities that each have many possible successors, resulting in a large data structure.

6   Conclusion

In this paper, we introduced the notion of *hyperquery*, which generalizes instance-spanning compliance constraints by allowing arbitrary calculations involving multiple traces from a log at the same time. We presented the concept of hyperprocessor, which evaluates a hyperquery incrementally at runtime and updates its output each time a new event is added to a log. We proposed a set of elementary hyperprocessors that can form the basis of complex hyperqueries. An implementation of these hyperprocessors as an extension of the BeepBeep event stream processing library makes it possible to efficiently evaluate hyperqueries at runtime, as confirmed by an experimental evaluation over both synthetic and real-world logs.

The monitoring of real-time evaluation of hyperqueries also leads to a number of interesting research questions that could be explored in future work. The first revolves around *anomaly detection*. Earlier works have shown how trend deviations in a stream can be detected in various ways [32]; however, these assume either a fixed reference trend to which each process instance is compared. The evaluation of hyperqueries could be explored as a complementary means of detecting trend deviations, this time by quantifying the dissimilarity of a set of traces in a log as they unfold in realtime.

The second is the design of *explainable* hypercompliance. In the same way that the streaming model lends itself to the automated establishment of links between specific output events of a flow graph and its inputs [19], one could imagine defining similar relationships for operators evaluating hyperqueries. Combined, these could prove a useful diagnostics tool, for example by pinpointing the specific process instances (and events of these instances) that cause a violation of hypercompliance.

Finally, hyperqueries themselves could be further generalized. The hyperqueries considered in the paper process all traces in a log regardless of their actual moment of occurrence; yet, there exist situations where ordering those logs would matter. For example, one could imagine a condition stating that if a bonus is given to a specific type of customer, then all *future* customers of the same type should get the bonus too. Such a property cannot be expressed over a set of traces, but rather on an ordered sequence of traces (i.e. not 2^{Σ^*}, but rather $(\Sigma^*)^*$).

References

1. van der Aa, H.: Complex event processing methods for process querying. In: Polyvyanyy, A. (ed.) Process Querying Methods, pp. 479–510. Springer, Cham (2022). https://doi.org/10.1007/978-3-030-92875-9_17
2. van der Aalst, W.M.P., de Beer, H.T., van Dongen, B.F.: Process mining and verification of properties: an approach based on temporal logic. In: Meersman, R., Tari, Z. (eds.) OTM 2005. LNCS, vol. 3760, pp. 130–147. Springer, Heidelberg (2005). https://doi.org/10.1007/11575771_11
3. Aamer, H., Montali, M., Van den Bussche, J.: What can database query processing do for instance-spanning constraints? In: Cabanillas, C., Garmann-Johnsen, N.F., Koschmider, A. (eds.) BPM 2022. Lecture Notes in Business Information Processing, vol. 460, pp. 132–144. Springer, Cham (2023). https://doi.org/10.1007/978-3-031-25383-6_11
4. Awad, A., Decker, G., Weske, M.: Efficient compliance checking using BPMN-Q and temporal logic. In: Dumas, M., Reichert, M., Shan, M.-C. (eds.) BPM 2008. LNCS, vol. 5240, pp. 326–341. Springer, Heidelberg (2008). https://doi.org/10.1007/978-3-540-85758-7_24
5. Awad, A., Weidlich, M., Weske, M.: Visually specifying compliance rules and explaining their violations for business processes. J. Vis. Lang. Comput. **22**(1), 30–55 (2011)

6. Betti, Q., Montreuil, B., Khoury, R., Hallé, S.: Smart contracts-enabled simulation for hyperconnected logistics. In: Khan, M.A., Quasim, M.T., Algarni, F., Alharthi, A. (eds.) Decentralised Internet of Things. SBD, vol. 71, pp. 109–149. Springer, Cham (2020). https://doi.org/10.1007/978-3-030-38677-1_6

7. Buijs, J.: Environmental permit application process ('WABO'), CoSeLoG project (version 1) [data set]. Technical report, Eindhoven University of Technology (2014). https://doi.org/10.4121/UUID:26ABA40D-8B2D-435B-B5AF-6D4BFBD7A270

8. Cabanillas, C., Baumgrass, A., Mendling, J., Rogetzer, P., Bellovoda, B.: Towards the enhancement of business process monitoring for complex logistics chains. In: Lohmann, N., Song, M., Wohed, P. (eds.) BPM 2013. LNBIP, vol. 171, pp. 305–317. Springer, Cham (2014). https://doi.org/10.1007/978-3-319-06257-0_24

9. Chesani, F., Mello, P., Montali, M., Riguzzi, F., Sebastianis, M., Storari, S.: Checking compliance of execution traces to business rules. In: Ardagna, D., Mecella, M., Yang, J. (eds.) BPM 2008. LNBIP, vol. 17, pp. 134–145. Springer, Heidelberg (2009). https://doi.org/10.1007/978-3-642-00328-8_13

10. Chesani, F., Mello, P., Montali, M., Torroni, P.: A logic-based, reactive calculus of events. Fundam. Informaticae **105**(1–2), 135–161 (2010)

11. Clarkson, M.R., Finkbeiner, B., Koleini, M., Micinski, K.K., Rabe, M.N., Sánchez, C.: Temporal logics for hyperproperties. In: Abadi, M., Kremer, S. (eds.) POST 2014. LNCS, vol. 8414, pp. 265–284. Springer, Heidelberg (2014). https://doi.org/10.1007/978-3-642-54792-8_15

12. Clarkson, M.R., Schneider, F.B.: Hyperproperties. J. Comput. Secur. **18**(6), 1157–1210 (2010)

13. De Giacomo, G., Felli, P., Montali, M., Perelli, G.: HyperLDL$_f$: a logic for checking properties of finite traces process logs. In: IJCAI, pp. 1859–1865. IJCAI Org (2021)

14. Fdhila, W., Gall, M., Rinderle-Ma, S., Mangler, J., Indiono, C.: Classification and formalization of instance-spanning constraints in process-driven applications. In: La Rosa, M., Loos, P., Pastor, O. (eds.) BPM 2016. LNCS, vol. 9850, pp. 348–364. Springer, Cham (2016). https://doi.org/10.1007/978-3-319-45348-4_20

15. Finkbeiner, B., Hahn, C., Stenger, M., Tentrup, L.: Monitoring hyperproperties. Formal Methods Syst. Des. **54**(3), 336–363 (2019)

16. Giacalone, M., Cusatelli, C., Santarcangelo, V.: Big data compliance for innovative clinical models. Big Data Res. **12**, 35–40 (2018)

17. Governatori, G., Hashmi, M., Lam, H.-P., Villata, S., Palmirani, M.: Semantic business process regulatory compliance checking using LegalRuleML. In: Blomqvist, E., Ciancarini, P., Poggi, F., Vitali, F. (eds.) EKAW 2016. LNCS (LNAI), vol. 10024, pp. 746–761. Springer, Cham (2016). https://doi.org/10.1007/978-3-319-49004-5_48

18. Governatori, G., Milosevic, Z., Sadiq, S.W.: Compliance checking between business processes and business contracts. In: EDOC, pp. 221–232. IEEE Computer Society (2006)

19. Hallé, S.: Explainable queries over event logs. In: EDOC, pp. 171–180. IEEE (2020)

20. Hallé, S., Khoury, R., Awesso, M.: Streamlining the inclusion of computer experiments in a research paper. Computer **51**(11), 78–89 (2018)

21. Hallé, S.: Event Stream Processing With BeepBeep 3: Log Crunching and Analysis Made Easy. Presses de l'Université du Québec (2018)

22. Hallé, S., Soueidi, C.: Benchmark lab for hypercompliance properties on event logs (2023). https://doi.org/10.5281/zenodo.8303080

23. Hashmi, M., Governatori, G., Lam, H., Wynn, M.T.: Are we done with business process compliance: state of the art and challenges ahead. Knowl. Inf. Syst. **57**(1), 79–133 (2018)

24. Heinlein, C.: Workflow and process synchronization with interaction expressions and graphs. In: ICDE, pp. 243–252. IEEE (2001)

25. Indiono, C., Mangler, J., Fdhila, W., Rinderle-Ma, S.: Rule-based runtime monitoring of instance-spanning constraints in process-aware information systems. In: Debruyne, C., et al. (eds.) OTM 2016. LNCS, vol. 10033, pp. 381–399. Springer, Cham (2016). https://doi.org/10.1007/978-3-319-48472-3_22

26. Ly, L.T., Maggi, F.M., Montali, M., Rinderle-Ma, S., van der Aalst, W.M.P.: Compliance monitoring in business processes: functionalities, application, and toolsupport. Inf. Syst. **54**, 209–234 (2015)

27. Maggi, F.M., Montali, M., van der Aalst, W.M.P.: An operational decision support framework for monitoring business constraints. In: de Lara, J., Zisman, A. (eds.) FASE 2012. LNCS, vol. 7212, pp. 146–162. Springer, Heidelberg (2012). https://doi.org/10.1007/978-3-642-28872-2_11

28. Maggi, F.M., Montali, M., Westergaard, M., van der Aalst, W.M.P.: Monitoring business constraints with linear temporal logic: an approach based on colored automata. In: Rinderle-Ma, S., Toumani, F., Wolf, K. (eds.) BPM 2011. LNCS, vol. 6896, pp. 132–147. Springer, Heidelberg (2011). https://doi.org/10.1007/978-3-642-23059-2_13

29. Plourde, M., Hallé, S.: Synthia: a generic and flexible data structure generator. In: ICSE, pp. 207–211. ACM/IEEE (2022)

30. Polyvyanyy, A., Ouyang, C., Barros, A., van der Aalst, W.M.P.: Process querying: enabling business intelligence through query-based process analytics. Decis. Support Syst. **100**, 41–56 (2017)

31. Rinderle-Ma, S., Gall, M., Fdhila, W., Mangler, J., Indiono, C.: Collecting examples for instance-spanning constraints. CoRR abs/1603.01523 (2016)

32. Roudjane, M., Rebaïne, D., Khoury, R., Hallé, S.: Detecting trend deviations with generic stream processing patterns. Inf. Syst. **101**, 101446 (2021)

33. Sani, M.F., van Zelst, S.J., van der Aalst, W.M.P.: Improving the performance of process discovery algorithms by instance selection. Comput. Sci. Inf. Syst. **17**(3), 927–958 (2020)

34. Saralaya, S., Saralaya, V., D'Souza, R.: Compliance management in business processes. In: Patnaik, S., Yang, X.-S., Tavana, M., Popentiu-Vlădicescu, F., Qiao, F. (eds.) Digital Business. LNDECT, vol. 21, pp. 53–91. Springer, Cham (2019). https://doi.org/10.1007/978-3-319-93940-7_3

35. Senderovich, A., Di Francescomarino, C., Ghidini, C., Jorbina, K., Maggi, F.M.: Intra and inter-case features in predictive process monitoring: a tale of two dimensions. In: Carmona, J., Engels, G., Kumar, A. (eds.) BPM 2017. LNCS, vol. 10445, pp. 306–323. Springer, Cham (2017). https://doi.org/10.1007/978-3-319-65000-5_18

36. van Dongen, B.: Real-life event logs – hospital log, version 1.4 [data set]. Technical report, Eindhoven University of Technology (2011). https://doi.org/10.4121/UUID:d9769f3d-0ab0-4fb8-803b-0d1120ffcf54

37. Warner, J., Atluri, V.: Inter-instance authorization constraints for secure workflow management. In: SACMAT, pp. 190–199 (2006)

Paving the Way for the Low-/No-Code Development of Digital Therapeutics: The DTxTAPP Framework

Thure Georg Weimann$^{(\boxtimes)}$

Research Group Digital Health, TU Dresden, Dresden, Germany
thure.weimann@tu-dresden.de

Abstract. Digital Therapeutics (DTx) are considered primarily patient-facing software applications that promise personalized behavioral treatments whenever and where needed. In recent years, the DTx market has seen strong growth due to reforms promoting the digital transformation of national healthcare systems, leading to competitive pressure among vendors and shorter times to market. To accelerate the development of DTx and deal with their complexity, so-called low-/no-code platforms that build on the ideas of model-driven engineering have moved into the focus of research and practice. However, research regarding the generic development of DTx is still in its infancy, and prior contributions mainly focused on specific modeling and development aspects. Following a design science research approach, a synergized framework is derived based on previous conceptualizations to provide a holistic view on DTx intervention modeling. The proposed framework describes how the intervention workflow modeling can be systematically structured, may help to organize existing intervention knowledge, and provides the foundation for a technical instantiation. After demonstrating the framework, implications for future research and practice are discussed.

Keywords: Digital health · Intervention modeling · Low-code development

1 Introduction

Driven by the modernization of reimbursement policies, digital health innovations have successively become an integral part of patient care in several countries. Especially Germany, which has long been behind in implementing a national electronic health record, has recently transformed into a global pioneer in digital therapeutics (DTx) [1]. In general, DTx can be understood as mobile or web applications primarily used by the patient (i.e., patient-facing) that aim to "prevent, manage, or treat a medical disease or disorder" [2]. Given that self-management support evolved as a significant challenge for successfully treating chronic diseases and reducing healthcare costs in the long run, DTx promise to close a gap in care and are, therefore, a fast-growing market [3, 4]. This growth has led to increased competition with multiple products for the same indication by different vendors and shorter times to market access for innovations [5].

© The Author(s), under exclusive license to Springer Nature Switzerland AG 2024
T. P. Sales et al. (Eds.): EDOC 2023 Workshops, LNBIP 498, pp. 265–280, 2024.
https://doi.org/10.1007/978-3-031-54712-6_16

Under the hood, DTx often provide digitalized health behavior change interventions grounded in theoretical and empirical evidence [6]. From an engineering perspective, DTx can be viewed as instances of "virtual coaches," i.e., (semi-) autonomous software agents that target behavioral transformations of the user towards a specific goal by continuously adapting the coaching actions to the patient's context (i.e., being context-aware) [7]. Although the actual DTx design is highly disease and patient-specific, there are common elements underlying these interventions. Identifying and abstracting these mechanisms could facilitate the engineering and understanding of generic low-/no-code development platforms (LNCDPs) that incorporate design methods for building high-quality applications for various disease contexts [8]. One typical building block of LNCDPs are tools to model the application workflow [9]. Transferred to digital health interventions, the workflow refers to the care pathway model, which is digitally supported by the DTx application and represents the actual "intelligence" of the system. Research in the field of DTx recently started to investigate specific aspects, such as modeling languages for formally describing health coaching plans or conversation dialogs [10, 11]. However, a holistic framework that unifies existing concepts is lacking. Such a framework may help to structure existing intervention knowledge and the developer's tasks systematically and may be technically supported by LNCDPs. Beyond accelerating the software development process of DTx, such systematic guidance may help to reduce the risk of faulty software applications that could jeopardize patient safety. Further, such a framework could serve as a starting point for a deeper analysis of LNCDPs in the field of DTx to identify shortcomings or limitations and opportunities for improvement. Therefore, the present paper aims to investigate the following research question: *How can the intervention workflow modeling of DTx be systematically structured and guided?*

The remainder of the paper is structured as follows. The next section describes the research methods in detail before the literature review results summarizing prior work are presented (Sect. 3). In Sect. 4, the proposed framework is derived based on the concepts identified in the literature and demonstrated (Sect. 5). The paper closes by discussing the proposed framework and implications for future research and practice.

2 Research Methods

To develop a framework to guide the intervention workflow modeling of DTx, the design science research (DSR) method, according to Peffers et al. [12], is followed. In the previous section, the overall research problem has been identified and motivated. Based on a systematic literature review, prior work's essential modeling aspects and shortcomings are determined to define objectives for the intended framework (Sect. 3). Therefore, the method by Webster & Watson [13] is followed. Focus of the literature review are existing conceptual contributions that addressed the modeling of the temporal logic in digital health interventions at a meta-level. A qualitative content analysis method (both inductive and deductive) is used to analyze the different contributions, as described by Mayring [14]. Afterward, a novel integrated framework is developed as a theoretical and conceptual artifact, demonstrated, and critically discussed.

3 Literature Review

A systematic literature search was conducted in PubMed, Scopus, and Web of Science to identify prior work that conceptually discussed modeling digital health interventions' temporal logic at a meta-level. Additionally, scientific publications of projects funded by the recently ended European Horizon 2020 grant program that investigated personalized coaching solutions for well-being and care were included as their project scopes fit this paper's research goal [15].

Table 1. Search string used for the literature review.

Concept	String	Fields
Conceptual artifact types	"model*" OR "framework*" OR "conceptual*" OR "method*"	Title
Behavior change	"behavior change*" OR "behaviour change*" OR "behavior intervention*" OR "behaviour intervention*" OR "behavioral intervention*" OR "behavioural intervention*" OR "coach*"	Title, Abstract
Technology and Digital health	"software" OR "digital" OR "ehealth" OR "e-health" OR "electronic health" OR "mhealth" OR "m-health" OR "mobile health" OR "technolog*"	Title, Abstract

The used search string combined DSR-related artifact types of interest with a focus on behavior change interventions in digital health (see Table 1). The literature search was conducted in April 2023 (updated in June) and included peer-reviewed journal articles and conference papers written in English from 2010 onwards. The literature search yielded 2084 results (PubMed: 505, Scopus: 864, and Web of Science: 715) and 1165 after duplicate removal. In the first step, the papers were screened for relevance based on title and abstract ($n = 928$ papers excluded). Afterward, a full-text screening of the remaining papers was conducted. Articles that did not propose generic development approaches related to patient-facing digital health applications' temporal logical flow (i.e., not guiding the workflow perspective specification) were excluded. Furthermore, papers that did not propose adaptive concepts for tailoring the intervention to the context of the patient (enabling personalized treatments) were excluded. Finally, $n = 7$ papers identified from the literature search were included in the final analysis. By screening the project websites of Horizon 2020 projects in the field of personalized coaching in medical care, $n = 3$ additional papers were identified and included. Therefore, the final analysis set comprised $n = 10$ papers.

To summarize prior work, identify essential concepts, and compare the different approaches, a concept matrix was created based on the deductive categories derived from previous research and inductively derived new categories or sub-categories based on the analyzed literature. As mentioned at the beginning of this manuscript, DTx can be considered an instance of the technological concept of virtual coaches (VCs) applied to the healthcare domain [16, 17]. A previous paper on VCs proposed a research framework that summarizes the abstract "high-level" building blocks [7]. Based on this framework, an initial set of categories was identified and refined with inductive content analysis. Following the qualitative content analysis method, the recording unit referred to the entire paper, the context unit to a paragraph, and the coding unit to a word. Six of the analyzed papers were published in 2020 or later, indicating the increasing relevance of generically describing the development of digital behavior change interventions. The earliest contribution to this field included in the analysis was the so-called Behavioral Intervention Technology Model (BIT) by Mohr et al. (2014) [18], followed by the Just-in-time adaptive intervention (JITAI) framework by Nahum-Shani et al. (2015) [19]. Measured by the citation count, the JITAI framework [19, 20] is the most dominating approach in the literature. It should be noted that several other contributions included in the analysis also refer to the seminal work on JITAIs by Nahum-Shani et al. [21–23]. The following paragraphs describe the concept matrix's categories (see Table 2). Note that "•" in the concept matrix means that the corresponding approach explicitly addressed the concept. In contrast, "○" means that the concept was recognized but is essentially not deeply embedded within the approach. Instead, it was rather viewed as a potential extension or opportunity for implementation. It is important to mention that some aspects have been formulated vaguely and leave room for interpretation.

Table 2. Concept matrix.

Ref.	Trigger	Sequential	Time Scales	Interv.-/Com.-Options	CA Cues	Media	Channel	Other	Dynamic Charact.	Rule-based	Machine Learning	Exceptions/Constr.	Aggregation	Get Current	Get History	Set Value	Outcomes	Tailoring Variables	Template/Instance	External flows/Serv.
[19, 20]	•		•	•		•	•	•	○	•	○	•	•	•	•		•	•	•	
[18]	•	•	•	•		•	•	•	○	•	○		•	•	•		•	•	•	○
[10]	•	•		•	•	•	•		•				•	•	•	•	•	•		
[11]	•	•	•	•	○				○	•	○	•	•	•	•			•	•	○
[21]	•	•		•		•	•	•	•		•							•	•	○
[22]	•	•		•				•	•					•	•		•	•		
[23]	•	•	•	•				•	•	○	○		○	○	○	○	•	•		
[24]	•			•		•	•	•	•	•	•	•	•	•	•	•	•	•	•	
[25]	•	•	•	•			•	•	•	•	•	•	•	•	•	•	•	•	•	

1) Temporal Flow: The first three categories of the concept matrix refer to the general time-based intervention flow (i.e., when a specific action should occur).

A) Triggers: A central conceptual building block of the JITAI framework are decision points (first sub-category) that can be considered events that trigger a certain intervention logic (decision rule). Generally, the conceptual idea of decision points can be found in all analyzed papers. As stated by Nahum-Shani et al., these decision points may occur in a defined interval (e.g., every 2 h starting from 9 a.m. to 6 p.m.), at a particular time of a day (midnight), a specific time after an intervention (e.g., X minutes after prompt) or in a random manner [20]. In addition, Mohr et al. [18] also consider the triggering of intervention logic based on task-completion events (e.g., finishing an educational module and receiving a reward) [18]. Furthermore, they also explicitly incorporate user-defined workflows (interventions triggered by the users themselves on demand) as part of their model. The approach described by Gand et al. [11] leverages the Business Process Model and Notation for formally describing coaching-related care pathways (BPMN4VC). They link "Timer Events" (particular time and date, activity duration, cyclic events defined with a min- and max frequency) to process activities.

B) Sequential Flow: The second sub-category related to the time-based intervention flow refers to explicitly modeling the sequence of actions following a decision point (i.e., sequential flow). In contrast to the approach by Gand et al., which models the intervention actions as a sequential flow consisting of multiple steps aligned in a temporal order (e.g., greeting, reminder, motivational assessment, reminder, etc.), the JITAI framework suggests a single-step relationship after a decision point (i.e., trigger – action). However, modeling sequential flows based on the JITAI framework is still not impossible. One approach for achieving this may be to concatenate decision rules and define decision points that trigger the following rule after the previous rule has been executed. Nonetheless, this approach is arguably not straightforward and significantly increases the number of decision points that need to be explicitly defined by the modeler. Similarly to the BPMN-based approach [11], Beinema et al. [10] proposed a new modeling language ("WOOL") for defining sequential conversational flows in the context of VCs. Likewise, several other papers suggested a sequential intervention flow modeling [18, 21–23, 25].

C) Time-scales: Overall, the different intervention elements may impact health outcomes at different time scales and may systematically vary during the intervention (e.g., stepped care). For example, the actual weight loss of an obese patient can be considered a distal outcome, and clinically significant changes occur over weeks and months. In contrast, the daily steps can be impacted on a tighter time scale (proximal outcome). Furthermore, when the VC instructs a physical activity workout, a new exercise may be prompted every minute, and the workout schedule is dynamically controlled based on continuously monitored parameters (e.g., heart rate). Consequently, the different intervention sub-models are linked to each other along the time-axis up to an aggregated and thus highly complex model including all features. The general idea of disassembling the disease-related mechanisms into sub-models linked to each other can be found in the work by Nahum-Shani et al. [19]. However, rather than representing the actual coaching intervention flows along these different time scales (hour, day, week, month, and year) as aggregating models, they use this "disassembling approach" to systemize and understand the dynamic relationship of different psychological and behavioral outcomes (proximal and distal). Mohr et al. also speak of "blocks of time" with corresponding workflows [18]. Likewise, Zhang et al. [23] recognized the need for different temporal scales based on a thorough analysis of several psychological theories. They proposed two levels: an "action level" and a more overarching "reflection level". Although the work by Gand et al. [11] does not explicitly suggest representing the coaching intervention as temporal aggregating BPMN models (e.g., the weekly pathway is broken down into a daily pathway), they consider the inclusion of sub-pathways and target variables (outcomes) along different time dimensions as an essential requirement (e.g., daily and weekly goals). The idea of time-scaling can also be found in the work by Beristain Iraola et al. [25].

2) Intervention and Communication Option (ICO) Repository: The actual repository of possible intervention options represents, along with outcome measures (intervention goals) and tailoring variables, the core of every DTx application. Therefore, it seems not surprising that all of the analyzed papers refer to it in some way. Generally speaking, the intervention options can be regarded as the technological instantiation of traditional behavior change techniques (e.g., feedback, monitoring, goal-setting, suggestions, education, motivation, and social support) [18, 26]. Driven by fast technological progress in the field of artificial intelligence (AI) in recent years, so-called conversational agents (CAs) are frequently used for the interface of VCs, including DTx [7, 17]. CAs aim to mimic interpersonal communication between the user and the system via text (chatbot), speech (voice-based), or combine verbal- and non-verbal behavior (embodied conversational agents or avatars) [27]. When using CAs, more generic messages, such as greeting the user or responses to frequently asked questions, become apparent but often do not directly impact the intervention outcomes. Therefore, the overarching term "communication options" will be used in the remainder of this paper.

3) Representation Configuration: A) CA-related Cues: Directly coupled with the use of CAs is the intervention and communication representation configuration in terms of social cues (e.g., giving the agent a name, providing an avatar with a specific design, animated gestures,...). However, only two analyzed papers describe the use of CAs and the deliberate configuration of CA-related cues [10, 21]. Overall, integrating social cues is much researched in information systems, and a growing knowledge base can be consulted for designing CAs within DTx [28]. **B) Media, C) Delivery Channel, and D) Other:** Several papers describe the representation configuration in terms of media (e.g., text message, audio, video, tactile, chart, etc.), the delivery channel (e.g., app notification, smartwatch, link to other resources,...) or the definition of other content representation characteristics such as complexity, intensity, dosage or aesthetic aspects [18, 20]. This implies that the ICOs are "tagged" with attributes that describe them appropriately.

4) Dynamic Intervention and Communication Option Characteristics: However, the ICOs may also be described in terms of attributes that change their values during the course of the intervention. For example, Zhang et al. [23] consider activation, habit, goal, and attribute values as dynamic characteristics of intervention options. This corresponds to the idea that the DTx application may explore algorithmically which intervention and communication options should be preferred for the user to personalize and optimize the interaction by assigning some kind of "utility values".

5) Decision-Making: Rule-based and **Machine-learning** approaches are discussed in the literature for selecting a specific ICO (i.e., decision-making). In general, selecting an ICO may occur on a categorical level (i.e., selecting the most suitable intervention option category and then randomly drawing a message) or on an instance level (directly selecting a particular message). While rule-based approaches are the most straightforward context adaptation mechanism concerning interpretability and clinical safety [29], machine-learning approaches could address their disadvantages of formally explicating the adaptation knowledge first and their missing possibility to automatically re-adapt the intervention logic to the user during the trajectory [20]. Although several authors ($n = 6$) mention machine learning approaches, most do not describe them as an integral part of their framework for modeling the intervention flow.

6) Exceptions and Constraints: Although one may define exceptions to explicitly not send an ICO to the user ("provide nothing") as part of decision rules (e.g., [20]), this concept may also be regarded separately, as was done by Gand et al. [11]. Consequently, exceptions and constraints can be considered a particular class of rules that forbid an intervention if the specified conditions are met and may propose an alternative action.

7) Value Functions: Closely related to determining a suitable ICO are value functions that serve as input for the decision-making algorithm or algorithmically adapt particular variables. They can be part of the algorithmic data pre-processing before inserting the data into a decision model, be part of any analytical decision model, or are executed afterward. In particular, a) aggregation functions (e.g., calculating a sum), b) functions for getting the most recent data and c) historical data, and d) functions to set a new value for a specific variable have been identified in the literature.

8) Outcomes: As mentioned, outcomes are one core component of every DTx application and represent the direction the system needs to act with suitable actions. In general, different types of outcomes are distinguished in the literature. For example, the framework by Nahum-Shani et al. [19] differentiates between proximal outcomes that are considered short-term goals (e.g., reducing daily stress level) and distal outcomes to be achieved in a larger time window (e.g., weight reduction, increased quality of life). Another perspective can be found by Mohr et al. [18]. They distinguish between clinical outcomes and usage-related outcomes. The latter addresses the idea that a digital behavior change intervention can only have an impact when the patient uses the application regularly (technology adherence). To tailor the intervention based on the outcomes, the specified constructs are operationalized and then measured passively (via sensors) or actively (via questionnaires) [4].

9) Tailoring Variables: Typically, the derivation of tailoring variables used by the decision models for selecting a suitable action goes hand in hand with the specification of outcome measures [20]. For example, the application may send the user a feedback notification (praise) when the daily step goal has reached a specific value. Nonetheless, there are often further tailoring variables that are not directly derived from the outcomes [18]. This can be (among many other examples) a particular time or weekday (e.g., propose a specific behavioral activity only on Monday), the weather forecast (e.g., suggest a running workout on a sunny day), or the user's preferences (e.g., user likes cycling more than running). Likewise, demographic baseline data can also be used to tailor the intervention (e.g., gender, age, etc.).

10) Templating: Notably, the work by Gand et al. [11] introduced the idea of "templating". They differentiate between templates of the intervention flow (pathway templates) and instantiations for individual patients (pathway instances). According to the understanding by Gand et al., pathway templates refer to the general intervention schedule and have an overarching character. In contrast, pathway instances develop adaptations to fit the individual patient's needs that may occur during model execution.

11) External Flows & Services: The framework described in [7] considers *external knowledge bases and services* as viable sources to set up and control the system's behavior. For instance, a DTx app may be used in a blended-care program combining on-site behavioral therapy (e.g., group therapy) with automated coaching elements for the remaining part of the patient's daily life. Therefore, the appointment timeline of the hospital information system may be integrated and synced with the DTx app to optimize the entire intervention workflow. However, the literature analysis revealed that only some works mentioned this concept by deriving events from (external) sources such as electronic medical records [18, 21], using interoperable data exchange standards [11].

4   Proposed Framework

As shown in Table 2, several aspects, such as integrating external services, templating, temporal scaling, using CAs, machine learning-based approaches, and value functions, are significantly underrepresented or have been not dedicatedly addressed. In particular, to the best of the author's knowledge, the interplay of the aspects above has yet to be studied on a conceptual level, underscoring the need for a novel holistic framework that synergizes and extends prior work. Based on the prior contributions, a novel framework was developed that integrates existing concepts. The derived concepts were transferred into central structuring levels for modeling the intervention workflow and structural elements within these levels. Overall, three dimensions (structuring levels) are distinguished in the proposed framework: workflow-related specifications of DTx, time-aggregation (TA), and patient pathways (PP) (together "DTxTAPP") (see Fig. 1). In the following subsections, the different dimensions and the included structural elements are explained in detail.

4.1   Dimension 1: Workflow-Related Specifications of DTx

The first dimension comprises general workflow-related aspects that underly DTx and is divided into seven layers which are closely coupled to each other:

- The specified *intervention outcomes and tailoring variables*,
- *decision rules* for selecting an intervention and communication option (ICO), along with *constraints* and *exceptions* to restrict ICOs,
- *advanced analytical models and algorithms* for enabling an automatic adaptation and complex processing tasks that go beyond decision rules (if needed),
- the *intervention and communication flow (IC flow)*,
- the configuration of *representation characteristics*,
- the *intervention and communication option repository (ICO repository)*, and
- *external flows and services.*

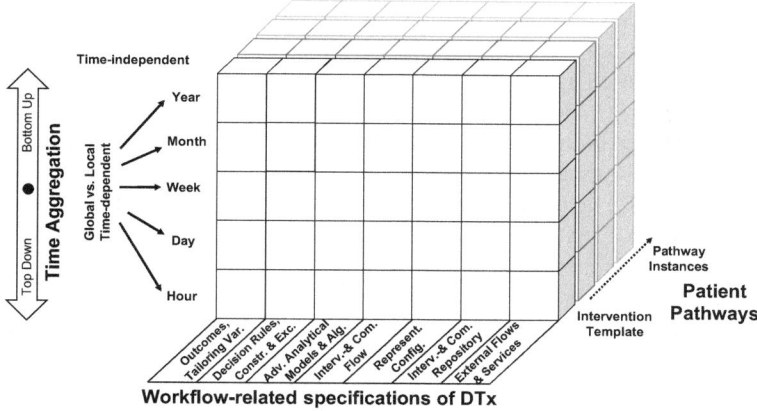

Fig. 1. The DTxTAPP-Framework.

In particular, the IC flow represents the most central aspect in this dimension and is the starting point for interaction with other levels mentioned above. About formally describing the IC flow, the works by Gand et al. [11] (BPMN4VC), Beinema et al. [10] (WOOL), and Mohr et al. [18] (finite-state machine notation) proposed new or adapted modeling notations. One drawback of the BPMN4VC approach by Gand et al. [11] is that the decision logic associated with certain activities (e.g., determining which type of feedback message [positive, negative, neutral] should be sent) is not explicitly represented in the model. One workaround could be to model these decisions directly with BPMN as part of the process flow. However, when decisions become complex, this may result in "spaghetti models" and is considered a misuse of BPMN in the literature [30]. An alternative and already used practice in other domains could be directly associating decision models with activities in the intervention process model. This aligns with the idea of using BPMN and DMN (decision model and notation) together [31]. In contrast to BPMN4VC, the WOOL approach directly models the rules and message texts of the CA within the model nodes, representing the different dialogue steps. Although this approach may improve model readability, the intervention options are scripted within the model nodes. Although scripting the messages of the VC directly within the model nodes is straightforward, the flexibility of re-arranging or extending dialogue fragments (and their internal rules) may be reduced. The work by Mohr et al. [18] proposed an approach based on finite-state machines, which models the different intervention elements as states and intervention steps as transitions. For transiting to the next intervention step (i.e., executing an intervention after a trigger or fulfilled condition), they propose a formal transition function ("intervention planner"). This transition function takes the intervention aims, the workflow, and data into account and then outputs an intervention element with certain characteristics (e.g., a specific coaching message). Conceptually, this idea can be regarded as similar to invoking the decision model (DMN) from the BPMN process when entering an activity node after a trigger occurred. Based on these considerations, the present manuscript proposes an approach corresponding to the idea of using BPMN and DMN in tandem, as this may reduce the complexity when model adjustments are needed (change decision logic independently of the overall intervention flow). Similar to the approach described by op den Akker et al. [24], a sequence of steps is executed to decide on an ICO. The decision model has access to the *current* (most recent) and *historical values* of tailoring variables via dedicated functions (*GetCurrent, GetHistorical*). These functions may have the variable name of interest as an argument and, in the case of historical time-series data, a specific time range of interest (e.g., last week, last month). The data can be pre-processed with a particular function (e.g., aggregation with *CalcSum, CalcMean*, etc.) before applying rules or inserting it into any other analytical function (e.g., machine learning model). The decision rule output could be either a specific intervention and communication option category *(ICC, e.g., "EncouragingPhysicalActivityMessage")*, a specific instance *(ICI, e.g., "Let's try something new today! A short walk can do wonders for your energy and mood.")* but may also be a set of attributes with corresponding values (e.g., activity = patient.activityPreference,...) that are used to look up an ICO from the repository. Additionally, the decision output could trigger a *SetValue* function to update a corresponding variable (e.g., update the daily step goal for the patient).

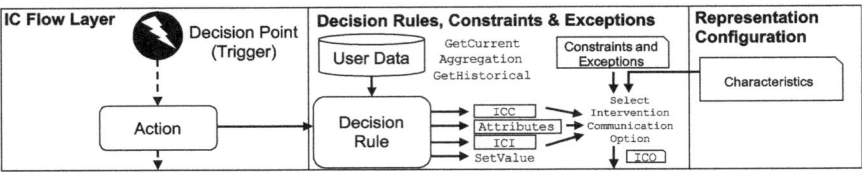

Fig. 2. Interplay of IC Flow, Decision Layer, and Representation Configuration.

For appropriately making a decision, current and/or historical data is used and aggregated (if needed). Based on the decision rule output, the *SelectInterventionCommunicationOption* function is invoked (similar to the "intervention planner" by Mohr et al. [18]) that also takes the representation characteristics and the constraints and exceptions into account to deliver an ICO to the user (or provide nothing if indicated). Within the *IC flow* layer, the decision points (triggers) are specified and serve as a starting point for a sequence of activities. In doing so, having multiple decision points with associated IC flows in this layer is also conceivable. Regarding the specified levels of *intervention outcome and tailoring variables*, it should be noted that these may be defined by the intervention modeler (e.g., health professional), the patients themselves (e.g., set individual daily step goals), the system automatically, or in a hybrid manner. The process of generically describing how the patients could define these values (e.g., via questionnaires) is beyond the scope of this work. However, in addition to manually defining or adapting the variable values, the intervention modeler may also define rules or functions that automatically update them via the *SetValue* function. Figure 2 depicts the interplay of the different layers for making a decision.

Furthermore, the time-based availability of ICOs may be controlled in a dedicated layer. For example, certain ICOs (e.g., educational content) could be activated based on specific events (e.g., successful completion of the previous module). Likewise, detailed patient questionnaires may pop up event-based depending on the disease scenario (e.g., every month) and only be available until successful completion. Beyond the IC flow layer, this layer is closely coupled with the representation configuration layer to determine where the ICOs should be presented (e.g., in a specific module of the DTx app).

When considering integrating CAs for the interface of DTx, the overall dialogue flow can be modeled in the IC flow layer. In this case, there is a continuous interplay between system outputs and user inputs, where the system outputs immediately depend on the previous user inputs. It can be helpful to deliberately use decision nodes (e.g., BPMN gateway) directly in the IC flow layer when the historical dialogue steps are relevant for future dialogue actions. Another option might be to define dialogue fragments separately from the IC flow as an ICO and then instantiate the fragments as one aggregated IC flow action (see Fig. 2). While the framework by Dhinagaran et al. [21] focuses on the development of rule-based CAs, the framework proposed in this paper could also describe how machine learning-based CAs (using machine learning-based natural language processing techniques) can be used within DTx. Particularly, user-driven dialogues may be started by defined triggers (e.g., the user asks a question or prompts the system to do something). The input may then be directly forwarded to the layer comprising *advanced analytical models and algorithms*, which may be associated with the *external flows and services* layer (external application programming interface, API). Using corresponding APIs, the external service may then return the analyzed user intent from the inserted text (via natural language understanding). The returned intent (e.g., a specific frequently asked question) may then be further processed rule-based (e.g., selecting the most suitable ICO based on the intent).

As indicated in the previous paragraph, a separate conceptual layer is dedicated to external flows and services that interfere with the other layers (notably the IC flow layer). One use case may be integrating the DTx app into conventional on-site care programs. For example, after a clinical visit on a particular day, a sequence of events conducted by the DTx app may be executed (e.g., repeat specific educational content from on-site group therapy with a quiz). Likewise, educational content may be unlocked incrementally as the patient progresses through the care program. Another example could be to match medication plans (dosing schedules) managed in the hospital information system with the DTx application. Based on the medication plan, reminders may be triggered within the IC flow layer to ensure medication adherence. To enable a seamless matching between an on-site program and the DTx app (blended care), this assumes interoperability between the systems involved. This may be achieved by rigorously building on established healthcare data exchange standards such as the Health Level 7 Fast Healthcare Interoperability Resources (FHIR) standard. From the analyzed papers, only the work by Gand et al. [11] explicitly refers to interoperability (FHIR) and thus provides at least the foundation for blended and integrated care scenarios.

Another aspect of the presented framework is the differentiation between decision rules for selecting an intervention and *constraints* and *exceptions* for deliberately reducing the selection space. These constraints set limits on ICOs and are either valid for the corresponding time window (locally, i.e., year, month, week, day, hour, or globally) or time-independent. Although these constraints can be, in principle, merged into the selection rules, a logical separation may allow for more flexibility and clarity when managed in a dedicated place. Consequently, the approach presented in this work endorses decoupling the constraints from the actual decision models whenever possible. For example, one may define a constraint on the daily level for the ICC "GoodMorningMessages" to ensure that only one good morning message is delivered to the user. This may be particularly relevant when multiple delivery channels are used for the intervention (e.g., chatbot and app notification). On a technical level, this implies keeping a record of the model execution state and performing aggregation operations on this record (e.g., calculating count for a specific ICC). This approach is related to the idea of integrating "exceptions" into pathway models by [11] or "provide nothing options" [20]. Within the context of the proposed framework, exceptions go beyond mere thresholds that forbid an ICO ("simple constraints", e.g., frequency of good morning messages should be less than or equal to 1) by proposing in a rule-based manner an alternative action. Note that this exception handling could be a "provide nothing" option.

4.2 Dimension 2: Time Aggregation

All of the mechanisms described in the first dimension of the DTxTAPP framework can be specified concerning a specific time window. This framework dimension is particularly inspired by Nahum-Shani et al. [19], who proposed to define disease-related factors and outcomes depending on their time-scaling (year, month, week, day, and hour). From the perspective of the intervention modeler, one may broadly distinguish between a "top-down" (starting with the highest time resolution), a "bottom-up" approach (starting with the most fine-grained resolution), or "in-between" for modeling the intervention. Within the presented framework, levels of specific outcomes and tailoring variables can be specified with a validity character for a particular time dimension. This time-scaling approach enables the modeling of specific days and assembling them into "higher level" weekly or monthly intervention building blocks. After this time window (e.g., after the first month), a re-adaptation may be necessary to map the patient to the IC flow to be executed in the next block. For example, the intervention outcomes (e.g., stress reduction in the last month) are evaluated, and the coaching strategy is changed or pursued depending on the patient's progress. A novel concept of the proposed framework, not found in the analyzed literature, is the differentiation between a *global and local model scope* about the time dimension. When mechanisms of the first framework dimension are specified globally, the IC flow and the associated layers are active across the *entire* course of the intervention. For instance, if specific decision points do not change over the course of the intervention, it would make sense to specify the IC flow with a global scope. In contrast, an example for a local model scope (i.e., active only for a specific time window) may be an "onboarding process" when the user opens the DTx app for the first time (trigger). The app may show particular questionnaires (e.g., demographic data, user preferences) for onboarding users. Consequently, this IC flow should be modeled with a local scope, as the onboarding process typically occurs once during the course of the intervention. Furthermore, a time-independent specification may also be differentiated in which there is no fixed modeling time window.

4.3 Dimension 3: Patient Pathway Templates and Instances

The third dimension of the proposed framework incorporates the idea of building general intervention templates that are instantiated for a particular patient [11]. This instantiated workflow of a specific patient (i.e., the patient pathway) includes dynamic characteristics (e.g., preference values for certain activities), specific constraints defined for this patient (e.g., sending no messages between 9 a.m. to 5 p.m. because the patient is at work and not receptive) along with adaptions from an original template (adaptations may be expert-, user- or system-defined). By building intervention workflow templates for different disease scenarios (e.g., obesity, diabetes, hypertension, depression) based on the framework, one could also address multimorbidity scenarios within one DTx app by merging them ("meta app" [17]). Since multimorbidity poses a significant and growing challenge [32], approaches that address these needs become relevant.

5   Demonstration

The proposed framework is intended to be applied across various health contexts. This case study example will illustrate how the framework could be used to model the intervention workflow of a virtual coaching application for obesity patients described in prior work [33]. The software application delivers a behavior change intervention focusing mainly on physical activity promotion and a healthy diet. Figure 3 exemplary shows a conceptual instantiation of the DTxTAPP framework for the first day of the fifth intervention week. Within the IC flow, four decision points are depicted. When the user opens the app, the virtual coach greets the user (depending on the time of day). Therefore, multiple rules are defined in the dedicated layer to select the most suitable greeting message category (ICC) based on the tailoring variable "TimeOfDay". The greeting message is randomly drawn from a corresponding message bank defined in the ICO repository. After a greeting message has been sent, multiple ICIs are sent to the user (day 29 specific message, a specific message to ask for the completion of a quality of life questionnaire along with an argument and link). Furthermore, the greeting message is linked with a waving gesture to be performed by the animated avatar representing the coach. On the right side of Fig. 3, greeting message constraints are defined, enforcing that a good morning message is only sent once per day. Further exceptions are defined if the patient significantly exceeds the recommended step goal (to avoid overexertion) and not exceed the daily calorie goal. Particularly noteworthy is the dialogue with ID 2, whose decision point is defined in an interval manner. If the decision point is triggered (every 2 h from 4 p.m. to 10 p.m.), a decision rule is executed, linked to an advanced analytical model for selecting a physical activity message. In this case, the analytical model is a bandit algorithm (a reinforcement learning algorithm) [29] that dynamically updates preference values based on the effect of a previously suggested ICO to successively learn which type of ICO should be preferred to improve the physical activity outcomes. It should be emphasized that this is only one example of how machine learning could be used within the DTxTAPP framework. Virtually any aspect within the different layers could be dynamically controlled using machine learning or other analytical functions (e.g., determining a suitable trigger timing or representation characteristics). In the external flows and service layer, a trigger is defined, associated with a reminder for the on-site group therapy (e.g., one week before the appointment). It should be noted that the depicted model refers to a patient pathway *template* of an obesity treatment program. However, assigning the patient's preference values to the ICOs pertains to the patient pathway *instance* perspective. Although Fig. 3 represents the daily level, decisions may also be made on the weekly or monthly level. For example, after the first month of the intervention program, it is evaluated if the patient's relative weight loss exceeds a defined threshold. Depending on this decision, the intervention workflow model "Week 5a" or "Week 5b" are executed, which differ in their strategies. Likewise, rather "unpredictable" events, such as decreasing system usage may be evaluated on the weekly level in order to intervene accordingly.

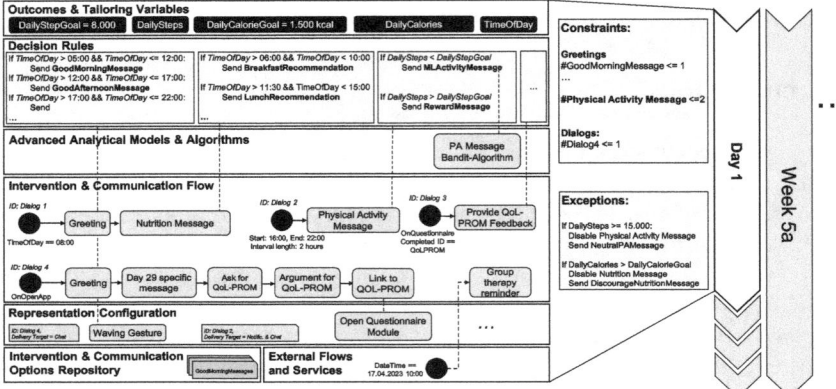

Fig. 3. Exemplary instantiation of the DTxTAPP framework (daily level).

6 Discussion and Conclusion

The present paper unified and extended existing approaches in a cohesive framework. Therefore, this work may be a further step toward the generic modeling of DTx. However, while the focus of this work was proposing a cohesive framework based on existing conceptual contributions (i.e., "theory-driven"), a dedicated analysis of the first existing LNCDPs in the field (e.g., [34]) should be addressed in future work. The proposed framework could then be used to guide a systematic analysis. Additionally, the framework needs to be evaluated beyond the described case study to justify its applicability in practice. The framework may support the modeler on both a conceptual and a technological level. On one hand, it could serve as a foundation to provide tool support in LNCDPs for the concepts unified in the framework. On the other hand, the framework may also help to organize the existing knowledge around the intervention workflow. The present work is part of broader research efforts on frameworks for guiding digital health behavior change interventions, such as recently reviewed by Pelly et al. [35], and particularly addresses the technical perspective regarding timing and adaptivity. Future research may propose a formal domain-specific modeling language addressing the framework's dimensions. Likewise, the proposed framework may be a part of an overarching development method to be derived in future work. Overall, this work contributes to a growing body of literature on DTx and may facilitate the development of effective interventions that could help patients in their daily lives.

References

1. Wang, C., Lee, C., Shin, H.: Digital therapeutics from bench to bedside. Npj Digit. Med. **6**, 38 (2023)
2. DTx Alliance: Digital Therapeutics Alliance. https://dtxalliance.org/. Accessed 27 Dec 2022
3. Holman, H., Lorig, K.: Patient self-management: a key to effectiveness and efficiency in care of chronic disease. Public Health Rep. **119**, 239–243 (2004)
4. Sim, I.: Mobile devices and health. N. Engl. J. Med. **381**, 956–968 (2019)
5. Prodan, A., et al.: Success factors for scaling up the adoption of digital therapeutics towards the realization of P5 medicine. Front. Med. **9**, 854665 (2022)
6. Nahum-Shani, I., Wetter, D.W., Murphy, S.A.: Adapting just-in-time interventions to vulnerability and receptivity: conceptual and methodological considerations. In: Digital Therapeutics for Mental Health and Addiction, pp. 77–87. Elsevier (2023)
7. Weimann, T.G., Schlieter, H., Brendel, A.B.: Virtual coaches: background, theories, and future research directions. Bus. Inf. Syst. Eng. **64**, 515–528 (2022). https://doi.org/10.1007/s12599-022-00757-9
8. Di Ruscio, D., Kolovos, D., de Lara, J., Pierantonio, A., Tisi, M., Wimmer, M.: Low-code development and model-driven engineering: two sides of the same coin? Softw. Syst. Model. **21**, 437–446 (2022). https://doi.org/10.1007/s10270-021-00970-2
9. Bock, A.C., Frank, U.: Low-code platform. Bus. Inf. Syst. Eng. **63**, 733–740 (2021). https://doi.org/10.1007/s12599-021-00726-8
10. Beinema, T., op den Akker, H., Hofs, D., van Schooten, B.: The WOOL dialogue platform: enabling interdisciplinary user-friendly development of dialogue for conversational agents. Open Res. Eur. **2**, 7 (2022)
11. Gand, K., Stark, J., Schlieter, H., Gißke, C., Burwitz, M.: Using clinical pathways to virtual coach patients for home rehabilitation. In: ICIS 2021 Proceedings (2021)
12. Peffers, K., Tuunanen, T., Rothenberger, M.A., Chatterjee, S.: A design science research methodology for information systems research. J. Manag. Inf. Syst. **24**, 45–77 (2007)
13. Webster, J., Watson, R.T.: Analyzing the past to prepare for the future: writing a literature review. MIS Q. **26**, xiii–xxiii (2002)
14. Mayring, P.: Qualitative Content Analysis. Forum Qual. Sozialforschung Forum Qual. Soc. Res. vol. 1, no. 2: Qualitative Methods in Various Disciplines I: Psychology (2000)
15. European Commission: Personalised coaching for well-being and care of people as they age (Horizon 2020). https://ec.europa.eu/info/funding-tenders/opportunities/portal/screen/opportunities/topic-details/sc1-pm-15-2017. Accessed 02 Mar 2022
16. Topol, E.J.: High-performance medicine: the convergence of human and artificial intelligence. Nat. Med. **25**, 44–56 (2019)
17. Fürstenau, D., Gersch, M., Schreiter, S.: Digital Therapeutics (DTx). Bus. Inf. Syst. Eng. **65**, 349–360 (2023). https://doi.org/10.1007/s12599-023-00804-z
18. Mohr, D.C., Schueller, S.M., Montague, E., Burns, M.N., Rashidi, P.: The behavioral intervention technology model: an integrated conceptual and technological framework for eHealth and mHealth interventions. J. Med. Internet Res. **16**, e146 (2014)
19. Nahum-Shani, I., Hekler, E.B., Spruijt-Metz, D.: Building health behavior models to guide the development of just-in-time adaptive interventions: a pragmatic framework. Health Psychol. **34**, 1209–1219 (2015)

20. Nahum-Shani, I., et al.: Just-in-time adaptive interventions (JITAIs) in mobile health: key components and design principles for ongoing health behavior support. Ann. Behav. Med. **52**, 446–462 (2018)
21. Dhinagaran, D.A., et al.: Designing, developing, evaluating, and implementing a smartphone-delivered, rule-based conversational agent (DISCOVER): development of a conceptual framework. JMIR MHealth UHealth **10**, e38740 (2022)
22. Baumel, A., Fleming, T., Schueller, S.M.: Digital micro interventions for behavioral and mental health gains: core components and conceptualization of digital micro intervention care. J. Med. Internet Res. **22**, e20631 (2020)
23. Zhang, C., Lakens, D., IJsselsteijn, W.A.: Theory integration for lifestyle behavior change in the digital age: an adaptive decision-making framework. J. Med. Internet Res. **23**, e17127 (2021)
24. op den Akker, H., Cabrita, M., op den Akker, R., Jones, V.M., Hermens, H.J.: Tailored motivational message generation: a model and practical framework for real-time physical activity coaching. J. Biomed. Inform. **55**, 104–115 (2015)
25. Beristain Iraola, A., et al.: User centered virtual coaching for older adults at home using SMART goal plans and I-change model. Int. J. Environ. Res. Public Health **18**, 6868 (2021)
26. Taj, F., Klein, M.C.A., van Halteren, A.: Digital health behavior change technology: bibliometric and scoping review of two decades of research. JMIR MHealth UHealth. **7**, e13311 (2019)
27. Seeger, A.-M., Pfeiffer, J., Heinzl, A.: Texting with human-like conversational agents: designing for anthropomorphism. J. Assoc. Inf. Syst. JAIS **22**(4), 8 (2020)
28. Feine, J., Gnewuch, U., Morana, S., Maedche, A.: A taxonomy of social cues for conversational agents. Int. J. Hum.-Comput. Stud. **132**, 138–161 (2019)
29. Philipp, P., Merkle, N., Gand, K., Gißke, C.: Continuous support for rehabilitation using machine learning. it-Inf. Technol. **61**, 273–284 (2019)
30. Batoulis, K., Meyer, A., Bazhenova, E., Decker, G., Weske, M.: Extracting decision logic from process models. In: Zdravkovic, J., Kirikova, M., Johannesson, P. (eds.) CAiSE 2015. LNCS, vol. 9097, pp. 349–366. Springer, Cham (2015). https://doi.org/10.1007/978-3-319-19069-3_22
31. Janssens, L., Bazhenova, E., De Smedt, J., Vanthienen, J., Denecker, M.: Consistent integration of decision (DMN) and process (BPMN) models. In: CAiSE Forum, pp. 121–128. Citeseer (2016)
32. Skou, S.T., et al.: Multimorbidity. Nat. Rev. Dis. Primer. **8**, 48 (2022)
33. Weimann, T., Schlieter, H., Fischer, M.: Designing an avatar-based virtual coach for obesity patients. In: Chandra Kruse, L., Seidel, S., Hausvik, G.I. (eds.) The Next Wave of Sociotechnical Design, pp. 52–57. Springer, Cham (2021)
34. Liu, S., La, H., Willms, A., Rhodes, R.E.: A "No-Code" app design platform for mobile health research: development and usability study. JMIR Form. Res. **6**, e38737 (2022)
35. Pelly, M., Fatehi, F., Liew, D., Verdejo-Garcia, A.: Novel behaviour change frameworks for digital health interventions: a critical review. J. Health Psychol. **28**, 970–983 (2023). https://doi.org/10.1177/13591053231164499

SecFlow: Adaptive Security-Aware Workflow Management System in Multi-cloud Environments

Nafiseh Soveizi$^{(\boxtimes)}$ ⓘ and Fatih Turkmen ⓘ

Information Systems Group, University of Groningen, Groningen, The Netherlands
{n.soveizi,f.turkmen}@rug.nl

Abstract. In this paper, we propose an architecture for a security-aware workflow management system (WfMS) we call SecFlow in answer to the recent developments of combining workflow management systems with Cloud environments and the still lacking abilities of such systems to ensure the security and privacy of cloud-based workflows. The SecFlow architecture focuses on full workflow life cycle coverage as, in addition to the existing approaches to design security-aware processes, there is a need to fill in the gap of maintaining security properties of workflows during their execution phase. To address this gap, we derive the requirements for such a security-aware WfMS and design a system architecture that meets these requirements. SecFlow integrates key functional components such as secure model construction, security-aware service selection, security violation detection, and adaptive response mechanisms while considering all potential malicious parties in multi-tenant and cloud-based WfMS.

Keywords: Security-aware workflows · Cloud-based workflows · Business and Scientific workflows · Workflow Adaptation

1 Introduction

In recent years, workflows are the commonly used application model to describe both business and scientific workflows. A workflow defines a series of computational tasks logically connected by data- and control-flow dependencies [1]. Using workflows to specify complex processes makes the management of such processes easier and more consistent in a structured, distributed, and automated manner. Workflows are managed by Workflow Management Systems (WfMSs) that are responsible for receiving the workflow input from its users and producing the output of each workflow execution (a.k.a. instance), and at the same time providing essential functionality to enable the execution of workflows such as task scheduling, service composition, managing the data- and control-flow dependencies, resource provisioning, and fault tolerance [2,3]. In addition to workflow modeling and execution, WfMSs play a crucial role in managing and analyzing operational processes. They serve as essential tools for enhancing effectiveness, efficiency, cost-effectiveness, quality, and productivity improvements [4,5].

© The Author(s), under exclusive license to Springer Nature Switzerland AG 2024
T. P. Sales et al. (Eds.): EDOC 2023 Workshops, LNBIP 498, pp. 281–297, 2024.
https://doi.org/10.1007/978-3-031-54712-6_17

The recent developments towards supporting data- and compute-intensive applications led to the need for flexible and scalable workflows and WfMS to fulfill users' requirements. Cloud-based WfMS is an effective solution providing the ability for the system to scale up or down resources as needed to meet changing demands. Besides, cloud-based solutions can also compensate for the limited processing capabilities of the users by outsourcing all or part of client-side operations to the cloud.

Cloud security significantly impacts the utilization of cloud services and infrastructures, particularly for workflows involving sensitive data and tasks [6, 7]. In fact, when a workflow or part of it is outsourced to the cloud, it will lead to increased security risks and make them vulnerable to malicious attacks. Deploying the entire WfMS on a semi-trusted or untrusted cloud further exacerbates the situation. Consequently, the security properties of workflows are inevitably affected. Therefore, it is crucial to identify potential malicious entities and other security threats within such systems and establish a secure architecture that efficiently addresses these risks through effective security mechanisms. This conclusion is based on the findings of a recent literature review of the security and privacy concerns in both scientific and business workflows [6] in which we investigated the current state of the art and its limitations. Our findings show that currently available research does not address security throughout the entire workflow lifecycle although it is essential in order to prevent cascading effects and the increased difficulty and cost associated with detecting and containing security issues in later phases. Furthermore, we could conclude that there is a widely unexplored area of research connected to detecting, predicting, and reacting to security violations during the execution time of cloud-based workflows.

To bridge this gap in the literature and tackle the challenges mentioned, our paper introduces SecFlow, a security-aware WfMS designed to address the essential requirements of such a system, with a primary focus on security and privacy. Towards this goal, the contributions of this paper are summarized as follows:

- We provide a classification of the possible security attacks on cloud-based workflows in our multi-tenant WfMS and thus establish the security requirements for a secure WfMS.
- We propose a security-aware functional architecture for a WfMS that meets the identified requirements and evaluate its performance.

By addressing the identified gaps in the state-of-the-art [6], our contribution focuses on developing a WfMS that effectively mitigates security risks in a multi-cloud environment. SecFlow provides comprehensive security measures throughout the entire workflow lifecycle and considers all potential malicious parties, thereby addressing a critical need in the field.

Our paper has the following structure: firstly, in Sect. 2, we will present the classification of the security vulnerabilities of a cloud-based WfMS and then discuss the potential countermeasures against them known from the literature. After that, the existing cloud-based and security-aware WfMSs are discussed in

Sect. 3. In Sect. 4, the proposed architecture is described in detail. We evaluate the proposed architecture in Sect. 5. Finally, Sect. 6 presents our conclusions.

2   Security in Cloud-Based Multi-tenant WfMSs

In this section, we examine the security vulnerabilities of a WfMS, following the Open Web Application Security Project (OWASP) terminology [8]. We begin by emphasizing the importance of sensitive resources, referred to as *Assets*, in multi-tenant WfMS and explore potential threats from attackers, known as *Actors*, within these environments. Furthermore, we analyze the impact of various attacks on the respective targets and explore the preventive measures, referred to as *Preventions* as well as the *Mitigations* commonly employed to minimize the impact of such attacks. To provide a clear overview of these security concerns, preventions, and mitigations, we present Fig. 2 as a concise visual representation of this classification.

2.1   Assets of Tenants

In multi-tenant WfMSs, the assets of tenants, which consist of sensitive resources, are the primary targets for potential attacks. This section discusses three valuable assets owned by each tenant.

The **Tenant's Metadata** includes sensitive data such as account information and the number of users. Unauthorized disclosure of this information can compromise the overall security of the tenant.

Each tenant has different users who need to undergo the authentication process to access tasks and resources. Compromising **Users' Metadata**, such as legitimate user account credentials, can lead to violations of Confidentiality, Integrity, and Availability (CIA) of the users' tasks.

The **Workflow** is the most significant asset in the WfMS and needs to be protected at different levels of abstraction. It encompasses the following assets:

Tasks: workflows consist of various types of tasks, including user tasks and service tasks. These tasks can be performed by users or outsourced to the cloud.

Intermediate data: another critical asset of workflows is the intermediate data generated by the tasks, which includes the data that the workflow exchanges with external services and users via a network.

Logic: workflow logic represents another important asset that should be protected from reconstruction and disclosure by third parties.

2.2   Potential Actors

In multi-tenant and cloud-based WfMS, various entities have the potential to compromise the assets of tenants at different phases of the workflow lifecycle. This section discusses the details of these potential actors. Figure 1 illustrates our adversary model within the system.

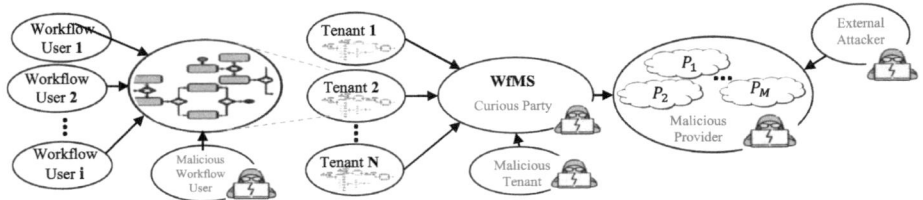

Fig. 1. Adversary model in cloud-based and multi-tenant WfMS

Workflow users encompass all parties involved in the workflow tasks, including roles, organizational units, or the entire organization. It is important to acknowledge that these users have the capability to engage in both intentional and unintentional malicious activities.

In a multi-tenant environment, **tenants** themselves have the potential to become threat actors. Malicious tenants can launch various attacks to compromise the assets of other tenants. Their objectives may involve unauthorized access to sensitive information, manipulation of tasks and data, or causing disruptions.

The cloud-based **WfMS** is responsible for providing essential functionality to manage the execution of the workflows which are submitted by tenants. While it is assumed to be semi-trusted and compliant with protocols, it may attempt to gather as much information as possible about tenants and their sensitive data.

Cloud providers, whose infrastructure and services are utilized by the WfMS for executing workflow tasks, can also be considered potential threat actors as semi-trusted parties. They have the ability to exploit tenants' assets, thus posing a significant security risk.

The shared nature of cloud infrastructure, where multiple users utilize computing and storage resources, introduces vulnerability to attacks. **External Attackers**, including malicious cloud provider users or individuals outside the cloud network (e.g., network attackers), exploit the Internet to execute disruptive attacks, thereby impacting the services available to legitimate users. In our specific case, these actors can target tenant assets during their execution within the cloud providers or even during data transfer processes.

2.3 Attacks and Countermeasures

This section categorizes potential attacks in cloud-based WfMS into three levels and examines the two existing groups of countermeasures that focus on prevention and mitigation controls against these attacks.

The potential categories of attacks in cloud-based WfMS [9] (see Fig. 2) are: a) Application-based attacks: the applications running on the cloud, such as the engine and tasks, are vulnerable to various attacks, including malware injection and protocol vulnerabilities. b) Network-based attacks: the internal network (a virtual private network) connecting cloud machines and the external network

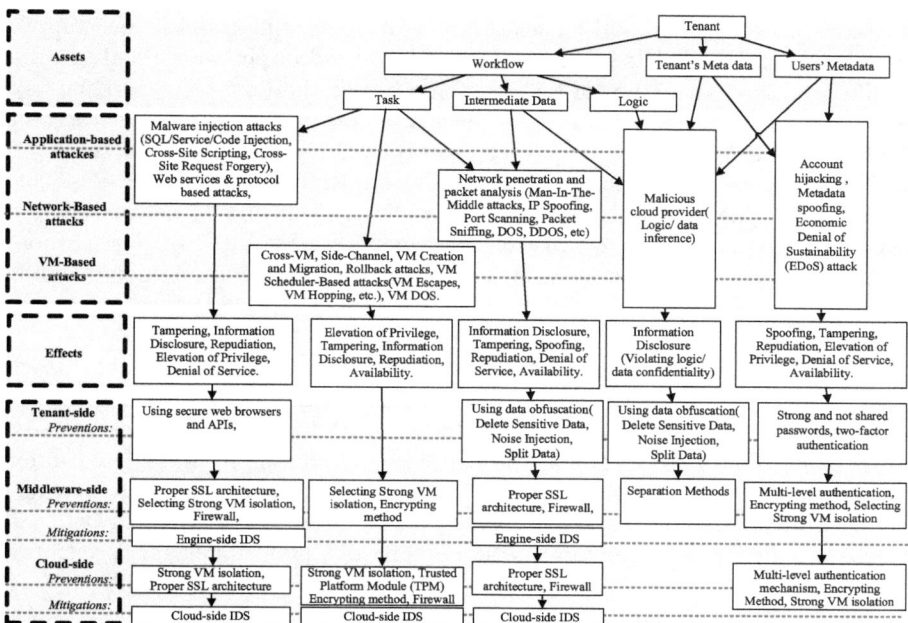

Fig. 2. A classification of the possible attacks in the cloud-based and multi-tenant WfMS organized according to assets, levels, effects, and prevention and mitigation approaches.

(internet) connecting the cloud front-end to users can be compromised. These attacks can violate the CIA of tasks and data. c) VM-based attacks: these attacks exploit vulnerabilities in Virtual Machines (VMs), compromising the CIA of tasks and affecting cloud services.

In what follows, we discuss the possible attacks as well as the possible prevention and mitigation approaches.

Malware injection attacks, including SQL/Service injection, Cross-site scripting (XSS), and Cross-site request forgery (CSRF), as well as attacks at the level of services or protocols are common threats that significantly impact the CIA of tasks. These attacks can also manipulate the control flow of victim processes. To mitigate these risks, clients should utilize secure interfaces/APIs when interacting with cloud systems. Furthermore, employing a secure implementation of protocols, robust encryption mechanisms, and HW-assisted Trusted Computing methods are crucial for improving security [9]. Implementing a web application firewall (WAF) can effectively address common web application-related attacks such as XSS and SQL injection [10]. Techniques for input validation and neutralization should be applied to sanitize user input [11]. Additionally, it is essential to have application-based intrusion detection systems (IDS) deployed on both the cloud and middleware side to detect abnormal user activities.

Network penetration and packet analysis are potential attacks that compromise the execution results of tasks, leading to eavesdropping, data leakage, and the unauthorized alteration of task contents before they are passed to the next task. To enhance security in such scenarios, employing secure socket methods like the SSL (Secure Sockets Layer) protocol [12] is recommended to ensure secure electronic transactions. Additionally, implementation of firewalls, such as packet-filtering, stateful and proxy firewalls, can effectively detect and prevent unauthorized access to sensitive intermediate data [10,13]. Furthermore, the application of machine learning techniques for detecting anomalous traffic [14] on both the cloud side and middleware side can provide further security enhancements.

Logic/data inference by a malicious cloud provider is another possible attack. It can occur when a dishonest provider administrator or high-privileged malicious cloud software combines knowledge of workflow logic to infer sensitive information. This knowledge can be collected by combining data from different workflow tasks or fragments, or by combining data from different workflow instances belonging to the same user/tenant. One solution to mitigate these attacks is splitting sensitive information among different clouds as a prevention control.

Account hijacking and metadata spoofing present significant threats to the sensitive data of users and tenants. These attacks can compromise the CIA of user and tenant responsibilities. Another attack to be aware of is Economic Denial of Sustainability (EDoS), which targets customers' economic resources by fraudulent billing for resource consumption [15]. These attacks can manifest at various levels, including the application, network, and VM levels. To mitigate these threats, prevention controls such as utilizing strong and unique passwords, implementing multi-level authentication mechanisms, employing encryption methods, and ensuring robust VM isolation [11,16] can help.

3   Related Work

In this section, we briefly present the existing cloud-based WfMSs that possess some kind of security awareness and how they can handle security requirements during different phases of the workflow lifecycle. More detailed discussion of these systems is available in [6].

A framework of a "mimic cloud workflow execution system" is proposed in [17] featuring three strategies: heterogeneity (diversification of physical servers, hypervisors, and operating systems), redundancy (Lagged Decision Mechanism), and dynamics (switching workflow execution environment). This system only covers the execution and monitoring phases of the workflow life cycle and cannot carry out adaptation of the process instances to react to security violations.

[18] developed a secure big data workflow management which they called Sec-DATAVIEW, based on DATAVIEW [22]. This system leverages the hardware-assisted trusted execution environments (TEEs) such as Intel Software Guard

Table 1. Different WfMSs regarding security concerns in the cloud.

Feature	[17], 2018	[18], 2019	[19], 2015	[20], 2016	[21], 2019
Workflow Type	Scientific	Scientific	Scientific	Business	Business
Multi-Tenancy	No	No	No	No	Yes
Workflow Targets	Intermediate Data	Intermediate Data, Task	Intermediate Data	Intermediate Data	Intermediate Data, Task
Covered Security Requirements	Data Integrity, Data Confidentiality	Data/Task Integrity, Data Confidentiality	Data Integrity	Data Confidentiality, Data Integrity, Authentication	Data Confidentiality, Task Confidentiality
Considered Attackers	Providers, External Attackers	Providers, External Attackers	External Attackers	External Attackers	Tenants
Covered Attacks Categories	Network-based, VM-based	Network-based, VM-based	Application-based	Network-based, Application-based	Application-based
Covered Phases of the Workflow Lifecycle	Execution, Monitoring	Execution, Monitoring	Execution, Monitoring	Modeling, Deployment	Execution, Monitoring

eXtensions (SGX) and AMD Secure Encrypted Virtualization (SEV) to protect the execution of big data workflows and the data used by them. They also proposed a secure architecture and the WCPAC (Workflow Code Provisioning and Communication) protocol for securing the execution of workflow tasks in remote worker nodes. This system is vulnerable to attacks like network traffic analysis, denial-of-service, side-channel attacks, and fault injections. Furthermore, it only protects workflows from possible attacks during execution, and if an attack occurs, it terminates the workflow execution. In other words, there is no alternative way to adapt the workflows to the detected violation in this system.

[19] extended the Kepler provenance module and added the Security Analysis Package (SAP) to it in order to analyze provenance information in the security context using three security properties: input validation, remote access validation, and data integrity. This module can only detect some of the Application-based attacks and does not offer any way of reacting to security violations during workflow execution. Besides, it does not consider providers as malicious actors.

[20] proposed a system named BPA-Sec4Cloud, which aims to provide a "holistic and integrated cloud-based solution" to address the automation of security-aware business processes from modelling to their deployment. The system does not cover the monitoring, analysis, and adaptation phases of the lifecycle. Similar to [19], the providers are not considered as malicious actors.

[21] presented a cloud workflow engine based on an extension of jBPM4 [23] that can support privacy protection between different tenant workflow instances in the cloud workflow systems. This system considers only malicious tenants as possible attackers and leaves out of scope attackers like service providers and users. Similarly, the solution cannot detect security violations in workflows and like others, does not allow for adaptations in the workflows as reaction to such violations.

We compare these WfMSs from different perspectives in Table 1 which shows that there is no WfMS that can protect all of the mentioned potential targets from all different types of actors (see Sect. 2).

4   System Architecture

This section introduces the architecture of our security-aware WfMS, *SecFlow*, which is specifically designed to protect workflows from various security violations throughout their whole lifecycle. Figure 4 provides a detailed view of the proposed architecture, highlighting its key modules such as the Tenant's Kernel, the Middleware, and the multi-cloud environment. We assume that the tenants' resources are cleanly isolated from each other and may be on the same cloud node; we also assume that the middleware is a logically centralized component that can be hosted by a third party. This deployment option we selected for our work offers the following benefits: (a) It separates workflow instances of different tenants at runtime, meeting their specific functional and non-functional requirements [21], within isolated environments (i.e. the *Tenant's Kernel*). This model also limits the amount of information the engine possesses about individual tenants. (b) It simplifies the cloud infrastructure for tenants. This is achieved by designing a logically centralized component – the *Middleware*, which facilitates informed decision-making for all tenants. The middleware component can be designed so as to be able to integrate with other middlewares, e.g. such that are used as communication backbones or service-oriented middlewares.

Other options of deploying *SecFlow* are also possible but not in the scope of this work.

To meet the requirements of a security-aware WfMS, our work focuses on implementing a comprehensive monitoring procedure to detect potential attacks in the considered deployment model. Figure 3 provides a basic overview of this monitoring procedure, illustrating the locations of monitoring modules and their areas of responsibility. This monitoring approach aims to preserve privacy, safeguard sensitive information, and provide the capability to detect all possible attacks. In this procedure, tenants play an active role in monitoring their users. Similarly, the Middleware component supervises the behavior of both the Clouds and the tenants, using behavioral patterns learned from both sides.

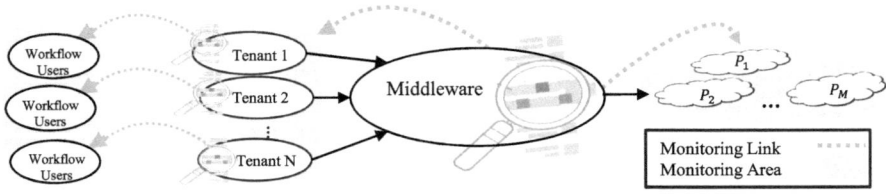

Fig. 3. General Overview of the Monitoring Procedure

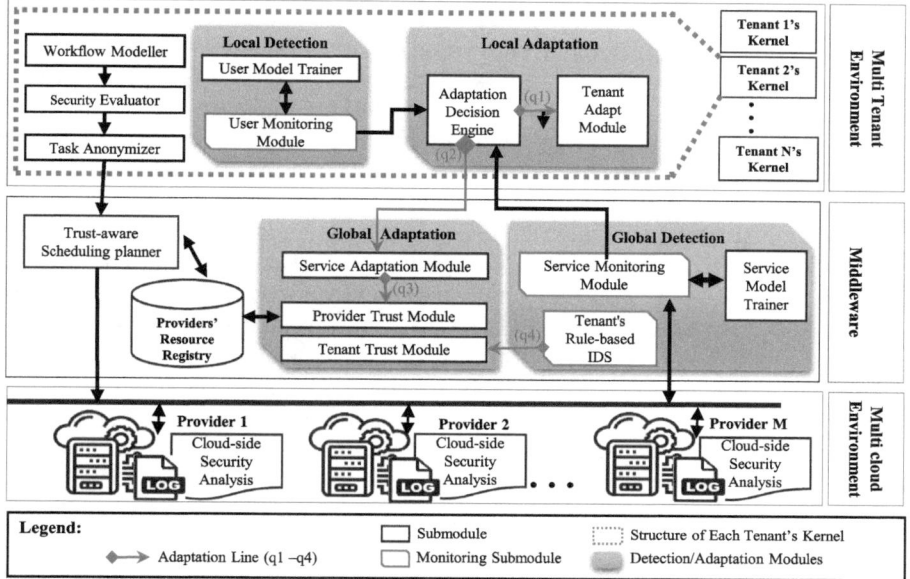

Fig. 4. The architecture of SecFlow

In the next sub-sections, we will describe the functionalities of the components of the *SecFlow* architecture (excluding the multi-cloud environment).

4.1   Multi-tenant Environment

Based on our assumption that each tenant has a cleanly separated version of the WfMS, the **Tenant's Kernel** provides an isolated environment for each tenant where they can model, analyze, execute, monitor, and adapt workflows based on their requirements and strategies. This ensures that the decisions and data of one tenant are protected from other tenants. It consists of the following five sub-modules.

1) ***Workflow Modeller:*** The Workflow Modeller module enables tenants to model their workflows in a secure and efficient way. During the modelling process, the security requirements (CIA) of each task are defined.
2) ***Security Evaluator:*** This module is responsible for defining the possible adaptation actions for each task in the workflow. It involves establishing a set of adaptation strategies, such as skipping, re-working, re-sequencing, and re-configuration, of each task in the workflow instances that determine which actions are feasible for each task in the event of a security violation. Furthermore, it assesses the potential impact of each adaptation action on the overall value of the workflow. To illustrate this, let's consider the scenario of skipping a certain task within a workflow to mitigate the impact of a specific

detected violation. Some tasks may be less critical, and skipping them may have minimal impact on the overall value of the workflow. However, for other tasks, such as authentication tasks, skipping is not a viable option in case of a violation, as they are crucial for maintaining the security of the workflow. By incorporating task-specific adaptations into the security evaluator module (after the modeling phase), it becomes possible to estimate the cost of each adaptation action in terms of execution time and select the optimal adaptation strategy that has the lowest cost and maximal value.

3) *Task Anonymizer:* This module employs obfuscation techniques to securely handle sensitive data and removes unnecessary information for task processing. The obfuscated information is retained in intermediate results for future tasks, as required. Tenants within this module utilize client-side obfuscation techniques, such as data removal, noise injection, and data splitting, along with conflict detection methods to address conflicts between data-minimization and security requirements [24].

4) *Tenant's Detection module (Local Detection):* Each tenant assumes the responsibility of training a machine learning model to detect malicious behavior among its users and monitors them based on this model. This approach not only ensures the security of each tenant's data associated with their users but also allows for customization based on the individual preferences of each tenant.

5) *Tenant's Adaptation module (Local Adaptation):* This module is responsible for selecting suitable adaptation actions according to the tenant's preferences and the run-time monitoring information, and performing these actions at the tenant level. The module comprises three sub-modules: a) *Adaptation Decision Engine* to assess the cost of potential adaptation actions and prioritize those with the lowest impact on the system. It considers factors like price, time, mitigation impact, and overall value to the workflow in response to the detected attacks. Dependencies between tasks are also considered to prevent the propagation of violations so that the subsequent tasks are appropriately adapted. Tenant or middleware level actions are invoked based on the nature of each adaptation (e.g., **q1** and **q2** in Fig. 4). b) *Tenant Adapt Module* designed to perform the adaptations selected by the decision engine while still allowing for customized adjustments (e.g., skipping tasks, re-sequencing processes, introducing new tasks to mitigate the impact) per violation. The submodule can also respond to identified instances of malicious user behavior through appropriate adaptation measures. These measures may include lowering the user's trust level or imposing restrictions on their access to specific tasks.

4.2   Middleware

This module is essential for ensuring the efficient management and scheduling of tasks for all tenants' kernels in the cloud environment. It monitors the behavior of the tenants and the cloud environment in order to detect any malicious activities that could potentially compromise the security of the workflow, and take appropriate actions based on the specific requirements of the submitted tasks. The module consists of three key components:

1) **Trust-aware Scheduling planner:** The primary function of this module is to efficiently schedule workflows and allocate appropriate cloud resources for each task, taking into consideration the specific requirements of individual tenants, such as cost, time, and security. The module integrates the regularly updated trustworthiness information of the providers received from the Provider Trust module into the scheduling process. It is also responsible for anonymizing the tenants' task specifications before transmitting them to the cloud for execution. This process is similar to the Task Anonymizer module, which operates on the tenant side.

2) **Global Monitoring and Detection:** This module is responsible for real-time monitoring of cloud behavior by analyzing the cloud log file and the network traffic data. It includes two main modules: a) *Service Model Trainer:* The main purpose of this submodule is to train a robust machine learning model that can detect any malicious behavior in the cloud by analyzing the real-time network traffic data and cloud log files. The model is trained by using various parameters such as protocol type, duration, and number of packets from the network traffic data sets. The cloud log file is also analyzed to extract information on CPU utilization, bandwidth consumption, and RAM utilization. b) *Service monitoring:* The Service Monitoring submodule uses the machine learning model trained by the Service Model Trainer module to detect any malicious activity in the cloud services and providers and network attacks. It continuously analyzes the real-time network traffic data and cloud log file, comparing them with the expected behavior derived from the trained model. In case of anomalies or suspicious activity, the module immediately raises an alert to the adaptation module of the corresponding tenant so that the appropriate measures are taken. c) *Tenant's Rule-based Intrusion Detection System (IDS)* encompasses a collection of predefined rules in identifying potential attacks originating from the tenants by using submitted workload patterns and specific thresholds established for each tenant. The IDS can detect any suspicious or malicious activities exhibited by tenants during specific time intervals. When a tenant's behavior matches the predefined rules, indicating a potential attack, the IDS promptly triggers an alert (shown as **q4** in Fig. 4).

3) **Global Adaptation:** The Global Adaptation module is critical for ensuring efficient adaptation at the level of the middleware in response to the detected violations or security threats. It comprises three submodules described in detail below:

   a) *Service Adaptation Module:* This submodule enables the adaptation of services chosen by the Adaptation Decision Engine. Operating at the middleware level, this module is responsible for implementing the necessary actions to meet the evolving requirements of tenants. These actions may involve modifying the selected services within the same provider or exploring alternative services from different providers that align with the tenant's specific needs. Then, based on the detected violation, the trust score/level of the service and provider will be updated (shown as **q3** in Fig. 4).

b) *Provider Trust Module:* This submodule updates the trust level of the providers based on any detected violations or security risks. The updated trust values are utilized by the Trust-aware scheduling planner to schedule upcoming workflow instances, thus enhancing the overall security and efficiency of the system. Additionally, this module may modify the Provider Prediction model to improve the monitoring of malicious provider behavior with greater precision.

c) *Tenant Trust Module:* Since the response to an attack in a tenant varies based on the attack's severity/impact, this submodule updates the tenant's trust level and takes corresponding actions, such as ignoring the alert (if trust falls below the defined threshold), isolating affected resources or activity blocking.

5   Evaluation

We implemented *SecFlow*[1] by extending the jBPM (Java Business Process Management) [23] engine and integrating it with the Cloudsim Plus [25] simulation tool. jBPM offers a pluggable architecture that allows for easy replacement of different module implementations. Additionally, the integration of the simulation framework Cloudsim Plus has allowed us to accurately model the complexities of a multi-cloud environment.

5.1   Experimental Setting

To evaluate our system, we utilized three distinct categories of process models: Small (3–10 tasks), Medium (10–50 tasks), and Large (50–100 tasks). Our scenario assumed the availability of 5 cloud providers, each offering 3 different services for the service tasks. The specifications of these services fell within the following ranges: Response time [1, 50], Cost [0.1, 10], and confidentiality, integrity, and availability [0, 1].

Table 2 provides an overview of the relative price and time associated with each adaptation type compared to the original task's response time (R) and price (P). The weights (W) are determined based on the workflow requirements provided. We utilize this table as a reference to determine the appropriate actions for each attack type (mitigated attackType) and its mitigation. To identify the optimal choice with minimal cost, we use Eq. 1 for computing the associated cost of each potential adaptation action. This equation factors in the price, time, and risk mitigation score specific to each adaptation action, while incorporating weights assigned by the tenant to prioritize their preferences.

---

[1] Our code will be available soon at *https://github.com/nafisesoezy/SecFlow.*

$$AdaptationCost(aa, t) = W_{price} \cdot (AdaptPrice(aa) + PriceOverhead(aa, t)) +$$
$$W_{time} \cdot (AdaptTime(aa) + TimeOverhead(aa, t)) -$$
$$W_{Security} \cdot MitigationScore(aa, t)$$

$$(1)$$

In Eq. 1, $AdaptPrice$, $AdaptTime$, and $MitigationScore$ represent the price, time, and risk mitigation score of the adaptation action aa, respectively. Additionally, $PriceOverhead$ and $TimeOverhead$ represent the adaptation price and time overhead specific to the adaptation action aa for a given task t.

The calculation of $MitigationScore(aa)$ follows Eq. 2. It considers the security requirements of task t (represented by obj_t), the impact of the detected attack a_i on the CIA aspects (represented by obj_{a_i}), and the mitigation impact of the adaptation action on each aspect (represented by obj_{aa}).

$$MitigationScore(aa, t, a_i) = \sum_{obj \in \{C, I, A\}} (1 - obj_t \cdot obj_{a_i}) * obj_{aa} \qquad (2)$$

In our experiments, we considered each adaptation action's mitigation impact (Table 2) and each attack's impact (Table 3) on the CIA.

Table 2. Cost of Different Adaptation Types

AdaptType	Late	Skip	ReExecute	Redundancy	Reconfig
Time	$T * T_{Late}$	0	$T_{BackupSrc}$	$T_{BackupSrc}$	$T * T_{reconfig}$
Price	P	0	$P_{BackupSrc}$	$P + P_{BackupSrc}$	$P * P_{reconfig}$
Mitigation Impact(C, I, A)	$(0.7, 0.6, 0.8)$	$(0.5, 0.4, 0.6)$	$(0.8, 0.9, 0.7)$	$(0.9, 0.8, 0.9)$	$(0.6, 0.7, 0.5)$
AttackType Mitigated	DOS	Probe	DOS, Probe, U2R, R2L	DOS, U2R	DOS, Probe, U2R, R2L

Table 3. Security Impact of different attackTypes

Attack type	DoS	Probe	U2R	R2L
Impact on C, I, A	0.56, 0.56, 0.56	0.22, 0.22, 0	0.56, 0.22, 0.22	0.56, 0.56, 0.22

5.2   Main Results

Figure 5 presents a snippet from the system's logfile, providing insights into the activities of two tenants. At timestamp 46:08, the logfile entry reveals that $tenant0$'s $userTask1$ exhibits no indications of malicious behavior, as verified by the conducted user monitoring. Additionally, the logfile captures an occurrence of a violation within $tenant1$'s $serviceTask_6$, associated with the utilization of $service4$ from the available multi-cloud services. The detected attack type is identified as a Denial of Service (DoS) attack. In response to this threat, the architecture selects the adaptation strategy of *Reexecute*. This excerpt from the logfile showcases the architecture's capability to dynamically detect attacks originating from diverse entities. It showcases the architecture's adaptive nature, as it seamlessly adjusts its response strategy according to the type, severity, and characteristics of the detected attack, as well as the specific task in which the attack occurs.

Timestamp	Tenant ID	Workflow ID	Instance ID	Task ID	Task Type	Monitoring Resulit	Targeted User/Service ID	Detected Attack Type	Selected Adaptation
46:08.0	tenant0	1	1	1	UserTask	Normal			
46:09.1	tenant0	1	1	2	ServiceTask	Normal			
46:23.5	tenant1	3	3	6	ServiceTask	Abnormal	4	dos	ReExecute
46:35.0	tenant1	3	4	15	ServiceTask	Abnormal	0	probe	Ignore the attack!
46:59.6	tenant0	1	4	29	ServiceTask	Normal			
48:18.3	tenant0	1	7	13	ServiceTask	Abnormal	0	dos	Late
48:57.0	tenant0	1	7	47	ServiceTask	Abnormal	0	dos	Ignore the attack!
55:16.2	tenant1	3	17	92	ServiceTask	Abnormal	2	u2r	ReExecute
56:30.9	tenant0	1	10	6	ServiceTask	Abnormal	2	probe	Skip
02:01.5	tenant0	1	4	27	ServiceTask	Abnormal	2	probe	ReConfiguration
03:00.3	tenant1	3	6	14	UserTask	Abnormal	16	Elevation of Privilege	Update User Trust

Fig. 5. Logfile Snippet in SecFlow

The results of our study are presented in Fig. 6, which shows figures of the normalized average time, price, and mitigation score. These metrics were evaluated across 100 executions of three process categories (small, medium, and large) at varying attack rates.

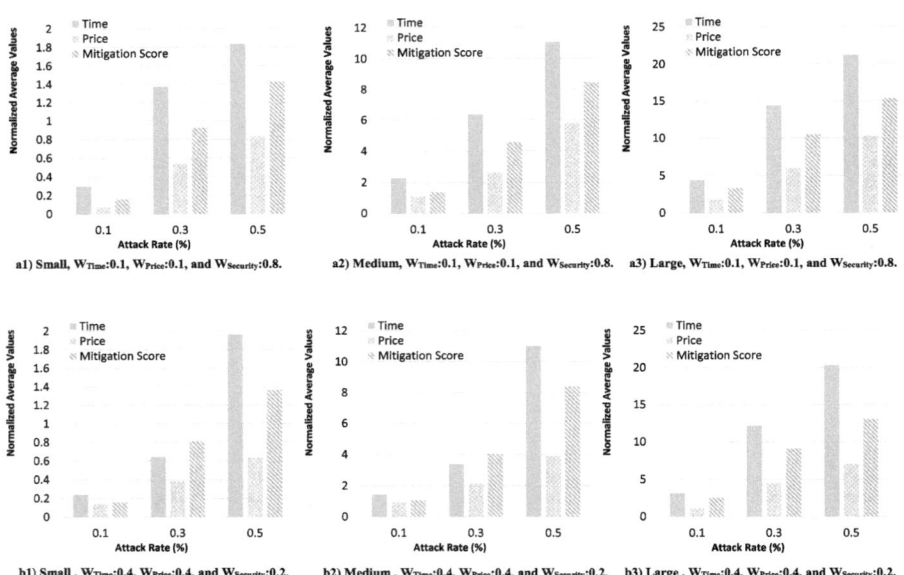

a1) Small, W_{Time}:0.1, W_{Price}:0.1, and $W_{Security}$:0.8.   a2) Medium, W_{Time}:0.1, W_{Price}:0.1, and $W_{Security}$:0.8.   a3) Large, W_{Time}:0.1, W_{Price}:0.1, and $W_{Security}$:0.8.

b1) Small , W_{Time}:0.4, W_{Price}:0.4, and $W_{Security}$:0.2.   b2) Medium , W_{Time}:0.4, W_{Price}:0.4, and $W_{Security}$:0.2.   b3) Large , W_{Time}:0.4, W_{Price}:0.4, and $W_{Security}$:0.2.

Fig. 6. Normalized Average Time, Price, and Mitigation Score for Different Process Sizes with Varying Weights

In Fig. 6a1, a2, and a3, we assigned weights of 0.1, 0.1, and 0.8 to time, price, and security respectively. Similarly, in Fig. 6b1, b2, and b3, the weights for time, price, and security were set as 0.4, 0.4, and 0.2, respectively.

Comparing these two sets of figures (Fig. 6), we observe that the adaptation actions in b1, b2, and b3 have a shorter time and lower price compared to a1, a2, and a3. This reflects the tenant's higher prioritization of time and price in b1, b2, and b3. However, the mitigation scores in b1, b2, and b3 are lower than that of a1, a2, and a3, indicating a lower emphasis on the selected adaptation actions' mitigation effectiveness.

The findings highlight the effectiveness of the Adaptation Decision Engine Module in enabling tenants to tailor their adaptation strategies to meet their unique needs. By considering factors such as time, cost, and the mitigation score associated with various adaptation actions, tenants can strike a well-balanced approach that aligns with their requirements.

6 Conclusion

In this paper, we introduced SecFlow, a security-aware architecture designed for WfMS in a multi-cloud environment. Unlike previous studies, SecFlow comprehensively addresses security and privacy concerns throughout the entire workflow lifecycle, with particular emphasis on the detection and reaction to violations that are positioned in the adaptation phases of workflows. By considering threats from various parties, SecFlow provides an extensive monitoring functionality of malicious behavior at different levels (e.g., tenant and middleware) and detects abnormal activities. By leveraging the collected monitoring information, many adaptations become possible for safeguarding user privacy and/or tenant confidentiality. The proposed architecture was implemented by extending the jBPM engine and integrating it with the Cloudsim Plus simulation tool. Experimental results demonstrate that SecFlow dynamically detects and responds to attacks while exhibiting good performance in terms of time, price, and mitigation score across workflows of different sizes.

As future work, we plan to extend the system's functionality to incorporate adaptive learning from past reactions and adaptations to violations. This enhancement will improve the overall effectiveness and responsiveness of SecFlow when securing and managing workflows in multi-cloud environments.

Acknowledgments. This work is partially funded by the HORIZON-KDT-JU-2022-1-IA project 101112089 AIMS5.0. The authors thank Dimka Karastoyanova for the input and contribution in most phases of this work.

References

1. Dumas, M., La Rosa, M., Mendling, J., Reijers, H.A.: Fundamentals of Business Process Management, vol. 37, no. 6, p. 517 (2018)

2. Li, X., et al.: Design and development of an adaptive workflow enabled spatial-temporal analytics framework. In: ICPADS - International Conference on Parallel and Distributed Systems, pp. 862–867 (2012). ISSN: 1521-9097

3. Rodriguez, M.A., Buyya, R.: Scientific Workflow Management System for Clouds, 1st edn., pp. 367–387. Elsevier Inc. (2017)

4. Meidan, A., et al.: A survey on business processes management suites. Comput. Stand. Interfaces **51**, 71–86 (2017)

5. Poola, D., et al.: A taxonomy and survey of fault-tolerant workflow management systems in cloud and distributed computing environments. In: Software Architecture for Big Data and The Cloud, pp. 285–320 (2017)

6. Soveizi, N., Turkmen, F., Karastoyanova, D.: Security and privacy concerns in cloud-based scientific and business workflows: a systematic review. Future Gener. Comput. Syst. **148**, 184–200 (2023)

7. Varshney, S., Sandhu, R., Gupta, P.K.: QoS based resource provisioning in cloud computing environment: a technical survey. In: Singh, M., Gupta, P., Tyagi, V., Flusser, J., Ören, T., Kashyap, R. (eds.) ICACDS 2019. CCIS, vol. 1046, pp. 711–723. Springer, Singapore (2019). https://doi.org/10.1007/978-981-13-9942-8_66

8. OWASP. Threat modeling cheat sheet (2022). https://cheatsheetseries.owasp.org/cheatsheets/Threat%20Modeling%20Cheat%20Sheet.html

9. Minhaj Ahmad Khan: A survey of security issues for cloud computing. J. Netw. Comput. Appl. **71**, 11–29 (2016)

10. Modi, C.N., Acha, K.: Virtualization layer security challenges and intrusion detection/prevention systems in cloud computing: a comprehensive review. J. Supercomput. **73**(3), 1192–1234 (2017). https://doi.org/10.1007/s11227-016-1805-9

11. Alhenaki, L., et al.: A survey on the security of cloud computing. In: ICCAIS 2019, pp. 1–7 (2019)

12. Hwang, G.H., Kao, Y.C., Hsiao, Y.C.: Scalable and trustworthy cross-enterprise WfMSs by cloud collaboration. In: Proceedings of the IEEE International Congress on Big Data 2013, pp. 70–77 (2013)

13. Maroua, N., Adel, A., Belhassen, Z.: A new formal proxy-based approach for secure distributed business process on the cloud. In: Proceedings of the International Conference on AINA 2018, pp. 973–980 (2018). ISSN: 1550-445X

14. Salman, T., et al.: Machine learning for anomaly detection and categorization in multi-cloud environments. In: CSCloud 2017, pp. 97–103 (2017)

15. Bhardwaj, A., et al.: Distributed denial of service attacks in cloud: state-of-the-art of scientific and commercial solutions. Comput. Sci. Rev. **39**, 100332 (2021)

16. Panda, D.R., Behera, S.K., Jena, D.: A survey on cloud computing security issues, attacks and countermeasures. In: Patnaik, S., Yang, X.S., Sethi, I. (eds.) Advances in Machine Learning and Computational Intelligence. AIS, pp. 513–524. Springer, Cham (2021). https://doi.org/10.1007/978-981-15-5243-4_47

17. Wang, Y., et al.: Scientific workflow execution system based on mimic defense in the cloud environment. Front. Inf. Technol. Electron. Eng. **19**(12), 1522–1536 (2018). ISSN: 2095-9230

18. Mofrad, S., et al.: SecDATAVIEW: a secure big data workflow management system for heterogeneous computing environments. In: ACM International Conference Proceeding Series, pp. 390–403 (2019)

19. Kim, D., Vouk, M.A.: Securing scientific workflows. In: Proceedings of the IEEE QRS-C 2015, pp. 95–104 (2015)

20. Lins, F., Damasceno, J., Medeiros, R., Sousa, E., Rosa, N.: Automation of service-based security-aware business processes in the Cloud. Computing **98**(9), 847–870 (2016). https://doi.org/10.1007/s00607-015-0476-3

21. Huang, H., et al.: Research on cloud workflow engine supporting three-level isolation and privacy protection, pp. 160–165 (2019)
22. Kashlev, A., Lu, S.: A system architecture for running big data workflows in the cloud. In: Proceedings of the International Conference on SCC, pp. 51–58 (2014)
23. jBPM: Business Process Management Suite. https://www.jbpm.org/
24. Ramadan, Q., Strüber, D., Salnitri, M., Jürjens, J., Riediger, V., Staab, S.: A semi-automated BPMN-based framework for detecting conflicts between security, data-minimization, and fairness requirements. Softw. Syst. Model. **19**(5), 1191–1227 (2020). https://doi.org/10.1007/s10270-020-00781-x
25. CloudSim Plus Contributors. CloudSim Plus. GitHub repository. https://github.com/manoelcampos/cloudsim-plus

On the Ability of Novice Modelers to Identify, Represent and Trace Strategic and Tactical Conceptual Elements in Business Process and Enterprise Modeling

Ghazaleh Aghakhani[1], Koen Heeren[2], Yves Wautelet[2(✉)]🆔, Stephan Poelmans[2], and Manuel Kolp[1]

[1] Université catholique de Louvain, Louvain-la-Neuve, Belgium
[2] KU Leuven, Leuven, Belgium
yves.wautelet@kuleuven.be

Abstract. Many software professionals think about Business Process Modeling (BPM) as a way of representing all of the steps and details of a daily work execution. BPM is nevertheless also devoted to defining the broad outlines of a particular process and how internal improvements (like automation or worker support) can align with an organization's business strategy. Business processes in their aggregated form (i.e. one entire business process represented by one black box element) do provide information on their scope (so can be seen as a tactical-level source of information) and, if mixed in a common representation with business objectives and goals, we can trace the impact of their execution, reengineering or IT-support on the strategy. Most of the work on the ability of novice modelers to represent a business process has focused on the operational perspective rather than the latter tactical and strategic ones. Evaluating the quality of higher level representations is also, to a large extend, an open issue. This paper aims to overview the performance of novice modelers when representing such tactical-level elements and tracing their strategic impact through a quasi-experiment. More specifically, subjects are given a complex case and have to draw a Business Use-Case Diagram which is a representation combining all of these elements. Results show that: (1) the proposed quality assessment is suitable when compared to a domain and modeling expert's solution; (2) the cognitive style of modelers has no impact on the quality of the representations they produce.

Keywords: Strategic Modeling · Tactical Modeling · Traceability · Model Quality

1 Introduction

A Business Process (BP) refers to the set of activities and tasks whose aim is the production of an output which brings value to the customer [1]. While BP representations are often associated with operational execution, they can also be envisaged in a more aggregated (tactical and strategic) fashion in order to model complementary dimensions. For

T. P. Sales et al. (Eds.): EDOC 2023 Workshops, LNBIP 498, pp. 298–314, 2024.
https://doi.org/10.1007/978-3-031-54712-6_18

differentiating functions, their careful IT support can indeed become an important tool to both create and maintain a competitive advantage as it plays a key role in a firm's daily operations and customer support. Packaged as IT services themselves components of the information system, software can support and automate custom BP execution [2].

The human component in both the creation and the understanding of BPs has been and continues to be a topic where much research is done [3–7]. As humans are prone to error and typically struggle with abstraction, errors during the modelling process could easily happen [7], which can cost both significant amounts of time and money in a software development process [8]. This is especially a significant issue when non-expert (i.e. novice) modelers are involved in projects [1]. Since there are a lot of 'moving parts' (i.e. large amounts of textual (interview-based) descriptions provided) when it comes to modeling BP, the way a person gathers and processes information, could conceivably play a role in their ability to produce high quality BP modeling. There is a limited number of studies regarding the link between the modeler's modeling style and BP model quality. This is especially the case when it comes to higher abstract levels (so non-operational). This paper will focus on the ability of novices on producing qualitative models at strategic level. To this end, we overview what quality elements could be applied to evaluate such representations, we conduct an experiment based on a real life case with master-level students in Business Information Management (BIM) at KULeuven campus Brussels with a basic training on software modeling to overview their performance in such representations. For this, we evaluate their performance on the basis of standard elements present in the case and a reference solution made by an expert; we also overview if the Cognitive Style (CS) of subjects has an impact on their performance. It could indeed be reasonable to hypothesize that the way someone gathers and analyses information (e.g. when presented with a business modeling exercise and a complex textual description) has a real effect on the output they create in the form of the quality of a produced model [9] especially for non-experienced modelers. This way of gathering and processing information can then be operationalized by their CS. This paper thus aims to answer two research questions: RQ1: *"How successful are novice modelers in producing tactical and strategic conceptual elements representations and ensuring their in-between traceability when compared to an expert solution?"* and RQ2: *"Does the CS of a novice modeler have an impact on the quality of their produced tactical and strategic-level BP models?"*.

2   Background and Related Work

2.1   Strategic and Tactical Modeling Using the Business Use Case Model

Goal-oriented requirements models can be used to model strategic and tactical elements. These models are more geared towards 'why' and 'what' questions instead of 'who', 'what' and 'how' in the operational layer. Models like i* [10] and KAOS [11] are semantically rich and suitable wrt this but not widely adopted. Based on the literature, the *Unified Modeling Language* (*UML*) [12] is by far the most industry adopted modeling notation. The Rational Unified Process (*RUP*) is a well known customizable and iterative software development process framework originally created by Rational Software and now maintained by IBM. The RUP aims to guide practitioners through the effort of software development with the help of a series of guidelines, artifacts etc. [13]. The RUP effectively acts as a guide on how to use UML. Specifically the *Business Use-Case Model (BUCM)* which is specified in the RUP documentation [14] is of interest as it can be used to represent both the strategic and tactical layer. BUCM is presented in the Rational UML Profile for business modeling, which is an extension of the UML use case model by adding business semantics [14]. It is defined as *"a model of the business goals and intended functions"* [14] and is valuable to anyone who aims to understand how the business interacts with its environment.

The BUCM consists of several elements. The *business goal (BG)* is defined as a certain business requirement that has to be satisfied which allows the planning of the activities of the business [13]. It represents the strategic abstraction level and can be further abstracted as the *business objective (BO)*. The main difference between the two is that BGs can be measured by key performance indicators, while a BO is too abstract to do so. A BG thus refines a BO [14]. An example of this would be the BO of sustainable management, which is then refined in the BG of *'reduce waste management by 20%'*. The *Business Use-Case (BUC)* represents the tactical level in the BUCM and is defined as *"a set of business use-case instances, where each instance is a sequence of actions a business performs that yields an observable result of value to a particular business actor"* [14]. BUCs are essentially BPs that involve both stakeholders in and outside of the business and focus on the value provided to these stakeholders and the business [13–15]. *Business actors (BA) and business workers (BW)* are connected to the BUCs and can be comprised of humans or software systems. The BA role is placed outside of the business but interacts with it through BUCs. A typical example is a customer. The BW plays a role inside the business and takes part in the BP that make up the BUCs (e.g. a procurement department employee). Both are linked to BUCs that they interact with through association links, indicating a relationship between the two [13–16].

2.2   Traceability and Levels of Abstraction

Traceability is defined in the RUP knowledge base as *"the ability to know and recognize that a particular model or code at any abstraction level, derives from something else, at a higher level of abstraction"* [13]. Traceability between different models allows for consistency [15] and facilitates changing requirements during software development [13]. **The Strategic Level** is the highest level of abstraction and provides an answer to the 'why' questions posed during development. It indicates general direction and long term strategy through goals and objectives of the organization or project. Additionally, it is important as it provides a good oversight or context for all stakeholders involved and facilitates the communication [17, 18]. Weske [19] also identifies the BGs as long term objectives and the business strategy as an overarching plan to reach those goals. In the context of this research, the strategic level will be modeled by means of the BUCM, allowing the use of BOs and BGs. **The Tactical Level** provides and answer to the 'what' and 'who' questions posed during development. The tactical level models the BP and resources that are available to the organization which will be used to achieve the BOs and BGs in the strategic level. It also shows how the different processes and roles interact with each other and provides an organizational view [16, 17, 20]. This level could be modeled by means of use-case diagrams as defined by UML, but in the context of this research, the tactical level will be modeled by means of the BUCM, allowing the use of BUCs. **The Operational Level** concerns specific tasks performed in realization of the (business) use cases or processes in the tactical level. This level answers the 'how' question and models the specific tasks for each stakeholder [17,20]. UML and BPMN [21] are most often used for the modeling of this level.

2.3 Modeling Quality Framework

The measurement of quality of conceptual and BP models remains a significant topic. Different guidelines, frameworks, and standards have been proposed over the years with the objective of measuring or improving model quality. Unfortunately, there is a lack in generally accepted way of measuring model quality especially at the strategic level [5].

Quality of BP models can be hard to define and many different definitions are proposed [22]. In the context of this research paper, quality will follow the interpretation of Dzepina & Lehner [23], equating the term of quality with the 'suitability for use'. They also state that *"To assess or evaluate quality, the assessors judging the quality (novices or experts in process modeling) as well as the intended purpose of the process model, need to be considered. Otherwise the same model can be understood in various ways, depending on who is evaluating it and for which purpose it is intended"* [23].

Despite the existence of different frameworks, there is still no generally accepted universal way of measuring BP model quality [5,24]. Finding suitable quality metrics can be challenging as researchers often use different definitions for quality and quality metrics [5]. A recent systematic literature review by De Meyer & Claes [25] combined recent literature on process model quality in their own *Comprehensive Process Model Quality Framework* (*CPMQF*) and found no less than 39 quality dimensions and 21 quality metrics used in various research papers to measure process model quality.

One of the modeling frameworks that is often discussed in research papers specifically addressing process modeling quality is SEQUAL [25]. The main idea behind it is that since models are essentially statements being made in a language, semiotic (or linguistic) quality properties can be applied to them to evaluate said models [26–28]. The framework is based on sets of statements, each representing different aspects of modeling. This include the *goals of modeling* (*G*), the *language extension or syntax* (*L*), the *domain* (*D*) of the modeling context, the *externalized model* (*M*), the *knowledge of stakeholders* (*K*), *social actor interpretation* (*I*) and *technical actor interpretation* (*T*). These statements can then be compared in relation to each other in order to define the conceptual modeling quality of a certain model on different levels [28–30]. However, the framework has some shortcomings. Usually it is hard for participants to make reliable quality evaluations based on the statement sets and thus, there are raising concerns about the reliability of such a quality evaluation [31].

These different levels of quality can be divided up in *physical quality*, which relates to *how well the modeler was able to externalize their domain knowledge in the model* and *how well the reader of the model can understand it*. The *empirical quality* indicates the *comprehensibility of the model* (e.g. the layout). The *syntactic quality*, which relates to *whether all the elements in the model use the correct syntax of the modeling language*. This could for example be checked by the formula dividing the set of statements in the M by the set of statements that apply by the correct syntax rules of the L. The semantic quality relates to the elements in the model being correct and relevant to the problem (aka validity) and whether the model contains all elements that would be correct in the context of the problem (aka completeness). The perceived semantic quality relates to the actors model interpretation and domain knowledge. Pragmatic quality indicates whether or not the reader of the model understands it. The social quality relates to the agreement on the model between different actors and finally the organizational quality relates to whether or not the original goal of modeling is actually fulfilled [29,30,32].

While the original SEQUAL framework serves as the basis for many variations and extensions, several shortcomings of the framework were identified. Moody et al. [31] trained participants of their experiment in the application of the framework, but found that it was hard for participants to make reliable quality evaluations based on the statement sets explained earlier and thus raising concerns about the reliability of such a quality evaluation. Krogstie et al. [29] added to this that it is likely only feasible to measure the syntactic quality level objectively, as other measures rely on participant opinions and are thus hard to evaluate objectively. They add to this that this would be a challenge for basically any framework trying to measure objective quality measures beyond the syntactic level [29]. In the context of this research and the case that will be given to respondents, the semantic and syntactic quality measures are the most relevant and feasible to measure. Specifically the semantic validity and correctness will be measured, as well as the syntactic correctness of the modeled BUCM elements. This paper will focus on the SEQUAL modeling framework as it is often discussed in research papers specifically addressing process modeling quality [25].

2.4 Modeler Experience Impact on Modeling Quality and Cognitive Style Index

Traditionally, conceptual models including BP models are made as an interplay between the domain expert and a system analyst (an expert in modeling techniques) [33]. Typically, unlike system analysts, domain experts have higher, detailed knowledge of the domain but often, slight powers of abstraction beyond that knowledge. Recently, BP modeling projects have expanded to company-wide initiatives in which novice modelers are increasingly active. The trend towards a growing involvement of novice modelers in process modeling projects results in various quality issues [34]. Recent studies reveal considerable weaknesses of process models from practice with reference to understanding and error probability [24,35–38]. The way someone gathers and analyses information (e.g. when presented with a business modeling exercise and a complex textual description) has a real effect on the output they create in the form of the quality of a produced model [9].

The CSI, designed by Allinson & Hayes [39] is a 38-item self-report questionnaire that allows a straightforward way of measuring ones CS. Every question is oriented towards the intuitive or analytic style and respondents simply have to respond whether they agree or disagree with the statements proposed. If they do not lean either way, they indicate that they are uncertain. Two points are given depending on the polarity of the question and a total of 76 points are able to be scored. Respondents can then be grouped into one of the five categories of CS, depending on their score [40].

People on the left side of the scale are considered to be intuitive (0–28) and the people leaning towards intuitive are considered quasi-intuitive (29–38). The adaptive category sits in between the intuitive and analytical categories (39–45) and indicates the ability to adapt to the situation, expressing qualities of both extremes. People leaning towards the analytic category are considered to be quasi-analytic (46–52) and the analytic category finds itself on the right side of the scale (53–76) [40]. The difference between intuitive and analytic is based on left and right brain theory [41]. The right side of the brain relates to the intuitive side of the CSI scale and to feeling-based judgements and open ended, creative approaches to problem solving and a global perspective. The left side of the brain relates to the analytic side. It relates to reasoning, attention to detail and analytical people prefer a methodical approach to problem solving [7, 39].

It can definitely be argued that both intuitive and analytical minded modelers have their place in an information systems development context. The interesting fact about this divide between intuitive and analytical is that it could be argued that due to intuitive people being better at seeing the 'big picture', might have an easier time to produce strategic BP models in particular as they allow a higher level of abstraction. However, in the context of this paper and the experiment that will be conducted, the hypothesis is that analytical respondents should have an easier time following the case instructions, are better suited to analyze the complex textual description and ultimately produce a higher quality model. This hypotheses will be tested in the paper.

3 The Experiment

3.1 Experiment Design

The experiment took place in a physical setting and respondents were given a general introduction as to what was to be expected. The attendance for the experiment was not obligatory and thus students were incentivized to attend by offering a maximum of 1,5 bonus points on their final grade for their *BP Management and Integrated Software Systems* (*BPMISS*) course. A half point was to be earned by simply attending and completing the entire experiment, whilst an extra point could be earned by creating a high quality model. Students were expected to need two hours to complete the entire experiment, however if needed could take longer if they wanted to.

Before starting the modelling experiment, students received the CSI questions to fill in part 0. In part 1, students were surveyed about their occupation, educational background, age and gender as well as their familiarity with UML, the business modeling discipline of the RUP and the BUCM. In part 2, respondents were provided a theory section concerning the RUP/UML BUCM which detailed all the necessary constructs, to be used as a reference while solving the TransLogisTIC case [42, 43] depicted in the next section. The whole experiment including part 1, part 2 and part 3 can be found in Appendix C[1]. Subjects were expected to have some basic knowledge of the BUCM as it was part of the course curriculum for the BPMISS course where some theoretical background was given. Also, all students had followed and passed a course about UML during the preceding semester. However it was to be expected that the majority of students would not actually have created a BUC diagram by themselves based on a complex textual description at that stage of the academic year. Because of this, a top-down

---

[1] The online appendix can be found at: https://data.mendeley.com/datasets/ccn327m4g4/1.

approach with six steps was provided during the explanation of the BUCM constructs to give the respondents guidance as to how to approach the creation of a BUC diagram. The following steps were: (i) *Identify the BO(s) and BG(s)*; (ii) *Identify the BUCs (and which BG they support)*; (iii) *Identify the business actor instances*; (iv) *Identify the business worker instances*; (v) *Identify the relationships between the different components*; (vi) *Bring everything together in a diagram.*

Following the theoretical examples based on the RUP/UML profile for business modeling, a small example ('Knitting shop') was provided and solved along the same six above steps. A physically drawn solution was provided as well. To end part two, respondents were surveyed about the clarity and understandability of the theory.

3.2   TransLogisTIC Case

The modeling exercise was provided by one of the authors and is based on a real life case he has been working on. Respondents were given the following introduction: *"You're hired as a business analyst working for a consultancy firm. You are currently working on a project, for which you're asked to model the strategic and tactical elements of the organization's BP on the basis of the following textual description. You need to model these levels using the BUCM. A summary of all elements (modeling constructs and links/relationships) that are needed is provided for you to use as a reference when modeling (see part 2)".*

The case revolved around the TransLogisTIC project relates to an organization adopting new IT system for managing its outbound logistics processes. Respondents were given a two-page textual description further clarifying the project to be represented. The first page mainly included information about the BOs and goals (i.e. the strategic level). The second page provided more information about business actors and workers involved in supply chain process and the BUCs they were involved in (i.e. the tactical level). The complete textual description can be found in Appendix C. In consistency with the top-down approach provided in the theory part, respondents were given steps that can guide them through modeling a high quality BUCM. These steps were: (i) *Identify the BO(s) and BG(s) from the point of view from TransLogisTIC*; (ii) *Identify at least 2 BOs and or goals which are not explicitly stated in the text, but are relevant in the context of the case (also include these in the drawing of your model in step 6)*; (iii) *Identify the BUCs (and which BG they support)*; (iv) *Identify the business worker(s)*; (v) *Identify the business actor(s)*; (vi) *Identify the relationships between the different components*; (vii) *Bring everything together in a diagram.*

To end the experiment, respondents were surveyed about the clarity of the case instructions, the perceived difficulty of modeling and finally their perceived ease of use and usefulness of the BUCM method.

3.3   Data Collection Through Variables

Modelers' Background. The first questionnaire of the experiment informed about the modeler's demographic characteristics and familiarity with modeling. Students were asked what their primary occupation was at the time of the experiment (*occupation*), what their educational background was (*edu*), their age (*age*) and gender (*gender*).

Familiarity with Modeling. This was then followed by questions inquiring about the familiarity with the UML (*fam_UML*), familiarity with the business modeling discipline of the RUP (*fam_BMRUP*) and finally the familiarity with the BUCM (*fam_BUCM*). Responses were recorded by means of a five-point Likert scale ranging from 1 to 5. With (1) 'Not at all', (2) 'Slightly', (3)'Moderately', (4) 'Very' and (5) as 'Extremely'. The coding of this Likert scale is the same for every subsequent subsection.

Clarity of Theory. After reading through the provided theory regarding the creation of a BUCM and the 'Knitting shop' example, respondents were asked to what extent certain concepts were clear to them. Responses were recorded by means of a five-point Likert scale ranging from 1 to 5. The questions inquired after the clarity of BOs (*clarity_BO*), BGs (*clarity_BG*), BUCs (*clarity_BUC*), business actors and workers (*clarity_BA clarity_BW*), association and dependency links (*clarity_association*; *clarity_dependency*) and finally the clarity of the provided example case (*clarity_example*).

Model Quality and Evaluation Metrics. As discussed earlier, several levels of quality are commonly used to perform quality assessment of conceptual models. In the context of this research and its limitations, the quality assessment of the produced BUCMs will be mainly focused on the semantic quality goals of *validity* and *completeness*. This means that the models will be graded based on whether or not the elements in the model are correct and relevant to the problem proposed in the TransLogisTIC case and whether or not the models show a sufficient degree of completeness compared to all the model elements that would be considered relevant and correct. Additionally, the proper notation of the language extension was graded in the form of checking for any illegal links between the modeling constructs (e.g. connecting a BA to the BO) as a measure of syntactic correctness or quality.

In order to have a representation of a model that is considered to be complete, a reference diagram was used as recommended by España et al. [44]. This reference was furnished by Yves Wautelet (see Appendix D), an expert in the context of the modeling notation and case. It is important to note that there is not one single correct model, however for the purpose of this research the reference diagram is considered to be correct and complete provides a high quality solution to the case. Having such a reference allowed the subject's answers to be graded in a consistent way.

Six semantic quality metrics were used to grade the models. The correct identification of the BO (*BO_identification*), the BGs (*BG_identification*), the BOs or goals which were not explicitly stated in the case but would be relevant in its context (*BOBG2_identification*), the BUCs (*BUC_identification*), the links between the BUCs (*BUClinkstoBG*), the business actors and workers (*BABW_identification*) and finally the syntactic metric in the presence of any illegal links between the elements (*Links_illegal*). As said, different interpretations of the case could result in different but equally correct solutions of the case. As a result, respondents could identify more elements in their diagram than there were in the reference one. More points than the reference diagram would have had could be obtained by providing elements that are correct and relevant for the case. This would, however, prove to be exception.

Regarding the BOs, BGs, BUCs and BWs, a point was given for every single correctly represented element (meaning it had the right description and was modeled correctly). Alternatively, a partial score of a half point was given when the modeled element was considered to be correct but not specific enough, overlapping with other elements or when for example a BA was correctly identified but modeled as a BW. The assessment of every single element on a separate basis was done to provide a more detailed score of the modeled elements. As the case proved to be complex, using a more strict method of scoring (e.g. giving zero or one when all use-cases were identified) would likely result in extremely low scores as most respondents would likely not able to replicate the completeness of the reference model. For the assessment of the links between the BUCs and BGs and the presence of illegal links a score was given on one, again with the possibility of receiving partial points. Partial points were for example given when most links were present and correct but some obvious connections were clearly missing or when arrows between elements were pointing the wrong way.

When applying this scoring method to the reference model, a total of 29 points were achievable with a higher score indicating a more complete, correct and thus higher quality model. A problem with simply summing up the points of all the variables was that certain elements like the BAs and BWs would be proportionally too large. To create a global score on 10 that properly measures the modeling of the strategic and tactical levels, the different scores of every variable were thus divided by the scores of the reference model, creating scores for every variable on 1 (or slightly more if respondents managed to be more complete than the reference model). This then allowed the application of weights that could put more importance on the BOs, goals and use-cases, as these are the core of the BUCM. Finally, the scores were converted to ones on 10 (*Quality_score*). An overview of the weights applied can be seen Table 1.

Table 1. Weights of scoring variables

Metrics	Weights
BO Identification	5.5%
BG Identification	22%
BO/BG2 identification	5.5%
BUC Identification	33%
BUC links to BG	11%
BA/BW Identification	11%
Illegal Links	11%

To add validity to the assumption that the total quality score is actually an appropriate indicator of model quality, an additional expert review score (*Expert_review*) of subject's awareness was provided by Yves Wautelet. Each model was independently graded, with a strong focus on correct interpretation and consistency in the models, **not** making use of the reference diagram. A correlation analysis was conducted between the quality score and expert review score with the assumption that if the calculated quality score actually is a good indicator of quality, it should also be highly correlated with the scores given by an expert reviewer.

Clarity of Case Instructions. Once the respondents finished the drawing of their model, they were asked to what extent the case instructions were clear (*case_instructions*) and to what extent the description of the TransLogisTIC case was clear (*case_description*) once again by means of a five-point Likert scale ranging from 1 to 5.

Perceived Ease of Modeling. The perceived difficulty of modeling the different components that make up the BUCM was also surveyed. On a five-point Likert scale respondents were asked to indicate how easy they found the modeling of BOs (*ease_BO*), BGs (*ease_BG*), BUCs (*ease_BUC*), links between BUCs and BG (*ease_BUCtoBG*), business actors and workers (*ease_BA*; *ease_BW*) and identifying the relationships between components (*ease_relationships*).

4   Results

The following two hypothesis are proposed as a basis for the experiment: *H1: If the proposed quality score is a suitable measurement for the model quality, then it will be strongly correlated to the score given by an expert reviewer. H2: Analytical modelers will achieve higher quality scores, compared to intuitive and adaptive modelers, because it is easier for them to follow the structured experiment approach and they are able to process complex information more easily.*

4.1   Respondents' Profile

Background. All 29 respondents (12 females and 17 males) indicated that their main occupation was *student*. When asked about their educational background or highest previous degree, nine respondents indicated having an academic bachelor in business administration with two other respondents having an academic bachelor in business engineering. Five respondents already obtained a master degree with two specializations in digital marketing, one in management and 2 master degrees were unspecified. Twelve students indicated having a professional bachelor with specializations in accountancy & tax (1), business & IT (1), marketing (2), financial management (1), teacher math & economics (1), event management (2), international entrepreneurship (1), logistics (1), office management (1) and two unspecified degrees.

Familiarity with Modeling Variables. As to be expected, not a single student considered themselves to be extremely proficient in any of the three variables presented. The familiarity with the UML is indicated to be at least moderately to very high for 89.7% of respondents with only 3 respondents (10.30%) indicating they were slightly familiar with the UML. Three respondents (10.30%) indicated not being familiar with the business modeling discipline of the RUP at all. The familiarity with the BUCM is moderate overall with 62% of respondents indicating being moderately or very familiar. Eleven respondents (37.90%) claimed to be only slightly familiar with the BUCM.

Cognitive Style of the Respondents. Following the theory presented by [39], 31% of the respondents are intuitive, 34.50% of them adaptive and 34.50% are analytic. Moreover, females are deemed to be more analytical than males. Allinson & Hayes [40] state that this difference in CS between male and female students does occur more often, but tends to reverse when students graduate and enter the workforce.

4.2 Analysis of the Representations

Individual Quality Metrics. This section is focused on the discussion of quality metrics. First, the descriptive statistics are discussed and an analysis per metric between the different CS groups is made. Following this, a correlation analysis of the global quality score and the score given by the expert reviewer is performed which is then followed by testing if any significant differences exist in the quality scores between the different CS groups. This is shown in Table 2.

In a nutshell, regarding the strategic level and identification of the BO, respondents did quite well with a mean of 0.62, indicating that the average respondent got the BO at least partially right. Identifying BGs proved to be a much more difficult task with a mean of 2.09. This means that of the seven BGs that were present in the textual description, respondents on average only managed to model slightly over 2 goals. For most respondents this was the result of confusing the objectives with goals, resulting in overlap of the two metrics. When presented with the question to model two BOs or BGs not explicitly in the text (BO/BG2 identification), respondents managed to find, on average one BO or BG that was relevant and correct in the context of the case. When looking at the tactical level, the modeling of the BUCs produced divergent results. On average respondents managed to model about half of the possible use-cases, however some people did not manage to model a single BUC, whilst other respondents managed to identify 11 BUCs. Linking BUCs to the correct BGs proved difficult as well. Not a single respondent managed to appropriately link their BUCs and BGs. Respondents tended to either draw their links either too fine-grained or course-grained, or simply made clearly false connections. Identifying the different BAs and BWs proved to be the easiest for respondents. The average respondents identified an average of 6.47 BAs and BWs. Finally, most respondents successfully avoided to draw illegal links (e.g.

Table 2. Individual Quality Metrics

	Min	Max	M	SD
BO identification	0	1	0.62	0.42
BG identification	0	6	2.09	1.57
BO/BG2 identification	0	2	0.97	0.84
BUC identification	0	11	4.86	3.65
BUC links to BG	0	0.5	0.17	0.24
BA/BW identification	1	10	6.47	2.87
Illegal links	0	1	0.85	0.36

connecting a business actor to a BO). Most errors were made by either not providing a direction to the links between constructs or simply missing links, causing for example a BUC to not be connected to anything in their model.

Table 3 shows the quality metrics by their respective CS category. A notable difference in the ability to identify the BGs can be seen between the analytical respondents (M = 2.55, SD = 1.54) and intuitive respondents (M = 1.22, SD = 0.97). Another remark is that connecting BUCs to the correct BG clearly did not go well for the intuitive respondents (M = 0.05, SD = 0.17).

In the following subsections the specific variables retained from the different parts of the experiment are specified. The complete experiment can be found in Appendix C, a complete list of variables can be found in Appendix B.

Table 3. Descriptive statistics quality metrics by cognitive style category

Cognitive Style	Intuitive		Adaptive		Analytic	
	M	SD	M	SD	M	SD
BO identification	0.61	0.42	0.55	0.44	0.70	0.42
BG identification	1.22	0.97	2.40	1.82	2.55	1.54
BO/BG2 identification	0.83	0.93	0.95	0.86	1.10	0.77
BUC identification	5.22	3.27	4.40	3.94	5.00	4.00
BUC links to BG	0.05	0.17	0.25	0.26	0.20	0.26
BA/BW Identification	6.61	2.40	5.95	3.01	6.85	3.31
Illegal Links	0.89	0.33	0.90	0.32	0.75	0.42

Total Quality Score. Because simply adding up the scores attained for every separate quality metric would result in certain metrics having too much weight (e.g. the identification of business actors and workers would make up 8 'easy' points of the maximum attainable 29 points), every score was divided by the amount of elements that were present for every metric in the reference model. This then allowed for the usage of weights to be applied to the different metrics and the conversion to a total quality score on 10. Next to this global score, an additional 'expert review' of student's representations score was provided by Yves Wautelet. The use of an expert reviewer can help immensely in assessing the quality of a model [44] and is routinely used in practice. While the calculated total quality score based on the provided quality metrics relies heavily on the semantic quality metrics validity and completeness, the score provided by Wautelet focused more on consistency and correctness of the models. Subsequently, it could be argued that if the correlation between both quality scores is high, it adds reliability and validity to the total quality score variable as a measurement for the quality of the produced representations.

The minimum and maximum for the total quality score were respectively 0.3 and 9.31. For the expert review score this was respectively 1 and 8 out of 10. In Table 4, the means and standard deviations are presented for both all the respondents between the three CS categories. When looking at the means of the total quality score between the

Table 4. Descriptive statistics of total quality score and expert review score. Note that N = 29, scores on 10.

	n	Total quality score		Expert review	
		M	SD	M	SD
All respondents	29	5.11	2.30	5.04	2.16
CSI 3 categories					
Intuitive	9	4.87	1.42	5.39	2.23
Adaptive	10	5.08	2.86	4.35	2.37
Analytic	10	5.37	2.53	5.40	1.93

three CS categories, a slight slope in average score is noticed. Analytic respondents (M = 5.37, SD = 2.53) scored slightly higher on average than adaptive respondents (M = 5.08, SD = 2.86) which in turn scored slightly higher than the intuitive respondents (M = 4.87, SD = 1.42). While this initially looks promising and to be a first indication of support for our second hypotheses, the same cannot be said for the expert review scores. Both the intuitive and adaptive respondents score more than a point higher on average compared to the mean of the adaptive respondent (M = 4.35, SD = 2.37).

Table 5. Pearson correlation analysis total quality score, expert review score and CSI score. Note that N=29, CSI score on scale of 0 to 76. Quality scores on scale from 0 to 10. $*p < 0.1, **p < 0.05, ***p < 0.01$

Variables	(1)	(2)	(3)
(1) Total quality score	1.000		
(2) Expert review score	0.793***	1.000	
(3) CSI score	0.017	0.002	1.000

As can be seen in Table 5, the Pearson correlation between the total quality score and expert review score can be considered to be strong and positive ($r = 0.793$, $p < .001$). No significant correlation was found between the two quality scores and the CSI score. This confirms H1. With both the KS and SW normality tests indicating that the total quality score variable follows a normal distribution, a one one-way ANOVA test can be performed to test whether there is a significant difference in the mean quality scores between the three CS groups. It revealed that there is no statistically significant difference in quality score between the three different CS groups ($F(2, 26) = 0.105$, p = .900). Two more tests were performed in search of a possible significant effect between groups, this time making use of the CS variable with two categories and the expert review score. First, an independent samples t-test was conducted to compare the total quality score for both intuitive and analytic respondents. No significant differences were found ($t(27) = 0.501$, p = .621) in scores for intuitive respondents (M = 5.34, SD = 1.69) and analytical respondents (M = 4.91, SD = 2.79). Because the KS and SW normality tests indicate that the expert review score does not follow a normal distribution, a KW test can be used to test the expert review scores between the three different CS categories. The results of the KW test (H(2) = 1.534, p = .464) indicate that the expert review scores do not differ significantly based on the modelers CS either. After conducting the above tests, H2 cannot be confirmed.

5 Discussion

RQ1: *"How successful are novice modelers in producing tactical and strategic conceptual elements representations and ensuring their in-between traceability when compared to an expert?"*. We can point out that there was some diversity in the ability of novice modelers to effectively produce a valid diagram but that, on average, the score was positive. Also, the proposed method of quality assessment for the produced models correlated strongly with the scores given by the expert reviewer. This indicates that the quality assessment could be deemed appropriate for its purpose.

RQ2: *"Does the CS of a novice modeler have an impact on the quality of their produced tactical and strategic-level BP models?"*. To answer this, it was hypothesized that analytical modelers would be more capable than intuitive and adaptive modelers at producing a high quality model, as a result of being better at gathering and processing complex information and being more at comfort with a methodical, logical approach. The analysis of the data shows that there is a significant difference in the perceived clarity of the experiment case description, as analytical modelers found the TransLogisTIC case description to be more clear than intuitive modelers. However, based on the findings, the significantly higher perceived clarity of the case description that the analytic respondents had did not result in a higher quality of their strategic level BP models compared to their intuitive counterparts.

The rest of this section presents the threats to the validity as presented in [45].

Construct Validity. The choice of the case can impact the results. TranslogisTIC is a rather advanced case with a natural language description, also students are not familiar with industrial work environments can impact the quality of their representations. The results did nevertheless not show too many issues in the modeling process and a total of 5 preliminary tests involving qualitative interviews were made with PhD students in conceptual modeling to envisage the feasibly and pinpoint the potential problems.

Internal Validity. The total paperwork furnished to the subjects was up to 5 pages for the CSI questionnaire, 6 pages for the case description and the questions and 8 for the experiment itself. A documentation and survey of this size can lead to fatigue with subjects finally trying to simply fill-in rather than trying to furnish their best possible answer. This was dealt with through: i) applying correctional penalties for guessing; ii) improving the subject's motivation by the possibility of gaining an additional bonus point on the basis of their performance for a course related to conceptual modeling.

External Validity. The group of respondents that took part in the experiment is composed of students only. While originally 33 respondents took part in the experiment, only 29 cases were ultimately available to analyze due to two respondents not being able to produce a representation and two cases containing missing values in the collected data. The sample size for this research is considered to be extremely low and any (in)significant results should be interpreted carefully as they could and probably should be considered to be unreliable. A second limitation concerning the group of respondents was the fact that every respondent was a student from the same master degree program in business information management, with presumably the same modelling background knowledge. If this experiment was conducted with business professionals, it could very well be that the results of both the BP model quality and modelling experience were significantly different.

6   Conclusion

Different reasons could cause the design of low quality models. One factor, rarely discussed in existing literature is the CS of the modeler creating the model. It is hypothesized, in this research, that analytical respondents would be more capable of producing high quality models as a result of paying more attention to detail and preferring a structured, methodical approach to dealing with complex descriptions. To test whether the CS had an effect on the quality of produced strategic BP models, an experiment was conducted. There were no significant differences between the familiarity of modeling between the three CS and all respondents were considered to be slightly to moderately familiar with modeling in general. The clarity of the theory provided, the perceived ease of modeling the case, the perceived usefulness and ease of use of the BUCM method all did not differ significantly between intuitive, adaptive or analytical respondents.

The main conclusions from this analysis are threefold. First, the proposed method of quality assessment for the produced models, correlated strongly with the scores given by the expert reviewer. This indicates that the quality assessment could be deemed appropriate for its purpose. Second, there was a significant difference found between the perceived clarity of the case description between intuitive and analytical respondents. The analytical respondents found the case description to be more clear. This, however, did not result in any significant difference in the quality of the models that were produced by analytical respondents compared to intuitive respondents, nor in any difference between the three categories. In conclusion, the effect of CS on the quality of produced strategic-level BP models did not present itself in this research, however due to the caveat of limited sample size, definitive conclusions should not be drawn and further research regarding this topic should be pursued.

References

1. Alotaibi, Y.: Business process modelling challenges and solutions: a literature review. J. Intell. Manuf. **27**(4), 701–723 (2016)
2. Wautelet, Y.: A model-driven it governance process based on the strategic impact evaluation of services. J. Syst. Softw. **149**, 462–475 (2019)
3. Aysolmaz, B., Reijers, H.A.: Use cases for understanding business process models. In: Dubois, E., Pohl, K. (eds.) CAiSE 2017. LNCS, vol. 10253, pp. 428–442. Springer, Cham (2017). https://doi.org/10.1007/978-3-319-59536-8_27

4. Figl, K., Recker, J.: Exploring cognitive style and task-specific preferences for process representations. Req. Eng. **21**(1), 63–85 (2016)
5. de Oca, I.M.-M., Snoeck, M., Reijers, H.A., Rodríguez-Morffi, A.: A systematic literature review of studies on business process modeling quality. Inf. SW Tech. **58**, 187–205 (2015)
6. Oppl, S.: Which concepts do inexperienced modelers use to model work?-an exploratory study. In: Proceedings of MKWI 2018 (2018)
7. Turetken, O., Vanderfeesten, I., Claes, J.: Cognitive style and business process model understanding. In: Metzger, A., Persson, A. (eds.) CAiSE 2017. LNBIP, vol. 286, pp. 72–84. Springer, Cham (2017). https://doi.org/10.1007/978-3-319-60048-2_7
8. Bolloju, N., Leung, F.S.: Assisting novice analysts in developing quality conceptual models with UML. Commun. ACM **49**(7), 108–112 (2006)
9. Dhillon, M.K., Dasgupta, S.: Individual differences and conceptual modeling task performance: examining the effects of cognitive style, self-efficacy, and application domain knowledge. In: Halpin, T., et al. (eds.) BPMDS/EMMSAD 2011. LNBIP, vol. 81, pp. 483–496. Springer, Heidelberg (2011). https://doi.org/10.1007/978-3-642-21759-3_35
10. Eric, S.: Social Modeling for Requirements Engineering. MIT Press, Cambridge (2011)
11. Van Lamsweerde, A.: Requirements Engineering: From System Goals to UML Models to Software, vol. 10. Wiley, Chichester (2009)
12. O. UML, OMG (2017) unified modeling language version 2.5.1 (2017)
13. Wahli, U., et al.: Building SOA solutions using the rational SDP. IBM (2007)
14. Johnston, S., et al.: Rational UML profile for business modeling. IBM Developer Works (2004). http://www.ibm.com/developerworks/rational/library/5167.html
15. Wautelet, Y., Poelmans, S.: Aligning the elements of the RUP/UML business use-case model and the BPMN business process diagram. In: Grünbacher, P., Perini, A. (eds.) REFSQ 2017. LNCS, vol. 10153, pp. 22–30. Springer, Cham (2017). https://doi.org/10.1007/978-3-319-54045-0_2
16. Wautelet, Y.: Using the RUP/UML business use case model for service development governance: a business and IT alignment based approach. In: 22nd IEEE Conference on Business Informatics, CBI, pp. 121–130. IEEE (2020)
17. Monsalve, C., April, A., Abran, A.: Business process modeling with levels of abstraction. In: IEEE Colombian Conference on Communication and Computing (IEEE COLCOM 2015), pp. 1–6. IEEE (2015)
18. Wautelet, Y., Poelmans, S.: An integrated enterprise modeling framework using the RUP/UML business use-case model and BPMN. In: Poels, G., Gailly, F., Serral Asensio, E., Snoeck, M. (eds.) PoEM 2017. LNBIP, vol. 305, pp. 299–315. Springer, Cham (2017). https://doi.org/10.1007/978-3-319-70241-4_20
19. Weske, M.: Business Process Management Architectures. Springer, Cham (2007)
20. Monsalve, C., April, A., Abran, A.: Requirements elicitation using BPM notations: focusing on the strategic level representation. ACACOS **11**, 235–241 (2011)
21. von Rosing, M., White, S., Cummins, F., de Man, H.: Business process model and notation-BPMN (2015)
22. Fettke, P.: How conceptual modeling is used. Commun. Assoc. Inf. Syst. **25**(1), 43 (2009)
23. Dzepina, A., Lehner, F.: Business process model quality-results from a SLR (2018)
24. Reijers, H.A., Freytag, T., Mendling, J., Eckleder, A.: Syntax highlighting in business process models. Decis. Support Syst. **51**(3), 339–349 (2011)
25. De Meyer, P., Claes, J.: An overview of process model quality literature-the comprehensive process model quality framework. arXiv preprint arXiv:1808.07930 (2018)
26. Krogstie, J.: A semiotic approach to quality in requirements specifications. In: Liu, K., Clarke, R.J., Andersen, P.B., Stamper, R.K., Abou-Zeid, E.-S. (eds.) Organizational Semiotics. ITIFIP, vol. 94, pp. 231–249. Springer, Boston (2002). https://doi.org/10.1007/978-0-387-35611-2_14

27. Krogstie, J.: Evaluating UML using a generic quality framework. In: UML and the Unified Process, pp. 1–22. IGI Global (2003)
28. Lindland, O.I., Sindre, G., Solvberg, A.: Understanding quality in conceptual modeling. IEEE Softw. **11**(2), 42–49 (1994)
29. Krogstie, J., Sindre, G., Jørgensen, H.: Process models representing knowledge for action: a revised quality framework. Eur. J. Inf. Syst. **15**(1), 91–102 (2006)
30. Nelson, H.J., Poels, G., Genero, M., Piattini, M.: A conceptual modeling quality framework. SW Qual. J. **20**(1), 201–228 (2012)
31. Moody, D.L., Sindre, G., Brasethvik, T., Solvberg, A.: Evaluating the quality of information models: empirical testing of a conceptual model quality framework. In: Proceedings of the 25th International Conference on SW Engineering, pp. 295–305. IEEE (2003)
32. Krogstie, J., Lindland, O.I., Sindre, G.: Defining quality aspects for conceptual models. In: Falkenberg, E.D., Hesse, W., Olivé, A. (eds.) Information System Concepts. IAICT, pp. 216–231. Springer, Boston, MA (1995). https://doi.org/10.1007/978-0-387-34870-4_22
33. Frederiks, P.J., Van der Weide, T.P.: Information modeling: the process and the required competencies of its participants. Data Knowl. Eng. **58**(1), 4–20 (2006)
34. Rosemann, M.: Potential pitfalls of process modeling: part A. BPM J. (2006)
35. Mendling, J., Reijers, H.A., Cardoso, J.: What makes process models understandable? In: Alonso, G., Dadam, P., Rosemann, M. (eds.) BPM 2007. LNCS, vol. 4714, pp. 48–63. Springer, Heidelberg (2007). https://doi.org/10.1007/978-3-540-75183-0_4
36. Mendling, J., Neumann, G., van der Aalst, W.: Understanding the occurrence of errors in process models based on metrics. In: Meersman, R., Tari, Z. (eds.) OTM 2007. LNCS, vol. 4803, pp. 113–130. Springer, Heidelberg (2007). https://doi.org/10.1007/978-3-540-76848-7_9
37. Mendling, J., Verbeek, H., van Dongen, B.F., van der Aalst, W.M., Neumann, G.: Detection and prediction of errors in EPCs of the SAP ref. model. Data Knwl. Eng. **64**(1), 312–329 (2008)
38. Mendling, J.: Metrics for Process Models. LNBIP, vol. 6. Springer, Heidelberg (2008). https://doi.org/10.1007/978-3-540-89224-3
39. Allinson, C.W., Hayes, J.: The cognitive style index: a measure of intuition-analysis for organizational research. J. Manag. Stud. **33**(1), 119–135 (1996)
40. Allinson, C., Hayes, J.: The cognitive style index: technical manual and user guide (2012)
41. Ornstein, R.E.: The psychology of consciousness (1972)
42. Wautelet, Y.: Representing, modeling and engineering a collaborative supply chain management platform. Int. J. Inf. Syst. Supply Chain Manag. **5**(3), 1–23 (2012)
43. Wautelet, Y., Kolp, M., Penserini, L.: Service-driven iterative software project management with I-Tropos. J. Univers. Comput. Sci. **24**(7), 975–1011 (2018)
44. España, S., Condori-Fernandez, N., González, A., Pastor, Ó.: Evaluating the completeness and granularity of functional requirements specifications: a controlled experiment. In: 2009 17th IEEE International Requirements Engineering Conference, pp. 161–170. IEEE (2009)
45. Wohlin, C., Runeson, P., Höst, M., Ohlsson, M.C., Regnell, B., Wesslén, A.: Experimentation in Software Engineering. Springer, Cham (2012). https://doi.org/10.1007/978-3-642-29044-2

Demonstrations Track

EDOC 2023 Demonstrations Track

Fadi Mohsen[1] and Stefan Schönig[2]

[1]University of Groningen, Groningen, The Netherlands
`f.f.m.mohsen@rug.nl`
[2]University of Regensburg, Regensburg, Germany
`stefan.schoenig@ur.de`

We are thrilled to introduce and enhance the Demonstration Track of the EDOC conference. This track presents an exceptional opportunity for researchers, practitioners, and innovators to exhibit their state-of-the-art solutions, prototypes, and practical implementations in the dynamic realm of Enterprise Design, Operations, and Computing.

The Demonstration Track stands as a vibrant platform, facilitating the exchange of valuable insights, innovative ideas, and the cultivation of collaborative relationships among the conference attendees. It perfectly complements the research presentations by providing a hands-on experience, thus bridging the gap between theoretical concepts and real-world applications. Participants have the chance to immerse themselves in interactive demonstrations, gaining a deeper understanding of the showcased advancements and fostering an environment of productive learning and growth.

Acknowledgments. We extend our gratitude to all authors who dedicated their time and expertise to prepare these engaging demonstrations. Their efforts play a pivotal role in enhancing the conference experience for all participants.

Furthermore, we extend our heartfelt gratitude to the esteemed members of the Program Committee for their invaluable contributions to the review process of the demos. Your dedication, expertise, and meticulous assessments have played a pivotal role in maintaining the high standards of quality and relevance that our conference upholds.

Demonstrations Track Organization

Demonstrations Track Chairs

Fadi Mohsen   University of Groningen, The Netherlands
Stefan Schönig   University of Regensburg, Germany

Program Committee

Agnes Koschmider   Kiel University, Germany
Martin Käppel   Universität Bayreuth, Germany
Leo Poss   University Regensburg, Germany
Stefan Schönig   University of Regensburg, Germany
Francesca Zerbato   University of St. Gallen, Switzerland

A Distributed In-Car Massage Application Based on Eclipse Chariott

Kevin Klein[1,2], Alexander Walz[1], and Steffen Becker[2]

[1] Mercedes-Benz AG, Sindelfingen, Germany
kevin.klein@iste.uni-stuttgart.de, alexander.walz@mercedes-benz.com
[2] Institute of Software Engineering, University of Stuttgart, Stuttgart, Germany
steffen.becker@iste.uni-stuttgart.de

Abstract. With the steadily increasing amount of software in modern cars, traditional electric/electronic (E/E) architectures reach their limit when it comes to deploying complex applications, which often require the integration of various sensors, processing units, and software components, as well as higher bandwidth and processing power. To cope with this issue, more powerful computing platforms are being employed. One of the many new software projects that try to solve the challenges associated with these new platforms is Chariott, which provides a metadata-driven communication middleware that fosters the communication of distributed in-car applications through a common interface. Software components can register with Chariott to advertise their functionality. Software components that are registered with Chariott, referred to as providers, can then be found via service discovery. Alternatively, Chariott offers an intent-based approach where a broker maintains a mapping of intents and providers that can fulfill requests for these intents. Contrary to interfaces that define required implementation details, intents capture only the high-level purpose of a request as well as the required data. In this demo paper, we present our massage seat use case that was specifically designed to evaluate the suitability of Chariott for distributed in-car applications as well as our evaluation results.

Keywords: In-Car Applications · Eclipse Chariott · Distributed Systems · Service-Oriented Architecture

1 Introduction

The rapid growth regarding the amount of software in cars started already more than fifteen years ago [2]. This trend continues and the current electric/electronic (E/E) architectures, based on dedicated electronic control units (ECUs), are not capable of meeting the increasing requirements of complex applications like advanced driver assistance systems (see Shaout et al. [7] for an overview of ADAS systems). Hence, newer architectures will incorporate embedded high-performance computing (eHPC) platforms [1]. Such eHPC platforms

T. P. Sales et al. (Eds.): EDOC 2023 Workshops, LNBIP 498, pp. 319–324, 2024.
https://doi.org/10.1007/978-3-031-54712-6_19

offer more computing power than traditional ECUs. Since such platforms usually comprise multiple eHPCs interlinked by some networking technology, each is likely assigned a different functionality. Consequently, deploying the involved software components where most effective is possible and complex features will be designed as distributed applications introducing related challenges like service discovery to the in-vehicle application development domain.

Eclipse Software Defined Vehicle [5] (Eclipse SDV) is a working group that focuses on providing a platform for the development of software as the basis for a scalable, modular, extensible, industry-ready vehicle software platform provided under an open-source license. To this end, the members of the working group can contribute software projects that aim to solve individual challenges. Eclipse Chariott [3] is a project organized within Eclipse SDV that provides a metadata-driven middleware that offers a common way to access the cars' hardware and sensors and provides a way for consumers to discover available functionality. Since Chariott is a new project, there are currently no known real-world scenarios where Chariott has been employed as a communication middleware and thus there is a lack of evaluation that further motivates our investigation.

Chariott implements the service-oriented architecture (SOA) paradigm, where service providers publish their services through a service discovery. Clients, which Chariott refers to as applications, can then look up these services [4]. To this extent, Chariott implements two approaches: (i) plain service discovery and (ii) intent-based brokering. Providers can register with Chariott by providing a namespace as well as additional metadata required for communication, e.g., the endpoint for direct communication with the provider. The registered providers can then be looked up by their namespace in order to open a direct communication channel. Furthermore, providers can specify the intents they support when they register. Chariott maintains a mapping of namespace and intent to the provider that can fulfill requests for that intent. Whenever a fulfillment request for a specific namespace and intent is sent to Chariott, the request is brokered and forwarded to the correct provider accordingly. Currently, Chariott supports the following intents:

- **Discover:** The discover intent can be used to retrieve the native interfaces of a provider. This is useful in case direct communication is preferred or even required, e.g., to minimize latency. Also, this intent has to be used in order to retrieve the streaming endpoint since Chariott does not support brokered streaming of events.
- **Inspect:** The inspect intent can be used to retrieve functionality, properties, and events of a provider.
- **Invoke:** The invoke intent can be used to invoke a method on a provider. In comparison to direct communication based on the result of a service discovery, the request is brokered through Chariott.
- **Subscribe:** When a streaming channel is opened by calling the native streaming endpoint of the provider a channel id is returned. In order to receive events through the channel identified by that id, a fulfillment request for the subscribe intent has to be sent.

- **Read:** The read intent can be used to read the value of a provider's property.
- **Write:** The write intent can be used to write a property to a provider.

To evaluate the suitability of Chariott for distributed in-car applications, we implemented an automotive scenario using Eclipse Chariott as communication middleware. The scenario was specifically designed to make use of multiple ECUs and is, thus, being used for validation purposes in this paper. Overall, we want to determine whether employing Chariott is an alternative to hard-wiring all of the involved software components.

2 System Overview and Use Case

The system architecture of our demonstration is depicted in Fig. 1. We chose a user-controllable massage seat as an evaluation basis for Eclipse Chariott. The seat contains a set of addressable air-filled bubbles with a modifiable filling level. Changing the filling level of specific bubbles over time creates the massage sequence. In a car, user-facing functionality is driven by a display. In our use case, this display is simulated by a web front end. Its main tasks are (i) to display a list of sequences that are available, (ii) to offer a button that starts a specific massage sequence from that list, and (iii) to visualize a changing filling level for verification purposes. The available sequences are stored on a controller. Its task is to return a list of available sequences to the display upon request and to initiate a specific massage sequence when requested through the display. The communication with the actual hardware happens through the Hardware Abstraction Layer (HAL). The actual seat is replaced by a seat simulation covering the required seat functionality. In summary, our application conceptually consists of four parts: (1) the web front end with the simulated display, (2) the Controller, (3) the Seat-Mock, and (4) the HAL. In a production environment, the events that reflect the changes concerning the air-filled bubbles would be brokered through the HAL as well. To simplify the implementation and because of the current architecture of Chariott, the described design was applied instead. The Controller has been implemented in Go whereas Python has been chosen as the programming language for the Seat-Mock and the HAL.

For the implementation, we define the following requirements: (i) Since not every car has a massage seat, our web front end must be capable of rendering a state where no massage functionality is available. Also, it must be possible to detect when such functionality becomes available and to react accordingly. (ii) Changes regarding the filling level of the air-filled bubbles must be made available in the correct order and with the delay between the individual steps taken into account. (iii) The list of available sequences must be available to the web front end. (iv) The web front end must be able to start the playback of an individual sequence.

The detection of the availability of the massage functionality has been implemented by regularly issuing a fulfillment request for the discover intent until the Seat-Mock becomes available. As soon as the service discovery of the massage functionality returned the Seat-Mock, the web front end renders the massage

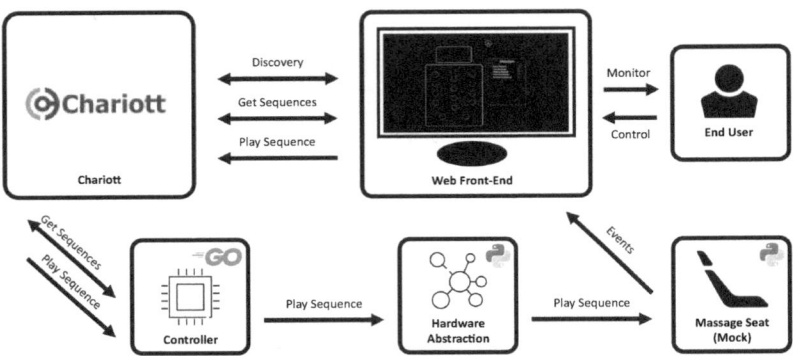

Fig. 1. Architecture and components of the massage seat use case.

functionality and needs to retrieve a list of available sequences. To this end, a fulfillment request with the invoke intent is issued to Chariott with the command name and potential parameters as metadata. Chariott then redirects the request to the Controller and returns the response with the list of available sequences back to the web front end. Starting a specific massage sequence is handled in the same fashion. As soon as a massage sequence is started, the Seat-Mock sends updates regarding the filling levels of the air-filled bubbles via the streaming channel to the web front end. This way, the delay between the individual steps of the massage sequence can be taken into account.

3 Discussion

Our goal was to evaluate whether Chariott can support the implementation of a distributed in-car application. Overall, it was possible to implement our massage seat use case based on Chariott as an alternative to hard-wiring all the components. Although the implementation was overall possible and Chariott implements useful concepts, we identified limitations that leave room for improvement.

Currently, Chariott does not offer a way to detect when new functionality becomes available. For this use case, this restriction was bypassed by regularly issuing a fulfillment request for the discover intent until the Seat-Mock is included in the response. The Seat-Mock has been chosen as a marker for the availability because the communication metadata of the Seat-Mock that is returned with the response is required later. Since service providers have to register with Chariott and Chariott is thus aware of new services as they register, Chariott can notify applications using well-established paradigms like pub/sub.

Furthermore, to receive sensor data via event streaming, Chariott requires that a direct communication channel between the application and the service provider is opened. This involves that the endpoint of the service provider is extracted from the response to the fulfillment request with the discover intent.

For more complex scenarios, this means that an application will need to maintain more than one streaming channel to receive all events it is interested in. The request brokering approach of Chariott can be extended such that events are also brokered between service providers and applications. Comparably, Guner et al. [6] propose a software architecture for context-aware IoT application development that employs a message broker to communication between requestors and providers. Additionally, receiving events requires a fulfillment request with the subscribe intent per opened channel and event source. When brokering events through Chariott, the amount of these requests can be reduced.

4   Conclusion and Outlook

We present our distributed in-car massage application that uses the Eclipse SDV project Chariott as communication middleware. Our goal was to evaluate whether employing Chariott as communication middleware can replace the hard-wiring of all of the involved software components. Chariott offers support for service discovery but can also act as a message broker. Our use case comprises four software components and was used to evaluate both concepts. Remote procedure calls to retrieve the available sequences were brokered through Chariott, whereas service discovery was used to determine the availability of the massage functionality in general, as well as the endpoints of software components that require direct communication. Overall, it was possible to replace the hard-wiring of the components with Chariott as communication middleware. Although Chariott implements useful concepts, there is still room left for improvement.

As a next step, Chariott could integrate a message broker to allow applications to subscribe to events of a provider without having to discover its endpoint upfront. This mechanism could also be used to inform applications about the availability of services after they register themselves with Chariott.

Furthermore, this evaluation did not cover all aspects that are relevant when applying a communication middleware technology in real-world scenarios. Further investigation could cover aspects related to the fields of security, latency, and scalability as well.

Acknowledgements. This publication was partially funded by the German Federal Ministry for Economic Affairs and Climate Action (BMWK) as part of the Software-Defined Car (SofDCar) project (19S21002).

References

1. Bello, L.L., Mariani, R., Mubeen, S., Saponara, S.: Recent advances and trends in on-board embedded and networked automotive systems. IEEE Trans. Ind. Inf. **15**(2), 1038–1051 (2019). https://doi.org/10.1109/tii.2018.2879544
2. Broy, M.: Challenges in automotive software engineering. In: Proceedings of the 28th International Conference on Software Engineering, ICSE 2006, pp. 33–42 (2006)
3. Eclipse Foundation: Chariott. https://sdv.eclipse.org. Accessed 26 Apr 2023

4. Eclipse Foundation: Chariott design specification. https://github.com/eclipse/chariott/blob/main/docs/design/README.md. Accessed 26 Apr 2023

5. Eclipse Foundation: Software Defined Vehicle. https://sdv.eclipse.org. Accessed 26 Apr 2023

6. Guner, A., Kurtel, K., Celikkan, U.: A message broker based architecture for context aware IoT application development. In: 2017 International Conference on Computer Science and Engineering (UBMK), pp. 233–238 (2017). https://doi.org/10.1109/UBMK.2017.8093381

7. Shaout, A., Colella, D., Awad, S.: Advanced driver assistance systems - past, present and future. In: 2011 Seventh International Computer Engineering Conference (ICENCO 2011), pp. 72–82 (2011). https://doi.org/10.1109/ICENCO.2011.6153935

Enabling 3D Simulation in ThingsBoard: A First Step Towards A Digital Twin Platform

Massimo Callisto De Donato, Flavio Corradini, Fabrizio Fornari[✉],
Barbara Re, and Matteo Romagnoli

School of Science and Technology, Computer Science Department,
University of Camerino, Via Madonna delle Carceri, 7, Camerino, Italy
{massimo.callisto,flavio.corradini,fabrizio.fornari,barbara.re,
matteo.romagnoli}@unicam.it

Abstract. Digital twin platforms enable the creation, management, and analysis of digital twins. However, most of the available platforms are distributed as proprietary software. Considering that available digital twin platforms often generate from former IoT platforms and that visualization and simulation are among the main characteristics of digital twins, we present an extension we developed to the ThingsBoard open-source IoT platform to support the design and development of 3D simulations. Here, we describe such a simulation mechanism and its application on a smart classroom use case. Our work represents a first step towards an open-source digital twin platform.

Keywords: digital twin · digital twin platform · 3D simulation

1 Introduction and Motivation

A digital twin is a virtual representation of a physical object, process, or system. It uses real-time data and simulations to mimic the behavior, characteristics, and interactions of its real-world counterpart [5,6].

The concept of a digital twin allows organizations to gain insights into the performance, maintenance, and optimization of physical assets and processes. It brings together various technologies, such as the Internet of Things (IoT), data analytics, artificial intelligence (AI), and cloud computing, to create a comprehensive and dynamic representation of the physical entity in the digital realm.

A digital twin platform is a technology solution that enables the creation, management, and analysis of digital twin models [8]. Essentially, Digital Twin platforms allow to combine data retrieved from the physical entity with the models that represent the physical entity. Several models can be defined to describe the physical entity such as *3D models, behavioral models, physical models, mathematical models*, etc. Through interactive controls, users can manipulate the digital counterpart, explore different perspectives, and gain a better understanding of its

T. P. Sales et al. (Eds.): EDOC 2023 Workshops, LNBIP 498, pp. 325–330, 2024.
https://doi.org/10.1007/978-3-031-54712-6_20

structure and functioning. In addition, those kind of models enable the possibility to conduct simulations to test various scenarios and identify potential issues before they occur in the physical world. In fact, by simulating the behavior of the physical entities, in different conditions and scenarios, users can predict how the entities will behave before implementing any change or making any decision. We report in Fig. 1 a conceptual representation of a Digital Twin Platform.

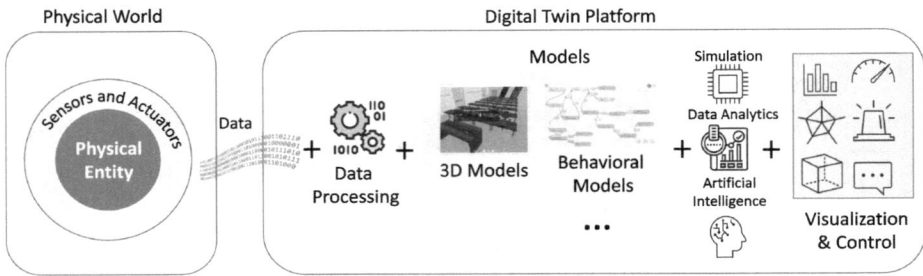

Fig. 1. Concept of a Digital Twin Platform

Several Digital Twin platforms have started to appear in the market such as *Azure Digital Twins*, *AWS IoT TwinMaker*, *iTwin Bentley*, and many others. They often generate from former IoT platforms and have different characteristics and provide different supports for Digital Twins [7,8]. However, to the best of our knowledge, a comprehensive open-source DT platform is not made available yet [4]. It is towards the development of such a DT platform that in this work we present an extension of the ThingsBoard IoT platform[1], to start integrating some of the main features of Digital Twins, especially referring to the support for 3D simulation. As recognized by recent works, ThingsBoard is among the most well-known open-source platforms for IoT applications [2,3], it provides a powerful set of tools for building and managing connected devices and applications. The platform implements a wide range of functionalities (device integration, big data storage, data processing, visualizations) defined to support both developers and businesses to quickly create scalable IoT solutions without the need for extensive coding. Thingsboard has been recognized as a good candidate for supporting digital twins [1]. Especially, it has been compared with other platforms and it emerged that ThingsBoard already implements a good portion of digital twin characteristics, but with a limited support for visualization and simulation [1]. Therefore, we extended ThingsBoard by adding the possibility to support and visualize 3D models associated with digital entities registered in the platform and with the possibility to design and execute 3D simulations.

The rest of the paper is structured as follows. Section 2 describes in detail the 3D simulation mechanism we defined. Section 3 describes the steps necessary to design a 3D simulation. Finally, Sect. 4 closes by reporting concluding remarks.

---

[1] https://thingsboard.io/.

2 3D Simulation with ThingsBoard

The 3D simulation design and execution rely on a *simulation widget* we developed. The widget allows to create and simulate real-world scenarios and analyze the behavior of IoT systems in a virtual environment. ThingsBoard widgets[2] are additional UI modules that easily integrate into any dashboard that can be created in ThingsBoard. They provide end-user functions such as data visualization, remote device control, alarms management, and display of static custom HTML content. ThingsBoard allows also the development and integration of customized widgets that add functionalities to the platform. Figure 2 represents the 3D simulation widget with the various components involved in the design and execution of a 3D simulation.

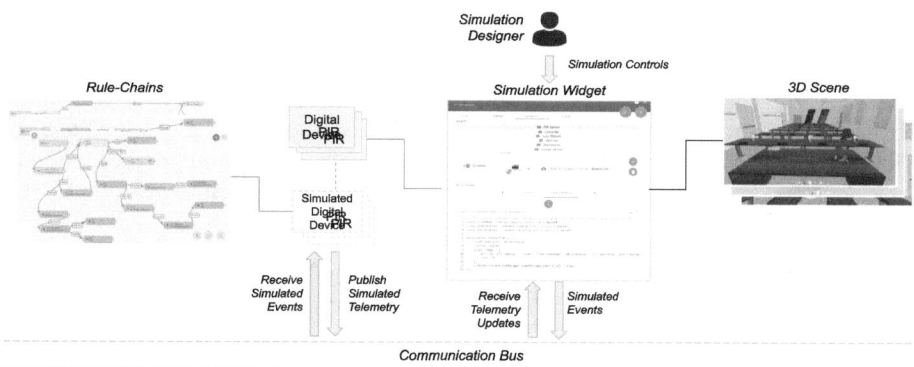

Fig. 2. Schematization of the 3D Simulation Mechanism.

ThingsBoard has a mechanism to define digital representations of IoT devices, we refer to them as *Digital Devices*. Such digital devices are enriched with attributes, treated as key-value pairs, that describe characteristics of the physical device such as *name, description, firmware version, latitude, longitude,* etc. In addition, telemetry data coming from the physical devices can be associated with the digital devices, i.e., in the case of an HVAC system such telemetry data can regard *temperature, humidity, status* (on/off), etc.

Among the components required to design and run a 3D simulation, we also included *Simulated Digital Devices*, see Fig. 2. Those devices inherit all the characteristics of digital devices, but they are the ones actually used for running the simulations. This distinction is required to avoid simulated telemetry data from overwriting real telemetries coming from the physical world and reflected on the digital device.

For creating a 3D simulation, the *Simulation Designer* needs to specify the digital devices and the simulated digital devices that he would like to involve

---

[2] https://thingsboard.io/docs/user-guide/ui/widget-library/.

in the simulation. Then, by means of the 3D simulation widget, the user can design a 3D simulation including the digital devices reported on the ThingsBoard platform. Some familiarity with the Three.js[3] library used for designing the *3D Scene* as well as the cannon-es[4] library used for handling the physics is required.

The device behavior is simulated by means of the ThingsBoard *rule engine* which is a tool for processing and analyzing data generated by physical devices and associated with digital ones. It allows users to define complex rules, named *Rule-Chains* in terms of connected control flows where certain conditions can trigger specific actions based on the data received. In our case, we proposed adopting such a tool for encoding the behavior of a digital device and associating such behavior to a simulated digital device.

When a simulation is activated by a user, simulated events in the simulated environment may occur. Such simulated events are published on a *communication bus* and received by the corresponding simulated digital devices which handle the event by updating their telemetry. If a rule-chain that predicates on that event is available then the rule-chain fires and the simulated behavior of the simulated digital device starts. Also, the execution of a rule-chain might cause the update of some telemetries associated with the simulated digital device. Such telemetries are then published on the communication bus and received by the simulation widget that will reflect those updates in the simulated environment.

3   Use Case

We used ThingsBoard and the 3D simulation mechanism previously introduced to simulate a smart classroom scenario inspired by the SAFE project [9] which involves smart furniture equipped with PIR devices for the detection of people in case of a seismic event.

By following the mechanism defined in Sect. 2 we first created the digital devices that represent the physical PIR devices of the SAFE scenario (*PIR-1*, *PIR-2*, and *PIR-3* in Fig. 3 part-a). Then, we defined the corresponding simulated digital devices (*SIM-PIR-1*, *SIM-PIR-2*, and *SIM-PIR-3*) to which we associated the simulated behavior encoded as ThingsBoard rule-chains.

To instantiate the widget, we followed the ThingsBoard's standard approach which required us to create a new dashboard specifying the digital devices we wanted to use in the simulation. Then, we added the new instance of the 3D simulation widget and we started the design process. In Fig. 3 part-b, we reported the widget configuration that we defined acting as *simulation designers* which includes the import of the 3D models[5] and the coding of the simulation scenario.

Using the 3D models of the devices and of the environment these devices populate (a classroom), we designed, by means of scripting, a 3D scene like the one reported in Fig. 4 and we programmed parts of its behavior to drive the

---

[3] https://threejs.org/.

[4] https://pmndrs.github.io/cannon-es/.

[5] 3D models have been created by means of third-party tools such as Blender and exported in glTF format.

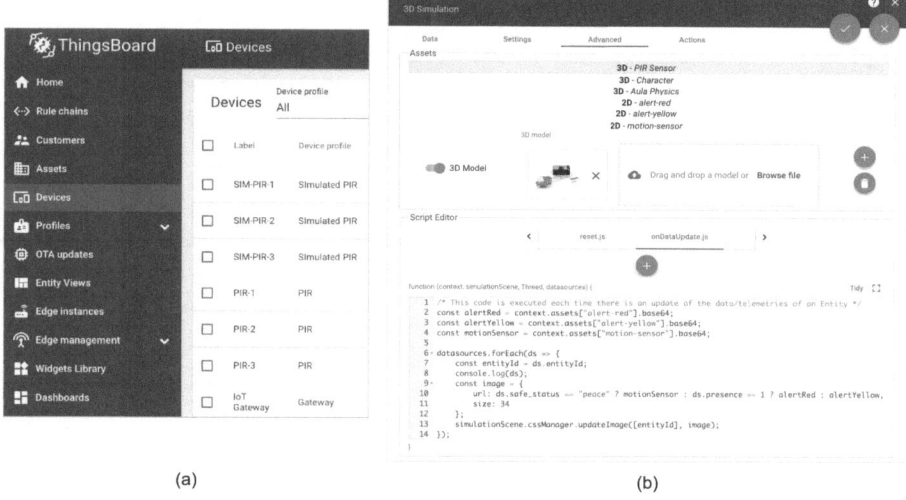

Fig. 3. Design a 3D Simulation with ThingsBoard: a) reports a list of digital devices and simulated digital devices; b) reports the configuration of the 3D simulation widget.

simulation's execution. In our use case, as shown in Fig. 5, the scene we designed intends to simulate the occurrence of a seismic event showing the change in the behavior of the simulated PIR devices when the presence of a person taking shelter under the smart furniture is detected. This kind of simulation allows for rapid prototyping of possible classroom scenarios, envisioning different furniture dispositions or different positions of the PIR devices. Especially, the simulation enabled us to evaluate the PIR behavior by inspecting the rule chains execution, assessing whether the devices behaved as expected.

Fig. 4. 3D model of the scene   **Fig. 5.** Running 3D simulation

4   Conclusion and Future Work

We presented a 3D simulation mechanism for extending the ThingsBoard platform so to start its transition towards a digital twin platform. A user can design his own 3D simulation of a cyber-physical system, include the digital devices of interest, and start the simulation from real telemetry data. We have shown the steps necessary to implement a 3D simulation by means of a smart classroom use case. Currently, designing a graphical simulation requires programming skills, therefore we envision to define alternative approaches to facilitate this step. We also plan to conduct an evaluation with users. Further details and the source code are available at https://pros.unicam.it/digitaltwin/dtplatform. A screencast showing the design of the 3D simulation introduced in this paper is available at https://youtu.be/up2fwEMH7Vg.

Acknowledgements. This work has been partially supported by the European Union - NextGenerationEU - National Recovery and Resilience Plan, Mission 4 Education and Research - Component 2 From research to business - Investment 1.5, ECS_00000041-VITALITY - Innovation, digitalisation and sustainability for the diffused economy in Central Italy.

References

1. Corradini, F., Fedeli, A., Fornari, F., Polini, A., Re, B.: DTMN a modelling notation for digital twins. In: Sales, T.P., Proper, H.A., Guizzardi, G., Montali, M., Maggi, F.M., Fonseca, C.M. (eds.) EDOC 2022. LNBIP, vol. 466, pp. 63–78. Springer, Cham (2022). https://doi.org/10.1007/978-3-031-26886-1_4
2. Corradini, F., Fedeli, A., Fornari, F., Polini, A., Re, B.: FloWare: a model-driven approach fostering reuse and customisation in IoT applications modelling and development. Softw. Syst. Model. **22**, 1–28 (2022)
3. Corradini, F., Fedeli, A., Fornari, F., Polini, A., Re, B., Ruschioni, L.: X-IoT: a model-driven approach to support IoT application portability across IoT platforms. Computing **105**, 1–25 (2023)
4. Fei, T., et al.: makeTwin: a reference architecture for digital twin software platform. Chinese J. Aeronaut. **37**, 1–18 (2023)
5. Grieves, M.: Intelligent digital twins and the development and management of complex systems. Digital Twin **2**(8), 1–8 (2022)
6. Grieves, M., Vickers, J.: Digital twin: mitigating unpredictable, undesirable emergent behavior in complex systems. In: Kahlen, J., Flumerfelt, S., Alves, A. (eds.) Transdisciplinary Perspectives on Complex Systems: New Findings and Approaches, pp. 85–113. Springer, Cham (2017). https://doi.org/10.1007/978-3-319-38756-7_4
7. Lehner, D., Pfeiffer, J., Tinsel, E., Strljic, M.M., Sint, S., Vierhauser, M., Wortmann, A., Wimmer, M.: Digital twin platforms: requirements, capabilities, and future prospects. IEEE Softw. **39**(2), 53–61 (2022)
8. Pfeiffer, J., Lehner, D., Wortmann, A., Wimmer, M.: Modeling capabilities of digital twin platforms - old wine in new bottles? J. Object Technol. **21**(3), 3:1–14 (2022)
9. Pietroni, L., Mascitti, J., Galloppo, D., et al.: The SAFE project: an interdisciplinary and intersectoral approach to innovation in Furniture Design. In: DS 118: Proceedings of NordDesign 2022, Copenhagen, Denmark, 16th-18th August 2022, pp. 1–12 (2022)

Adaptive Process Log Generation and Analysis with *Next(Log)* and *ML.Log*

Dyllan Cartwright[✉], Radu Andrei Sterie[✉],
Arash Yadegari Ghahderijani[✉][iD], and Dimka Karastoyanova[✉][iD]

Information Systems Group, University of Groningen, Groningen, The Netherlands
{a.yadegari.ghahderijani,d.karastoyanova}@rug.nl

Abstract. In this paper we present a tool for adaptive process log generation and analysis of the correlation between KPI (Key Performance Indicator) values and changes in adaptive processes. The tool features a component called *Next(Log)* helping users to generate initial business process logs using any preferred method and subsequently allows them to adapt these logs based on their own defined rules while ensuring an intuitive and coherent user interface. The adapted logs are then used for log analysis with the *ML.Log* component, which employs machine learning techniques to find patterns of matching KPI values and adaptation injections in the logs. The tool therefore supports the research on the challenges imposed by the lack of sufficient amount of data from adaptive process logs and the open issues in identifying at what KPIs values changes are required and what kind of changes would have the best impact on the process performance at run time.

Keywords: Runtime process adaptation · Adaptive process log generation · KPI-to-adaptation correlation · Synthetic process event logs

1 Introduction

Runtime process adaptation is one of the ways to enable autonomous process performance improvement [3] for augmented processes [2] enacted by process-aware information systems. Significant research results of the fields of process mining, predictive and prescriptive process monitoring [6] have established the fundamentals of learning from available process event logs for discovering processes and identifying potential KPI violations in process behaviour. One of the significant challenges this kind of research faces is the lack of available process event logs, and in particular such that containing known adaptations of any of the process dimensions - control and data flow, activity implementations and changes in (human) resource availability. The other challenge the community is facing is the matching of the reasons for changes made in processes to concrete adaptation actions. *If we can learn what reasons for changes have been and their impact on the process performance, only then we can recommend (automatically*

© The Author(s), under exclusive license to Springer Nature Switzerland AG 2024
T. P. Sales et al. (Eds.): EDOC 2023 Workshops, LNBIP 498, pp. 331–337, 2024.
https://doi.org/10.1007/978-3-031-54712-6_21

or not) a specific adaptation action to be enacted into the affected running process instance.

In this paper we present a tool that has two main objectives: 1) to generate synthetic event logs of adaptive processes to alleviate the impact of the challenge mentioned above and 2) to analyse the adapted logs to identify correlations between the adaptations made and the KPIs values for which an adaptation was needed. The process logs it generates, using its *Next(Log)* component, are based on existing process event logs and are subsequently extended with control flow adaptation events following rules that users can define using the tool. The analysis of the extended logs the tool can perform, using its *ML.Log* component, is based on several well-known ML (Machine Learning) algorithms and identify the value of the KPIs that present a reason for an adaptation.

Our tool allows for user friendly adaptive log generation by easy import of original process logs and intuitive adaptation rule definitions based on formal grammar implemented in a rule editor. Furthermore, the tool automates the adaptive process log analysis pipeline and its architecture allows for future extensions of the algorithms used for that purpose.

We present our tool along the following paper structure: The tool's architecture and implementation are presented in Sect. 2. We show an example of adaptive process log generation and analysis in Sect. 3 and in Sect. 4 we discuss the limitations of the current version of the prototype. We conclude the paper and point to future improvements in Sect. 5.

2   Tool Components and Implementation

The key components of the tool[1] (see Fig. 1) are the *Next(Log)* component for generating adaptations in process logs based on predefined rules and the log analysis tool *ML.Log* that can use adaptive process logs to discover correlation between adaptations on the one hand and the reasons for the adaptations, like specific values of KPIs, on the other.

Next(Log) is a flexible tool designed to generate and adapt business process logs[2]. Its key component is a 'Rules Editor' page, which allows users to define custom rules for log adaptation. The tool provides a user-friendly interface, making it intuitive to define these adaption rules. Users can create rules that apply to specific traces and are built upon the trace's KPI metrics, for example, duration and cost.

Next(Log) was written in Python and used PySide6 for creating the user interface, a Python binding for the Qt framework. The PLY (Python Lex-Yacc) library was used to create a simple parser for the user-defined rules. Finally, the xml library in Python was utilised to interpret both the MXML and BPMN files, which are currently the only allowed input formats for process models and process event logs.

---

[1] The tool is available in https://github.com/aryadegari/Next-ML-Log/.

[2] The initial logs will need to be provided in MXML format. *Next(Log)* has only been tested on synthetic logs generated by the BIMP simulator.

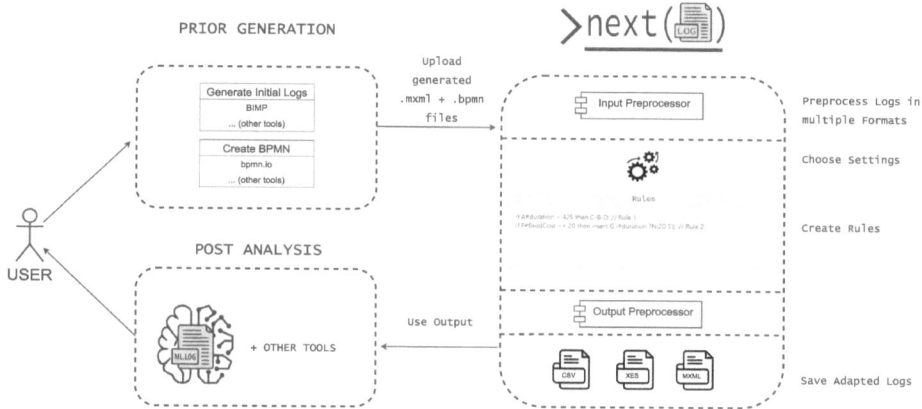

Fig. 1. Architecture of the Tool.

ML.Log is an application for using machine learning methods on adaptive business process logs. It automated the data processing pipeline and thus enables the user to easily use different machine learning models, find the best parameters, save the models for future use and test saved models on different logs.

ML.Log was also written in Python with PySide6. The software utilises the popular Python library Scikit-learn to build various machine learning models, including Decision Trees, Random Forest Classifiers, and K-Nearest Neighbours (KNN). Additionally, the sklearn-glvq module was employed to develop GLVQ models. For visualisation, Graphviz and Matplotlib were used.

3   Example of Generating and Analysing an Adaptive Process Log

In the following section, we will demonstrate a very straightforward example of adapting business process logs using *Next(Log)*, followed by *ML.Log*'s analysis of the adapted logs. A demonstration video is available[3].

Log Adaption with *Next(Log)*

Suppose we had the process model shown in Fig. 2, with the following user-defined rule[4] focusing on time as KPI:

```
if C#duration > 575 then insert K (#duration ?N(100 15));
```

The above rule can be interpreted as follows: For each trace in the initial logs, if the duration of event C was greater than 575 s, then introduce a new event K immediately after C. The duration of event K is sampled from a normal distribution with $\mu = 100$ s and $\sigma = 15$ s.

---

[3] https://doi.org/10.6084/m9.figshare.24082083.v1.

[4] To see all possible rules that can be made and their notation/formal grammar, please refer to [1].

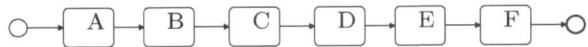

Fig. 2. Sample process model (`X#duration` $\sim N(500, 50)$ $\forall$ X $\in$ {A,..,F})

In Tables 1 and 2 we present the original process log and the adapted log using the adaptation rule from above. The presented results have undergone filtering, resulting in the exclusion of numerous traces and columns. This selection aims to try highlight elements for demonstration purposes.

Table 1. Original Logs

trace_id	C#duration	D#start_time	K#duration	_End#start_time	_End@duration	_Path
184	520.272	2023-07-19T22:02:36.535	0	2023-07-22T22:51:24.642	2877.945	"_Start,A,B,C,D,E,F,_End"
27	576.532	2023-07-18T08:37:50.625	0	2023-07-19T17:25:32.212	2981.662	"_Start,A,B,C,D,E,F,_End"
30	478.811	2023-07-18T09:52:33.449	0	2023-07-19T19:59:50.737	3013.945	"_Start,A,B,C,D,E,F,_End"
167	603.946	2023-07-19T18:43:35.746	0	2023-07-22T20:14:34.943	3018.123	"_Start,A,B,C,D,E,F,_End"

Table 2. Adapted Logs

trace_id	C#duration	D#start_time	K#duration	_End#start_time	_End@duration	_Path	_Label
184	520.272	2023-07-19T22:02:36.535	0	2023-07-22T22:51:24.642	2877.945	"_Start,A,B,C,D,E,F,_End"	0
27	576.532	2023-07-18T08:39:32.704908	102.079	2023-07-19T17:27:14.291908	3083.741908	"_Start,A,B,C,K,D,E,F,_End"	1
30	478.811	2023-07-18T09:52:33.449	0	2023-07-19T19:59:50.737	3013.945	"_Start,A,B,C,D,E,F,_End"	0
167	603.946	2023-07-19T18:45:20.822520	105.076	2023-07-22T20:16:20.019520	3123.19952	"_Start,A,B,C,K,D,E,F,_End"	1

Traces 27 and 167 trigger the specified rule. The "_Path" column updates correctly, indicating the adapted sequence of events. The "_Label" column is also updated to indicate whether an adaptation occurred or not. Additionally, the insertion of event K is observed, with its `duration` randomly sampled from $N(100, 15)$. Furthermore, `_End#start_time` and `_End@duration` are updated appropriately in response to the adaptation.

Adaptive Process Log Analysis with *ML.Log*

After adapting the logs shown in Table 2, we conducted an analysis using the machine learning techniques implemented by *ML.Log*. The results of this analysis are presented below (see Table 3).

Figure 3 represents the decision-making rule that has been retrieved by the Random Forest model as the best performing one and as visualized by the tool, while in Fig. 4 we show the results of the KNN algorithm.

For a detailed analysis of the results, you may refer to [5], which evaluates the performance of all four models using different metrics such as F1 score, recall, and accuracy, providing a quantitative measure of their performance with different logs.

Table 3. Classification Reports for Given Logs.

Model		precision	recall	f1-score	support
Random Forest	class 0	1.00	1.00	1.00	276
	class 1	1.00	1.00	1.00	24
	macro avg	1.00	1.00	1.00	300
	weighted avg	1.00	1.00	1.00	300
Decision Tree	class 0	1.00	0.99	0.99	276
	class 1	0.92	0.96	0.94	24
	macro avg	0.96	0.98	0.97	300
	weighted avg	0.99	0.99	0.99	300
KNN	class 0	0.99	1.00	0.99	276
	class 1	1.00	0.83	0.91	24
	macro avg	0.99	0.92	0.95	300
	weighted avg	0.99	0.99	0.99	300
GLVQ	class 0	0.95	1.00	0.97	276
	class 1	1.00	0.33	0.50	24
	macro avg	0.97	0.67	0.74	300
	weighted avg	0.95	0.95	0.93	300

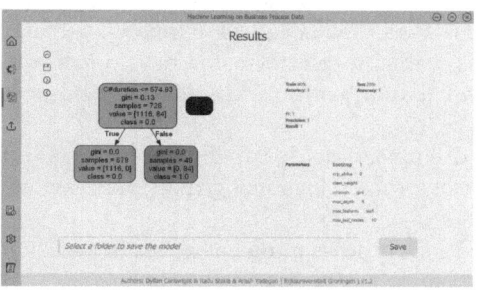

Fig. 3. Visualisation of a found Tree using a Random Forest Classifier in *ML.Log*.

Fig. 4. Visualisation of the Labels assigned by a KNN model found within *ML.Log*.

4   Maturity

Both components of the tool have some limitations which we will discuss here.

Firstly, *Next(Log)* assumes that user-defined rules do not overlap (i.e. maximum of one rule may apply to each process case), as overlapping rules may lead to unpredictable and ambiguous outcomes. Secondly, while it is designed to work with any standard BPMN and MXML files, it has been predominantly tested with files generated by specific tools (bpmn.io and BIMP), and minor issues may arise when using other generative tools. Moreover, the tool assumes there are no loops within the process models, and is limited to parallel and exclusive (XOR) gateways. Additionally, it does not support nesting of gateways within process models.

The current implementation of *ML.Log* includes GLVQ, KNN, Decision Trees, and Random Forest as the four implemented machine learning models, evaluated using various metrics for performance assessment. However, the limited selection of models and performance metrics may not encompass the full range of possible insights.

5   Conclusions

In this paper we presented a tool for adaptive process log generation and analysis. The current version of the tool has two components: i) *Next(Log)*: based on a BPMN process model and a corresponding process log it allows for extending the logs with different process adaptation, simulating the fact that process instances have been adapted during their execution; ii) *ML.Log* automates the data processing pipeline for analysis of the adapted process logs - currently the analysis is based on several ML algorithms.

More specifically, the objective of *Next(Log)* was to enable users to generate initial business process logs using their preferred method and subsequently adapt them based on custom rules. As demonstrated earlier and in [1], all adapted logs performed as intended. While the current version lacks the ability to create more complex adaptations, *Next(Log)* is designed so that it can be extended further. With improvements, it could serve as a valuable platform for developers and researchers to test, build and integrate with analysis tools like *ML.Log* and be a catalyst for exciting research in the field.

The objective of *ML.Log* was to find connections between adaptations and their impact on KPIs in adaptive business process logs using multiple machine learning techniques.

As the tool is currently requiring a BPMN process model as input in addition to a corresponding process log, in order to improve its usability, in future the tool can be extended with a process discovery component based on existing process discovery algorithms like PM4PY, so that the process model is discovered from the process event logs. Integration with approaches like e.g. [4] and [6] will draw upon works in prescriptive process monitoring and analytics.

References

1. Cartwright, D.: A tool for log generation of adaptive business processes. B.Sc. thesis, University of Groningen (2023). https://fse.studenttheses.ub.rug.nl/31012/
2. Dumas, M., et al.: Augmented business process management systems: a research manifesto. CoRR abs/2201.12855 (2022). https://arxiv.org/abs/2201.12855

3. Ghahderijani, A.Y., Karastoyanova, D.: Autonomic process performance improvement. In: EDOC Workshops 2021, pp. 299–307. IEEE (2021). https://doi.org/10.1109/EDOCW52865.2021.00061
4. de Leoni, M., Dees, M., Reulink, L.: Design and evaluation of a process-aware recommender system based on prescriptive analytics. In: ICPM 2020, pp. 9–16 (2020). https://doi.org/10.1109/ICPM49681.2020.00013
5. Sterie, R.A.: Adaptive business process analysis using machine learning algorithms. B.Sc. thesis, University of Groningen (2023). https://fse.studenttheses.ub.rug.nl/31141
6. Yadegari Ghahderijani, A.: Change recommendation in business processes. In: Troya, J., et al. (eds.) ICSOC 2022. LNCS, vol. 13821, pp. 334–340. Springer, Cham (2023). https://doi.org/10.1007/978-3-031-26507-5_29

Doctoral Consortium

EDOC 2023 Doctoral Consortium

Irene Vanderfeesten[1] and Maria-Eugenia Iacob[2]

[1]Faculty of Business and Economics, KU Leuven, Belgium
irene.vanderfeesten@kuleuven.be
[2]Department of Industrial Engineering and Business Information Systems, University of
Twente, The Netherlands
m.e.iacob@utwente.nl

The Doctoral Consortium (DC) of EDOC is a forum of exchange organized to encourage PhD students to present their early work and exchange ideas and experiences with other researchers in their fields. Senior researchers provide feedback on the work presented and give advice on managing research projects. The DC is also a place to establish a social network with peers in the field of the conference.

For the DC of EDOC 2023, we accepted four submissions for presentation and discussion at the DC session of the conference. Each of the submissions was reviewed by at least three members of the Program Committee and was assigned a senior researcher as tutor to lead the discussion on the research proposal at the DC session. Each of the participants was also asked to review another submission and provide feedback.

We would like to thank the tutors Colin Atkinson, Paul Grefen and Dimka Karastoyanova for their excellent feedback and engaging discussions. We also thank the other PhD students and colleagues in the audience for their support and active participation in the DC session. It was a valuable, fruitful and enjoyable meeting.

Doctoral Consortium Organization

Doctoral Consortium Chairs

Irene Vanderfeesten   KU Leuven, Belgium
Maria Iacob   University of Twente, The Netherlands

Program Committee

João Paulo Almeida   Federal University of Espírito Santo, Brazil
Colin Atkinson   University of Mannheim, Germany
Paul Grefen   Eindhoven University of Technology,
        The Netherlands
Georg Grossmann   University of South Australia, Australia
Sylvain Hallé   Université du Québec à Chicoutimi,
        Canada
Selmin Nurcan   Université Paris 1 Panthéon - Sorbonne,
        France
Estefanía Serral Asensio   KU Leuven, Belgium

An ESG Metrics Management System for Sustainable Financial System

Mingqin Yu[✉]

The University of New South Wales, Sydney, NSW 2052, Australia
mingqin.yu@unsw.edu.au

Abstract. Climate change risks permeate all economic sectors [1]. As Environmental, Social, and Governance (ESG) initiatives expand and reporting obligations adapt to the dynamic evolution of ESG, several challenges arise. There is a pressing demand for tools that address these ESG-related deficiencies, data infrastructure challenges, and technical constraints while enhancing domain expertise engagement. In our research, we design top-down architecture and framework to serve and satisfy ESG user requirements among jurisdictions and guide bottom-up ESG data infrastructure. In addition, we define the nature of the ESG analytic data pipeline, embedding models and metrics. Our contribution will lay on three aspects. **First**, our research shed light on sustainable financial systems' framework and architecture development, especially ESG services for decision-making and disclosure. **Second**, our ESG analytics data pipeline design assists ESG data infrastructure development. **Last but not least**, our research mitigates misrepresenting the ESG concept and fragmentation of ESG terminology.

Keywords: ESG Metrics · ESG Indicator · Ontology-Based Data Pipeline · Sustainable Financial System Framework · Risk Management

1 Introduction

Environmental, Social, and Governance (ESG) considerations are now central to global decision-making, given the severe consequences of climate change and the pressing need to cap global warming within 2 °C of pre-industrial levels [2]. Recognizing the vital interplay of emissions, global temperatures, and macroeconomic consequences, as shown in models like DICE and scenario like NGFS, there's a drive toward sustainable integration both at the macro and micro levels [3]. This shift is evident in investment management, where ESG criteria are becoming pivotal. Stakeholders are seeking consistent, transparent, and actionable climate-related information to inform their decisions.

However, a myriad of challenges persists. Diverse reporting obligations stemming from varying regulators and standard setters [4,5], combined with corporate commitments to various frameworks complicate the landscape [6]. These complexities lead to misrepresentations, greenwashing, and confusion in ESG disclosures, highlighting the need for standardization and streamlined processes. Additionally, the current ESG landscape faces five primary engineering problems, ranging from inconsistency in terminology to challenges in data pipeline and framework development [7–9].

To address these challenges, our research endeavors to bridge the gap between theoretical requirements and practical applications. We seek to refine ESG nomenclature, design data pipelines at a high level, and formulate comprehensive frameworks that foster transparent ESG decision-making. Ultimately, our work aims to promote ethical business conduct, efficient financial analysis, and informed decision-making, ensuring alignment with globally recognized ESG standards and initiatives.

2   Literature Review

2.1   ESG Background

The investment industry has experienced a significant shift towards incorporating Environmental, Social, and Governance (ESG) considerations, primarily due to the far-reaching implications of climate change across all economic sectors [1]. This transition is guided by an array of initiatives (UNEP, UNEP FI and so on) [2], including governmental and regulatory efforts, international and regional standards, industry-led endeavors, and developments within stock exchanges.

The burgeoning interest in ESG issues, fueled by key initiatives, has led to the widespread adoption of ESG reporting frameworks (IFRS SI, TFCD and so on) [5] in recent years. However, this rapid proliferation presents unique challenges for regulators and entities adhering to these frameworks. These challenges arise from variances in the reporting frameworks, differing definitions, diverse metrics, and disparities in data availability.

In an increasingly diversified range of scenarios and reporting frameworks guiding the formulation and execution of ESG benchmarks, engagement with pertinent ESG data emerges as a central issue. The primary ESG data refers to the raw information collected directly from its source. Secondary ESG data is information that has been interpreted or processed, deduced or calculated in some way from the primary ESG data [8].

2.2   ESG Metrics

In the context of this study, our main focus is on 'secondary Data', which encompasses aggregated ESG metrics. These metrics adhere to the standards mandated by ESG reporting frameworks like TCFD, TNFD, and PRI Climate Metrics, among others. We employ macro-level [10] scenario requirements as a roadmap for devising these metrics. This composite dataset comprises three core components: ESG Metrics, ESG Indicators and ESG Models. ESG indicators are the specific, **measurable data points** contributing to broader ESG metrics. An ESG model is a structured framework that helps businesses and investors evaluate a company's ESG performance, alongside traditional financial metrics, to make informed decisions and strategies grounded on sustainability and ethical practices. It encompasses assessments of a company's impact on the environment, its social responsibilities, and the quality of its governance policies.

ESG metrics refer to a set of metrics that aim to capture as accurately as possible a firm's performance on a given ESG issue [11]. These metrics are inherently **multi-dimensional** and could encompass aspects such as greenhouse gas emissions, water usage, incidents related to worker safety, board diversity, executive compensation, and more. The exact metrics employed may vary based on the company, sector, and the adopted ESG framework or standard.

2.3   The Challenge of ESG Metrics

The current ESG metrics are plagued with challenges stemming from business necessities and contentious research outcomes as evidenced in the works of Widyawati (2021), Christensen (2022), and Kotsantonis (2019) [6, 9, 11]. The specific issues are as follows:

- ESG Metric Disagreements: the uncertainty or standard deviation in ESG ratings among providers arises from controversial ESG research results.
- Lack of Future-oriented Indicators: the current ESG metrics lack a clear taxonomy, complicating the categorisation of ESG issues under the environmental, social, or governance domains.
- Measurement and Modelling Complexity: the opacity in ESG measurement and modelling can lead to misconceptions and misinterpretations.
- Indicator-Metric Discrepancies: there is a conflict between input indicators and output metrics, such as a low correlation between low carbon emissions and high ESG scores.

Our research emphasizes the engineering of ESG metrics and the construction of a data pipeline. In doing so, we identified the following challenges associated with building the data pipeline:

- Interconnectedness and Semantic Depth: ESG metrics often interrelate in complex ways, demanding more than surface-level connections.
- Harmonization Across Sources: ESG data comes from global sources, each with different reporting standards and formats, necessitating a common ground.
- Dynamic Evolvability: the ESG landscape is evolving. New issues emerge, and standards shift, requiring a system that can adapt.
- Transparency and Traceability: stakeholders demand clear data lineages and sources due to the significant implications of ESG scores.
- Addressing Ambiguities: ESG data is subjective. Different regions and organizations might rate the same metric differently.
- Multidimensionality: ESG covers a broad spectrum of metrics, from carbon footprints to workplace diversity, all of which need integration.

3   Research Framework

3.1   Identify Research Questions and Objectives of Solution

Utilizing the Design Science Research (DSR) Methodology [12], our approach emphasizes designing and assessing innovative solutions tailored to real-world issues (Fig. 1).

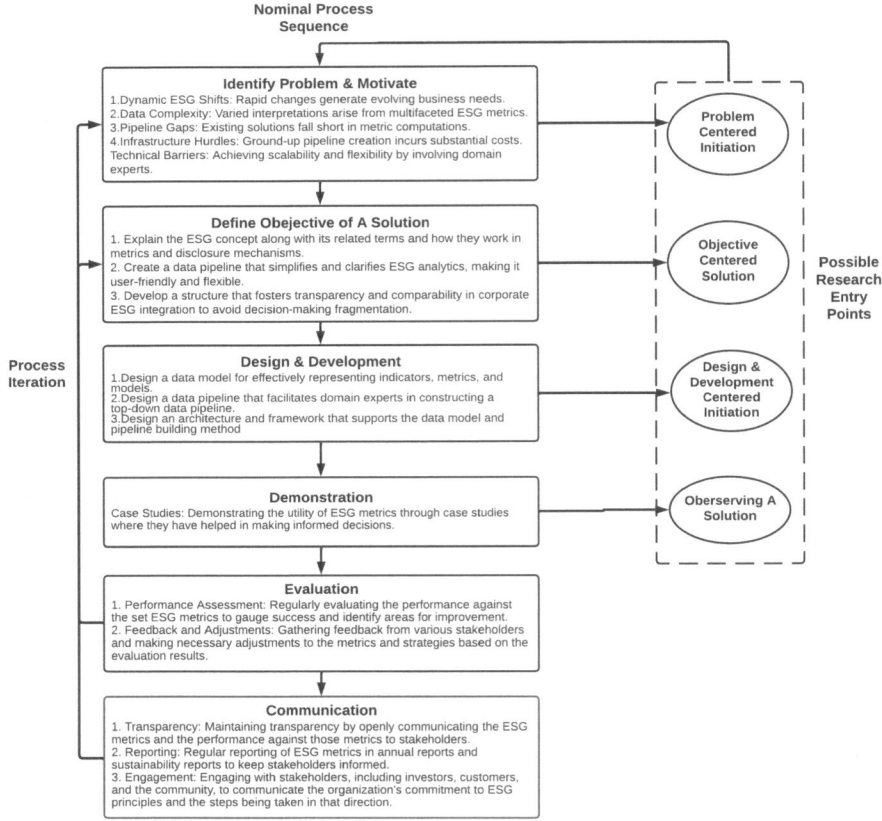

Fig. 1. ESG Design Iteration Process [12]

From a thorough literature review, we've derived the following research questions and their corresponding objective of solution:

– Q1: How can we define and govern ESG metrics models in a manner that is independent of specific data sources or ESG Providers?
  Our method involves using an ESG Framework and Scenario as guidelines, employing a top-down methodology to define metrics and models, which in turn guide the computation using indicators.

– Q2: How can we empower a domain expert to design a data pipeline supporting large-scale ESG data analytics?
  We propose an agile technique customized to facilitate domain expert involvement in the modelling and implementation process.
– Q3: How can a flexible architecture and framework be designed for an ESG metric management system?
  Our approach includes an analysis of business requirements to design a top-down data pipeline, engagement of bottom-up indicator experts, and using Macro scenarios and micro ESG frameworks as guides. This architecture accommodates the integration of transformer, statistical, and ML models to ensure technical feasibility.

3.2   Research Steps

Within the scope of DSR, the following artifacts will be crafted during our research:

– A data model for effective representation of indicators, metrics, and models.
– A method that facilitates domain experts in constructing a top-down data pipeline.
– An architecture and framework that underpins the data model and pipeline-building method.

Demonstrating the utility of ESG metrics through case studies where they have helped in making informed decisions. Evaluation involves performance Assessment, Feedback and Adjustments. For communication, engaging with stakeholders, including investors, asset managers, and other stakeholders, to communicate the organization's commitment to ESG principles and the steps being taken in that direction.

Leveraging the Design Science Research (DSR) methodology, we iteratively refine our design based on business requirements and existing knowledge. This iterative process involves model enhancement, data pipeline development, and architectural refinements to eventually construct microservices demonstrating with case studies and evaluating via feedback and adjustment with the engagement with stakeholders.

This research aims to devise an innovative, collaborative tool for ESG metric management, which will facilitate identifying and tracking metrics essential for fostering sustainable financial systems.

4   Conclusion

Our research provides a comprehensive exploration of the Environmental, Social, and Governance (ESG) arena, combining industry insights with academic viewpoints. We aim to simplify ESG data by demystifying metrics, indicators, and dimensions, with an emphasis on disclosure-based information. We are developing a method that facilitates domain experts in constructing a top-down data pipeline. Additionally, we are constructing a universally applicable framework to enhance ESG integration services and minimize fragmentation in corporate decision-making and risk management.

The expected outcomes of this study will mitigate ESG integration risk and sustainable portfolio analysis challenges. We aim to simplify complex reporting obligations arising from diverse jurisdictional regulations and tackle the widespread issue of inconsistent metrics and unclear measurements in ESG integration. Our goal is to standardize and clarify these elements, addressing significant barriers in ESG data management and reporting.

References

1. Australian Prudential Regulation Authority. Prudential practice guide: draft cpg 229 climate change financial risks (2021)
2. Hänsel, M.C., et al.: Climate economics support for the un climate targets. Nat. Clim. Change **10**(8), 781–789 (2020)
3. Dietz, S., Bowen, A., Dixon, C., Gradwell, P.: 'climate value at risk' of global financial assets. Nat. Clim. Chang. **6**(7), 676–679 (2016)
4. Financial Stability Board et al. Recommendations of the task force on climate-related financial disclosures 92017)
5. Financial Stability Board et al. Task force on climate-related financial disclosures: 2022 status report (2022)
6. Christensen, D.M., Serafeim, G., Sikochi, A.: Why is corporate virtue in the eye of the beholder? the case of ESG ratings. Account. Rev. **97**(1), 147–175 (2022)
7. Avramov, D., Cheng, S., Lioui, A., Tarelli, A.: Sustainable investing with ESG rating uncertainty. J. Financ. Econ. **145**(2), 642–664 (2022)
8. OECD. ESG ratings and climate transition. (06) (2022)
9. Widyawati, L.: Measurement concerns and agreement of environmental social governance ratings. Account. Financ. **61**, 1589–1623 (2021)
10. Nordhaus, W.: Evolution of modeling of the economics of global warming: changes in the dice model, 1992–2017. Clim. Change **148**(4), 623–640 (2018)
11. Kotsantonis, S., Serafeim, G.: Four things no one will tell you about ESG data. J. Appl. Corp. Financ. **31**(2), 50–58 (2019)
12. Peffers, K., Tuunanen, T., Rothenberger, M.A., Chatterjee, S.: A design science research methodology for information systems research. J. Manage. Inf. Syst. **24**(3), 45–77 (2007)

Anomaly Detection and Categorization for a Data Quality Management Framework in Financial Regulatory Reporting

Aya Tafech$^{(\boxtimes)}$ (iD)

University of New South Wales, Sydney, NSW 2052, Australia
a.tafech@unsw.edu.au

Abstract. Financial institutions are subject to stringent regulatory reporting requirements to manage operational risk in international financial markets. Producing accurate and timely reports has raised challenges in current data processes of big data heterogeneity, system interoperability and enterprise-wide management. Data quality management is a key concern, with current approaches being time-consuming, expensive, and risky. This research proposes to design, develop, and evaluate a Financial Reporting Data Quality Framework that allows non-IT data consumers to contextualize data observations. The framework will use anomaly algorithms to detect and categorize observations as genuine business activities or data quality issues. To ensure sustainability and ongoing relevance, the framework will also embed an update mechanism.

Keywords: Big Data · Data Quality · Financial Regulatory Reporting · Anomaly detection algorithms · Machine Learning

1 Introduction

The 2007–08 Global Financial Crisis spurred the need for more robust financial markets, with increased requirements for operational management contingencies. The Basel Committee on Banking Supervision (BCBS) noted international deficiencies in banks' operations to perform accurate and timely aggregation of risk exposures. This sentiment was echoed by domestic, government-endorsed agencies that are the primary regulators of financial institutions (FIs) within the jurisdiction they operate.

Regulators require FIs to submit regulatory reports (RRs) that demonstrate operation is within mandated risk-accepted levels maintainable during a crisis. Regulators, aware of the reliance on quality data processes for accurate RRs, have introduced data management frameworks and requirements. The Bank of International Settlements (BIS), used as primary guidance for domestic regulators, released the BCBS239 standard in 2013 to identify data aggregation used for decision-making as a risk management area requiring improvement [1].

While there are many challenges as FIs attempt to meet current regulations, financial regulators have emphasized that future data risk management regulations will be even more stringent. The BIS envisions a global standard for data infrastructure to operate in real-time, providing granular insights to reduce operational risk management internationally as domestic financial markets become more intertwined [2].

To address this, the research will design a framework that uses artificial intelligence to identify anomalous data points throughout a financial regulatory Big Data process and then categorize these observations as either data quality (DQ) issues or not, i.e., provide context to the observation. The framework will integrate into existing FI data architectures and maintain relevance as processes evolve. The overall contribution of this research is to offer a scalable and sustainable alternative to the current state manual/static approaches to DQ detection (DQD). As FIs become increasingly more data-driven, robust data processes underpin the stability of financial markets worldwide. Current and future regulatory expectations highlight the risks of inadequate data management and the need for better DQ management in our financial systems. The rest of this paper is structured as follows: Sect. 2 contains a summarized literature review and research questions to be addressed; Sect. 3 details the proposed research methodology, expected outcome and evaluation criteria; and Sect. 4 offers concluding remarks on the research, expected benefits and next steps.

2   Literature Survey

As mentioned in the introduction, many FIs are pivoting towards a data-drive mindset, embedding data strategy into IT infrastructure to ensure regulatory requirements are met. A key aspect is data quality management and monitoring (DQMM) as modern financial markets have led FIs to deal with 'Big Data'. Coupled with complex enterprise data architecture, low interoperability, and a mix of internal and third-party systems, strategic, cost-effective, and efficient enterprise DQMM is difficult [3].

'Big Data' refers to a large volume of heterogenous data that grows rapidly [4]. Adjacently, DQ is defined as data fit for use from the data consumer's perspective and is typically represented dimensionally and measured through metrics [4]. DQMM has been driven by academic and industry-based frameworks that have utilized different dimensions or industry-specific data processes [5]. These DQMM frameworks provide a high-level approach, but industry application is limited. Specific dimensions and metrics may not be equally significant in the dataflow [4] and focus too much on structured data, which may negate these approaches as unstructured data becomes more common in the financial sector [5]. There is also a reliance on data sampling and profiling to reduce processing which may distort enterprise level DQMM [4].

DQMM is further challenged due to many handover points and roles in the dataflow and limited upstream visibility. Data consumers first need to raise data observations to be contextualized, i.e., what does an observation represent. To categorize the observation as a DQ issue requires engagement between many technical and business teams, delaying data validation and issue resolution [6]. Automated DQ assessment and improvement methods have been developed for enterprise data systems to reduce time consuming and manual DQD processes. However, implementing across an enterprise's big data infrastructure is difficult due to data heterogeneity, system interoperability and confidentiality [7]. Current industry-developed solutions successfully use anomaly detection algorithms as a sustainable solution in big datasets [8]. However, compared to in-house solutions, industry products raise concerns around enterprise interoperability, scalability as data needs grow, ongoing licensing and maintenance costs, security of data, and customization to suit all data users [3, 9].

Another key challenge for DQMM is that an FI will typically have highly heterogenous data sources due to new or changing regulations, products, and technology [10]. Equally, data use is extremely varied, leading to many data consumers with varying DQ requirements. FIs typically support risk management, data controls and data integration with a centralized enterprise data architecture. This leads to a bow-tie architecture, where data flows from producer to processing to consumer [10], relying on elastic computation for horizontal scalability, transparency, and parallel and efficient pre-processing. Orchestration and metadata management also become integral to overcome data heterogeneity of data producers and consumers.

Since BCBS239, the design of an FI data architecture that supports DQMM has been an academic and industry focus. The BIS's BCBS239 implementation review found no FIs were fully compliant [7], sighting difficulties in integrating legacy IT and third-party systems, complex lineage and inherent non-standardization when aggregating data [3]. Proposed solutions focus on BCBS239 compliance, data standardization, open-source frameworks, technological longevity and reducing cost [2, 9].

A common challenge of these solutions is understanding data transformations with a complex lineage and identifying genuine DQ issues throughout the architecture to support business and reporting functions [11]. Typical DQ issues include missing/incorrect data used for key reporting functions, inconsistency between data sources, and changes in metadata throughout data transformations [12]. These issues are exacerbated in larger datasets, leading to more data roles and complex organizational management [13]. As FIs become more data-driven, there is an increasing reliance on big DQMM. Coupled with the ever-increasing nature of big data and typically complex data architectures, FIs' current approach is not viable in the long-term.

Table 1 summarizes the identified challenges and research questions.

Table 1. Identified existing challenges and research questions.

Identified existing challenges	Research question
A lack of context when data consumers observe data anomalies, which can lead to mislabeling these observations as DQ issues or non-DQ issues	RQ1: How can the context be represented when FIs use anomaly detection for DQ detection as a means for data consumers to contextualize data observations in big datasets used for regulatory reporting?
A lack of focus on novel data architecture to support big DQD	RQ2: How can an FI's data architecture integrate DQ detection as proposed in RQ1?
A lack of control, modification, and maintenance of a DQ detection process used by non-IT experts	RQ3: How can the architecture (proposed in RQ2) be maintained as business context (proposed in RQ1) changes without requiring continual or manual update?

3   Research Methodology and Expected Outcome

This research will apply the Design Science Research Methodology (DSRM) framework, utilizing iterations, where interim evaluations act as a primary guidance to address design questions [14]. DSRM has been chosen as the research aims to develop an artifact in the form of a framework with solution elements that address the research questions. The solution framework is the 'Financial Reporting Data Quality Framework' (FRDQF). It will have four high-level components:

1. An approach that will focus on how to integrate anomaly detection into an existing financial reporting data architecture,
2. A knowledge base with a model repository and representation of historic data anomalies, data transformations and data elements,
3. An implementation mechanism where each model represents an anomaly categorization algorithm that determines if data observations are DQ issues or not and a change management mechanism to update the knowledge base as processes, datasets, regulations, and requirements evolve, and
4. A user experience solution for data consumers to interface with the framework, including capabilities to explore the categorized anomalies and provide any business knowledge regarding anomaly observations.

These components will interact as shown in Fig. 1. The final product of this research will be the conceptual framework design and implementation in a prototype environment to demonstrate and evaluate its performance.

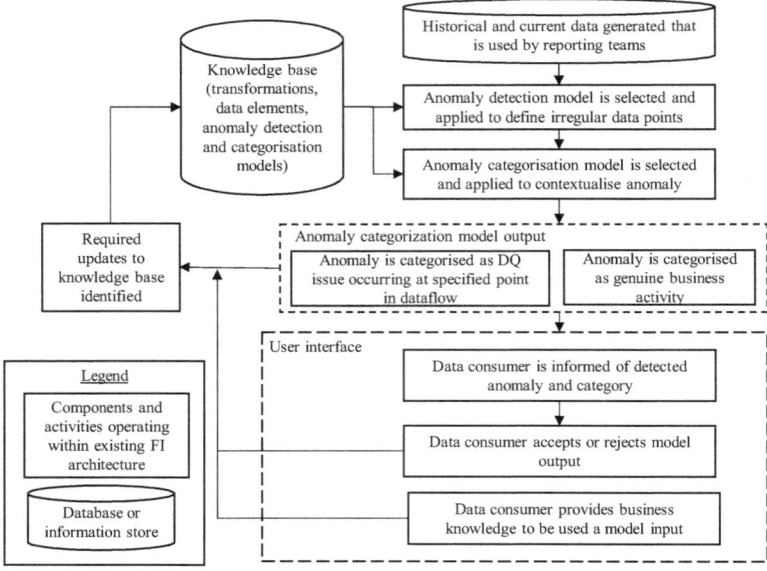

Fig. 1. High-level representation of the Financial Reporting Data Quality Framework (FRDQF)

DSRM will be applied in three steps. Initially, the problem is identified to define the solution objectives that address the gap identified in the literature review and inform the design and development of the framework, followed by demonstration and evaluation. Interim evaluations will be completed for the design, development, and integration of each component into the framework. Evaluation will be completed by testing the framework performance in a prototype environment and validated comparatively to current industry practice. The overall research steps are detailed in Table 2.

Table 2. Research steps to produce the FRDQF

Iteration	DSMR step	Action
#1	Design and development	Component 1 Part of component 2 - initial knowledge base development Part of component 3 - anomaly detection model
	Demonstration	Using large public financial dataset in a prototype enterprise environment
	Evaluation	Does the solution design detect anomalies, comparably to traditional methods, that are reflective of DQ issues in financial data? Is the solution interoperable with typical FI architecture?
#2	Design and development	Link components 2 and 3 developed in iteration #1 Part of component 3 - anomaly categorization model
	Demonstration	Using subset of financial enterprise-like data in a prototype environment
	Evaluation	Iteration #1 criteria Does the solution allow data consumers to contextualize the data?
#3	Design and development	Part of component 3 - knowledge base update mechanism Interaction between knowledge base and all models (C2 and C3) Component 4
	Demonstration	Using subset of financial enterprise data in a prototype environment with an existing architecture
	Evaluation	Iteration #2 criteria Is the solution deemed by industry experts to be more strategic and scalable than current DQMM methods for financial reporting data processes?

4 Conclusion

Financial data processes are key for FIs to operate within prescribed risk levels and maintain worldwide financial market stability. Regulators have raised concerns with current and future enterprise DQ management in these processes, citing issues of interoperability, big data, skill diversity and longevity as regulation, markets and products evolve. This research proposes the Financial Report Data Quality Framework to address these concerns and provide FIs with a scalable and sustainable solution.

The work completed to date has focused on evaluating current academic and industry approaches and defining the high-level components of the framework. Next steps will further develop the framework, demonstrate its application, and evaluate its performance in a realistic financial enterprise data process used for regulatory reporting.

The benefit of this framework is to provide data consumers with full transparency to contextualize the data received. This research will view a DQ issue as a categorized anomaly, in that the solution will detect unusual data patterns then determine what the observation represents. At a high-level, the data observation (i.e., anomaly) can be a real event originating from the source data or a data quality issue.

References

1. The Basel Committee on Banking Supervision: Basel Committee on Banking Supervision Principles for effective risk data aggregation and risk reporting (2013)
2. Moir, A., Broadbent, B., Woods, S.: Transforming data collection from the UK financial sector. Bank of England (2020)
3. Dyck, M.: From compliance to risk management: implementing BCBS 239 (2021)
4. Elouataoui, W., Alaoui, I.E., Gahi, Y.: Data quality in the era of big data: a global review (2022)
5. Cichy, C., Rass, S.: An overview of data quality frameworks. IEEE Access **7**, 24634–24648 (2019). https://doi.org/10.1109/ACCESS.2019.2899751
6. Poon, L., Farshidi, S., Li, N., Zhao, Z.: Unsupervised anomaly detection in data quality control. In: Proceedings of 2021 IEEE International Conference on Big Data, Big Data 2021, pp. 2327–2336 (2021). https://doi.org/10.1109/BIGDATA52589.2021.9671672
7. The Basel Committee on Banking Supervision: Progress in adopting the Principles for effective risk data aggregation and risk reporting (2020)
8. Bakumenko, A., Elragal, A.: Detecting anomalies in financial data using machine learning algorithms. Systems **10**, 130, 10, 130 (2022). https://doi.org/10.3390/SYSTEMS10050130
9. Bank of England: New economy, new finance, new bank (2019)
10. Munar, A., Chiner, E., Sales, I.: A big data financial information management architecture for global banking. In: 2014 International Conference on Future Internet of Things and Cloud (2014). https://doi.org/10.1109/FiCloud.2014.68
11. Hasan, M.M., Popp, J., Oláh, J.: Current landscape and influence of big data on finance. J. Big Data **7** (2020). https://doi.org/10.1186/s40537-020-00291-z
12. O'connor, L.: Data Quality Management and Financial Services (2007)
13. Khaleel, M.Y., Hamad, M.M.: Data quality management for big data applications. In: Proceedings of the International Conference on Developments in eSystems Engineering, DeSE, October-2019, pp. 357–362 (2019). https://doi.org/10.1109/DESE.2019.00072
14. Peffers, K., Tuunanen, T., Rothenberger, M.A., Chatterjee, S.: A design science research methodology for information systems research. J. Manag. Inf. Syst. **24**, 45–77 (2007). https://doi.org/10.2753/MIS0742-1222240302

Towards a Knowledge Base and Design and Action Theory for Intelligence Amplification

Jean Paul Sebastian Piest$^{(\boxtimes)}$

University of Twente, Drienerlolaan 5, 7522 NB Enschede, The Netherlands
j.p.s.piest@utwente.nl

Abstract. This short paper positions my doctoral research within the field of information systems, and, more specifically, to the EDOC community in preparation for the doctoral symposium. The research topic of my doctoral research is the design and implementation of Intelligence Amplification (IA) applications. Although extensively researched, there is no consensus in literature regarding the definition of IA, design knowledge is scattered across disciplines, and no routine design exists for IA applications. Therefore, the main aim of my doctoral research is two-fold to (1) establish a knowledge base for IA, as a foundation to (2) develop a design and action theory for IA. The knowledge base will be developed using established design science research methodologies and frameworks. Design knowledge regarding IA will be identified, analysed, and synthesized based on a systematic literature review using the PRISMA 2020 statement. The knowledge base will serve as a foundation for the design and action theory for IA. Action design research will be utilized to iteratively develop and evaluate an IA design method and practical design tools to help professionals and practitioners design and implement IA applications in the context of Industry 5.0 and Society 5.0.

Keywords: Knowledge Base · Design Theory · Design Method · Intelligence Amplification · Information Systems · Design Science Research · Systematic Literature Review · Action Design Research · Society 5.0 · Industry 5.0

1 Introduction

In today's information society, the physical, social, and digital worlds are converging and increasingly interconnected. Real-time data from sensors drive big data analytics and the development of highly personalized, Artificial Intelligence (AI)-infused, smart products and services. Technological advancements provide opportunities for innovation, which result in transformation challenges for organizations (e.g., changing work structures, processes and skill sets of workers), and are increasingly affecting the daily lives of people. The latter is, amongst other developments, illustrated by 'citizen-AI tools' like ChatGPT.

The above-mentioned societal transition towards a *"supersmart society"* has been described as Society 5.0. Society 5.0 was first introduced in Japan as part of its Fifth Science and Technology Basic Plan [1]. Here, Society 5.0 is defined as: *"a human-centered*

T. P. Sales et al. (Eds.): EDOC 2023 Workshops, LNBIP 498, pp. 355–362, 2024.
https://doi.org/10.1007/978-3-031-54712-6_24

society that balances economic advancement with the resolution of social problems by a system that highly integrates cyberspace and physical space." In Europe, a similar, but somewhat different, transition is currently in progress from the current industrial revolution (Industry 4.0), based on cyber-physical systems, towards a *"sustainable, human-centric and resilient European Industry"* (Industry 5.0) [2].

A recent comparison study of [3] emphasizes that, although the main perspectives and realization paths may be different, human-centred design and the large-scale use of (emerging) technology are instrumental to realize human-cyber-physical systems (Industry 5.0) and the super smart Society 5.0. In this context, Intelligence Amplification (IA) is an interesting topic, which connects the context to the topic of this paper.

The term IA can be traced back to the 1950s and was first introduced by William Ross Ashby in his work Introduction to Cybernetics [4]. In the last chapters of this seminal work, Ashby relates the concept of power-amplification to the amplification of sound, regulation, the human brain, and intelligence. Over time, various definitions and disciplinary views have been developed regarding IA. Common synonyms, amongst others, are augmented intelligence, extended cognition, and human-centred AI. Although extensively researched, at present, there is no general accepted definition for IA (P1) and design knowledge is scattered across literature and (sub-)disciplines (P2). At present, no routine design exists for the design and implementation of IA-applications (P3). These three problems will be investigated and treated within this doctoral research project, which is currently at the end of the second year.

Since the definition of IA varies among researchers and disciplines, it is important to clarify how the term is defined in this doctoral research project. IA is defined as "the effective use of information technology in augmenting human intelligence in a given context" [5]. This definition 1) relates to the discipline of Information Systems (IS) research, in which artifacts are studied in context as part of a broader socio-technological environment, 2) emphasizes the augmentation of human intelligence, which clearly sets IA apart from AI, 3) can easily be developed into or incorporated in Design Science Research (DSR) and Action Design Research (ADR), which are the underlying research methodologies for this doctoral research project, and 4) is short and comprehensible, which makes it suitable for designers and practitioners to use.

The research underpinning this paper is based on the disciplinary perspective of IS, and, more specifically, the topic of Design Science (DS) and the research paradigm of DSR. In short, IS can be seen as a discipline that is concerned with *"the use of information-technology artifacts in human-machine systems"* [6]. DS can be defined as *"the design and investigation of artifacts in context"* [7]. DSR aims to contribute to the knowledge base of foundational knowledge and methodologies [6, 8]. Design is both studied and applied in several scientific disciplines. In parallel, design is practiced and developed in professional communities. The focus on developing knowledge and methodologies distinguishes DS from design practice.

A distinct feature of the IS discipline and, more specifically, the EDOC tradition, is its mission to unite researchers and professionals. Therefore, the aim of the doctoral research, that is positioned in this doctoral symposium paper, is two-fold to: (1) establish a knowledge base for IA, as a foundation to (2) develop a design and action theory for IA. Subsequently, the Main Research Question (MRQ) of the research is defined as following: *How can a knowledge base and design and action theory for IA effectively support IS professionals and practitioners to design, construct, implement, and evaluate IA applications?*

The remainder of this paper is structured as follows. Section 2 highlights relevant work. Section 3 presents the research design and questions. Section 4 concludes by summarizing the envisioned contributions and (intermediate) results of the research.

2 Related Work

This section contains related work about DSR knowledge bases and design theorizing.

2.1 DSR Knowledge Bases and Contributions

A distinct feature of DSR is its connection to knowledge bases and application environments, involving both the production and consumption of descriptive (Ω omega) and prescriptive (Λ lambda) knowledge [6]. More specifically, the anatomy of knowledge bases in IS comprise formal (kernel) theories, mid-range or practitioner-in-use theories, design theories, and justification knowledge [9]. Next to design theorizing, the contribution of IS research to practice is an important aspect of DSR [6].

The DSR framework for knowledge contribution [6], depicted in Fig. 1, including its communication scheme, were selected to position and communicate the DSR knowledge contributions of this doctoral research project. DSR project results and outputs can be assessed, amongst other approaches, by level of abstraction, completeness, and knowledge maturity, more specifically, by assessing: (1) situated implementations of artifacts, (2) nascent design theory, and (3) well-developed design theory about embedded phenomena [6]. Significant DSR contributions typically require the involvement of multiple researchers over several years and result in a number of (intermediate) research results during its evolvement [6].

At present, no knowledge base exists regarding IA. Therefore, the DSR framework for knowledge contribution and the anatomy for knowledge bases [7] will be utilized within this research project to identify, categorize, and analyse existing descriptive and prescriptive knowledge related to the design and implementation of IA. This will create a foundation for the design and action theory for IA and a baseline for cumulative knowledge development.

2.2 Design Theorizing

The role of theory and design theorizing in DSR are much debated topics [6]. One problem is to understand how DSR relates to human knowledge [8]. Another problem is to understand and appreciate artifacts developed by IS professionals and practitioners as DSR contributions [8]. Here, related works exist regarding the nature of theory in IS [6], and, more specifically, regarding the anatomy of a design theory [10].

The nature of theory consists of different forms of knowledge [6, 9] and the type of theory that formalizes design knowledge in DSR is called a design theory [6, 8, 9]. More specifically, a taxonomy has been developed to categorizes five types of theories:

(1) theory for analysing, (2) theory for explaining, (3) theory for predicting, (4) theory for explaining and predicting, and (5) theory for design and action [6].

Within the current research project, the focus lies on the development of a type-five theory, which aims to generalize prescriptive knowledge for the design and action of IA [10]. More specifically, the anatomy of a design theory will be used, consisting of the following eight building blocks: (1) purpose and scope, (2) constructs, (3) principles of form and function, (4) artifact mutability, (5) testable propositions, (6) justification theory (kernel theories), (7) principles of implementation, and (8) expository instantiation [10].

3   Research Design and Questions

This section provides a synopsis of the research design and methodology.

3.1   Extended DSR Knowledge Base Framework

In line with related work regarding DSR knowledge bases and design theorizing, this research is based on the DSR knowledge base framework of [8], depicted in Fig. 1.

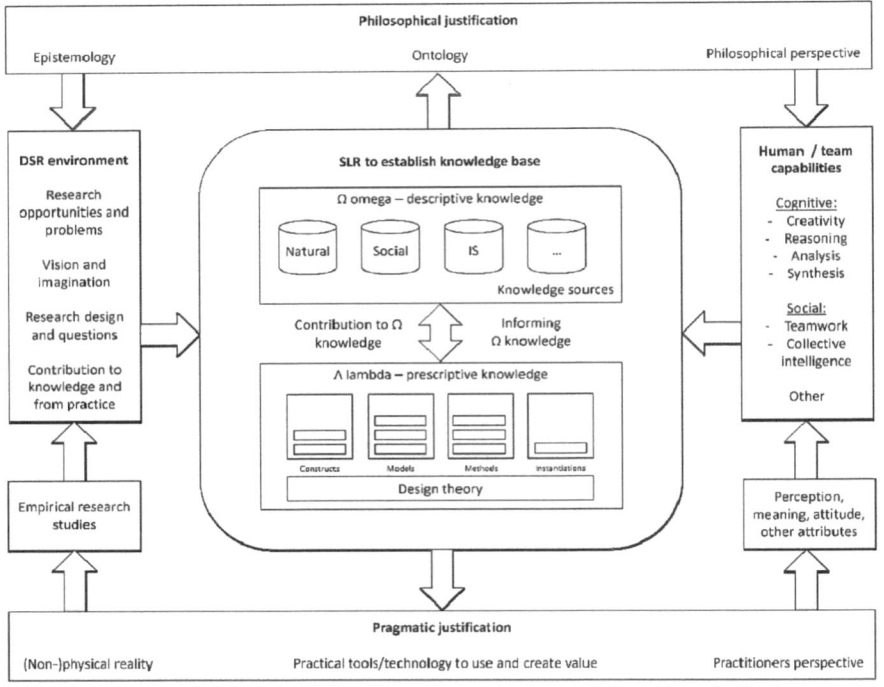

Fig. 1. Extended DSR knowledge base framework (adapted from [8]).

This research is based on a pluralistic philosophical perspective and disciplinary knowledge regarding design theorizing in the field of IS. Established DSR methodologies have been selected to develop the knowledge base and design and action theory for IA. A Systematic Literature Review (SLR) is conducted using the PRISMA 2020 statement (https://www.prisma-statement.org/) regarding the design of IA. More specifically, the aim of this SLR is to identify and categorise relevant descriptive (Ω omega) and prescriptive (Λ lambda) knowledge related to the design and implementation of IA-applications to establish a novel DSR knowledge base to serve as the foundation for the IA design and action theory and cumulative knowledge development.

The DSR knowledge base framework is extended with a layer for philosophical (top) and pragmatic justification (bottom). Philosophical perspectives influence, amongst other aspects, the research design, the interpretation of results, and the communication of truth claims [8]. Several ontological and epistemological positions and philosophical perspectives have been developed over time [6–10]. Whereas ontological and epistemological positions differ per scientific field and DSR project, it is important to accompany each contribution to the DSR knowledge base with philosophical justification knowledge. As the IS discipline aims to unite researchers and professionals, it is important that the DSR knowledge base provides useful, relevant, and reusable knowledge. Therefore, ADR will be utilized to iteratively develop a IA design method and supporting tools. Additionally, it is important to incorporate empirical research studies and perspectives of practitioners.

3.2 Research Questions and Approach

This subsection explains which Research Questions (RQs) guided the research. Table 1 presents the RQs that were formulated based on the MRQ and research design.

First, a DSR environment was established based on the DSR framework of [8] by identifying research problems and opportunities for knowledge contributions (see P1–3 in the Sect. 1). Additionally, the value for IS professionals and practitioners has been positioned within the context of Society 5.0 and Industry 5.0. This first step resulted in the MRQ, guiding RQs, and overall research design.

Second, the current state-of-the-art was investigated based on a SLR. Following the research design, ΩQ1–2 were formulated to investigate knowledge sources and existing knowledge bases for informing Ω knowledge to provide grounding. ΛQ1–2 were formulated to identify and explore existing Λ knowledge, including situated artifacts, design knowledge, and (nascent) design theories. The anatomy of knowledge bases [9] has been selected to categorise, analyse, and synthesise existing knowledge.

Third, a knowledge base will be developed using established DSR frameworks [8] and the anatomy for knowledge bases [9], guided by KQ1. This creates a foundation for the design and action theory for IA [10], guided by KQ2.

Fourth, practical design tools were developed and evaluated with IS professionals and practitioners using ADR and case-based research as part of this doctoral research project (EQ1). Additionally, the established extended DSR knowledge base framework [8] is utilized to develop understanding of the novelty and (potential) knowledge contribution of situated artifacts from related research projects (EQ2) as well as existing empirical research studies (EQ3).

Fifth, a philosophical perspective was developed to extend the DSR knowledge base framework [8]. Here, the results of both the SLR and case based research were be

Table 1. Overview of research questions that guided the research activities.

Dimension	ID	Research question
Ω knowledge	ΩQ1	What is the current state of the art regarding the design of IA?
	ΩQ2	What are the main concepts related to IA?
Λ knowledge	ΛQ1	Which situated artifacts, design knowledge and/or theories exist related to IA?
	ΛQ2	Which constructs, models, and methods are used to design, construct, and evaluate IA applications?
Knowledge contributions	KQ1	How can a knowledge base for IA be established?
	KQ2	How can a design and action theory for IA be developed?
Practitioners perspective	EQ1	How can the knowledge base, and design and action theory support IS professionals and practitioners with the design, construction, and evaluation of IA applications?
	EQ2	How can knowledge contributions from related research projects be incorporated in the knowledge base for IA?
	EQ3	How can contributions from existing empirical research studies be incorporated in the knowledge base for IA?
Philosophical perspective	PQ1	Which ontologies, epistemologies, and philosophical perspectives exist regarding IA?
	PQ2	How can philosophical perspectives to IA be incorporated in the DSR environment and knowledge base?

utilized to identify ontological and epistemological positions regarding IA (PQ1). Additionally, the philosophical perspectives of researchers were included as philosophical justifications in the established knowledge base for IA (PQ2).

4 Envisioned Contributions and Intermediate Results

This doctoral research project aims to position, demonstrate, and evaluate: (1) a novel DSR knowledge base regarding IA, that serves as the foundation for (2) a design and action theory for IA. This section highlights (intermediate) results.

During the first year, the SLR has been preregistered [11] and completed (176 articles in sample). Based on the analysis of 20 definitions, the main concepts related to IA have been identified as a starting point to develop an ontology. Furthermore, an extensive body of knowledge has been identified and categorised, including four articles with generic constructs, 29 articles with relevant models, and 23 articles with methods. Additionally, 54 articles were found containing IA applications and 18 studies contained empirical research studies. Four articles contain design theories.

During the second year, the problem investigation was completed and the treatment design for the knowledge base for IA was verified. Current work in progress aims to instantiate the knowledge base for IA by developing an online interactive online environment, containing the results from the SLR, to make the design knowledge better accessible and actionable for IS scholars and professionals.

Throughout the first and second year, the first ADR cycles have been completed to develop an IA design canvas [5], supporting IA design workshop [12], IA design canvas tutorial [13], and IA design method [14]. The IA design canvas aims to support and ease the design processes related to IA applications, especially during the first stages of a DSR project, and improve communication with experts and involved stakeholders. The IA design canvas and workshop approach have been empirically tested by means of an in-company workshop with four practitioners and three design workshops involving 25 practitioners representing 14 organizations. Based on the workshop outcomes and user surveys, a set of four guiding design principles were derived to effectively use the IA design canvas. Utilizing ADR in several iterations, the workshop design was improved and the duration was reduced from four hours to two hours while delivering similar results.

The IA canvas has been incorporated within the Adaptive Integrated Digital Architecture Framework (AIDAF) design thinking approach to explore the potential use for prototyping and enterprise software development [14]. Furthermore, the use of the IA design canvas was mapped to the four design activities and six principles of the ISO 9241-210:2019 standard for human-centred design of interactive systems.

Several DSR projects have been initiated to validate and evaluate the IA design canvas and supporting workshop, tutorial, and design method, with IS professionals and practitioners for the design of IA-applications in transportation, logistics, and healthcare in the context of Industry 5.0 and Society 5.0.

The current status will be presented in more detail during the doctorial symposium. Here, the author would like to discuss the treatment design for the interactive knowledge base system as well as possible (future) use cases for IA.

References

1. Cabinet Office. (2015). The 5th science and technology basic plan. https://www8.cao.go.jp/cstp/kihonkeikaku/5basicplan_en.pdf. Accessed 20 Nov 2023
2. European Commission. (2023). Industry 5.0. https://research-and-innovation.ec.europa.eu/research-area/industrial-research-and-innovation/industry-50_en. Accessed 20 Nov 2023
3. Huang, S., Wang, B., Li, X., Zheng, P., Mourtzis, D., Wang, L.: Industry 5.0 and society 5.0—comparison, complementation and co-evolution. J. Manuf. Syst. **64**(July), 424–428 (2022). https://doi.org/10.1016/j.jmsy.2022.07.010
4. Ashby, W.R.: An introduction to cybernetics (1957)
5. Piest, J.P.S., Iacob, M.E., Wouterse, M.J.T.: Designing intelligence amplification: a design canvas for practitioners. In: Proceedings of the 8th IHIET 2022: Artificial Intelligence & Future Applications, vol. 68, pp. 68–76 (2022). https://doi.org/10.54941/ahfe1002739
6. Gregor, S.: The nature of theory in information systems. MIS Q. Manag. Inf. Syst. **30**(3), 611–642 (2006). https://doi.org/10.2307/25148742
7. Wieringa, R.J.: Design Science Methodology for Information Systems and Software Engineering. Springer, Berlin, Heidelberg (2014). https://doi.org/10.1007/978-3-662-43839-8
8. Gregor, S., Hevner, A.R.: Positioning and presenting design science research for maximum impact. MISQ **37**(2), 337–355 (2013). https://doi.org/10.25300/MISQ/2013/37.2.01

9. Gaß, O., Koppenhagen, N., Biegel, H., Mädche, A., Müller, B.: Anatomy of knowledge bases used in design science research: a literature review. In: Peffers, K., Rothenberger, M., Kuechler, B. (eds.) Design Science Research in Information Systems. Advances in Theory and Practice. DESRIST 2012. LNCS, vol. 7286, pp. 328–344. Springer, Berlin, Heidelberg (2012). https://doi.org/10.1007/978-3-642-29863-9_24

10. Gregor, S., Jones, D.: The anatomy of a design theory. J. Assoc. Inf. Syst. **8**(5), 312–335 (2007). https://doi.org/10.17705/1jais.00129

11. Piest, J.P.S.: Review of design theories, methods, frameworks and case studies for intelligence amplification (2023). https://doi.org/10.17605/OSF.IO/RQN8C

12. Piest, J.P.S., Iacob, M.E., Wouterse, M.J.T.: Designing intelligence amplification: organizing a design canvas workshop. In: Proceedings of the 8th IHIET 2022: Artificial Intelligence & Future Applications, vol. 68, pp. 247–251 (2022). https://doi.org/10.54941/ahfe1002739

13. Piest, J.P.S., Iacob, M.E., Wouterse, M.J.T.: Tutorial: conceptualizing intelligence amplification in human-centred AI applications using the design canvas. In: Proceedings of the 10th IHIET, vol. 70, pp. 129–138 (2023). https://doi.org/10.54941/ahfe1002937

14. Piest, J.P.S., Masuda, Y., Nakamura, O., Karaca, K.: Human-centred design thinking using the intelligence amplification design canvas and the adaptive integrated digital architecture framework. In: Zimmermann, A., Howlett, R., Jain, L.C. (eds.) Human Centred Intelligent Systems. KES-HCIS 2023. SIST, vol. 359, pp. 153–163. Springer, Singapore (2023). https://doi.org/10.1007/978-981-99-3424-9_15

Trusted Provenance of Collaborative, Adaptive, Process-Based Data Processing Pipelines

Ludwig Stage[✉]

Information Systems Group, University of Groningen, Groningen, The Netherlands
l.stage@rug.nl

Abstract. The abundance of data nowadays provides a lot of opportunities to gain insights in many domains. *Data processing pipelines* are one of the ways used to automate different data processing approaches and are widely used by both industry and academia. In many cases data and processing are available in distributed environments and the workflow technology is a suitable one to deal with the automation of data processing pipelines and support at the same time collaborative, trial-and-error experimentation in term of pipeline architecture for different application and scientific domains. In addition to the need for flexibility during the execution of the pipelines, there is a lack of trust in such collaborative settings where interactions cross organisational boundaries. Capturing provenance information related to the pipeline execution and the processed data is common and certainly a first step towards enabling trusted collaborations. However, current solutions do not capture change of any aspect of the processing pipelines themselves or changes in the data used, and thus do not allow for provenance of change. Therefore, the objective of this work is to investigate how provenance of workflow or data change during execution can be enabled. As a first step we have developed a preliminary architecture of a service – the Provenance Holder – which enables *provenance of collaborative, adaptive data processing pipelines in a trusted manner*. In our future work, we will focus on the concepts necessary to enable trusted provenance of change, as well as on the detailed service design, realization and evaluation.

Keywords: Provenance of Change · Reproducibility · Trust · Collaborative Processes · Data Processing Pipelines · Workflow evolution provenance · Provenance of ad-hoc workflow change

1 Introduction and Motivation

Data-driven research and development in and for enterprises is currently one of the most investigated topics with specific focus on data analysis, simulations, machine learning algorithms and AI. In the scope of such initiatives, both, academic and industrial research and development in different domains show great

T. P. Sales et al. (Eds.): EDOC 2023 Workshops, LNBIP 498, pp. 363–370, 2024.
https://doi.org/10.1007/978-3-031-54712-6_25

effort in automation and deployment of data processing in enterprise computing environments in order to leverage operational improvement opportunities and to profit from the available data.

Automation of computations and data processing is done by using data processing pipelines. One major challenge of this automation is the identification of the best approach towards the actual automation of such pipelines since they can be implemented using different methodologies and technologies. Furthermore, integration of computational resources, the ability to use data from different sources in different formats and varying quality properties, the flexibility of data pipelines, the modularity and reusability of individual steps, the ability to enable collaborative modelling and execution of data processing pipelines, as well as their provenance and reproducibility are hard requirements. Consequently, there are a lot of research results in literature on the application of different technologies and concepts in different domains such as eScience, scientific computing and workflows, data science, intelligent systems, business processes, etc.

The topic of *provenance*[1] has been researched predominantly in the field of scientific experiments and scientific workflows, which led to the definition of the characteristics of Findable Accessible Interoperable Reusable (FAIR) results [1,2] and Robust Accountable Reproducible Explained (RARE) experiments [1]. In this field, scientific experiments are considered to be of good provenance if they are reproducible. Enabling reproducibility of experiment results, typically by means of tracking the data through all processing, analysis and interpretation steps of the experiment, has been one of the main objectives of scientific workflow systems, in addition to the actual automation of scientific experiments. The importance of provenance in in-silico experiments has been identified and discussed and approaches have been partly implemented more recently in e.g. [3–6] and are relevant to enabling the provenance of data processing pipelines. Furthermore, there are initiatives towards standardization of representing provenance information for the purposes of both modeling provenance information and establishing an interchangeable format for such information, e.g. PROV-DM[2].

To the best of our knowledge, the ability to reproduce the changes on either workflow or choreography models or instances made by collaborating organisations in the course of running their data processing pipelines in a trusted manner, has not been the subject of other works. Towards closing this gap in research, we propose a solution [7], called *Provenance Holder service*, that has to track and record all changes made on choreography and/or workflow models or instances to support their provenance in a trusted manner and allow collaborating organisations to retrace and reproduce their data processing pipelines exactly the same way as they have been carried out, including all changes made on both data and software used during the execution.

The contributions we intend with this work are: (i) A workflow provenance taxonomy to account for adaptation based on existing taxonomies from literature, (ii) Identification of provenance requirements for the Provenance Holder

---

[1] "The provenance of digital objects represents their origins."[2].
[2] https://www.w3.org/TR/prov-primer/.

service, (iii) Detailed definition of the properties of the Provenance Holder service that will guarantee trusted provenance of collaborative, adaptive data processing pipelines, (iv) functional architecture, which is generic in nature and
applicable in any application domain and is easy to integrate with other flexible
Management System (WfMS) systems, (v) concepts and data structures necessary for capturing the adaptations, and (vi) an implementation as a proof of
concept and its evaluation. We also intend to explicitly identify (vii) the *prereq-*
uisites for employing the Provenance Holder with other WfMS environments,
namely the ability to support the trial-and-error manner of experimenting (as
in e.g. Model-as-you-go-approach [8] or ability to change and propagate change
in choreographies [9]) and the ability to provide workflow monitoring data that
allows for data and workflow provenance in a trusted manner [7].

2   Scope and Research Questions

In the scope of our work are automated data processing pipelines, which use only
software implementations of computational and data transformation tasks and
excludes data processing pipelines in which participation of physical devices (e.g.
microscopes, wet labs, sensors and actuators) is directly visible in the pipeline.
We aim at enabling the *provenance of flexible, a.k.a. adaptive, data processing*
pipelines that are carried out in collaboration among identifiable organisational
entities. The matter of *trust among the collaborating parties* is of utmost importance in the context of our work, in particular because of the need to capture
the origins of change that can be carried out by any of the participating parties
at any point in the execution of the pipelines.

Our technology of choice for modelling and running collaborative data processing pipelines is *service-based, adaptable processes, both workflows and chore-*
ographies, that are well known from the field of Business Process Management
(BPM) [10] and conventional Workflow Management Technology [11] and for
their beneficial properties such as modularity, reusability, interpretability, transactional support, scalability and reliability.

We have identified four requirements on the Provenance Holder [7,12] in order
to be enable reproducible, trusted and adaptive collaborations (cf. Table 1).

Table 1. Provenance Holder Requirements adopted from [7,12]

Requirement	Description
R1	**Adaptability** to adhere to the adaptability of experiments
R2	**Provenance** to enable FAIR results [1]
R3	**Reproducibility** for RARE experiments [1]
R4	**Trust** among collaborating parties to also enable accountability

To the best of our knowledge, the ability to reproduce the changes on
either workflow or choreography models or instances made by collaborating

organisations in the course of running their data processing pipelines in a trusted manner, has not been the subject of other works. We call this type of provenance *"trusted provenance of change"*. Based on the existing taxonomies for provenance as summarized by [4], to accommodate the provenance of adaptation, we identified which new types of provenance need to be considered (cf. Fig. 1).

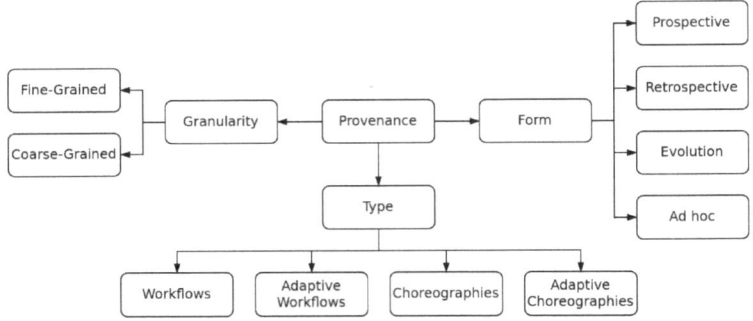

Fig. 1. Workflow Provenance types taxonomy adopted from [4] and [13]

With our work we aim to answer four research questions (cf. Table 2).

Table 2. Research questions

RQ1	How can we bring traceability, reproducibility, accountability and trust to Automated, Collaborative and Adaptive, Process-based Data Processing Pipelines?
RQ2	What does a system look like that provides traceability, reproducibility, accountability and trust for Automated, Collaborative and Adaptive, Process-based Data Processing Pipelines?
RQ3	What are the requirements on such a system?
RQ4	What are the prerequisites for the environment such a system is to be integrated?

3   Provenance Holder Properties and Architecture

The Provenance Holder is a service responsible for collecting all information necessary to ensure provenance and reproducibility of and trust in the collaborative adaptations and enabling the four properties (cf. Table 3). We aim at providing a generic, reusable and non-intrusive solution across different scenarios and separation of concerns [14]. We realize P1 via electronic signature, P2 with (trusted) timestamping, we will investigate how P3 can be enabled using non-interactive zero knowledge proofs ([15], as it presents a systematic overview over the greater topic of verifiable privacy-preserving computations), and P4 by linking provenance information objects.

Table 3. Provenance Holder Properties and their mapping to statements made by choreography participants. In the statement column the pronoun **It** is information about either of the following: result, origin/predecessor or change. The text in bold highlights where the focus of each property lies. Adopted from [13].

Property	Statement by participant	Description
P1	"**I** know it"	A result/change/predecessor can be attributed to a certain identifiable entity, i.e. choreography participant
P2	"I knew it **before**"	A result/change/predecessor has been available/known or has happened at or before a certain point in time
P3	"I **actually** know it"	Prove that participants know of a result/change/predecessor (without information disclosure)
P4	"I know **where it came from**"	Participants have knowledge of the predecessor of a result/change/ predecessor

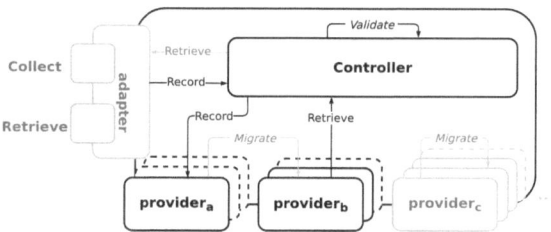

Fig. 2. Provenance Holder Architecture: components, external operations and internal methods, implemented ones are solid black (adopted from [13])

The Provenance Holder service provides *two main operations* as part of its interface (cf. Fig. 2): 1) **Collect** provenance data and 2) **Retrieve** provenance information; we call these operations also external operations. The controller, the adapter and one or more provenance providers are the *components of the Provenance Holder* and they carry out four *interaction scenarios* in order to realize the two externally provided operations of the Provenance Holder service. The interaction scenarios are always combinations of several of the internal methods[3]; the (internal) methods are: *Record, Retrieve, Validate* and *Migrate*.

---

[3] We use the term *method* for disambiguation purposes only.

The *adapter* is the component ensuring the *integration* of the Provenance Holder with other systems and provides the two external operations: *Collect* and *Retrieve*. Its actual design and implementation are specific for the system with which it has to work to enable the integration and correct communication.

Providers or *provenance providers* have to implement three methods, *record, retrieve and migrate*, certain requirements to fulfil, and ultimately store the provenance information. The implementation characteristics and complexity strongly depend on the employed (storage) technology and the needs of different workflow types also come into play when deciding which technology to use.

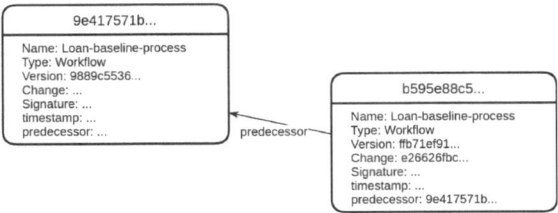

Fig. 3. Provenance Information objects representing a change [13]

The *controller* is in charge of the interaction between the adapter and the provenance providers so that the Provenance Holder can provide the provenance service operations to each workflow and choreography. The controller combines the four methods: record, validate, retrieve and migrate into the realization of the two operations provided by the Provenance Holder: Collect and Retrieve. For the *collect provenance data operation* the controller receives, validates and relays the provenance information to the providers. For the *operation retrieve provenance information*, it combines the methods retrieve and validate. Data structures to capture and store provenance information, e.g. of change, had to be defined and supported by all components (cf. Fig. 3). During the execution and adaptation of workflows and choreographies the Provenance Holder constantly collects provenance data on a very detailed level, including on per-workflow-activity level. The *Record* method selects appropriate provider components for a certain workflow type out of the available providers and uses them to store the provenance information. Data is validated (with the validation method) before it is actually handed over to a provider for storage. The *Retrieve* method is used to fetch the desired provenance information from the provider components via their interfaces. The actual data retrieval is done by each provider itself and returned to the *retrieve* method. After retrieval, the information is validated before it is handed over to the adapter component, i.e. the Provenance Holder's interface implementation. The *validation* method is called during *Recording* to verify the signature and identify the signee the data is "recorded". If the signature verification fails due to an invalid signature or an unknown signee, the information will not be "recorded". When calling the *Retrieve* method, the provenance information is fetched from the provenance provider and then validated. The *Migrate* method is only used if stored information has to be transferred to a new provider type or instance, in case such an addition or change is desired/needed and provides the ability to retrieve all stored provenance information from a provider at once. Migrations can be triggered both automatically or manually by an administrator; the actual procedure for migration is out of scope of our work as related work like [16] is available.

4   Conclusions and Future Work

The goal of this work is to support trusted provenance in collaborative, adaptive, process-based data processing pipelines. We currently provide the concepts of capturing provenance of change in such pipelines as well as the architecture of the corresponding system, including the detailed design of the controller and provider components of the Provenance Holder. The prototypical implementation of these components and properties P1, P2 and P4 is available at https://github.com/ProvenanceHolder/ProvenanceHolder.

Refining the concepts, identification of the adapter requirements, its detailed architecture and implementation are the future steps in our research. This also includes the identification and differentiation of change, its capturing and visualisation, how changes are communicated and all supporting data structures. Subsequently we will work towards the evaluation and extension of both, the approach and the proof-of-concept implementation.

We recognise that the approach and its realization is not only applicable to Scientific Workflows, but also to Workflows and to process-based data processing pipelines in general. Furthermore, we do not rule out the possibility that the approach may also go beyond this. These are two of the reasons why we will be following a generic research path and at the same time we have a specific use case.

References

1. Mesirov, J.P.: Accessible reproducible research. Science **27**, 415–416 (2010)
2. Wilkinson, M., et al.: The fair guiding principles for scientific data management and stewardship. Sci. Data **3**, 1–9 (2016)
3. Atkinson, M., et al.: Scientific workflows: past, present and future. Future Gener. Comput. Syst. **75**, 216–227 (2017)
4. Herschel, M., et al.: A survey on provenance - what for? what form? what from? Int. J. Very Large Data Bases (VLDB J.) **26**, 881–906 (2017)
5. Alper, P., et al.: Enhancing and abstracting scientific workflow provenance for data publishing. In: Proceedings of the Joint EDBT/ICDT Workshops (2013)
6. Freire, J., Chirigati, F.S.: Provenance and the different flavors of reproducibility. IEEE Data Eng. Bull. **41**, 15 (2018)
7. Stage, L., Karastoyanova, D.: Provenance holder: bringing provenance, reproducibility and trust to flexible scientific workflows and choreographies. In: Di Francescomarino, C., Dijkman, R., Zdun, U. (eds.) BPM2019. LNBIP, vol. 362, pp. 664–675. Springer, Cham (2019). https://doi.org/10.1007/978-3-030-37453-2_53

8. Sonntag, M., Karastoyanova, D.: Model-as-you-go: an approach for an advanced infrastructure for scientific workflows. J. Grid Comput. **11**, 553–583 (2013)

9. Fdhila, W., et al.: Dealing with change in process choreographies: design and implementation of propagation algorithms. Inf. Syst. **49**, 1–24 (2015)

10. Weske, M.: Business Process Management - Concepts, Languages, Architectures, 3rd edn. Springer, Heidelberg (2019)

11. Leymann, F., Roller, D.: Production Workflow: Concepts and Techniques. Prentice Hall PTR, Hoboken (2000)

12. Karastoyanova, D., Stage, L.: Towards collaborative and reproducible scientific experiments on blockchain. In: Matulevičius, R., Dijkman, R. (eds.) CAiSE 2018. LNBIP, vol. 316, pp. 144–149. Springer, Cham (2018). https://doi.org/10.1007/978-3-319-92898-2_12

13. Stage, L., Karastoyanova, D.: Trusted provenance of automated, collaborative and adaptive data processing pipelines (2023). https://doi.org/10.48550/arXiv.2310.11442. Accessed 26 Nov 2023

14. Dijkstra, E.W.: On the role of scientific thought. In: Selected Writings on Computing: A Personal Perspective. Texts and Monographs in Computer Science. Springer, New York (1982). https://doi.org/10.1007/978-1-4612-5695-3_12

15. Bontekoe, T., Karastoyanova, D., Turkmen, F.: Verifiable privacy-preserving computing (2023). https://doi.org/10.48550/arXiv.2309.08248. Accessed 13 Oct 2023

16. Strauch, S., et al.: Migrating enterprise applications to the cloud: methodology and evaluation. Int. J. Big Data Intell. **5**, 127–140 (2014)

Author Index

T. P. Sales et al. (Eds.): EDOC 2023 Workshops, LNBIP 498, pp. 371–372, 2024.
https://doi.org/10.1007/978-3-031-54712-6